From Surface Collection to Prehistoric Lifeways

FROM SURFACE COLLECTION TO PREHISTORIC LIFEWAYS

MAKING SENSE OF THE MULTI-PERIOD SITE OF ORLOVO, SOUTH EAST BULGARIA

Edited by John Chapman

with contributions by

Bisserka Gaydarska, Ana Raduntcheva, Ruslan Kostov, Irko Petrov,
Elena Georgieva and Yvonne Beadnell

Oxbow Books

Oxford and Oakville

Published by
Oxbow Books, Oxford

ISBN 978-1-84217-391-6

A CIP record for this book is available from the British Library

This book is available direct from

Oxbow Books, Oxford, UK
(Phone: 01865-241249, Fax: 01865-794449)

and

The David Brown Book Company
PO Box 511, Oakville, CT 06779, USA
(Phone: 860-945-9329; Fax: 860-945-9468)

or from our website

www.oxbowbooks.com

Library of Congress Cataloging-in-Publication Data

From surface collection to prehistoric lifeways : making sense of the multi-period site of Orlovo, south east Bulgaria / edited by John Chapman ; with contributions by Bisserka Gaydarska ... [et al.].
      p. cm.
   Includes bibliographical references.
   ISBN 978-1-84217-391-6
   1. Orlovo Site (Bulgaria) 2. Antiquities, Prehistoric--Bulgaria--Khaskovo Region. 3. Khaskovo Region (Bulgaria)--Antiquities. 4. Khaskovo Region (Bulgaria)--Antiquities--Collection and preservation. 5. Material culture--Bulgaria--Khaskovo Region--History--To 1500. 6. Prehistoric peoples--Bulgaria--Khaskovo Region--Social life and customs. 7. Community life--Bulgaria--Khaskovo Region--History--To 1500. 8. Social archaeology--Bulgaria--Khaskovo Region. 9. Neolithic period--Bulgaria--Khaskovo Region. 10. Copper age--Bulgaria--Khaskovo Region. I. Chapman, John, 1951- II. Gaydarska, Bisserka.
   GN845.B8F76 2010
   949.9'6--dc22
                        2010018124

Printed in Great Britain by
The Short Run Press, Exeter

Contents

List of Figures

List of Plates

List of Tables

Preface

We dedicate this book to the memory of the inspiring Haskovo archaeologist, Dimcho Aladzhov (1930–2010)
One of the finest field archaeologists of his generation.

This volume had its origins in the collaborative research in the Eastern Rhodopes (the 'Rocky Landscapes' Project) and the tell of Dolnoslav (The 'Dolnoslav Figurine Project') that three of the authors – Ana Raduntcheva, John Chapman and Bisserka Gaydarska – have carried out from the late 1990s onwards. It was Sanja who first drew the attention of John and Bisserka to the outstandingly interesting surface collection from the site of Orlovo, curated in the Historical Museum of Haskovo. Our first visit to meet the Keeper of Archaeology, Mr. Irko Petrov, was in August 2006. We agreed to return in the winter of 2006/7 to begin a detailed study of the finds. Since the research could not be completed in this visit, we returned in Easter 2007, this time with two other colleagues. The first was Dr. Ruslan Kostov, a geologist and mineralogist, who had previously worked with John and Bisserka on the petrology of the miniature polished stone axe and the pumice in the Omurtag hoard (Gaydarska *et al.* 2004), as well as with several other prominent Bulgarian prehistorians. The second was Elena Georgieva, an illustrator who had worked with John and Bisserka on the Dolnoslav figurines. The team of six is jointly responsible for the research presented in this book, as well as for the specialist tasks for which each person was responsible:- the site environment and cultural context – Irko Petrov, John Chapman and Ruslan Kostov; the figurines – Ana Raduntcheva and Bisserka Gaydarska; the polished stone axes – Bisserka Gaydarska and Ruslan Kostov; the ornaments – John Chapman and Ruslan Kostov; the museum documentation and photography – Irko Petrov; and the line drawings – Elena Georgieva. The seventh memebr of the team, Yvonne Beadnell (Durham) added new illustrations

The authors would like to record our collective and/or individual thanks to those who have made a substantial contribution to this publication:- the Bulgarian Academy of Sciences for funding (JCC and BG); the British Academy for funding (JCC and BG); Durham University for funding and research time abroad (JCC); Haskovo District Council, for support to the Project (IP); and the Haskovo Police Force, for providing an escort for the site visit, Colonel Branimir Mitkov, whom we also thank. John and Bisserka are grateful for the kind invitation from Fotis Ifantidis and Marianna Nikolaidou to speak about Orlovo at their EAA session on *Spondylus* at the Zadar Annual Meeting, September 2007. Several Durham and Bulgarian colleagues have helped in the research: we should like to thank Robin Skeates (advice on artifact biographies), Judy Allen (for her help with plant taxa); Georgi Nehrisov (discussions on aspects of Rhodopean prehistory); Erich Claßen, Alasdair Whittle, Eva Lenneis, Burcin Erdogu, Antiklia Moundrea-Agrafioti and Onur Ozbek (help with polished stone axe parallels) and Dr Kathie Way, Natural History Museum (for her kind identification of shell species). We are particularly grateful to Alasdair Whittle who read the entire book and made valuable comments about settlements, personhood and exchange networks. The skills of our publishing team at Oxbow Books – Clare Litt and Tara Evans – have made the production of this book far easier than we could have imagined.

The Orlovo objects have now been placed back in their quaint wooden containers, nestling in the locked cupboards of the Keeper of Archaeology in the Regional Historical Museum of Haskovo. The microscopes, geological lenses and thin-section equipment have been stored and the computer programmes for post-collection analysis have been switched off. No more e-mails will be sent between the authors, or between the authors and their colleagues, to elicit answers to factual enquiries or comments on ideas and new interpretations. No more of the endless short walks between two adjoining upstairs rooms in a house near Durham City – consulting, discussing, disagreeing, calming nerves, stimulating the two principal authors to work and re-work the interpretations of this fascinating collection. This book has taken part of a two-year period at a busy time of our lives – a Research Assessment Exercise (RAE) in Durham, a major new exhibition in the National Natural History Museum in Sofia, new excavations on Rhodopean sanctuaries, complete renovations of the Haskovo Museum, *etc.*, *etc*. We hope that the Orlovo collections will feature strongly in the new display on the prehistory of the Haskovo region.

It has been a pleasure to work with our group of authors – friends and colleagues as well as professionals, mostly working at a distance from each other but always in virtual contact. We hope that each reader will gain a sense of the excitement of this extraordinary site which all of us have encountered during this research.

John Chapman and Bisserka Gaydarska, on behalf of the authors

Introduction

Excavation and fieldwalking – irreconcilable results?

Archaeology in the 21st century is a complex and tangled web of irreconcilable theories and barely integrated methodologies. Since none of the grand set of theories purporting to be paradigms (traditional, processual, post-processual) has been replaced in the desired Kuhnian framework (Kuhn 1962), there is a chaotic network of competing theoretical claims and counter-claims (Fletcher 1989), which leaves some archaeologists baffled and demotivated, others excited at the prospect of further change. The barely concealed antagonism between humanistic and scientific archaeology, Andy Jones notwithstanding (Jones 2002), is hardly conducive to the resolution of theoretical conflicts.

One of the most deeply-running faults in archaeology separates archaeological field survey and interpretatative archaeology. On the one hand, field survey has developed a strong suit in methodologies, whether intra-site gridded collections (e.g. the Maddle Farm Project: Gaffney and Tingle 1989), intra-site combination of artifactual and geophysical data (e.g. Bertók *et al.* 2000), regional transect sampling (e.g. the Ager Tarraconensis Project: Millett *et al.* 1995), integration with regional palaeo-environmental reconstructions (e.g. the Neothermal Dalmatia Project: Chapman *et al.* 1996), integration with a GIS platform (e.g. the Upper Tisza Project: Chapman *et al.* 2003; Gillings 1998) or a combination of all of these (e.g. the Boeotia Project: Bintliff 1991; 2000; Bintliff *et al.* 2006). However, the close attention paid to sampling has never managed to fill the void of the absence of detailed contextual data – a problem heightened by the narrow range of artifactual data recovered by traditional fieldwalking – generally, small, worn sherds, abraded lithics and (for later periods) brick and tile (but see Bintliff *et al.* 2000). It could be argued that the lively innovations in field survey methodologies amount to collective compensation for the lack of truly contextual data and for the narrowness of the artifactual sample.

On the other hand, interpretative archaeologies have moved forward, based, in the vast majority of cases (for an exception, see Tilley's work on the Nämsforsen rock-art complex: Tilley 1991), on excavated samples from closely defined site contexts. One of the principal breakthroughs in Hodder's research programme at Çatalhöyük is the expansion of archaeological theory to the trench, encapsulated in his telling aphorism – "interpretation at the point of the trowel" (Hodder 1999). On an admittedly high-rolling budget, Hodder (2005) has demonstrated that excavation, scientific analysis and interpretation form recursive relationships, with the target of the completion of analyses of samples from very recently excavated contexts within 24 hours, so that the results can be fed back into the on-going understanding of excavations of related contexts. While the Çatal experience is currently remote from the strategies of most other excavations, it shows the drive for detailed contexual interpretation is taking excavation even further from field survey. Indeed, it is hard to imagine a way of expanding interpretative theory-building into field survey programmes.

Although accurate and comforting, the observation that field survey and interpretative archaeology are not inherently opposing strategies but merely two successive stages in the understanding of a regional landscape does not narrow the gap for what can be said about sites that have been investigated in these two different ways. But what of field collections that produce radically different data – data that resemble excavated samples but without the contextual information? In artifact-rich periods / areas of the world, one would expect to find sites which offer the potential to approach, if not the basis for detailed contextual interpretation, then at least the quantity and variety of artifacts that enable a more nuanced understanding of on-site social practices and their wider social and spatial settings. Such sites would offer an excellent opportunity to overcome some of the limitations of traditional intra-site artifact analyses by the articulation of more recent theoretical agendas, such as the study of artifact biographies and the creation of personhood, with more traditional site- and region-based concerns with production, distribution and consumption.

We have been fortunate enough to encounter such a site in South East Bulgaria. The prehistoric site of Orlovo has been investigated neither by excavation nor by systematic field walking but by repeated field visits, over many years, and the collection of objects exposed by the plough. The result is an extraordinarily rich and diverse collection of objects whose contexts are poorly known but whose diversity reminds us not so much of an excavated settlement as an excavated Chalcolithic cemetery such as Durankulak (Todorova 2002).

This collection has challenged us to develop an approach in which theory was integrated with methodology to propose as complete an interpretation of the site as could be done from an unstructured surface collection. Thus, our primary aim is to shed light on the worlds of the Neolithic and Chalcolithic communities of the Balkans through the prism of a single site with its remarkable assemblage of surface artifacts. We also discovered, through our reading of the literature on the find classes at Orlovo – figurines, personal ornaments and polished stone tools – that the latter two finds categories are, for the most part, heavily under-theorised and sometimes seriously neglected in favour of the key find category under most frequent investigation – decorated pottery. This neglect provided us with an opportunity to pursue a key objective – the re-evaluation of these three finds categories in terms of their relation to social practices. A second objective is to characterise through exemplification a coherent methodology for assemblages such as Orlovo. It is the generic nature of these aims and objectives that makes the Orlovo collection of more than regional or national value – but rather a European example of what can – and what cannot – be said of an artifact-rich site in an artifact-rich region.

In this introduction, we continue with an outline of the periods in question – the Balkan Neolithic and Copper Age – using this summary to explain the possibility of a phenomenon such as Orlovo. We then discuss the historical background of methods of investigation prevalent in Bulgarian archaeology, before turning to the theoretical and methodological approaches which we intend to utilise to inform our interpretations of the Orlovo materials. We conclude this chapter with a summary of the structure of this short book.

Setting the scene – the Balkan Neolithic and Chalcolithic

First studied systematically by V. Gordon Childe in his masterpiece "The Danube in prehistory" (1929), the communities who lived in the Balkans between 7000 and 4000 Cal. BC (Fig. I.1) have now been the focus of intensive and increasingly inter-disciplinary research for the last forty years (Tringham 1971; Hodder 1990; Whittle 1996; Bailey 2000; Chapman and Gaydarska 2006).

Dwelling between the warm, dry Mediterranean zones of the Aegean and Anatolia and the cooler and snowier Central European heartlands, these communities created distinctive social formations that left enduring marks on today's landscapes. These groups lived in a mosaic of settings, dominated except for two large Danubian plains by mountainous regions reaching to almost 3,000 m in height (the word 'Balkan' is the Turkish term for 'mountain') (Fig. I.2). This topographic setting not only provided a suite of complementary resources – summer pasture, metals, lithics and stones for tools in the mountains; alluvial gold, potting clay and arable lands in the lowlands – but also created the potential for symbolic differentiation of these two zones through the cross-referencing of values in each zone to the people, places and things in the other.

One of the key trends in these millennia concerned the high value attributed to the exotic, especially if that was represented by objects of striking colour and brilliance (Plates 5–8). Thus, the preference, wherever possible, for long-term sedentary lifeways was often in counterpoise with strategies for bringing distinctive objects from remote places back to the settlement for local 'domestication'. There was also a tendency to use parts of the fiercest wild animals –aurochs metapodia and wild boar bristles – to create intimate objects, such as spoons for eating and the painted decoration on serving vessels. In objects as well as in places, there was a tension between home and away, lowland and upland, that introduced the opportunities for framing social contrasts and similarities.

One suite of object categories in this period was rarely made in anything but local materials – usually fired clay. Ritual items were created in such profusion, most commonly as anthropomorphic figurines (Fig. 2.1; Plates 3–4) but also in a huge variety of other forms, including 'altars' and model 'shrines'. These finds become increasingly prominent with time, reaching a climax in quantity and diversity in the Late Copper Age (5th millennium Cal. BC). The probability is that we are talking about communities with highly ritualised domestic lifeways, since this material culture is most commonly associated with, and deposited in, the family house. We can also identify, especially in long-term tell settlements, an over-arching ancestral principle that groups live where their ancestors have lived – in particular vertically superposed above the ancestral houses. This apparently egalitarian, but essentially gerontocratic, principle generated contradictions with those emergent individuals and households whose personal skills and labour investment generated differences that could potentially be expressed by material means. The potential for display became strongest in the Copper Age, when new metals such as gold and copper gave new opportunities for the use of visual culture. It is in this phase that communal cemeteries became more frequent, as places apart from the settlements – perhaps places where open and competitive display was possible.

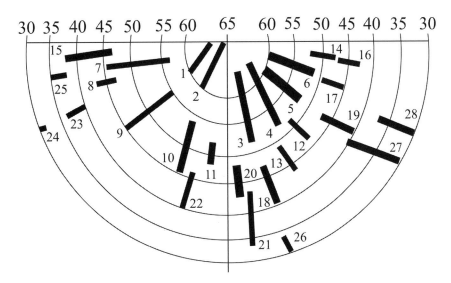

Figure I.1. Time-line for Balkan Neolithic and Chalcolithic groups. Key: 1. Early Neolithic of Marmara and Turkish Thrace; 2. Early Neolithic of Northern Greece; 3. Karanovo I–II; 4. Starčevo; 5. Criş; 6. Körös; 7. Middle Neolithic of Greek Macedonia; 8. Late Neolithic of Greek Macedonia; 9. Karanovo III–IV–V; 10. Early Vinča; 11. Alföld Linear Pottery; 12. Dudeşti; 13. Boian; 14. Early Hamangia (Late Neolithic); 15. Karanovo VI; 16. Varna cemetery; 17. Late Hamangia (Copper Age); 18. Gumelniţa; 19. Cucuteni A / Tripolye B1; 20. Hungarian Late Neolithic; 21. Hungarian Early–Middle Copper Age; 22. Late Vinča; 23. Sitagroi III; 24. Sitagroi IV; 25. Pevets; 26. Baden; 27. Cucuteni AB–B; 28. Tripolye C

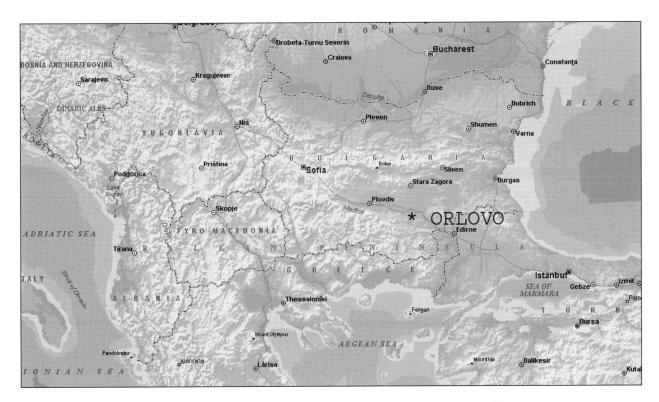

Figure I.2. Location map of South East Europe, showing Orlovo (starred)

Cemeteries such as Varna (Ivanov 1991) and Durankulak (Todorova 2002) are found to display greater accumulations of distinctive objects than ever before, suggesting that the days of ancestral equality were finally – or perhaps only temporarily – over.

A key thread connecting themes of exoticity, ritual and display in the later prehistoric Balkans concerns the emergence of different categories of persons – categories that simply did not exist in previous millennia (e.g. no-one talks about shepherds in the Palaeolithic!). These categories emerged at the same time as their practices developed – especially in two great bursts of innovation. The first was the spread of farming from Anatolia and Greece, while, in the early part of the Copper Age, a second wave of new categories of person can be identified, more closely related to metals. These two peaks in the creation of personhood led to one of the most distinctive features of the Neolithic and Copper Age – the emergence of a far wider range of categories of person than had been known before. Given the importance of visual display, the exotic, colour and brilliance, it is not surprising that this had material consequences, especially in the Copper Age but also in the Early Neolithic, in terms of material symbols and markers of relationships between, as much as personal identities for, these new classes of person (cf. the material entanglements of Hodder 2005a).

We can thus identify several reasons why a high density of objects may have been deposited at individual settlement sites – the use of a wider variety of materials embodying colour and brilliance, the environmental mosaic enabling the availability of many kinds of exotica for settlements, the huge and increasing variety of objects of vital importance for ritual practices, the growing diachronic tendency towards accumulation of objects and, finally but perhaps most significantly, the emergence of a wider range of categories of person than had ever been seen before in the Balkans, each with material consequences for their identity. Naturally, the question remains for later discussion: "why was it precisely at Orlovo, and other sites, that such an accumulation of objects was found?"

A short history of Bulgarian field practices

If we have earlier (p. 1) made the distinction between fieldwalking and excavation in terms of their potential and relation to archaeological theory and method, there can be no doubt that the key practice in the archaeological profession in the Balkans is excavation. The vast majority of funding has been devoted to excavation, the greatest attention is paid to new finds from excavation, it is newly excavated material that makes the sparks fly at conferences, and the status of the archaeologist is intimately related to the sites of her/his excavation. This *status quo* – evident for at least a generation of prehistorians – has led to an imbalance

between excavation and field survey that typifies the Balkans but must seem strange to Western eyes.

Ever since the 1960s, if not the 1940s (e.g. the survey projects of Ward Perkins in Italy: 1962; 1964; Ward Perkins *et al.* 1968), archaeology in the Mediterranean has benefited hugely from large-scale field survey of varying degrees of intensity and/or systematic coverage. Two volumes demonstrate the potential of this approach for a deeper knowledge of settlement trajectories and economic developments – Keller and Rupp's (1983) "Archaeological survey in the Mediterranean" and Barker and Lloyd's (1991) "Roman landscapes". Both volumes are replete with reports on site-based, local and regional survey projects that provide the basis for more intensive excavations, while the most interesting chapters integrate palaeo-environmental reconstructions, subsistence and land-use data with the survey findings (e.g. Branigan 1983; King 1983; Mills 1983; Bintliff 1991; Chapman and Shiel 1991: 1993; De Maria 1991; Rowland and Dyson 1991). These volumes show how field survey evolved into a fundamental part of the process of archaeological research.

Bulgarian prehistory has very largely missed out on this stage of European archaeological development, partly because of the military and security issues arising from map-based projects prior to 1989 and the Podgoritsa Project post-1989 (Bailey *et al.* 1998) but mostly because of the passion for digging. Two major field programmes have been developed in Bulgaria: the Bulgarian Academy of Sciences programme "The Archaeological Map of Bulgaria" (AKB) – started in 1990 – and the parallel initiative of the National Institute for Cultural Monuments (NIMK) – started in the 1970s and devolved to the level of (county) Historical Museums (Gaydarska 2007: 32). The aim of the former was a computer-based interactive database which now contains more than 14,000 archaeological sites of all periods (p.c., G. Nehrisov). The aim of the latter was to provide maps of all archaeological sites, based almost entirely on archive data and field prospection. However, the two principles of data collection were extensive, unsystematic collection through local informants and walking in areas of proven site occurrence. Ten volumes for NIMK have been produced out of 26 possible mapping regions. The best of the museum contributions provide a very good starting-point for more intensive investigations (e.g. the Targovishte volume: Dremsizova-Nelchinova *et al.* 1991). However, other museums, such as Haskovo, have produced their own, independent gazetteers (Aladzhov 1997). While those managing the AKB would encourage more professionals to use this wide-ranging resource, in effect, energetic archaeologists have used the NIMK and similar volumes as guides to finding the most promising sites for excavation. In themselves, these volumes lack detailed fieldwalking data and accurate recording of site locations. Most site locations are recorded in the form "x km North East of the village of Y" (cf. the more precise locational recording in AKB). To the best of our knowledge, there are no examples of intra-site gridded collections in the NIMK volumes that could be used to decide on further, more intensive field research. The results of both projects, therefore, represent an archaeological resource of enormous but under-utilised potential.

One of the key developments in the 1990s in all East European countries has been the planning and (usually) completion of new nets of motorways and fuel pipelines. Built into all such schemes has been an archaeological fieldwork component, in which surface survey takes place in an area rather wider than the pipeline, railway track or motorway line. These surface data can potentially be used in a variety of interesting ways – e.g. in interactive comparison with the results of excavations to assess the quality of predictive modelling. In Bulgaria, this large quantity of field survey data has so far been used to locate places of future excavation and not for its own sake at all. A good example is the Bulgarian Railways (NKZhI) survey and excavation project (Nikolov, V. *et al.* 2006), which reports on the excavations carried out at nine of the sites identified through fieldwalking the line of the track.

A welcome exception to the under-use of surface information is the recent volume on the settlement history of the Yantra valley (Krauß 2006), in which not only is there detailed, extensive and systematic field walking of part of the study area of 1,000 km² (2006, 145–6) but there is also a key level of the research design based upon intra-site gridded collections. The results of such intra-site analysis is used to document settlement patterns from the Early Neolithic to the Early Iron Age with a special focus on pedological inter-relations with settlement structure.

A further implication of the downgrading of field survey results to a third-class level in the hierarchy of knowledge about the past – below barrow-diggers' treasures and more serious excavated finds – is that the surface materials collected from the unsystematic surveys have rarely been utilised in further studies. Such collections share two main disadvantages. The lack of excavation context for the surface finds means that they are, by definition, hard to date. Moreover, the lack of spatial context in collection records means that it is rarely possible to provide any data on probable spatial associations. These collections often exist in museum stores as rather sad mementoes of past field visits and the heavily under-utilised source of typological dating for surface scatters.

The history of inter-disciplinary studies in Bulgaria is an interesting story. The BAN National Institute of Archaeology has had a Department of Inter-disciplinary studies since 1977, with a house journal – "Interdistsiplinarni Issledvaniya" published since 1978. Archaeological scientists have made major progress in palaeo-magnetics (Kovacheva 1995), archaeobotany (Popova 1995; Marinova 2006), faunal studies (Spassov and Iliev 2002), lithic use-wear analysis

(Gurova 2001) and other fields of research. Moreover, palynologists have completed a series of important studies taking site-based and local human impacts into account as much as regional vegetational histories (Bozhilova and Beug 1992; Bozhilova and Filipova 1975; Filipova-Marinova 2003; Kreutz *et al.* 2005). However, it is rare to find such researchers considering surface collections of the kind that are the focus of attention in this volume. There is a widely-held view that scarce scientific resources should be targeted on the most promising archaeological materials from secure, excavated contexts. While there is sense in this view, at the same time some surface collections would appear to merit the application of specialist skills.

In summary, there is little local precedent for an appropriate methodology for the study of a surface collection of the kind discussed in this book. We are limited by the nature of the methods of object retrieval – unstructured collection lacking in spatial co-ordinates – and the main advances that we can pursue pertain to scientific analyses and the systematic study of prehistoric artifacts . We have already stated that the second objective of this book is to develop strategies of research appropriate to artifact-rich surface collections of the kind that may well exist in other museums.

Artifact biographies and personhood

We have suggested earlier (p. 1) that there is a gulf between method-based fieldwalking practices and theory-based interpretative archaeological practices. However, we also maintain that the relevance of much interpretative theory to artifact-rich surface collections is revealed by working through the big issues present in the details of material culture – the 'macro in the micro'. Admittedly, the lack of stratified context of a polished serpentinite axe-pendant denies the possibility of an understanding of the circumstances of its deposition. But deposition in no way reflects or post-dicts (viz., the opposite of 'pre-dicts') the life and times of an object that began life in high in the Eastern Rhodopes, was flaked, ground and polished – possibly in different places by different people – before damage through use entailed a reduction in size, re-sharpening and then perforation – again perhaps by yet other persons – as a much smaller object that was used in almost direct contact with possibly yet another person's body (cf. Skeates' (1995) study of Italian 'axe-amulets'). The mid-life of an object is particularly hard to seize, unless the traces of changes in mid-life are inscribed onto the object's 'skin' and not removed by later 'operations'. But the identification of such mid-life traces can offer special insights, which, though enriched by knowledge of depositional context, do not depend upon it (for the mid-lives of figurines and shell rings, see Chapman and Gaydarska 2006). The challenge here is to develop for the whole of the life-course the principle that all artifacts that embody practice – figurines, ornaments and stone tools – are in themselves meaningful (Burkitt 1999).

Ornaments are a special class of objects whose biography portrays the tension between the values of the group and the identity of the person wearing that ornament. Emphasising the communal aspect, Newell *et al.* (1990: 79) propose that ornaments are "the patterned insignia of group membership and signs of the internal ordering and structure of that group". Many of these insights are equally applicable to polished stone display axes; individual axes would have been associated with particular persons, and vice versa, as an objectification of their personae. The personal aspect of ornaments cannot, however, be ignored, since ornaments are so adjusted to the proportions of the human body, and so close to it, that they become an indissociable part of that specific social persona (Riggins 1994). Linking the personal and the communal is Powers' (2006) observation that artifacts are the material templates of a scale of values, expressed through style – the visual expression of cultural priorities. Objects do not simply signify something else, whether society, gender or identity – they have material agency, as part of what constitutes and forms lives (Miller, D. 2005: 2).

One visually significant aspect of style concerns the materials used to fashion an ornament, a figurine or a polished stone tool. The material of an object provides insights into the relationship between persons, exotic origins and distance (Ingold 2007). The world of prehistoric communities may usefully be divided into three zones: the familiar zone of our own settlement and community area; the strange zone of foreign or alien places, beings and things; and, in between the others, the zone of otherness, inhabited by people not belonging to our community but who shared artefacts and symbols with us (Neustupný, 1998; Whittle 2003; for a Balkan example, see Chapman 2007). An emphasis on local place-value and the Familiar could be conveyed by the selection of freshwater molluscs from the local river for necklace elements, while associations of the Other and the Foreign could be highlighted by preferences for ornaments made of marine molluscs or upland rocks. While the Familiar was an inescapable part of local identity, those aspects of nature brought from afar required 'domestication' before their safe use so close to the bodies of local settlers (Chapman 2003). This taming implies a reduction of the dangers of Foreign materials by its transformation into material culture. This was achieved in two ways: aesthetically, by the creation of regular, harmonious form (Helms 1993, 70–5); and socially, through the co-emergence of contexts of use, such as an array of public performances, with the appearance of the objects themselves.

It would be surprising if, in periods characterised by the emergence of new types of person and animal and the concomitant development of many new forms of relationship, there was no attempt to represent these different and varied bodies in new or extended ways. The principal representations in the Neolithic and Copper Age comprise the small-scale rendering of humans, animals, birds and reptiles known as 'figurines'. The materials used in these images vary from the most common – fired clay – to the rarest – gold and silver, with a range of stones and shells in between. Recent approaches to anthropomorphic figurines have moved significantly away from the traditional emphasis on the Earth Goddess or Great Mother Goddess (Gimbutas 1989; 1989a; Monah 1997) to consider representations of persons (Hansen 2007), the meaning of decoration (Biehl 2003), size, materiality and portability (Bailey 2005), gender relations (Hamilton in Hamilton *et al.* 1996) and the relationships between personhood and deliberate fragmentation (Chapman and Gaydarska 2006). Particularly relevant to the assemblage under consideration are the two contrasting means of creating personhood as documented by the Neolithic figurines of the Hamangia group and those of the Final Copper Age. There are three stages in the dominant form of Late Neolithic Hamangia personhood, all materialised in the biographies of Hamangia figurines: birth as an androgynous person, the shedding of one gender to become a single-genedered adult; and an old age characterised by renewed androgyny (Chapman and Gaydarska 2006, 183). There are three quite different stages in the dominant life-course of a Late Copper Age Dolnoslav person, which are also found in anthropomorphic images: birth as a person without gender atrributes; the gradual growth of one gender, predominantly female; and the fading away of that gender in post-menopausal women. The key difference between the two forms of personhood is that, in Hamangia, both genders are inherited from birth, while, in Dolnoslav, the emphasis is on taking gender as a characteristic of growth and maturation. These two concepts of personhood are radically different from each other and each can be found more widely in Balkan prehistory. Each has significant implications for the meaning of personhood in Neolithic and Copper Age communities.

The emergence of persons through their life course – or personhood – is an area in which the tangled relationships between bodies, objects and places are fundamental. Just as the identity of a thing comes from the persons contributing to its creation and life, so personhood can be characterised, at least partly, through the material world that evinces it. Part of this material world comprises the place(s) where the person grows up – whether an isolated homestead with no prior settlement history or a large community living on a tell where the ancestors had lived before for many generations. It is also formed by the nature of the material objects that are present, whether made locally or introduced through exchange or procurement. Thus, embodied practices and skills learnt in the early years become the basis for different classes of persons. There are two phases in Bulgarian prehistory in which there are dramatic increases in the variety of classes of person – the Early Neolithic and the Copper Age. Both phases of creating personhood define important changes in the political economy of production, distribution and consumption in the Neolithic and Copper Age.

Political economy

Production

It is important to recognise a range of distinctive embodied skills in persons in the pre-farming period (Ingold 2000) (Table I.1). For some of these activities, such as the making of composite microlithic tools for bows-and-arrows, large string bags and grater-boards, there are long and complex *chaînes opératoires* which involve multiple authorship and where the technology can be seen as a metaphor for society (Finlay 2003). Almost all of the types of person in foraging lifestyle can be recognised in the early farming period but there are almost 30 new types of person whose existence is predicated upon the production of new kinds of structures or objects (Table I.2). Three of these new classes of persons actually combine many skills that are unlikely to have developed within one person – farming, pottery-making and building. There must have been key co-ordinating roles for all three forms of production, each of which comprised a very complex multi-authored suite of practices. At this stage, it will be important to investigate the possibility of the development of specialised skills, which may lead to intensification of production.

In the Copper Age, there is strong continuity in the types of person found in the pre-farming and the farming periods but a further major diversification in personhood takes place, much but not all of it related to the production of lithic and metal objects and the intensification of salt production (Table I.3). While the production of Chalcolithic superblades indicates investment in large fixed facilities and community skills, there are also signs of intensification of

domestic lithic production of smaller, less complex tools, as at Late Chalcolithic Sedlare, in the Eastern Rhodopes (Raduntcheva 1997). Further changes to many traditional practices, such as woodworking, building, figurine-making and ornament-making, meant that 'Neolithic' types of person were often different in the Chalcolithic. It is important to be clear that new types of person do not necessarily mean specialists, whether part-time or full-time. The implication is that different embodied skills are developed in tune with the demand for new and expanded kinds of productive labour. By the Late Copper Age, these techniques of the body are so varied that it would be impossible for a single household family to embrace the full range of these skills, let alone a single individual. We are thus dealing with a highly diversified suite of embodied skills, suggesting that the identities of many Chalcolithic persons were negotiated against a complex scale of values determined by the combination of place-value, personal status and skill and object-value. In making comparisons between each other, persons would have found that some of their skills overlapped with others – some perhaps with many people – while other skills were special and highly valued. This complex, overlapping categorisation of persons was found in the analysis of Late Copper Age pottery production in prehistoric Bulgaria (Chapman and Gaydarska 2006, Ch. 2). In this period, it would be surprising if one did not find craft specialisation and intensified production in many locales.

Distribution

Social anthropology illustrates, in admirable detail, that exchange networks are basic to the settlement and continued dwelling of any region. In this sense, any individual site is located in a radiating net of contacts between kin, friends, neighbours and relative strangers who participate in varying

Table I.1. Kinds of person in hunter-gatherer-fisher societies

Kind of person	Archaeological evidence	Site example
Hunter	projectile points; wild animal bones	Schela Cladovei
Shellfish collector	shellfish as food debris	Trieste caves
Fisher(wo)man	fish bones as food debris; fish-traps; hooks; harpoons; carp-stunning batons	Lepenski Vir
Plant gatherer	plant food remains; pollen of edible sp.	Ezero pollen diagram
Basket-maker	impressions of basketry on pottery	East Gravettian (Kostienski)
Grater-board maker	high densities of microliths	Lepenski Vir
Bow-and-arrow maker	arrowheads	Pobiti Kamani
Flint-knapper	production debris;	Pobiti Kamani
Resource collector	resources from all zones outside the immediate site locale	Cuina Turcului
Long-distance specialist	exotic materials or finished objects	Lepenski Vir
Warrior	weapons; defensive structures	Iron Gates Mesolithic
Shaman	totemic rituals	Star Carr (UK)

Table I.2. Additional kinds of person in early farming societies

Kind of person	Archaeological evidence	Site example
Farmer	cultivated grain; crop weeds	Azmashka mogila
Ditch-digger	field boundaries	Ceithi Fields (Ireland)
Hoe-user	stone hoe-blades; soil micro- morphological traces of hoeing	Linearbandkeramik
Ploughman	stone or antler plough-shares; soil micro-morphological or macro-traces of ploughmarks	Cascioarele Belgian LBK South Street (UK)
Fence-maker	round fields	Dubravica
Weeding team	purity of archaeo-botanical sample	Chavdar
Animal keeper		
Cowboy	animal bones	Ovcharovo-Gorata
Swineherd	animal bones	Ovcharovo-Gorata
Goatherd	animal bones	Ovcharovo-Gorata
Shepherd	animal bones	Ovcharovo-Gorata
Builder		
Thatcher	thatch-impressions on roofing debris	Opovo–Bajbuk
Plasterer	preserved daub	Sofia–Slatina
Painter	traces of paint on plastered walls	Porodin
Wood-worker	size of structural post-holes	Stara Zagora–Ok. Bolnitsa
Wattle-maker	wattle impressions on wall daub	Sofia–Slatina
Potter		
Clay preparer	clay vessels; stored piles of raw clay	???
Vessel former	clay vessels	Pernik
Pot-painter	decorated clay vessels	Rakitovo
Pot-decorator	decorated clay vessels	Kardzhali
Figurine-maker	fired clay, bone and stone figurines	Azmashka mogila
Figurine-knapper	deliberate fragmentation of figurines	Anza
Spinner	spindle-whorls	Rakitovo
Weaver	loom-weights, mat impressions	Divostin I
Brewer	isotopic traces of alcohol; traces of pollen of sweet plants (mead) or honey	???
Cheese-maker	isotopic traces of milk lipids	Schela Cladovei
Ornament-maker	finely made stone and shell artifacts	Kardzhali

Table I.3. Additional kinds of person in Copper Age societies

Kind of person	Archaeological evidence	Site example
Miner	mines	
Copper miner	copper mine	Mechi Kladenets
Salt miner	salt mine	Provadia
Flint miner	flint mine	Razgrad
Gold-panner	objects made of alluvial gold	exact source ???
Salt-boiler / briquetage-maker	briquetage	Cucuteni
Basket-maker	mat impressions	Divostin
Rope-maker	rope impressions	???
Copper smelter	objects made of smelted copper	Durankulak
Mould-maker	metal objects made in a mould	Varna I
Sheet metal-maker	sheet copper or gold objects	Varna I
Metal wire-maker	copper or gold wire objects	Varna I
Specialist for gold-painting	vessels with gold-painting	Varna I
Bone figurine-maker	bone figurines	Hotnitsa
Antler tool specialist	specialised antler tools	Căscioarele

ways in the material exchanges that characterise the network (Godelier 1999; Sahlins 1974; Strathern, M. 1988). The alternative to the gift exchange of valued exotic items is direct procurement by long-distance specialists (Helms 1993) whose aim it is to 'deliver the goods' rather than maintaining inalienable relations. The detail of the precise mode of transmission must be documented on a case-by-case level but there is strong evidence that the exotic, often from distances of several hundred km, was fundamental to social structure and the creation of personhood (Sherratt 1972; Chapman 2007).

Nonetheless, the complementary distribution of resources in the Balkans – notably between upland and lowland zones – laid the basis for intra-regional and inter-regional exchange networks from the pre-farming period onwards, rising to a crescendo in the Late Copper Age (Chapman 2008). Six categories can be distinguished in such exchange networks: lithics, semi-precious stones, shells, ceramics, copper and gold. We are still suffering from only a partial knowledge of the sources of many of these materials, of which two examples suffice. The high-quality yellow-brown spotted flint utilised in the Early Neolithic of Greece and the Balkans for macro-blades has not yet been sourced, despite an extensive programme of field reconnaissance (Gurova 2004; Tsonev 2004; Bonsall 2009). Equally, the origin(s) of the gold used to such stunning effect in the Varna Eneolithic cemetery continues stubbornly to elude detection (Éluère and Raub 1991; cf. Redfern 2007). The data on sourcing copper, shells, ceramics and some semi-precious stones are more reliable and provide a framework with which to understand raw materials in surface collections (Pernicka *et al.* 1997; Gale *et al.* 2000; Kostov 2007; Chapman 2008).

Consumption

While there is a small number of sites with direct evidence of production, it is often difficult to specify the ways in which distribution has occurred – how long the material took to travel between source and end-point, through how many pairs of hands did the materials pass and what changes in the meaning of the object occurred along the way? What confronts us from the vast majority of sites is the final phase of an object's biography. The detailed investigation of the depositional and post-depositional circumstances (viz., taphonomy) is a starting-point in the study of the way that an artifact has died – whether loss in the settlement (gold rings), settlement discard because broken (pottery) or consumed (empty shells), off-site loss (more gold coins), breakage through use (working adzes) or discard (lithics), deliberate fragmentation with re-use 'after the break' (fired clay figurines) or deliberate deposit with some structuring (hoards, pit deposits, grave goods) – to quote selectively from a far wider range of possibilities.

The rule of thumb in Balkan prehistory is that the incidence and significance of formal deposits (cemeteries, hoards, burnt house assemblages, etc.) increases through time, as does the formation of object sets of varying types (Chapman 2000). This gives the surface assemblage under study an added interest, since there is a possibility of an intensive deposition of ornaments, axes and figurines at a *settlement* site of as yet uncertain date. Thus far, the introductory chapter has provided an overview of the theoretical approaches which we intend to use to fulfill the main aim of the book – the interpretation of an assemblage of prehistoric objects which lack an excavation context. The Neolithic and Chalcolithic are characterised by *both* new categories of persons co-emerging first with early farming practices and later with developments in gold and copper metallurgy *and* new forms of personhood, as materialised in fired clay anthropomorphic images. A key way of creating personal identities was participation in social networks in three spatial zones – the Familiar Zone, the Other Zone and the Foreign Zone- from each of which raw materials were actively sought and utilised. The approach of identifying artifact biographies leads to the study of production, distribution and consumption, in each of which objects showed material agency in daily practices.

But the methods which are capable of relating surface finds to past lifeways are not immediately apparent. In an attempt to unravel these relationships, we turn to the methodology of studying surface collections.

Methodologies for surface assemblages

One key aspect of the investigation of a surface collection is the accurate ascription of the site to a phase or phases of deposition. Since there has been no systematic collection of pottery from the site of Orlovo, we must turn to the non-ceramic objects for the main clues to their chronological range.

The absence of stratigraphic contexts for the ornaments from Orlovo leaves few strategies for the establishment of a probable chronology. All things considered, the typological comparison of form and raw material with the widest possible range of sites in the Balkans and Central Europe is probably the best method for producing at least a series of general probabilities for date ranges of each object type and, eventually, the whole assemblage (cf. Milojčić' (1949) principle of comparative stratigraphy). An important additional factor is the context of objects from other dated sites. If there are no examples of, e.g. Ornament Type 3A from Copper Age graves but a group of well-dated parallels from Neolithic settlements, the likely inference is that the Orlovo settlement finds are more likely to date from the Neolithic than the Copper Age. While accepting the weakness of such an inference for any single artifact type, the strength of the Orlovo assemblage is that its relatively large number of types among the figurines, the ornaments and the stone tools provides the opportunity for combined inferences of greater reliability.

It should be emphasised that the chronology on which this study is based must rely not so much on Bayesian modelling of calibrated 14C dates (e.g. Bayliss and Whittle 2007) but on their visual inspection, since the stages in the cultural sequence of each region are out of step with each other – often very seriously (e.g. the 'Late Neolithic' of Eastern Hungary partly overlaps with the 'Late Copper Age' of North Eastern Bulgaria)(see Fig I.1). For the purposes of this comparison, the somewhat arbitrary date of 4750 Cal. BC is used for the local transition (i.e., the region surrounding Orlovo) from the Neolithic to the Copper Age (Higham *et al.* 2007; Boyadzhiev 1995). The range of sites included for comparisons with the Orlovo assemblage includes all major cemeteries and hoards and a sample of major settlements from the Neolithic and Copper Age in Bulgaria, Romania, Moldova, the Ukraine, Hungary, Serbia, Croatia, FYROM, Northern Greece, Bosnia-Hercegovina and Slovenia. In the case of the figurines, reliance is placed upon Hansen's (2007) study of Near Eastern and Anatolian figurines. The existence of special possibilities and constraints for each category of object means that the methodologies for each will be presented separately.

Figurines

The methodology presented here for the study of a surface collection of figurines is centred on typology and chronology. The fragmentary state of the collection made it very difficult to define the types of figurines, even though a very flexible typological scheme was applied – a division into body parts (cf. Gaydarska *et al.* 2007, p. 174). There were two major difficulties – the differentiation between certain extremities that might have been leg(s), base(s) or the terminal(s) of vessels, and between anthropomorphic, zoomorphic and ornithomorphic heads and/or terminals. The classification of body parts utilised at Dolnoslav was modified only insofar as rare parts (e.g. a single hip) were affiliated to more common types (e.g. legs). A detailed description of each figurine is provided in the Catalogue (pp. 130–137).

In terms of chronological attribution, figurines from hundreds of excavated sites, comprising well over 2,000 examples, were used as a comparative basis. The type of sites and the type of their investigations significantly vary, as does the quality and quantity of the published material. The preference for complete and exciting figurines and the paucity of usable graphic illustration is a well-known pattern of publication in the Balkans that substantially reduces the possibilities for comparison. Nonetheless, the vast geographical area that was covered – from the Near East to Central Europe, together with the availability of an indispensable new publication – Hansen's monumental coverage of figurines from the Near East, South East and Central Europe (2007) – have ensured a relatively high representativity of the *comparanda*.

The approach used takes as a basic spatial grid three kinds of comparisons: (a) figurines with parallels found within the same 'culture area'; (b) figurines with parallels from within the Balkans; and (c) figurines with analogies from outside the Balkans. The assessment of similarity for categories (a) and (b) figurines depends upon the degree of specificity in the analogy: general parallels score '1*', closer parallels score '2*' while specific analogies score '3*'. For category (c) figurines, only very good matches are considered and, in fact, there is only one such case that poses interesting questions – a head from Ain Ghazal, Jordan. If common types, such as upper torsos of standing undecorated figurines with breasts, have long-distance parallels (e.g. a figurine fragment with a general analogue from Tepe Sarab, Iran) they are not taken into account.

Because of the highly fragmentary nature of the material, the figurines are very difficult to relate to any of the typological schemes commonly in use (e.g. Todorova 1980), especially when it comes to morphological comparisons to establish chronological relations. It is also a methodological issue – you may have a very uncharacteristic head attached to a characteristic body: the importance (hence date and interpretation) comes from the body, while, if it is only a head, the interest is reduced and it is not published. Even if single heads are published, there are many possible body forms and hence many different dates and interpretations – especially for zoomorphic and other terminals. The issue of ambiguity arises again: similar uncharacteristic terminals can be interpreted as human heads or as zoomorphic heads or terminals. For example, the head from Zorlențu Mare interpreted by Hansen as human (2007: Abb. 112: 2) has a parallel from Harmanli interpreted by Băčvarov as zoomophic: (2005, Fig. 2:1). Single parts like legs and hands are mostly very uncharacteristic and make sense only if attached to a body; there are many uncharacteristic legs from tell Sudievo that may relate to our equally uncharacteristic legs (Kunchev and Kuncheva 1993). If they are decorated, then ornaments become important but it is very rare to have a 100% match of both ornamental style and motifs.

In order to make sense of a claimed long-distance parallel such as similar heads from Orlovo and Ain Ghazal, the best practice would be to have both figurines in hand. As this is not the case, we can only rely on the striking similarity visible from the photo of the Orlovo example (Plate 4f) and the drawing of the Levantine example (Hansen 2007, Tafel 13: 11). Links between the Balkans and North West Turkey and Anatolia are sought for, indeed over-exploited, in the Balkan literature (Gatsov 2000; Raduntcheva 2003), while failing to provide any sense of how such links could have worked in practice. On a different occasion, we were faced with a similar, curious and far from straightforward case of a pumice stone found in a context that is 1000 to 1560 km away from any possible volcanic source (Gaydarska *et al.* 2004, Fig. 1). Given that the distance between Orlovo and

Ain Ghazal is over 2,500 km, it appears that we have two possibilities. The heads present a general concept of a head design and the similarity established by the visual means of a photo and a drawing is no more than a coincidence, suggesting no direct transfer of know-how or skills between the past societies. Alternatively, the Orlovo head was produced somewhere in the Levant area and was exchanged or given as a gift by a number of different societies until it had reached its final destination in South East Bulgaria. The long and complex biography acquired en route by such a figurine head would have conveyed a sense of significance and reputation. It would be unwise to deny the possibility that the figurine was brought as a personal belonging or by a long-distance specialist but, in the present state of research, it is very difficult to support such a hypothesis.

Given the above limitations of the collection and the published comparative data, the following strategy was adopted. Every figurine was visually compared to every published relevant part and any observable similarity was rated from one to three, with three marking the highest degree of similarity. The figurines with multiple, specific parallels were considered as the most secure base for dating. These Group A examples were identified as having relatively stable chronology, since in at least two sites, the analogue figurine was given the same date. The next most reliable Group was Group B comprised figurines with multiple parallels but without similar dates at different sites; thus a date range rather than a single period was identified. The same importance was assigned to figurines with a single specific (3*) parallel. The least reliable parallels comprised Group C figurines, with single analogues that have 1* or 2* degrees of similarity.

Ornaments

Turning to ornaments, the lack of context for the ornaments in this surface assemblage denies us the most fundamental possibility in the study of ornaments – the knowedge of juxtaposition of elements in a set. This means that the unit of analysis for surface collections is not the set – the 'necklace of stone beads' or the 'shell girdle' – but the individual stone bead or shell pendant itself. This atomistic approach disallows some but not all of the methodologies proposed for the study of Copper Age ornaments by Todorova and Vajsov (2001) in the most comprehensive study of Balkan prehistoric ornaments published to date. The most serious losses are the possibilities to study the relationship between the parts of the sets (e.g. girdles: Todorova and Vajsov 2001:84–86) and the relationships between the ornament and the parts of the body (2001, Abb. 4).

However, this still leaves a variety of approaches for individual ornaments. The most obvious, first stage in the study is the identification of the material from which the object is made and, if possible, the source(s) of that material.

In the sample under study, the wide variety of both shell species and stone types used for ornaments is a primary characteristic of the assemblage and it was unthinkable to pursue this study without collaboration with natural scientists (molluscan experts and geologists).

One of the few limitations of the Todorova and Vajsov (2001) volume is the paucity of discussion of the techniques of production used for Copper Age jewellery. The emphasis throughout the book is on the final form of the ornaments, in their final depositional context. The only mention of an ornament workshop refers to the famous *Spondylus* workshop at the Gumelniţa tell of Hârşova (Galbenu 1963; for an alternative account, see Chapman 2000, 97–8). As we shall see later (see below, pp. 113–4), this limitation is a reflection of the Balkan evidence – there are very few places linked to local ornament production. Thus, the second stage of the ornament study is a consideration of the *chaîne opératoire* for each raw material. Developed out of concepts of Mauss (1936) and Leroi-Gourhan (1964), this technique has a long history in French Palaeolithic research (Geneste 1985; Audouze 1999) and has now been adopted outside lithic studies as a basic way to integrate technology and theories of social practices (Dobres 2000:164–211; Dobres and Robb 2000; for *Spondylus / Glycymeris* shells, see Tsuneki 1989 or Miller, M. 2003; for figurines, see Gaydarska et al, 2007). Essentially, the method seeks to identify different stages in the production chain that leads from the raw material to the final product (and beyond!) by a recognition of the débitage that is distinctive for each stage. The most appropriate *chaîne* for the surface ornaments is a highly simplified division into four stages – (1) the raw material, (2) half-finished forms, (3) complete objects and (4) fragmented objects. Recognition of all four stages in this simplified chain for a shell species would lead to the inference of local production of the ornaments in this particular raw material. By contrast, the occurrence of only Stage 3 objects could indicate exchange of such ornaments into the site, without being able to rule out (or indeed rule in) local on-site production. Within this approach, there is scope for the recognition of specific techniques of making, such as the facetting and fine polishing of marble beads, or the selection of natural decorative features to diversify shell beads and rings. In this way, ornaments as end-products display the division and quantity of embodied labour.

A third stage in the investigation is one that dominates the Todorova and Vajsov (2001) book – the typological division of the material. Unsurprisingly, much of their work is directly applicable to the finds in question. Moreover, there is an established and cross-culturally applicable terminology for ornaments (Kenoyer 1991:82, reproduced here as Table I.4).

In addition, the *chaîne opératoire* approach leads naturally to the derivation of types from the four stages. The establishment of ornament types facilitates the cross-

Table I.4. Definition of basic ornament types (based on Kenoyer 1991: 82)

Type of ornament	Definition
Bead	any object that is perforated along its major axis, generally worn on a cord or a wire, sewn onto clothing or used as an ornament
Pendant	any object that is perforated or scored at one end and is hung or attached to a cord or wire, sewn onto clothing or used as an ornament.
Bangle	any circlet (closed or open) made of a continuous homogenous material that can be worn on the arm or ankle
Bracelet	any circlet made of components such as beads, chain or cord, etc., that can be worn on the arm or ankle

correlation of types with raw materials, leading to inferences about the degree of specialised choice in ornament-making (viz., the finding that all axe-pendants were made of serpentinite would suggest specialised choice, though not necessarily specialised making!). It is a *sine qua non* of typological studies that the better the typology, the more informative subsequent research stages will be.

The fourth stage in surface ornament research is dependent upon the third, typological stage and concerns external comparison with other assemblages. This stage is especially important for a surface collection, since there are no internal mechanisms for chronological attribution. Two factors facilitiate the inter-site ornament comparison: the use of individual ornaments as the basis for typology and the usually complete nature of the objects under study. This means that it is possible, in a very high percentage of cases, to assign a potential parallel to an ornament type or reject it as too different. This was clearly not the case for either figurines or polished stone tools (see pp. 35–8 and 99–100).

Perusal of the published literature reveals five ways in which ornaments are 'published', which are listed here in order of increasingly utility (sadly, inversely proportional to frequency!): (1) an ornament type mentioned in the text but not illustrated (e.g. Slatino: Chohadzhiev 2006:39); (2) a *Typentafel* of ornaments, usually schematised and with individual ornaments drawn at a small scale (e.g. Goljamo Delchevo: Todorova 1975, Obr. 39); (3) photograph(s) of an individual ornament with a summary description (e.g. chapters in the Ecsegfalva 23 report: Choyke 2007; Oross and Whittle 2007; Starnini *et al.* 2007); (4) line drawings at an appropriate scale with a full description and consideration of the site context (e.g. Sitagroi: Nikolaidou 2003); and (5) a period / region synthesis with full description and illustration of the ornaments, together with a discussion of their cultural contexts (e.g. Bulgarian Copper Age ornaments: Todorova and Vajsov 2001). A succesful inter-site comparative study depends upon at least a number of Type 3 and 4 studies from each period, in a time range 7000–3000 Cal. BC – subdivided into 500–year blocks, and each region in South East and Central Europe. These core studies should be supplemented by a further group of

Type 1 and 2 studies for each period / region, to give added breadth if not depth to the comparison. The limitation of the evidence increases the higher the proportion of Type 1 and 2 studies, insofar as it increases the uncertainty of whether or not the actual type under consideration is represented at another site. But it is only fair to point out that there are probably many examples of half-finished ornaments and shell objects that have not even reached level (1) in the publication ladder because they have been considered as of insufficient importance to merit publication. Thus, when we state that there are few parallels for 'bead blanks', this may well signify their paucity in publications, not necessarily a genuine rarity in the past!

The final inference of probable date for an individual type relies on the range of both positive and negative occurrences at other dated sites or horizons. A clear majority of close analogies in one 500–year block, with only one or a few occurrences outside this period, enables a strong chronological inference; greater spatial proximity to the site also increases the probability of relevance. At a higher level of inference, a comparison of the sum total of chronological inferences for each individual ornament type enables a judgment on the probable chronological distribution of ornament deposition. As with seasonal indicators at a settlement (e.g. Star Carr: Legge and Rowley-Conwy 1988), there will be close analogies diagnostic of a specific period which permit a strong inference of deposition at that period, irrespective of other general diachronic patterns.

The fifth and final stage in the ornament study is the interpretation of the findings of the other four stages, in line with the theoretical approaches outlined above (pp. 77–79).

The wide-ranging search for analogies for the figurines and the ornaments has yielded valuable spatial data, which can be used to characterise the main regions with which strong social networks have been developed. An initial screening of the number of sites per region is necessary to define, if not to reduce, the bias in the frequency of parallels caused by differential site exavation and/or publication. The type of discovery context for analogies – whether settlement, cemetery or hoard – is also a sign of the extent of social significance of the material culture in question.

Polished stone tools

Polished stone tools from excavations constitute part of a class of finds which is rarely studied in depth, and especially, from a mineralogical and petrographical point of view in Bulgarian prehistory (Kunchev 2000; Kostov and Pelevina 2006; Kostov 2007; Anastasova 2008; Kostov and Machev 2008) and only occasionally in the Balkans as a whole. Most of the publications of such types of artifacts consist of brief descriptions, rarely accompanied by petrological analysis (but see Draguşeni: Muraru 2000) and usually very poorly illustrated. Line drawings of shape, longitudinal and cross sections are exceptional, the rule being of presenting black and white photographs of low quality. The scale of illustrations and the size of tools are not a common feature in the publications, nor is the total number of tools and separate types of tools (e.g. axes or chisels) found within a site. Very few site reports provide any systematic information on tool size (exceptions include Sitagroi (Elster 2003) and Divostin (Prinz 1988)), while data on tool weight or object colour are even less common. Even the typology of ground and polished stone tools generally remains at a common-sense level, with divisions between 'axes', 'adzes' and 'chisels', and the contrast between categories such as 'working axes' vs. 'miniature axes'. Moreover, there are very few sites from which all ground stone tools are published (an exception is the catalogue of the Durankulak cemetery: Todorova 2002 *et al.*). Usually, a selection of tools is presented based on the choice of the excavator (e.g. Goliamo Delchevo: Todorova *et al.* 1975) or the assemblage is typified and presented by several unified types (e.g. Ovcharovo: Todorova *et al.* 1983). This sequence of unfortunate facts makes any new investigation of ground stone tools very difficult in terms of comparative study and consideration of tradition and innovation. In addition, the impression is that there is a slower rate of change in polished stone tools than for figurines and ornaments, leading to the rarity of distinctive type-fossils. An example is the blanket chronological label "Neolithic–Chalcolithic" for the high-quality photographs of polished stone axes in the Stara Zagora Regional Museum collections (Kalchev 2005). These last two factors led to the lack of fine-grained chronology that could be established for figurines and personal ornaments, as much as a less nuanced pattern of inter-regional contacts.

In this report, we seek to rescue polished stone tools from their comparative neglect. We cannot readily extend the *chaîne opératoire* approach used for figurines and ornaments to the polished stone assemblage, since there is little *débitage* from the stages of production. Instead, we focus on artifact biographies and the ways in which the agency of the object can bring about change in prehistoric lifeways. The objects' place of origin and the quality of the available stone resources are linked in a dynamic way to the persons making, distributing, using and depositing the tools. Rather than a reliance on precise, abstract typology, the tool groups that we propose relate to the perception of a specific tool size in relation to past experience of making and anticipated uses and the contexts of everyday *habitus*. A multi-variate approach is favoured, in which variables such as production techniques, raw material, colour, wear and damage are related to each other to produce a rich and dense account of why people in the region made the specific tools that they did and changed their forms part-way into their lives.

The structure of the book

It is our contention that the surface collection studied in this book is of some significance for the prehistory not only of South East Bulgaria but also for European prehistory as a whole and that its study and publication are a research priority. It was for this reason that, together with our Bulgarian colleagues Dr.Sc. Ana Raduntcheva, Mr. Irko Petrov and Dr. Ruslan I. Kostov, and our two illustrators, Ms. Yvonne Beadnell and Ms. Elena Georgieva, we have completed the study of these extraordinary finds. In this book, we should like to present our results.

Following the thematic introduction, we set the site itself in its local and regional context in Chapter 1, both in terms of the environment past and present and the cultural contexts. In the next three chapters, we take a close look at the assemblage, with the figurines studied in Chapter 2, the ornaments in Chapter 3 and the polished stone tools in Chapter 4, while the small number of Other finds is discussed in Appendix 2. Each chapter examining the finds shares a common approach to the issue of the date of the main phases of deposition – a local, regional and inter-regional comparison of the finds with other cognate assemblages, using a broad diachronic span of 7000–3000 Cal. BC and a spatial network stretching from the Ukraine to Western Hungary (East–West) and from Greece to Northern Romania (South – North). But there are specific differences between these three chapters in other respects; the emphasis on raw materials and their sources for the ornament chapter; the portrayal of clear or ambiguous objects (anthropomorphic, zoomorphic or ornitho-zoomorphic), as well as questions of decoration and costume in the figurine chapter; and the relationship between form, raw material and function in the polished stone tools chapter.

The analyses of the separate finds classes comes together in the central chapter of the book – Chapter 5, where an attempt is made to interpret the human, animal and bird images, the ornaments and the polished stone display tools in terms of an overarching framework of personhood and political economy. The text concludes with a chapter re-stating the main findings. The basic data on the surface assemblage are presented in the catalogue of finds, which is supplemented by a limited set of photographs and line drawings (here, Appendix 1). The small assemblage of 'Other Finds' is presented in Appendix 2. The full set of archive photographs is accessible through the Durham University Department of Archaeology web page via John Chapman's research profile (URL: http://www.durham.ac.uk/archaeology/research/

1. The Site of Orlovo in its Local and Regional Context

The multi-period prehistoric settlement of Orlovo – Orlovska Chuka (Plate 1a) is located in the south-east part of Bulgaria, just North of the Rhodopes mountain range. In modern terms, the site is located 0.8 km North East of the North Eastern edge of the village of Orlovo, some 12 km South of the town of Haskovo and 25 km North North East of the town of Kardzhali (Plate 2a). The latitude of the site is 41° 57' 28", the longitude is 25° 29' 51" and by far the greater part of the site lies at an altitude of 230–235 masl. It was discovered in the 1980s by Dimitur Aladzhov (Aladzhov 1997, 200–201), as part of the Haskovo Museum's independent field survey to provide the basis for a regional settlement history. The Neolithic–Chalcolithic part of the complex covers an area of 1.5 ha and is partly overlain by a 5 m-high Thracian barrow (Plate 1b).

The site and its environment

Site topography

The Turkish toponym of the site –'Giurush' – means a 'very flat place'. The site lies on a high (65 m) terrace of the Harmanlijska reka (Fig. 1.1). It covers several low rises in an East–West series that form the high terrace. The terrace forms an abrupt slope to the North of the site, constraining access to the high-quality pasture of the floodplain (Plate 1c). By contrast, the ground slopes gently to the South, providing excellent arable land (Plate 1a).

Geology

The geological background of the Orlovo site (Plate 2b) is represented by two formations: the Paleogene ($2Pg_23$) coal-bearing and sandy formation and the Neogene (ahN_{1-2}) Akhmatovo formation (Boyanov *et al.* 1989; 1992).

Southeast of the Orlovo site and near the village of Knizhovnik are outcropping Precambrian metamorphic rocks. They are represented by the Zhulti Chal formation and Lessovo-type gneiss-granites – both rock formations belonging to the Pra-Rhodope Super Group (Boyanov *et al.* 1989).

The Zhulti Chal formation is some 600–700 m in thickness and composed of fine- to medium-grained biotitic and biotite-muscovitic gneisses, gneiss-schists, schists, amphibolites (in cases with pieces of metamorphosed ultrabasic rocks, serpentinites) and graphite-bearing quartzites. Typical for the formation is the presence of garnet. Later dykes, with a dioritic porphyritic or lamprophyric composition, have been metamorphosed (Boyanov *et al.* 1992, 11–12).

Among the gneiss-granites which are of a uniform grain structure and granoblastic texture are common xenoliths of amphibolites, serpentinites and gneisses (Boyanov *et al.* 1992, 13). Their composition is of quartz, plagioclase (oligoclase), microcline and biotite, in cases substituted by sericite, chlorite and a second generation of quartz. They are a product of a regional metamorphism in the amphibolite facies. Porphyroblastic gneisses are known 6–7 km to the East of the site.

The Paleogene coal-bearing and sandy formation is widespread around the village of Orlovo. At its base, there is a layer of conglomerates of a mostly quartz composition and in some cases with gneiss pebbles, followed next by a multiple alternation of yellow-brown or grey sandstones and aleurolites together with conglomerates (Boyanov *et al.* 1992, 27; see also Goranov and Atanasov 1989). Along the coal-bearing horizons, the colour of the sediments is dark gray and black.

The Neogene sedimentary rocks of the Akhmatovo formation have a transgressive and discordant horizontal position overlying the ancient metamorphic rocks and Paleogene sediments (Boyanov *et al.* 1992, 44). They are usually pale gray in colour, but yellowish and red hues are also observed. Their composition includes sands, sandstones, clays, limestones and gravels, the most important being the fine- to medium-grained sandstones or loosely-termed sandstones with a clay cement. The mineral composition of the sand is represented by quartz, feldspar, mica, as well as pieces of metamorphic and volcanic rocks, quartz and pegmatite – all with rounded or rough forms. The thickness of the formation has been estimated from 120–150 m to

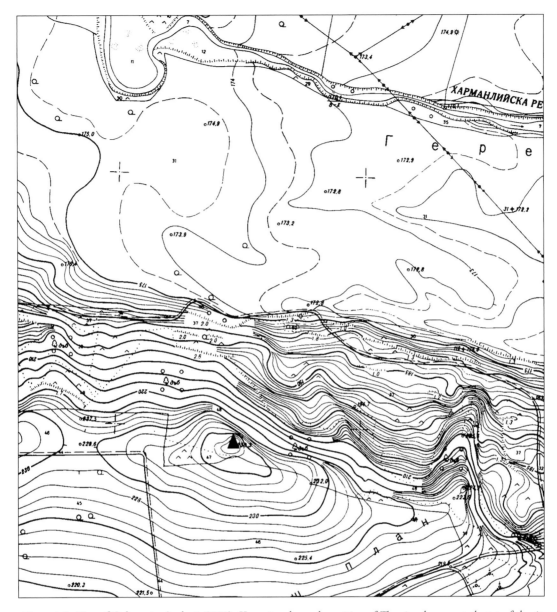

Figure 1.1. Map of Orlovo site (scale: 1:5000). Key: triangle marks position of Thracian barrow at the top of the site

about 350 m and has been related to three mega-cycles of formation (Meotian, Pont-Dacian and Upper Pliocene) (Dragomanov *et al.* 1984).

Along the river valleys, there are Quaternary and modern alluvial-proluvial sediments (Holocene) (aQh). The alluvial sediments can vary in thickness up to 30 m, as in the case of stretches of the Maritsa River.

From a tectonic point of view, the Orlovo site is located in the large Harmanli Block with superimposed Paleogene depressions. Small faults with a NW-SE orientation are observed SW of the village of Knizhovnik, but they are covered by sediments at the archaeological site.

The ore field closest to the site is the Spahievo lead-zinc ore field (Maneva 1988), which is located about 18 km to the West. This ore field includes one of the few sources of turquoise in Bulgaria.

Non-metallic mineral raw materials in the area are white granular quartz veins to the East in the village of Bryagovo, coal layers, zeolite-bearing volcanic tuffs, halloysite-kaolinite clays at Gorni Glavanak and very plastic clays with a 10 m thickness of the layers near the town of Harmanli. Bitumen-bearing schists (shale oil) with a 20–60 m thickness have been described South of the villages of Orlovo and Mandra (Minchev *et al.* 1964). The Eastern Rhodopes are also well

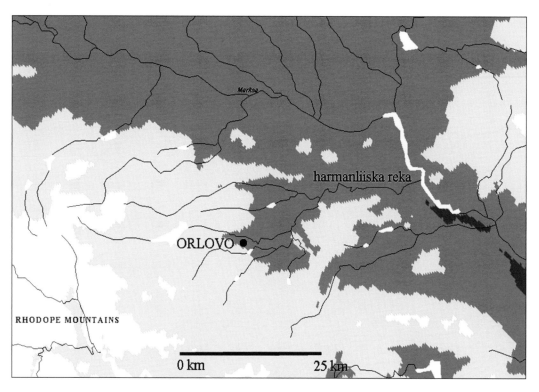

Figure 1.2. Hydrological network of the Haskovo area

known as a source for precious and decorative minerals and aggregates – mainly the different varieties of quartz (including amethyst) or chalcedony (including the agates), opal, jasper and related rocks (Petrusenko and Kostov 1992).

Hydrology and geomorphology

The Harmanlijska reka is a second-order tributary of the river Maritsa, which it joins some 35 km downstream of the site of Orlovo (at the modern town of Harmanli) (Fig. 1.2). This river is now sluggish, with a low sediment load, which has been strongly affected by the construction of the Thrakiets reservoir 12 km upstream. The river has its sources 35 km upstream of the site, in the Chukata hills, which are foothills of the Eastern Rhodopes.

To the South of the site is the Beklovska River, with the small Knizhovnik dam located just 1–2 km East of the village of Orlovo. Both the Harmanlijska river and its tributary, the Beklovska River, as well as other small rivers, have their origin in the Chukata Range in the Northern part of the Eastern Rhodopes.

From a geomorphological point of view, the Orlovo site is located in the Upper Thracian sub-region of the Thracian–Strandja region of South Bulgaria and related to the Haskovo Hills region (*Geografiya na Bulgaria* 2002, 395–396).

Communications

In terms of communications, there are no obvious hindrances to movement either way along the river valley, while mobility north across the Thracian Plain is equally unconstrained. However, movement to the South is an entirely different question (Plate 2a). Penetration into the Eastern Rhodopes is readily made, if slow, by following the ridge-top routes between the Virovitsa and Tsiganska streams (the modern villages of Gorno Vojvodino and Most) through to the valley of the river Perperek. Passage South of the Perperek valley to the Aegean drainage is somewhat harder, requiring the crossing of complex upland topography and dense vegetation both in the valleys and on the ridges but not as challenging as the high-mountain terrain of the Central or the West Rhodopes. An alternative route to the Aegean – longer but far easier – is to travel downstream to the river Maritsa and follow that river to the sea – a trip of ca. 100 km.

Modern soils

According to a general soil map of Bulgaria, the Haskovo–Orlovo area falls within a mixture of thicker, more fertile soils – mostly cinnomonic forest soils – of the Central Thracian–Tundja soil province of the Balkan-Mediterranean soil Subregion (*Geografiya na Bulgaria* 2002, 305) and the shallower rankers, lithosols and smolnitsa of the Haskovo

Svilengrad 52 masl

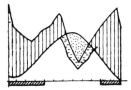

Mladinovo 330 masl

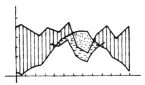

Dzhebel 326 masl

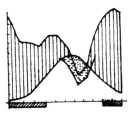

Figure 1.3. Water balance diagram for Svilengrad, Mladinovo and Dzhebel, January–December (source: Bondev 1991). Key: vertical hatching:excess precipitation; dotted areas: potential deficit; horizontal dashes: deficit in precipitation

Hills zone (*Geografiya na Bulgaria.* 2002, 304; see also Sarafov 2000, maps p. 49, 51, 53). The floodplain of the Harmanlijska reka is covered in alluvial meadow soils.

Modern climate

The modern climatic data are based upon records kept at eight local weather stations in South East Bulgaria over periods between 28 and 58 years (Bondev 1991, 20–46). The modern climate of the region may be characterised as a transitional Continental climatic zone, with long, dry summers and cold, rainy winters. The effect of altitude is only moderately strong in a comparison of the climate in the Orlovo area with that of the surrounding Thracian plain and the Eastern Rhodopes. Mean temperatures for the Haskovo region in July reach a mean 23–24° and for January +1° to 0° (*Geografiya na Bulgaria* 2002, 170–171). The average year's amplitude of temperature (the difference between the average temperatures in January and July) for the last

70 years of the 20th century AD is 21–23° (*Geografiya na Bulgaria* 2002, 148).

The three weather stations of Svilengrad, Mladinovo and Dzhebel (Fig. 1.3) indicate similar trends in seasonal climate, with longer summer water imbalances at Svilengrad, the lowest-lying of the three, and spring and winter peaks in precipitation at Svilengrad and Dzhebel. However, the precipitation is high in all months except July and August at Mladinovo – at a similar altitude to that of Dzhebel (Bondev 1991, figs 12, 14 and 18). The length of drought periods for the full set of eight weather stations (Bondev 1991, tab. 1) indicates a weak correlation with altitude (Fig. 1.4), with little reduction in the length of droughts at Kardzhali despite its location in an inter-montane basin. Interpolation of the altitude of Orlovo (230–235 masl) into this chart indicates the likelihood of a 2–3 month period of summer drought in the valley of the Harmanlijska reka.

These climatic parameters are important for providing a framework for understanding the agricultural potential of these regions in comparison to the climatic features of the Near Eastern, Levantine and Anatolian source areas for the major Neolithic cereal cultivars of South East Europe – viz., the mountains of the subtropics from 25° to 45° North, with their cold winters, wet springs and autumns, as well as hot dry summers (Hawkes 1969, 21). The climatic data also provide support for the notion of a possible summer grazing problem for lowland communities with a strong emphasis on pastoralism. The location of Orlovo at an ecological boundary between the lowlands and the uplands may assume more importance in such periods.

Modern vegetation

As with most lowland areas in modern Bulgaria, there have been major anthropogenic effects on the prehistoric forest since the Iron Age (Chapman *et al.* 2009). These effects include the expansion of cultivation in the post-War era, so that much of the territory around the site continues to be under intensive arable cultivation. There are remnants of lowland forest cover near the site, as near Sirakovo, 15 km West of the site. The major forested areas, however, lies South of Orlovo, in the foothills of the Eastern Rhodopes (Plate 1d).

In his major survey of the vegetation of Bulgaria, Bondev (1991, 96–97, 119, 134 and Karta 1) outlines three vegetational zones whose remains are represented in the modern anthropogenically-altered flora: flood-plain forests including small-leaved elm (*Ulmus minor* Mill.), Caucasian ash (*Fraxinus oxycarpa* Willd.) and long-thorned oak (*Quercus pedunculiflora* C. Koch); lower terraces, with mixed oak forests of *Quercus cerris* L. (Turkey oak) and *Quercus frainetto* Ten. (Hungarian oak); and higher terraces, with similar mixed oak forest but with elements of the Mediterranean flora such as juniper (*Juniperus oxycedrus*

L.), bladder senna (*Colutea arborescens* L.) and false senna (*Coronilla emerus* L.).

The regional topographical context

The Orlovo site lies close to an ecological boundary, marked by the Northern edge of the foothills of the Eastern Rhodopes (Plate 2a). In this part of the Rhodopes, the boundary of the first range from the Thracian Plain travelling South – the modern 'Chukata' – lies less than 10 km South West of the site. Thus, all of the notional 5–km territory of the Orlovo site is located in a largely arable zone with high potential for pastoralism. Within one day's round trip (10 km maximum distance from the site), there is access to additional pasture, as well as upland stone resources. Longer visits of up to 20 km would have been necessary to access the full range of rock sources for tools and ornaments. Thus, the site occupies an important place on the Southern margins of the arable zone of the Thracian Plain and just North of the Northern margins of an upland zone rich in rocks and minerals. This is, of course, also the case for the Haskovo region as a whole, making the region of considerable interest in prehistoric exchange between upland and lowland zones with complementary resources (cf. Sherratt 1972; Chapman 1981).

However, there is a paradox about the Eastern Rhodopes: while proclaiming itself in terms of its topography, vegetation, soils and, most particularly geology, the Eastern Rhodopes contains a number of inter-montane basins which are only 100–120 m higher than the Southernmost parts of the Thracian Plain, such as the Orlovo area. While both the Central and Western Rhodopes boast mountain peaks over 2000 m in altitude (Goljam Sjutkya at 2,186 m; Goljam Perelik at 2,191 m), the highest peak in the Eastern Rhodope is Tikla, with a peak rising to 744 m. The terrain of the Kardzhali basin varies from 350–500 masl, while that of the Krumovgrad basin is similar. Thus the Eastern Rhodopes are not so much classic mountain terrain as rolling foothills with a sizeable proportion of flat, fertile land.

Palaeo-environment

Direct data for the palaeo-environment of the Haskovo region and the Orlovo site are not as yet available. Recent motorway projects have begun to incorporate palaeo-environmental investigations: examples include the short reports on the natural environment of the Vinitsa area near Purvomaj (Kenderova and Sarafov 2006), the Keramlaka area near Krum, Dimitrovgrad (Evtimova *et al.* 2006, 267–8), the Brantiite area near Svilengrad (Kenderova in Nehrisov 2006, 397–8 and 454) and the short discussion of the immediate environs of Yabulkovo (Leshtakov 2004, 85–86). However, these reports present few generalised findings that could be applied to a wider area than that investigated.

The findings of a recent palaeo-environmental project in which pollen cores were extracted from the Ezero-dipsis marsh, near Nova Zagora, and the Göl Baba palaeo-meander, near Edirne in North Western Turkish Thrace showed that, during the millennia of particular interest – 7000–3000 Cal BC, the palaeo-climate was too dry for continuous sedimentation throughout the year (Magyari *et al.* 2008). This meant that the pollen records for the Neolithic and Chalcolithic were missing from the core. Nonetheless, this cautionary tale indicates that the mid-Holocene temperatures were several degrees C higher than the modern temperatures and that precipitation was probably lower than today.

A multivariate study of the pollen diagrams available in Bulgaria up to 2000 (Gaydarska 2007, chapter 4) provides a generalised reconstruction of vegetation history for the Thracian lowlands. The main features of the mid-Holocene forests are long-lasting mesoxerophyllic oak and hornbeam forests from the 7th millennium Cal. BC onwards, with some evidence for an increase in hornbeam (*Carpinus betulus*) between 6400 and 3900 Cal BC but no increases in hazel (*Corylus*) or beech (*Fagus sylvatica*) in this period (2007, 66–67).

The local and regional context of Orlovo

The date of the Orlovo occupations

The site is considered to be an extended Neolithic–Chalcolithic flat site, measuring 250 × 60m (Aladzhov 1997, 200–201)(Fig. 1.1). Since there was no interest shown in the pottery from Orlovo, none was collected by the villagers, although Aladzhov claims to have collected Early and Late Neolithic pottery and illustrates a Chalcolithic figurine head (1997, 200–201 and Obr. 96). There is therefore no relative chronology for settlement phases based upon the traditional ceramic typology. An Easter 2007 visit to the site by the authors, in the presence of the Haskovo District Police Force, revealed surface scatters of lithic débitage (including carnelian-type stones) and Late Neolithic and Chalcolithic pottery in varying concentrations along the highest part of the terrace, produced by recent shallow ploughing.

The issue of site chronology is discussed extensively in Chapters 2–6 of the book, as a fundamental question for the interpretation of this assemblage.

Other sites in the valley of the Harmanlijksa reka

The principal source for the archaeology of the Harmanlijska reka is Aladzhov (1997), supplemented by recent motorway investigations (e.g. Ignatov *et al.* 2006). It should, however, be recalled that these are minimum numbers, in the absence of intensive, systematic fieldwalking in the valley.

In addition to Orlovo, a small number of prehistoric settlements has been found, consisting of both tells and flat sites (Fig. 1.5). This includes three Early–Late Neolithic

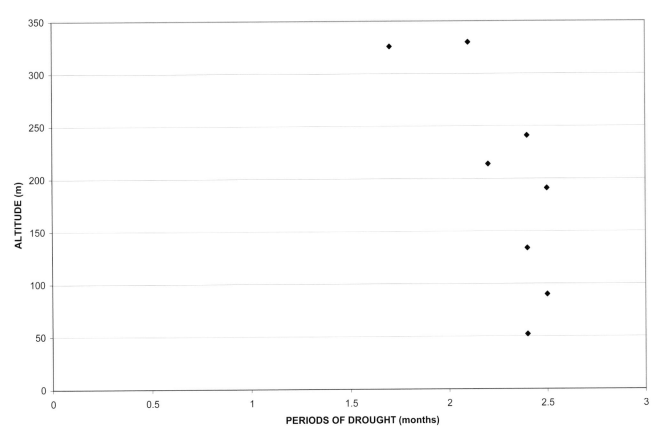

Figure 1.4. Altitude vs. drought periods, Haskovo lowlands and Eastern Rhodopes

sites – two tells at Konush and Dinevo 1 and one flat sites at Nikolovo. In the Copper Age, the Konush tell was abandoned but occupations were renewed at the Dinevo 1 tell and the Nikolovo flat site. However, two new open Copper Age sites were founded, at Dinevo 2 and Stojkovo. Only three sites showed signs of renewed occupation in the Bronze Age – the Dinevo 1 tell and the Stojkovo and Nikolovo open sites. There was no renewed occupation in the Bronze Age at Dinevo 2 but, equally, there was no new settlement in the Bronze Age – only renewed occupations at well-known places. In summary, minimum site numbers varied from 3 (Neolithic) to 4 (Copper Age) to 3 (Bronze Age), with varying rates of renewed occupation.

It will be important to establish the date of the first occupation at the Orlovo site, in terms of its likely social relations with the three other Early Neolithic sites – two tells and one flat site. One aspect of this question concerns the potential position of Orlovo as a founder community in the Harmanlijska reka or, instead, in a subsidiary social position in relation to earlier sites with a prior history of dwelling (cf. Kopytoff 1987, esp. pp. 12–23). Another interesting issue is the rate at which place-value would have

accumulated (Chapman 1997) at the Orlovo settlement. Moreover, we could enquire whether or not there are periods in the Neolithic and Chalcolithic when Orlovo would have seemed to be an 'ancestral' settlement in comparison with other, newly occupied places. It should be recalled that the location of the Thracian barrow (Plate 1b) on part of the long-abandoned Orlovo site can be read as a reference to the 'ancestral' qualities of that place.

Settlement spacings can be given only a maximum value for the linear, along-the-valley distance; with systematic, intensive survey, these values would certainly decrease! Given the presently known settlement network, and assuming deposition at Orlovo occurred both in the Neolithic and the Chalcolithic, the values varied from 4–12 km in the Neolithic (mean = 8.3 km); 2–13 km in the Copper Age (mean = 8 km); and 7–24 km in the Bronze Age (mean = 15.5 km). These figures are broadly comparable for the Sokolitsa valley in the Maritsa Iztok settlement network, some 20–35 km to the North East (Gaydarska 2007: Chapter 5), where the Neolithic inter-site distances varied from 8–14 km (mean = 11 km) while the Copper Age distances varied between 1 and 14 km (mean = 7 km). This

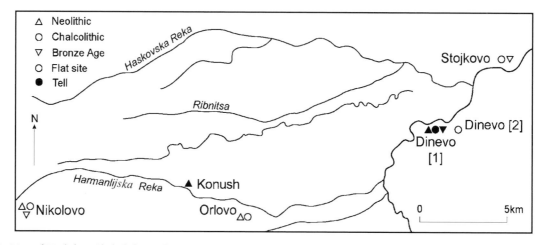

Figure 1.5. Map of Neolithic, Chalcolithic and Bronze Age flat sites and tells in the Harmanlijska reka (based upon data in Aladzhov 1997)

suggests that the Orlovo community was within a one- to two-hour walk of their nearest neighbours – a time-distance that opened up the possibilities for reasonably intensive contact and interaction at the local level, as well as the development of social networks validated and sustained by gift exchange of prestige objects.

Settlement in the South Eastern Thracian plain and the Eastern Rhodopes

One interesting part of the changing face of Bulgarian prehistory in the last decade has been the balance of research interest and knowledge about tells vs. flat sites. The importance of tells was recognised in the early years of the last century (Seure and Degrand 1906), in at least two senses: an accumulation of well-preserved and often spectacular finds, as well as a stratigraphic key to chronological developments. This position was strengthened by the Karanovo excavations, whose sequence was enshrined in the conference paper that Georgi Georgiev read to the Prague UISPP (Georgiev 1961; cf. later chronological revisions by V. Nikolov 1998), as much as by the often poor-quality discoveries made on those few flat sites that were excavated. There have been fewer large-scale investigations of flat sites, which were more common in the uplands, as well as in Western and in Northern Bulgaria. The site of Nova Zagora–Hlebozavoda is a good example of a large Karanovo IV (Late Neolithic) flat settlement within the main tell concentration in Thrace (Kunchev and Kuncheva 1988).

However, road builders have taken on the cost implications of excavating tells, so that very few motorway routes have crossed mounds (for a narrow escape, see the case of Polgár-Csőszhalom in Hungary: Raczky *et al.* 2002). Instead, the large-scale rescue excavations spawned by motorway construction have often hit large open sites of a previously

unknown kind. In South East Thrace, two classic examples of the large-scale, multi-period flat site, sometimes dominated by pit deposition, are Yabulkovo (Leshtakov 2004; 2006; Leshtakov *et al.* 2006) and Ljubimets (Nikolov *et al.* 2001; Nikolov 2002). It is in the context of these large multi-period flat sites that the Orlovo site can be recognised as a specific kind of archaeological monument, with its own characteristics and features. One principal feature is that these newly recognised flat sites are large sites by prehistoric standards in South East Bulgaria. So it is that the Karanovo IV period – once poorly known because poorly represented on excavated tells – is now becoming much better known because of its focus at many large open sites (e.g. Dimitrov, M. 1976; Todorova 1995).

In view of the lack of systematic, intensive field survey, it is difficult to gain an accurate picture of the changing settlement dynamics in the Upper Thracian Plain. Leshtakov (2004: 86 and Fig. 1) claims that there were small numbers of Early Neolithic settlements, with an increase in the number of sites – whether open-air and tell sites is not specified – in the Middle Neolithic (Karanovo III) and Late Neolithic (Karanovo IV) and the highest site densities, up to that phase, in the Early Chalcolithic (Karanovo V). Leshtakov relates the high densities of settlement to the fertility of the area, the good riverine communications and the ready availability of rocks and minerals (trachyandesites, quartz varieties and polymetallic ore sources). The typical feature of Late Copper Age (Karanovo VI) settlement in the Upper Thracian plain was a peak in site numbers, often comprising tells (Todorova 1978; Raduntcheva 2003).

The archaeology of upland regions has traditionally been regarded with mistrust, caused by the unspoken assumption that the inferior status and conservative nature of modern upland populations is mirrored in prehistory. However, the active role of regional Historical Museums, such as in

Kardzhali, and the popular media attention on 'Thracian' Orphic shrines such as Perperikon (Ovcharov 2005), has led to a renaissance of Eastern Rhodopean prehistory in the last decade. This new interest has benefited, if not always directly, from the hard-won insights of scholars such as Ana Raduntcheva and Georgi Nehrisov who have been working over a longer period in the region – the former on prehistoric settlement and the prehistoric foundations of later Thracian sanctuaries (Raduntcheva 1990; 1999), the latter on all aspects of the Iron Age, including megalithic monuments and, more recently, pre- and proto-historic gold mining at Ada Tepe (Nehrisov 2003; 2007). In addition, Late Copper Age and later settlements have been excavated under the aegis of the major infra-structural project at Makaza, near the planned Bulgarian–Greek border crossing (Boyadzhijev and Nehrisov 2008; Boyadzhijev Ya. and K. 2008).

We are thus in a position to demonstrate that there were two principal phases of uplands occupation before the Bronze Age: an early phase dated to the Early Neolithic and a late phase, dated to the Later Copper Age. At present, it remains difficult to identify finds dating to the intervening phases, which last from ca. 5300 to 4500 Cal BC. This would appear to be a good case of punctuated settlement that is so common in upland zones. A classic example is the Zemplén Mountains of North East Hungary, with settlement in the Middle Neolithic and then again in the Late Bronze Age but apparently lacking any intervening discard for a period of 2,500 years (4700–1500 Cal BC) (Chapman *et al.* 2010).

In the early phase, settlers were established in the Eastern Rhodopes not only at nascent tells, such as Sedlare (Raduntcheva 1997) but also at multi-phase flat sites such as Krumovgrad, with its wide range of tools as well as figurines and a marble phallus (Kunchev and Chohadzhiev 1994), and Kardzhali, with its nephrite stonework attesting to links with Neolithic Anatolia and Greece (Peïkov 1972). There is also an early interest in rocky landscapes, as seen in the swallow-hole deposition at Pchelarovo, North of Kardzhali, where richly ornamented objects from the Early Neolithic (and again later in the Later Copper Age) were deposited in a sink-hole in the local limestone (material in Regional Historical Museum, Kardzhali). Local deposits of agates and chalcedony were also exploited in the Early Neolithic, at sites such as the Kerez kaja rock-shelter, Podkova and Svinarnika (Zlateva-Uzunova 2004), although, intriguingly, the author suggests on the basis of lithic typology that there may also have been a Karanovo III occupation at the last-named (2004, 19). None of these sites is claimed as a specialised lithic workshop site – rather as reflecting periodic seasonal visits by mobile populations (2004, 19).

It is important to determine whether or not there was Early Neolithic deposition at Orlovo, so as to establish whether or not Orlovo was related to the early settlement of the Eastern Rhodopes. Whatever the answer to this question, the three

independently documented Early Neolithic settlements in the Harmanlijska reka would have been linked through social networks to the early phase of upland settlement.

The de-coupling that may have occurred in the Early Neolithic between Orlovo and settlements in the Eastern Rhodopes is certainly present in the Late Neolithic period. This is a time when deposition is attested at Orlovo and other settlements in the valley but there is little if no sign as yet of Rhodopean settlement.

This de-coupling is reversed in the Late Chalcolithic, when there is a dramatic surge of settlement in both the lowland plains and the upland zone (Todorova 1978). Both tells and flat sites are occupied in greater numbers than at any previous period and the quantity and diversity of deposited objects in this so-called 'Climax Copper Age' reaches new heights (Chapman and Gaydarska 2006). The research of Ana Raduntcheva on upland Chalcolithic sanctuaries (1990, 1999) has shown that many of the so-called 'Thracian' sanctuaries started their active life far earlier than the 1st millennium BC, with deposition of Late Chalcolithic materials in rock niches and fissures. At some upland peak sites, such as Perperikon, there is evidence of a Late Chalcolithic occupation layer (Raduntcheva 1997, 199 and figs 22–23), betokening more than only summer visits and seasonal acts of deposition. There is probably a middle way between the functionalist claims of Vassil Nikolov, for whom upland pottery represents nothing more than the material traces of summer transhumance (p.c., V. Nikolov) and Ana Raduntcheva, who has seen symbolic forces in most of the Rhodopean rock outcrops. We suggest that the upland zone took on a new significance for lowland communities in the Late Copper Age, not only as a zone of raw materials unavailable from the lowland valleys but also as the setting for places of symbolic significance, emphasised by foci of material deposition such as Pchelarovo. In return, the stone materials taken into the lowland zone presenced the rocky landscapes which gave such stone to the upland voyagers, enabling the creation of enduring symbolic links between the two zones. There is also the movement of pigments from upland to lowland zones, such as the white colourant taken from Belen Tash and used at the Dolnoslav tell (Raduntcheva 2002). It was into such a developed network of social, symbolic and material linkages that the Orlovo settlement became embedded in the Late Copper Age.

The assemblage in context

The surface collections from Orlovo have been made available to the museum by collectors from the village, who have returned many times, collected finds from the hoed strips between rows of vines (hand-hoeing to a depth of 0.20 has been reported) and brought in what amounts to a substantial surface assemblage. Aladzhov (1997) claims that the surface finds from the site came from three different zones – figurines from one zone, shell ornaments from another and polished stone axes and ornaments from yet a third; evaluation of this claim awaits further fieldwork.

The assemblage is divided into three main parts: (a) the fired clay figurines; (b) the ornaments mainly of shell and stone; and (c) the ground and polished stone tools. It should be underlined that the Orlovo collection is unusually rich and diverse. The overall totals of objects amounts to 130 figurines – 124 fired clay and six of ground and/or polished stone, 709 ornaments and 71 ground and/or polished stone tools, as well as nine other finds. The figurine types comprised 105 anthropomorphic examples, 10 zoomorphic, four ornithomorphic, five ornitho-zoomorphic, one leg that could be anthropomorphic or zoomorphic and five zoomorphic terminals to vessels.

There is not a single site in the East Balkans with such a surface collection of ornaments; indeed, the only examples of larger ornament assemblages derived from ornament hoards dating to the Neolithic and the Chalcolithic (Chapman 2000, chapter 4). Indeed, there are many settlement sites with a far smaller and less varied collection of ornaments and/or polished stone tools and/or figurines (Tables 1.1–1.2).

These data indicate that the Orlovo assemblage is both rich and diversified and that few other settlements have such a large quantity of *all three* artifact classes. The principal exception to this is the Final Chalcolithic tell of Dolnoslav, where an enormous amount of material culture

was deposited prior to the abandonment of the final phase structures (Gaydarska *et al.* 2007).

Two of the defining characteristics of the Balkan and Hungarian Neolithic and Copper Age are the quantity and diversity of miniature representations ('figurines') made in many materials but most often fired clay. Although there is a small number of graves in which figurines have been deposited (Bánffy 1990/1; Chapman 2000, 72–75), there is an overwhelming preference for disposal in the land of the living, viz. the settlement domain. This fits the notion that Orlovo is a settlement site rather than a burial site, although it is possible that part of the flat site was given over to burials for part of its occupation and that the village collector(s) targeted this zone as producing the 'richest' finds. Comparative data on the quantities of figurines discovered in excavated sites and surface collections can be more readily achieved using data from the Vinča culture (Chapman 1981, 74), rather than for the Bulgarian sequence. The largest number of figurines from a settlement excavation amounts to over 2,000 pieces from the metropolitan tell of Vinča – Belo Brdo – the most important tell in the culture (Srejović 1968; Chapman 1998). In terms of surface assemblages of figurines, there is only one site whose total approaches that of the Orlovo collection – the multi-phase Early Vinča upland settlement of Zorlenţu Mare, in South West Romania (Comşa and Rauţ 1969). Here, a total of over 100 fired clay anthropomorphs was found after shallow ploughing – a larger total than was ever recovered in the subsequent

Table 1.1. Object totals from totally excavated Neo-Chalcolithic settlements

Site Name	Figurines	Ornaments	Polished Stonework
Rakitovo (Early Neolithic)	32	3?	>51
Endrőd 119 (Early Neolithic)	38	31	???
Usoe (Middle/Late Neolithic)	228	?	???
Ovcharovo (Chalcolithic)	131	??	???
Vinitsa (Chalcolithic)	26	39	150
Hăbăşeşti (Chalcolithic)	175 + Z-ms	?	300
Truşeşti (Chalcolithic)	255	0	120

Table 1.2. Object totals from partially excavated Neo-Chalcolithic settlements

Site Name	Figurines	Ornaments	Polished Stonework
Obre I (Early Neolithic)	3	3	96
Sitagroi (MN–EBA)	250	992	171
Selevac (Middle Neolithic)	339	45	118
Parţa tell (Middle Neolithic)	> 15	>17	>68
Obre II (Late Neolithic)	18	28	>170
Dolnoslav (Chalcolithic)	500	??	???
Târpeşti (Chalcolithic)	>80	>30	<400
Draguşeni (Chalcolithic)	211	13	157
Divostin II (Late Neo)	107	10	238

excavations (Lazarovici 1973). The Vinča figurine data are limited by its lack of on-site contexts but nonetheless provides a sense of the range of variation in the density of figurine deposition (Chapman 1981, fig. 95). Comparison of the Orlovo data with the Vinča statistics confirms Orlovo as one of the sites with frequent ritual practices involving the use and deposition of figurines.

Perhaps the best parallels for the range of ornaments and small polished stonework derive not from settlements but from cemeteries. The famous Chalcolithic cemeteries of Durankulak (Todorova 2002) and Varna (Ivanov and Avramova 2000) both contain numerous parallels for many of the Orlovo types, giving a strong indication that at least part of the Orlovo finds were made and deposited in the Late Copper Age. However, there is a range of ornaments and small polished stonework from settlements in both the Neolithic and Copper Age – not so well-known or well-published, perhaps, but nevertheless indicative that personal ornaments were an important part of the whole Neolithic–Chalcolithic cycle, from the late 7th to the late 4th millennium Cal. BC.

The incidence of ground and polished stone axes is extremely difficult to gauge, since this category of objects rarely receives the attention in either analysis or publication that it merits. A preliminary literature search indicates that these same completely excavated tells publish frequencies up to 150 stone axes, adzes and chisels. However, museum collections such as Vratsa (North West Bulgaria) display a large number of ground and polished stone tools from sites ranging in date from the Early Neolithic to the Late Copper Age, often with medium to heavy use-wear traces. Moreover, part of the unpublished reserve collection in Haskovo Museum consists of an estimated 1,000 polished stone axes from the full range of prehistoric sites in the region. However, most of these examples represent 'working' axes with medium to strong use-wear and often heavily damaged blades and butts. The Orlovo collection is dominated by small polished stone tools with little or no use-wear, suggesting a rather different type of 'display' assemblage.

Chapter summary

The Orlovo site would appear to fit into the recently-established pattern of large, open sites with multiple occupations, though whether or not the communities on these sites created vastly different, or alternative, lifeways from those practised on tells remains an open and important research question – and a question to which the Orlovo assemblage can make a contribution. Whatever the precise dating of the deposition at Orlovo – perhaps the largest of the to-be-solved research questions emerging from this discussion – the community would have participated in social networks linking neighbouring sites in the valley of the Harmanlijska reka and beyond. There may be a disjunction between the early (Early Neolithic) phase of settlement in the Eastern Rhodopes and the paucity of Early Neolithic material at Orlovo. This disjunction is certainly present in the Late Neolithic (Karanovo III–IV), when there there are few, if any, signs of Rhodopean settlement but a clear focus of deposition at Orlovo. It is only in the Late Copper Age that the deposition at Orlovo is coeval with the second phase of upland settlement in the Eastern Rhodopes, as well as a dramatic increase in lowland settlement over the whole of the Thracian plain.

The Orlovo assemblage consist of three main concentrations of material – a varied suite of figurines normally deposited in the domestic domain; an unusually rich and varied set of personal ornaments in stone, shell and other materials – itself usually characteristic of the mortuary zone but with more muted settlement occurrences as well; and a collection of small-scale polished stone tools – often display objects – typifying both the domestic and the mortuary zones. It is the quantity and diversity of the surface collection, as much as its analogies in the two major Neolithic and Chalcolithic domains – the domestic and the mortuary – that make Orlovo such an unusual site and such a challenging site to interpret.

2. The Fired Clay Figurines

Introduction

In the typical manner of a Balkan Neolithic – Chalcolithic figurine assemblage, the Orlovo figurines (Fig. 2.1) consist of a mixture of types of image – those with a reasonably clear attribution (viz., clearly anthropomorphic, patently zoomorphic, probably ornitho-morphic) and those with a moderate or strong degree of ambiguity in the type (viz., human–animal, human–bird or animal–bird combinations). The underlying characteristic of this surface assemblage – a high degree of fragmentation – makes a strong contribution to this ambiguity and to the difficulties of both internal classification and external comparisons (for details, see above, pp. 10–11). We begin with internal classification.

Types, size and gender

The body part classification of the Orlovo figurines presents some striking results (Fig. 2.2). The dominant type appears to be the head, which is very rare (if not unique!) on Balkan prehistoric sites (Fig. 2.2 and Plate 4). When broken, a figurine usually can produce many different body parts but only one head, hence the well observed pattern, as at Dolnoslav (Gaydarska *et al.* 2007), of a less frequent distribution of heads. The majority of heads in Orlovo suggests either that there were many more body parts originally deposited on-site or that a different discard practice was followed in Orlovo. The lack of archaeological investigation in Orlovo prevents from evaluation of any of the above possibilities but it is nonetheless clear from their numbers and variety that figurines played an important social role in the life of the settlement. If the first interpretation is accepted, then the total number of figurines could well be doubled or even tripled, thus confirming figurines as an important element in the everyday life of the Orlovo occupants (cf. the often small number of figurines deposited in completely excavated tells: see above, p. 22 and Table 1.1). If the second interpretation is preferred, the special emphasis on the head may be connected to the type of activity performed on-site – that may have been executed by the hands but interacted with cognitive processes in the brain.

The distribution of the remaining types of figurines is not a surprise, apart from the relatively low presence of legs. In the context of the above discussed distribution of heads, one is tempted to suggest that heads were deposited on production sites, while legs were associated with middens (e.g. Dolnoslav: Gaydarska *et al.* 2007).

Another way of considering the body part distribution begins by distinguishing between human and non-human effigies. A quarter of the studied material can be characterised as zoomorphic and/or ornithomorphic figurines, suggesting ambiguity is an important feature in this assemblage. More than a half of the non-human figurines are heads (Fig. 1c), again raising the issue of ambiguity over the kind of body – human or not – to which they were once attached. A basic division was established between beaked faces, classed as ornithomorphs, and horned heads, classed as zoomorphs (Plate 4). However, the majority of the zoo/ornithomorphic heads was identified as such not because of a resemblance to a certain species but because of the lack of definitely human traits.

Even though relatively few in number (n = 37), the zoomorphs and ornitho-morphs can be grouped in as many as nine categories:

1. Ornitho-morphic heads with no bodies (e.g. Inv. 2789/1, 3 or 4)
2. Zoo-morphic heads with no bodies (Fig. 2.1c:? hedgehog)
3. Heads that could be classed as anthropomorphic or ornitho-morphic, with no attached anthropomorphic bodies (e.g. Inv. 3354/1 or 2)
4. Heads that could be classed as anthropomorphic or ornitho-morphic, with attached anthropomorphic bodies (e.g. Inv. 3261)
5. Heads that were either zoo-morphic or ornitho-morphic (e.g. Inv. 3344/3)
6. Zoo-morphic heads attached to a zoo-morphic body (Plate 3b: ? ram; Inv. 3425/2 – ? rabbit)
7. Zoo-morphic bodies with no heads (zoo-morphic or anything else) (Fig. 2.1f)
8. Zoo-morphic terminals, sometimes attached to a large vessel fragment (e.g. Inv. 3058/1, 4, 6 or 7)

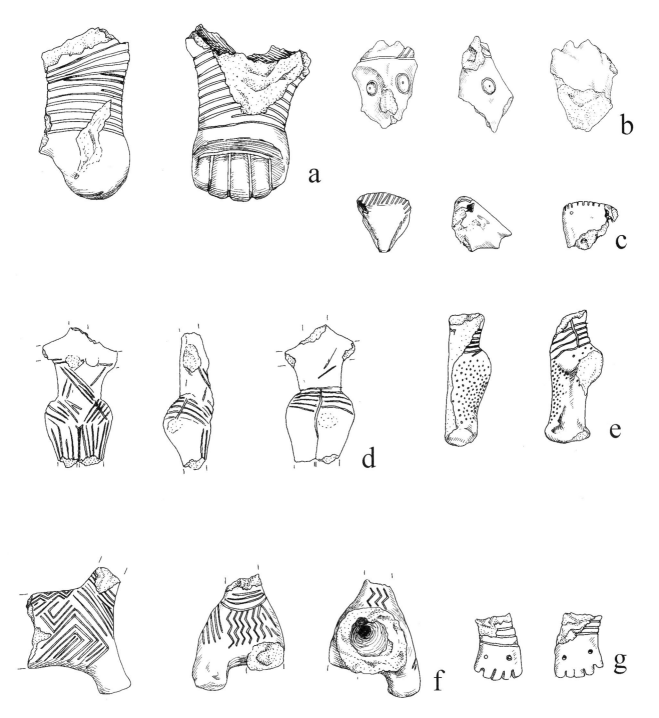

Figure 2.1. Figurines: (a) Inv. 3319; (b) Inv. 3520/3; (c) Inv. 2789/2; (d) Inv. 2743; (e) Inv. 3217/3; (f) Inv. 2750; (g) Inv. 3061/2 (drawn by Elena Georgieva)

9. Vessel terminals that could be either zoo-morphic or ornitho-morphic (e.g. Inv. 2998 and 2999)

Since we shall not be able to identify the kind of heads once attached to now headless bodies, we can only refer for guidance to that small number of images with both heads and torsos. Here an interesting pattern is observable: there are no examples of hydrid categories such as may have been formed by putting a zoo-morphic head on an anthropomorphic body or an anthropomorphic head on a zoo-morphic or

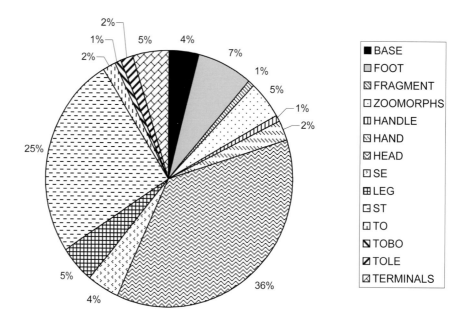

Figure 2.2. Frequency of figurines by body parts. Key: SE – seated; ST – standing; TO – torso; TOBO – torso and bottom; TOLE – torso and legs

ornitho-morphic body. There was the possibility of modelling ornitho-morphic heads on anthropomorphic bodies (Classes 3 and 4 above) but that is the principal evidence so far for hybrid images (but see below the discussion on decoration: pp. 31–5). What the collection does indicate is ambiguity, especially between zoo-morphs and ornitho-morphs (found in two classes) and also between ornitho-morphs and anthropomorphs (1 class only) and anthropomorphs and zoo-morphs (1 class only). These results suggest that the Orlovo inhabitants had a quite specific categorisation system for humans and for the natural world, in which there were blurred distinctions between what we may readily take to be entirely separate 'biological' species. There is also a high proportion of images interpreted as zoo-morphs that cannot be identified as to species. The possible exceptions include three rams, a rabbit and a hedgehog. Interestingly, ornitho-morphs present entirely generic forms with no details enabling an attribution to species of bird.

The use of masks on several Orlovo figurines (Inv. 3280, 3307/1, 3342/1 and 3354/2) indicates another means by which ritual performance may have involved changing identities. A final aspect of difference represented in the Orlovo figurines concerns the variation in the number of toes on figurines. While the biological norm of five fingers or toes is found in four examples (e.g. Fig 2.1a, g), four toes are found in one example (Inv. 3061/7) and two possible others (Inv. 3346/8 and 10), while six toes are shown on one example (Inv. 3346/7).

Turning to anthropomorphs, two-thirds of the collection

(68%) demonstrate more or less secure anthropomorphic features: almost 1/3 (29%) are heads only or heads with attached neck or torso (Plate 4). Therefore, even when the potential non-human heads are excluded, the relative presence of heads remains high. Such a pattern reinforces the importance of deciding between the two suggested hypotheses. A higher than expected value was found for standing figurines, representing 38% of the assemblage. This may be due to the recovery pattern or to some practice-based preference in the past; again, it is difficult to evaluate the hypotheses.

The fragmentary nature of the sample is confirmed by the size of the fragments. Most of them are between 19 and 78 mm in length and between 12 and 65 mm in width, with only three examples over 70 mm in width (Fig. 2.3). However, it should be mentioned that most of the figurines are produced as small images, as is visible from the proportions of the surviving fragments. There is only one example of a hand that is very large (length 93mm, width 72mm, thickness 52mm) and apparently belongs to a monumental figurine (Fig. 2.1a: Inv. 3319: this hand has a parallel on a vessel lid in Goljamo Delchevo: see below, pp. 35–8). Miniaturisation in general, and of human effigies in particular, was discussed in length by Bailey (2005) but the reason for the production of miniatures of different size remained unaddressed. The most obvious answer is that size was related to the available raw material and the type of figurine (? person) that the maker wished to create. While not underestimating the role of raw material, we would

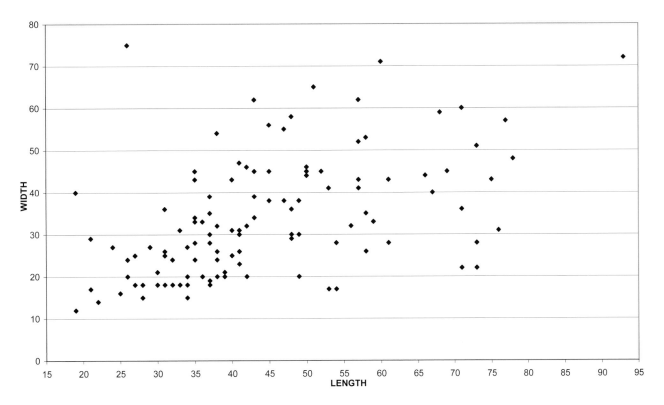

Figure 2.3. Size of figurine fragments

suggest that figurines and their size cannot be divorced from their "own" environment, whether it is miniature furniture (e.g. the scene from Ovcharovo) or other domestic and/or ceremonial equipment (e.g. polypod vessels, exotic objects, lamps, etc.). There will have been appropriate sizes to make figurines, leading to greater precision in making and in social categorization. In addition, size can reduce or enhance the potential for fragmentation, with large objects broken into many more fragments than small, dense figurines.

The overwhelming number of heads, together with the terminals, bases and the non-human effigies, predetermines the majority of figurines with no gender information (73%: Fig. 2.4). Among the remaining 27%, neither the dominance of female figurines nor the symbolic (? token) occurrence of a sole male figurine come as major surprises. The relatively low percent of unsexed examples, however, is indicative for a gendering strategy in which clear gender divisions were constructed wherever possible. Needless to say, the interpretation of such a strategy may be challenged if more figurines are recovered from the site.

Techniques of making (and breaking)

One positive side effect of the fragmentary state of the collection is the opportunity to glimpse the way the figurines

were made. The relatively high percentage of heads naturally limits the information how the body was made. All but one of the leg parts, together with three feet fragments, one torso with legs and possibly one seated and one standing figurine show evidence for production of the image in two halves (Plate 3a: Inv. 3312/1). The fragmentation pattern of figurines made in two halves is usually a very flat break along the surface of attachment that is believed to be one of the weakest parts, together with necks and the ankles. Using the best documented cases, nine figurines were initially made as left and right parts, which were later joined and attached to their respective heads. In only one case (Plate 3f: Inv. 3238/1), we are presented with the example of front and back halves. In another case (Inv. 3345/1), the shape of the breasts suggests that they were made separately and then attached to the body, rather than modelled from the torso.

The alternative technique of production is the modelling of the desired shape from a single ball of clay. The final step involves coating the core with a relatively thin (2mm) layer of clay before firing. At least two figurines are made with such a technique (Plate 4a: Inv. 3307/2; Plate 4g: Inv. 3346/9), with a further 19 as possible candidates.

Incision, perforation and modelling are common techniques for conveying different design details of the face and/or the head. However, each technique is used

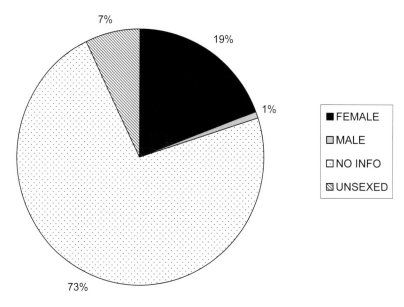

Figure 2.4. Gender attribution of Orlovo figurines

independently on other parts of the body. The most commonly utilised is incision, that is used for costume design and for outlining body parts such as buttocks and legs (e.g. Fig. 2.1d: Inv. 2743; Plate 3a: Inv. 3312/1). In at least 15 cases (plus a further possible five), perforation may have been performed for suspension – to be worn around the neck, on the clothes or for hanging in the house (e.g. Plate 3g: Inv. 3520/6). In two cases, the place of the perforation is unusual for suspension and it is not obviously related to the construction (a peg hole) or the design of the figurine (Plate 3c: Inv. 3311/3). A tempting suggestion is that we are presented with examples of post-manufacturing (and post-breaking) manipulation to convey injury and/or practices more readily associated with black magic (cf. Drașovean 1998 for the Banatean Vinča figurines). A very specific type of modelling was used to produce a clay figurine that looks like a bone figurine, where the schematic head and lower part are compensated by elaborated arms/upper torso (Plate 4i: Inv. 2988). Another example of schematic design is the regular triangular head (Plate 4d: Inv. 3346/6) that stands in contrast with the possibly ambiguous but yet clearly made head designs of the rest of the collection. There are two figurines that may have been deliberately designed to be fixed at different ends. In the case of Inv. 3307/1 (Plate 4c), the head has a hole to facilitate attachment to different bodies, while the perforation in the base of Inv. 3636 would have facilitated attachment to a stick or a staff.

Almost a half of the figurines bear traces of irregular firing easily recognizable by the different colour of the core and the surface. There are several possible reasons for such a pattern – the poor quality of the clay, the inexperience of

the maker – perhaps still an apprentice, incidents during firing or the choice to fire the figurine at a low temperature to resemble other poorly-fired objects. Figurine makers were usually careful in the process of modelling, since there is only one example of finger impressions left on the shoulder of Inv. 2998.

Despite the fragmentary state of the collection, the distribution of fragments with a certain number of breaks is not much different from the distribution registered on fragments recovered from a completely excavated site like Dolnoslav (Fig. 2.5a–b). The most numerous are fragments with two or three breaks, that constitute 52% of the whole collection. There are slightly fewer fragments with one break in comparison with Dolnoslav but this is compensated by the greater number of figurines with more than three breaks. The lack of substantial difference suggests that fragmentation was not necessarily caused by off-site and taphonomic factors but rather that figurine parts were initially deposited as fragments at different stages of the fragmentation chain (Chapman and Gaydarska 2006, 120, 142).

Surface colour

Typically, the figurines from Orlovo have been fired in a bonfire rather than in any device with specially controlled firing, as indicated by the colour variations on most of the surfaces. The surface colour variations compare well with coarse wares that have been bonfire-fired. The range of colours covers the light end of the spectrum – a beige–light brown colour – to the dark end of the range – dark grey. There is a clear preference for brown–dark brown figurines, followed by orange–red

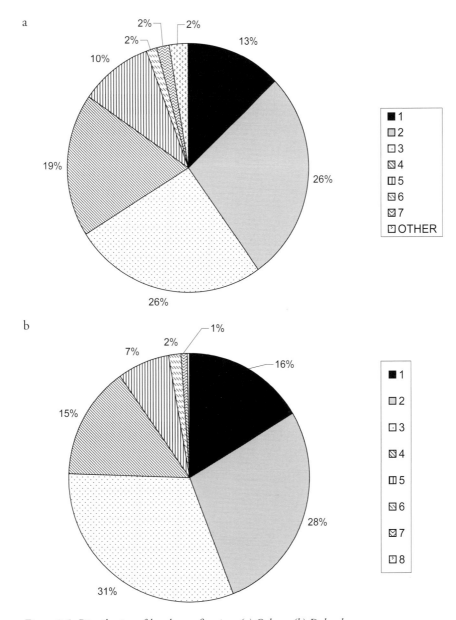

Figure 2.5. Distribution of breaks per figurine: (a) Orlovo; (b) Dolnoslav.

surfaces, dark grey surfaces, light grey–grey surfaces and, least commonly, beige–light brown colours (Fig. 2.6a). There is a moderately strong contrast between the surface colours of the anthropomorphic and the non-anthropomorphic figurines. The most frequent anthropomorphic figurine colours are equally divided between orange–red and brown–dark brown (Fig. 2.6b), while zoomorphic and ornithomorphic figurines are overwhelmingly dominated by brown–dark brown colours (Fig. 2.6c). The overall contrast in figurine colours concerns the earth colours, which are predominant over greys of various strengths, and the colours of the axes and the ornaments, which are rarely earth-coloured.

Wear and surface treatment

It is a general perception that a surface collection should have suffered a lot of damage and wear, and therefore would contain little or no information for wear achieved in the past and the surface treatment especially of clay objects. The figurines from Orlovo clearly disprove such a point of view. Only 16% of the figurines are either rough or worn, leaving the vast majority with surviving burnished and/or smoothed surface (Fig. 2.7). Such a pattern suggests that the on-site dynamics of taphonomy are currently poorly understood. In any case, it is difficult to claim any type of

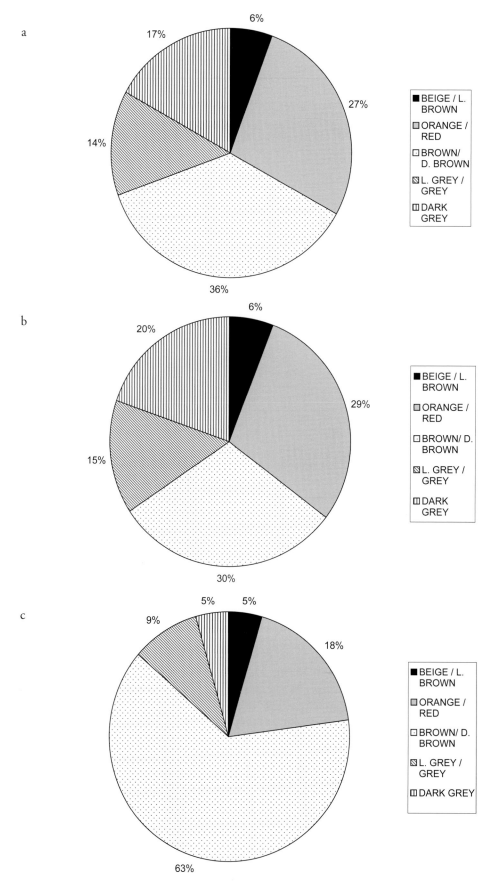

Figure 2.6. Surface colour of figurines: (a) all figurines; (b) anthropomorphic figurines; (c) non-anthropomorphic figurines.

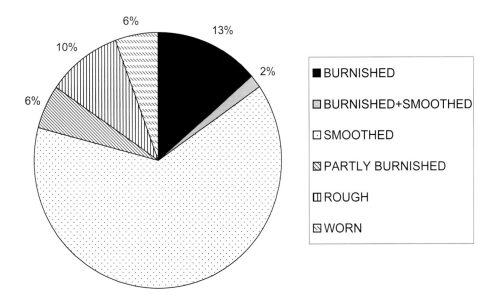

Figure 2.7. Distribution of surface treatment, wear and damage on Orlovo figurines

wear or damage on the clay figurines are entirely caused by long-term exposure to the elements on the surface. The large number of burnished and/or smoothed fragments is indicative of artifact preservation against all commonsense assumptions. In addition, the wear pattern on the few fragments with wear can be related not to surface wear or plough damage but to a particular use of the body parts. For example, some heads (e.g. Plate 4a: Inv. 3307/2) have wear on the back or the top as if they were constantly laid down or continuously rubbed, while some legs and the feet (Plate 4h: Inv. 3346/4) have specific wear on the feet as if caused by walking. Such 'characteristic' wear was noted also on figurines from Dolnoslav (Chapman and Gaydarska 2006, 131–132), thus suggesting that the fragments from Orlovo have been worn as a result of manipulations with the figurines during their participation in different social practices. However, it would be unwise to exclude the possibility of external wear caused by occasional exposure to weather conditions and erosion. The eroded face of Inv. 3369/1 (Plate 4e) or the rough surface of eight other fragments and, in particular, the rough and worn surface of four other fragments are the obvious candidates for wear that cannot be readily associated with intentional use of the figurines.

In summary, the figurines from Orlovo were carefully smoothed and, in some cases, burnished for aesthetic and social purposes. Intensive or long-term targeted use has caused some wear on a few figurines, while a small minority of the others was affected by the exposure on the ground surface.

Figurine Decoration

Many archaeologists may share the expectation that little decoration would have survived in a collection of surface figurines, exposed as they were to the elements and agricultural disturbance for decades if not longer. It may come as a surprise to colleagues that, in point of fact, the decoration has survived on a relatively high proportion of figurines – not quite half. It is even more surprising that normally fugitive decorative elements, such as the white incrustation, used to highlight incised lines, and red paint, crusted onto figurine surfaces after firing, have both survived in this remarkable assemblage. These factors, together with the absence of any plough damage or modern fractures on the figurines, lead us to believe that this assemblage may have been preserved rather better than one would normally expect.

While none of the six non-fired clay figurines was decorated, the number of decorated fired clay figurines comprises 55 examples out of a total of 124 (or 44%). Decoration was found on 47 anthropomorphs (or 44%), the only anthropomorphic/zoomorphic leg, three zoomorphs (or 30%), one ornithomorph (or 25%), one zoomorph/ornithomorph (or 20%) and one zoomorphic terminal (or 20%). There was no categorical difference between humans who could bear decoration and birds and animals that were naturally undecorated. Moreover, broadly similar styles of decoration and decorative motifs were used for human, animals, birds and ambiguous species, although rarely in the intensive manner occasionally found in anthropomorphs. We begin with the anthropomorphs.

Figure 2.8. Placement of decorative motifs, Orlovo figurines (front of body); numbers = motif numbers (drawn by Yvonne Beadnell)

The Orlovo figurine decoration utilises four different decorative styles, which can be combined to produce four additional styles. The basic styles are crusted decoration (n = 1), in which usually red paint is crusted onto a zone of the skin after firing, leaving a colour contrast; dotted decoration (n = 1), in which multiple small pinpricks are made in the skin; incised decoration (n = 28), where the sharp edge of a flint blade or some similar tool is cut into the skin; and incrusted decoration (n = 1), by which usually white carbonate material is pressed into an incision to fill the line, leaving a colour contrast. The combinations consist of crusted and incised decoration (n = 1), crusted, incised and incrusted decoration (n = 4), dotted and incised decoration (n = 3) and incised and incrusted decoration (n = 16). It

becomes clear that incision, with or without incrustation, is the commonest decorative style.

At a more detailed level, each decorative style is depicted by one or more decorative motifs, which can often be placed in several different places on the body in different examples (Figs. 2.8–9). Although every part of the body is emphasised by the addition of decoration, the three principal body zones thus treated are the head-and-neck, the torso and the legs. There is a clear preference for rectilinear decoration over curvilinear, both in terms of the number of motifs (28 cf. three) and the locations of the decoration (seven cf. three). The two most strongly expressed motif choices comprise elaborate textile motifs and oblique lines in various combinations. The elaborate textile motifs are reminiscent of

Back

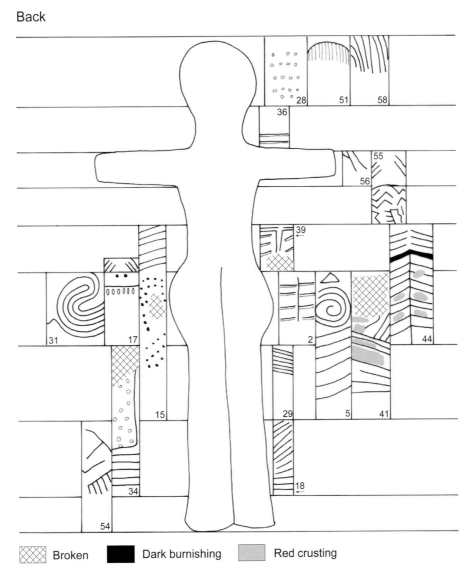

XXXX Broken   ■ Dark burnishing   ▨ Red crusting

Figure 2.9. Placement of decorative motifs, Orlovo figurines (back of body); numbers = motif numbers (drawn by Yvonne Beadnell)

the finely designed incised decoration on Tisza coarse wares in the Hungarian Late Neolithic – motifs considered to be derived from woven patterns (Banner 1930; Korek 1989, Chapman and Richter 2010).

One obvious limitation of the Orlovo collection is the high rate of fragmentation that most of the figurines have suffered (see above, pp. 26–7). This constrains our understanding of the meaning of the decoration because the elements are so often incomplete: an example is Inv. No. 3310, where the beginning of a row of parallel incised lines below the breasts of a female figurine has been broken off, leaving us too little to decide whether the lines represented clothing. But while there are no complete figurines in the collection, there are only a handful of examples where fragmentation completely denies the possibility of interpretation. There are far more examples where the interpretation of the decoration is ambiguous (e.g. Inv. 3313/5, which could represent skin decoration or possible clothing). Finally, there is a group of figurines where the decorated area is large enough (e.g. Inv. 3011/B), or the decoration is sufficiently complex (e.g. Inv. 3520/7), to make a positive interpretation.

In the context of the Orlovo assemblage, decoration is taken to mean the artificial and structured modification of an object's surface – here the human or animal or bird's skin – to produce a desired and communicable effect. This definition leaves open a variety of communicable effects, such as the emphasis on an existing body part, the depiction of coiffure, the representation of ornaments, the portrayal of tattooing or other bodily decorations, the annotation of a body with a special, possibly ritualised, sign and the depiction of clothing.

Interestingly, all of the examples of an added emphasis placed on body parts related to the eye, which was emphasised by an incised and white incrusted line (Plate 4f: Inv. 3058/2), by the addition of incised and white incrusted eyebrows (Inv. 3342/7) or by the crusting of red paint on an area adjoining the eye (Inv. 3354/1). Such an emphasis on the eye is known in other media, such as the Late Copper Age fired clay 'altars' with ocular motifs, where the right and left eyes are always rendered in different ways (Kamarev 2005).

The depiction of coiffure is well-known amongst figurines from all phases of the Neolithic and Chalcolithic cycle, from the rod-head figurines of the earliest farming period onwards (Nandris 1970; Kokkinidou and Nikolaidou 1996; Chapman and Gaydarska 2006). The most elaborate example of hair-style is Inv. No. 3309 (Plate 4b), with swirls and garlands of hair on the back and sides. Rather less refined coiffure is illustrated by Inv. 3520/3 (Fig. 2.1b), with a simple pattern of wide incised oblique lines.

There are only two possible examples of the representation of an ornament on an anthropomorph. The first is the diamond-shaped incision on the top of an anthropomorphic head (Plate 4c: Inv. 3307/1), which cannot indicate a hair-style but may portray a hair-ornament. The second example is the arm fragment (Fig. 2.1g: Inv. 3061/2) with three parallel lines on the wrist that may well indicate a bracelet, perhaps of the shell ring type found at the site. However, these lines may also indicate a cuff, if Orlovo shirts or blouses had such subtleties.

Tattooing marks are difficult to detect and hard to interpret in the figurine corpus but may be represented by the dotted decoration style at Orlovo. The making of this unusual style in a fired clay figurine – through the use of a bone needle/awl or a similar tool to make small depressions in the skin – bears a very close resemblance to the act of tattooing onto human skin. This decorative style is limited to four examples, three of which are combined with incised lines (Fig. 2.1e: Inv. 3217/3; Plate 3d: Inv. 3482/4; Plate 4e: 3369/1). In the last example, the dotting covers the head and neck, while the legs bear dotted decoration in the remaining cases.

The category 'other body decoration' may be seen as a residual place for examples of decorations that cannot be clearly interpreted. Thus, isolated placing of incised lines without any obvious reference to bodily divisions may pertain to motifs painted on, or scored into, the skin. Examples include Inv. 3262, with incised and incrusted lozenges, rectangles and a lunate placed on the cheeks, and Inv. 3058/5, with its incrustation on the right side of the head, that resembles skin-painting more than anything else. The

most elaborate example is Inv. 3354/1, with a combination of three decorative styles: an incised cruciform motif on the top of the head, red crusted decoration near the right eye and vertical parallel incised and white incrusted lines on the neck.

The only example of a possible incised sign is found on the front torso of the anthropomorph Inv. 3520/6: a set of five incised lines abutting against an oblique incised line, on the upper torso of a female figurine (Plate 3g). Since the figurine is also wearing clothing, as shown by the rear torso, it is likely that the sign is woven into, or painted onto, the front of the garment. This distinctive motif has few close published parallels in the Balkans, with absences notable in the Chalcolithic imagery of North West Bulgaria (Biehl 2003), the Greek Neolithic site of Achilleion (Gimbutas 1989), the Vinča sites of Selevac (Milojković 1990), Divostin (Letica 1988), Gradac (Stalio 1972) and Rast (Dumitescu, V. 1980), as well as the entire Cucuteni-Tripolye corpus (Monah 1997). The closest parallel to this sign on a figurine is known from the Late Neolithic tell of Öcsöd–Kovashalom, in the Alföld Plain (Hansen 2007, Vol. II, Taf. 236/1). The Öcsöd example has six, rather than five, vertical incised lines abutting on an only slightly oblique incised line, on the front of an anthropomorph with no gender information. More distant parallels can be found in the Early Neolithic at Méhtelek, Northeast Hungary (Hansen 2007, II, Taf. 128/3 and 5) and Ostrovul Golu, in the Iron Gates region (Hansen 2007, II, Taf. 134/4 and 135/2), as well as the Late Vinča site of Jakovo-Kormadin (Tasić 1973, 64 and T. XXV/84). Two general parallels occur at Sitagroi – one in Level II and one in Level III (Gimbutas 1986, 266 and fig. 9.87; 241 and fig. 9.31). Three instances of the exact parallel for the sign are found on the Early Vinča pottery at Turdaş, in Transylvania – two on pottery bases and one on the wall of a vessel (Makkay 1969, motif A23/18–19 and A26/1). However, there are no analogies for this sign on either decorated Neolithic lamps from Bulgaria (Nikolov, V. 2007) or Neolithic and Chalcolithic stamp-seals from Hungary and the Balkans (Makkay 1984, 2005). This range of general parallels, with identical analogies on a different medium in Transylvania and one very similar example in Hungary, shows the wide range of social networks in which the inhabitants of Orlovo participated.

The study of the clothing worn by anthropomorphs depends upon a match between the location and form of the decoration and the contours, divisions and segments of the human body. In the Orlovo collection, there are 16 examples where the decoration is highly suggestive of clothing of one sort or another (Table 2.1). These bodily images are portrayed as wearing upper garments (blouses *or* shirts, with sleeves and neck-line), lower garments (skirts *or* trousers; open skirts *or* open trousers; aprons with belts) and garments covering most of, or all of, the body (dresses *or* blouses + skirts *or* shirts + trousers). There is also a possibility that the large, half-life-size and Inv. 3319 (Fig. 2.1a) may be wearing mittens. We present below (Fig. 2.10) speculative reconstructions of how some of these costumes may have looked, in the spirit of the Vučedol people (Miličević 1988) rather more than the Boian ladies (Comşa 1974, 172–3) or the LBK males and females (Lüning 2005, 2006).

The decoration on non-human images is, in general, less elaborate and reticulated than that ornamenting people. Seven examples are known, most of them with close analogies in the anthropomorphic range of decoration. One ornithomorph (Plate 3e: Inv. 2789/3) has incised plumage on its head and neck. The bristles on what has been identified as a hedgehog (Fig. 2.1c: Inv. 2789/2) have been incised with short straight lines. Similarly, a zoomorph that may well be a caprine has incised slashes on both flanks of the body, presumably representing wool or hair (Plate 3b: Inv. 3057). Four of the non-human images have decoration that would probably be interpreted as clothing on anthropomorphs. The simplest decoration appears on the necks of two images – a zoomorphic terminal (Inv. 3058/6) and a zoomorph / ornithormorph (Inv. 3520/2) – the former with horizontal and vertical lines, the latter with horizontal lines round the neck. The most complex textile decoration appears on the front legs and both flanks of a zoomorph (Fig. 2.1f: Inv. 2750). An image that could be an anthropomorph or a zoomorph (Inv. 3217/1) has incised horizontal lines on the lower leg, which could be the bottom of trousers.

It is interesting that the most complex decoration known from the human images is also found on one of the zoomorphs – the textiles that have the best analogy in complex Tisza incision (Banner 1930; Korek 1989). This would suggest that the identity of some animals was closely related to the identities of their owners, as depicted in the clothes that they wore. We can hardly escape from the notion that humans were anthropomorphising some of their animals and birds by clothing them in garments that would have been recognisable to members of their community. There is also an equally strong tendency to emphasise the natural features of the animals or birds, which in the case of plumage is comparable to human hair but in the case of bristles or wool is not.

In summary, a limited number of decorative styles has been used at Orlovo to create a varied suite of decorative motifs to communicate a wide range of information to the viewers about the forms of humans, animals, birds and ambiguous creatures. While clothing is particularly emphasised in the group of anthropomorphs, it is also used for animals and birds, while the natural features of the latter are highlighted more often than for humans. There are only two examples of the probable representation of ornaments on anthropomorphs – one of which can be linked to the actual ornaments deposited at Orlovo.

Relative chronology and regional patterning

The application of the methodology for the analysis of analogies between the Orlovo figurines and figurines from other sites has produced some robust results. Almost 70% of all the Orlovo figurines (86 out of 124) have shown some similarity with other excavated miniature effigies from the sites listed below (Table 2.2). Only 23% have more or less secure parallels – the 29 out of 124 that form Group A according to the methodology described above (p. 11). In Group A, 42% are found only at Neolithic sites, 41% only at Copper Age sites and 17% in both phases. A more detailed examination of the chronological distribution shows that there are two peaks – in the Late Neolithic and in the

Table 2.1. Clothing as indicated by figurine decoration

Museum Inv no	Place on Body	Decorative Style	Type of Garment
3011/a	Torso	Incision	Shirt OR blouse
3520/6	Front and back of torso	Complex incision + incrusted	Shirt OR blouse
2743	Torso and hips	Complex incision	Dress OR shirt + trousers
3238/1	Torso and leg	Crusted + Incision + Incrusted	Dress OR shirt + trousers
3313/4	Torso + hips + legs	Complex incision	Shirt + trousers OR blouse + skirt
3011/B	Torso + hips + legs	Complex incision	Shirt + trousers OR blouse + skirt
3238/2	Arm	Incision	Shirt / blouse sleeves
3319	Hand	Incision	Mittens
3313/1	Hips and legs	Incision	Open trousers / skirt
3345/2	Hips and legs	Complex incision + incrusted	Apron + belt
3346/3	Legs	Incision	Trousers
3313/3	Legs	Complex incision	Trousers or footwear
3219/1	Legs	Complex incision	Skirt OR trousers
3482/4	Legs	Dotting + incision	Skirt OR trousers
3520/7	Legs	Crusted + complex incision + Incrusted	Trousers

Figure 2.10. Imaginative reconstructions of Orlovo female costume (drawn by Yvonne Beadnell)

Late Copper Age. The latter peak is not surprising, given the well known popularity of miniature images during the Chalcolithic, but the presence of figurines with close Late Neolithic analogies is significant. However, two further facts are noteworthy. The first is the high relative proportion of Neolithic figurines (almost half of the Group A examples) and in particular the presence of Early Neolithic examples. Since Early Neolithic figurines are generally rare, and certainly fewer in number in comparison to the Copper Age figurines, their value should be considered in the light of their relative paucity. The second important point is the relatively few examples of figurines found in both periods (Neolithic and Chalcolithic) – a chronological relationship

rarely confirmed by the other artifacts in the museum collection (see below, pp. 103–4).

Such a pattern is, however, compensated by the distribution of the 30 Group B figurines, where most of the analogues can be found in both the Neolithic and the Copper Age. This result is to be expected, given the less specific analogies, and this result is indeed confirmed by the chronology of the polished stone tools and the ornaments (see below, pp. 103–4). A more detailed consideration reveals that 7% of the figurines are common from the beginning of the Neolithic till the end of the Copper Age, a fact that adds to the already observed pattern in Group A, thus suggesting the existence of a small range of sustained figurine designs

Table 2.2. List of sites used for analogies to the Orlovo figurines

Site Name	Zone	Timespan of Parallels	Type of Excavation
Ain Ghazal	Levant	PPNB	Tell excavation
Asagi Pinar	Turkey	Middle–Late Neolithic	Tell excavation
Achilleion	Greece	Early–Middle Neolithic	Tell excavation
Otzaki magoula	Greece	Early Neolithic	Tell excavation
Anzabegovo	FYROM	Early Neolithic	Multi-phase flat site excavation
Mogila	FYROM	Early Neolithic	Tell excavation
Porodin	FYROM	Early Neolithic	Tell excavation
Galabnik	SW Bulg	Early Neolithic	Tell excavation
Karanovo	SE Bulg	Early Neolithic	Tell excavation
Rakitovo	SE Bulg	Early Neolithic	Multi-layer flat site excavation
Zauan	Romania	Early Neolithic	Flat site excavation
Mužla Čenkov	Slovakia	Middle Neolithic	Flat site excavation
Gradeshnitsa	NW Bulg	Neolithic–CA	Several flat site excavations
Harmanli	SE Bulg	Late Neolithic	Flat site excavation
Hlebozavoda	SE Bulg	Late Neolithic	Flat site excavation
Kaloyanovets	SE Bulg	Late Neolithic	Tell excavation
Kurilo	SW Bulg	Late Neolithic–Early Copper Age	Tell excavation
Kapitan Dimitrievo	SE Bulg	Middle–Late Neolithic	Tell excavation
Ljubimets	SE Bulg	Late Neolithic	Extended flat site excavation
Podgoritsa	NE Bulg	Late Neolithic	Tell excavation
Usoe	NE Bulg	Late Neolithic	Flat site excavation
Veselinovo	SE Bulg	Middle Neolithic	Tell excavation
Yasa Tepe	SE Bulg	Neolithic	Tell excavation
Cernavoda	Romania	Middle Neolithic	Flat site excavation
Farcasul de Sus	Romania	Middle–Late Neolithic	Multi-layer flat site excavation
Rast	Romania	Middle Neolithic	Flat site excavation
Zorlenţu Mare	Romania	Middle Neolithic	Multi-layer flat site excavation
Gradac	Serbia	Late Neolithic	Enclosed site excavation
Predionica	Kosova	Middle Neolithic	Multi-layer flat site excavation
Vinča–Belo Brdo	Serbia	Middle–Late Neolithic	Tell excavation
Dikili Tash	Greece	Late Copper Age	Tell excavation
Sitagroi	Greece	Late Copper Age	Tell excavation
Borovan	NW Bulg	Early Copper Age	Flat site excavation
Goljamo Delchevo	NE Bulg	Late Copper Age	Tell excavation
Kirilovo	SE Bulg	Late Copper Age	Tell excavation
Kolena	SE Bulg	Copper Age	Flat site or tell excavation
Krivodol	NW Bulg	Late Copper Age	Flat site excavation
Omurtag	NE Bulg	Late Copper Age	Tell excavation
Pernik	SW Bulg	Early–Late Copper Age	Multi-layer flat site excavation
Salmanovo	NE Bulg	Late Copper Age	Tell excavation
Sedlare	SE Bulg	Late Copper Age	Tell excavation
Slatino	SW Bulg	Early Copper Age	Multi-layer flat site excavation
Targovishte	NE Bulg	Late Copper Age	Tell excavation
Telish	NW Bulg	Early Copper Age	Multi-layer flat site excavation
Vinitsa	NE Bulg	Late Copper Age	Tell excavation
Yunatsite	SE Bulg	Late Copper Age	Tell excavation
Radovanu	Romania	Early Copper Age	Multi-layer flat site excavation
Căscioarele	Romania	Late Copper Age	Tell excavation
Gumelniţa	Romania	Late Copper Age	Tell excavation
Helep'e	Romania	Copper Age	Flat site excavation
Măriuţa	Romania	Late Copper Age	Tell excavation
Pianul de Jos	Romania	Copper Age	Multi-layer flat site excavation
Pietrele	Romania	Late Copper Age	Tell excavation
Valea Argovei	Romania	Late Copper Age	Flat site excavation
Vidra	Romania	Copper Age	Tell excavation
Vladiceasca	Romania	Late Copper Age	Multi-layer flat site excavation
Divostin	Serbia	Copper Age	Multi-layer flat site excavation
Kaloyanovets	SE Bulg	Late Neolithic	Tell excavation
Azmak	SE Bulg	Early and Late Copper Age	Tell excavation
Bereketska tell	SE Bulg	Late Neolithic	Tell excavation
Stara Zagora Spa tell	SE Bulg	Late Copper Age	Tell excavation
Obrutchishte	SE Bulg	Late Neolthic	Flat site excavation
Regional Hospital, Stara Zagora	SE Bulg	Early Neolithic	Tell excavation
Gudjova tell	SE Bulg	Late Copper Age	Tell excavation

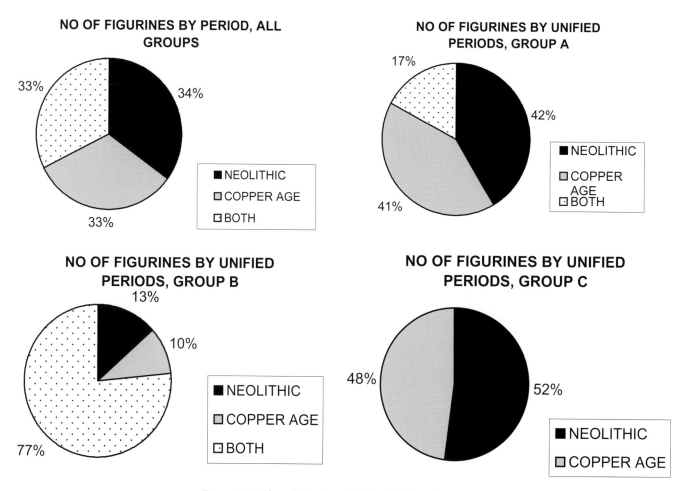

Figure 2.11. Chronological parallels for the Orlovo figurines

popular for nearly 2,000 years. It is also very interesting that none of the figurines from Group B can be explicitly and uniquely dated to the LCA. This means that there are types of figurines that have appeared in earlier periods but so far have been found at only LCA sites, therefore were dated to the LCA and probably overlooked the opportunity of possible similarities with earlier figurines. Alternatively, the body parts in question are so uncharacteristic or common that a more specific chronology is not possible.

The most interesting results of the chronological pattern of the 27 Group C figurines are the peaks during the LN and LCA already observed in Group A and supported by other material culture from the site. What is striking is the predominance of Neolithic figurines over Chalcolithic figurines, a pattern to our knowledge unregistered so far on any multi-period site. Given that the Chalcolithic, and especially the Late Chalcolithic, is considered as the climax period for the production and consumption of figurines, the expectation at a site with multiple occupations would be the discard of many more Chalcolithic than Neolithic figurines. But is that the case in Orlovo?

The combined data of all three groups have produced a somewhat surprising result – there are as many figurines with 'Neolithic only' analogies as there are figurines with 'Copper Age only' parallels as figurines with analogies in both periods (Fig. 2.11) The importance of such a pattern should not be over-estimated, given the methodology of comparative dating but it would be unwise not to flag the possibility of a breakthrough in our knowledge of figurine demand and production in the Balkans. This may be an echo of the diachronic development in figurine use at the Vinča-Belo Brdo tell, with a peak in the B and C layers and lower frequencies in the A and D levels (Chapman 1981). This result may be explained by a decline in the ritual significance of the Vinča tell in the Late Vinča phase, when ritual innovations were found elsewhere in the network.

The spatial distribution of the figurine parallels has also produced somewhat surprising results (Fig. 2.12). While domination of similarities from Southeast Bulgaria is to be expected, the high percentage of parallels with Northeast Bulgaria and especially with Romania, including the relatively remote Moldavia, is a strong indication for widely

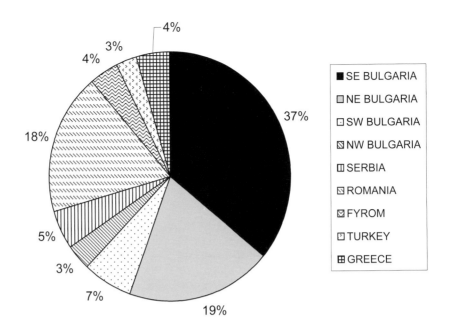

Figure 2.12. Spatial distribution of analogies for the Orlovo figurines

shared networks of ritual interaction. Although not that numerous, the parallels from the other neighbouring regions support such a pattern. The generally weak links to western Bulgaria is primarily due to the state of archaeological investigation in that part of the country.

On the basis of the comparative method for establishing the chronology of the Orlovo figurines, the site was occupied in all major phases of later prehistory, from the early 6th millennium BC (Early Neolithic) to the end of the 5th millennium BC (Late Copper Age), with occupational peaks during the Late Neolithic and the Late Copper Age. These analyses suggest periods in the history of the Orlovo settlement in which figurine discard was high and other periods where figurine discard was much less frequent. Whether these variations in figurine discard are related to different lengths of occupation in different phases, to variations in the rate of figurine production or to changes in the intensity of ritual practices is currently difficult to evaluate for a surface assemblage.

3. The Ornaments

Introduction

A total of just under 700 items relating to personal ornaments has been recovered from the surface of the Orlovo site – including raw materials for making ornaments, débitage from these practices, the end-products (complete ornaments) and fragments of ornaments. Approximately one-third of the items comprise objects made from the marine shell *Spondylus gaederopus*, another third is composed of *Cyclope* while the final third consists of very variable raw materials, including broadly similar frequencies of marine *Dentalium* shells, Other Shell species and Stone together with bone, antler and tooth ornaments (Fig. 3.1). Full identification of the wide range of marine and freshwater shell species indicates a total of 11 molluscan species – all but two of them marine species (Table 3.1). A total of 12 different kinds of stone, including one fragment of coal, has been utilised. A special discovery at Orlovo is the first recorded use, in Balkan prehistory, of the decorative bluish-green mineral turquoise (Kostov *et al.* 2007). Animal products were also utilised, such as bone, red deer canines and their imitations, as well as wild boar incisors. Only two ornaments were made of fired clay. The total number of raw materials amounts to 28, with a reduction to 27 in consideration of the mixed 'stone' category – 'volcanic rock or volcanic tuff'. This figure indicates the very wide range of raw materials – rock types, animal parts and molluscan species – that has been deposited at Orlovo.

Classes of raw material

The wide range of raw materials from which ornaments were, or could have been, made marks out the Orlovo assemblage as distinctive for the Neolithic–Eneolithic periods in Bulgaria. The raw materials may be divided into three groups – molluscan remains, stone and other materials.

Molluscan remains

In the following Table 3.1, the ecology and likely sources of the molluscan species found in the Orlovo assemblage are presented.

Stone

The location of the Orlovo site on the Northern edge of the Eastern Rhodope Mountains gives relatively easy access to a wide range of rocks, some of which may well have been collected locally (Plate 2). A dozen rock types have been identified, mostly by visual inspection, in the Orlovo assemblage (Table 3.2) relating to both ornaments and stone tools. The details of the lithic sources are as relevant for the stone tools (Chapter 4) as for the stone ornaments.

The majority of ornaments was made of marble, while volcanic rocks and tuffs were the next most popular stone for ornaments. Perhaps surprisingly, in third place came ornaments of turquoise – of extreme rarity in Balkan prehistory. A further six lithic materials were used occasionally for ornaments and are represented each by one example.

Volcanic rock and tuff

The most probable source for the large quantity of artifacts made of varieties of volcanic rock (of medium-acid volcanism of an Eocene and Oligocene age) or volcanic tuff can be either their abundant distribution to the South, in the Eastern Rhodopes, or the availability of fragments of pebbles of the same composition found along local river beds or in the Tertiary conglomerates in the formations around the site. Exchange or more remote sources of lithic material cannot be excluded. The volcanic rocks in the region usually are related to an acid or medium-acid volcanism of an Oligocene age (Boyanov *et al.* 1992). The volcanic tuffs are loosely lithified rocks composed of pyroclastic material (with a high percentage of volcanic glass), formed during volcano eruptions. In certain cases, they have undergone changes forming soft white to greenish zeolite-bearing rocks – monomineral zeolitites of a mainly clinoptilolite or mordenite composition (Djurova and Aleksiev 1989).

Sedimentary rock (sandstone; limestone; clays)

Sandstone and limestone are widespread in the sedimentary sequences of the Paleogene and Neogene formations in the

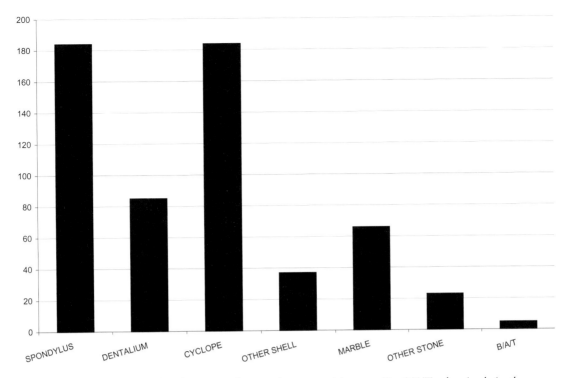

Figure 3.1. Total number of ornaments by general raw material groups. Key: B/A/T = bone/antler/teeth

region (see above, pp. 14–16). Clays of a halloysite-kaolinite composition have been identified stretching in a broad band across the Eastern Rhodopes – from the village of Dabovets in the Haskovo region to the village of Most in the Kardzhali region (including the well-known deposit at the village of Glavanak). Bentonite-type clay (of a montmorillonite composition) is known near the town of Kardzhali.

Metamorphic and metasomatic rocks (marble; schist; amphibolite; serpentinite; jasper-like rock)

Schists and fine-coursed gneiss-granites are localized in outcrops near the Orlovo site to the East (see above, p. 14). Marble is known from a lot of localities among the metamorphic complexes in the most Southerly and South-eastern parts of the Eastern Rhodopes, but it has no current economic value.

The serpentinite bodies (serpentinized ultrabasic rocks) are localized in the same part of the Eastern Rhodopes as small bodies outcropping on the surface. The best known and largest deposits are at Dobromirsti near Zlatograd, Golyamo Kamenyane about 10 km South of the town of Krumovgrad, Yakovitsa near the village of Drangovo and Brusevsti about 10 km South of the town of Madjarovo. According to the petrographic descriptions, the serpentinized rocks are of a harzburgite, peridotite and dunite (in some

cases, pyroxenite) composition. The serpentinites contain anthophillitic asbestos and picrolitic asbestos, as well as talc mineralisations.

The pendant (Fig. 3.12f: Inv. 3859/1) made of picrolite is the first find reported as yet from the territory of Bulgaria. Picrolite is a parallel-fiber aggregate of serpentine minerals (serpentinite of columnar or coarsely fibrous form) with a grayish-green silky texture and a cat's eye-like effect after polishing (chatoyant effect). Picrolite used as a raw material in the manufacture of prehistoric artifacts is well known from the island of Cyprus (Xenophontos 1991).

The Eastern Rhodopes are one of the main sources of jasper and jasper-like rocks in Bulgaria (Petrusenko and Kostov 1992). Such rocks of a predominantly metasomatic origin are related to the volcanic activity or post-volcanic hydrothermal changes upon volcanic and other kind of rocks (for the classification of jasper and related rocks, see Kostov 2006).

Vein mineral (turquoise)

Turquoise $CuAl_6(PO_4)_4(OH)_8.4H_2O$ is a copper-bearing phosphate mineral with a distinctive blue or bluish-green colour. It crystallizes in the Triclinic system, but it is rare to observe crystals. The hardness of the mineral on the Mohs scale is 5–6. Turquoise is found in copper-bearing

Table 3.1. Ecological contexts of molluscs deposited at Orlovo

Species name	Common name	Family	Habitat	Current distribution
Cerastoderma edule (formerly *Cardium edule*)	Common cockle	marine bivalve	middle and lower shores; burrows into soft sand, mud and muddy gravel to depths of less than 5 cm. Often found in huge numbers in estuaries and other sheltered inlets	western Barents Sea and Norway in the north, to Spain and Portugal; reaches as far south as Senegal in West Africa
Glycymeris sp.	dog cockle	marine bivalve	shallow burrower in fine shell gravels or sandy/muddy gravels and can be found offshore to approximately 100 m depth	from North Sea to Mediterranean (Aegean and Black Sea)
Ostrea edulis	European flat oyster	marine bivalve	rock outcrops at depths up to 20 m	the coast of Norway to the Mediterranean Sea, and into the Black Sea
Spondylus gaederopus	spiny oyster	marine bivalve	rock outcrops to a depth of 30 m, can be washed up on beaches	Aegean, Central and Western Mediterranean
Cerithium vulgatum	turret shell	marine gastropod	on sandy and shelly bottoms to 3–25 m	Atlantic coast of South Europe, Mediterranean, Aegean, Marmara and Black Seas
Conus sp.	Cone shell	marine gastropod	shallow, intertidal habitats to extremely deepwater	tropical oceans around the world, as well as the Mediterranean
Theodoxus sp.		freshwater gastropod	in or near freshwater streams	mostly tropical but also Mediterranean
Cyclope neritea		marine scaphopod	soft bottoms, sand of coastal area	Mediterranean (SW Europe–Black Sea)
Dentalium sp.		marine scaphopod	sea bed	Mediterranean
Marginella sp.		marine snail (univalve)	shallow, warm water, often washed up on beaches	Mediterranean (Aegean and Black Sea)
Melanoides sp.		freshwater snail	shallow slow running water (0.6–1.2m in depth), on a substrate consisting of soft mud, or soft mud and sand, or in areas rich in detritus and silt	southern Europe and Mediterranean

Table 3.2. Geological context of sources of rocks used at Orlovo

Genetic Type of Lithic Material	Tools	Ornaments
1. Igneous rocks – total	51	17
1.1. Volcanic rock	24	1
1.2. Volcanic tuff	27	16
2. Sedimentary rock (sandstone; limestone)	3	1
3. Metamorphic and metasomatic rocks – total	16	18
3.1. Marble; schist; amphibolite	3	14
3.2. Serpentinite (including picrolite)	2	3
3.3. Jasper-like rock	11	1
4. Vein mineral (turquoise)	–	8
5. Biogemmological materials (shell; bone; tooth; coal)	–	32+

and lead-zinc-copper regions (related usually to porphyry copper type deposits) with or without zones of secondary copper enrichment and oxidation zones.

Turquoise as a mineral species has been reported from the territory of Bulgaria for the first time from the Spahievo lead-zinc deposit (Spahievo ore field) at the boundary of the oxidation zone and the zone of secondary sulphide enrichment. Here, the main minerals are listed as being galena, sphalerite, hydrogoethite, chalcopyrite, bornite, chalcocite, quartz, kaolinite, wavellite and adular (Kounov *et al.* 1977). On the Balkan Peninsula so far, three sources of turquoise have been reported: (1) the Spahievo ore field (Haskovo district), related to the Obichnik deposit (Kardzhali district) in the East Rhodopes, Bulgaria; (2) the

Kilkis region in Greece; and (3) the area near the Bor copper deposit in North East Serbia (Kostov *et al.* 2007).

The mineral has been valued for its sky-blue colour as a gemmological material since prehistoric and later times in different cultures. At the time of Pliny the Elder and in Medieval times, the mineral was known as *callais*. Major areas for its early exploitation and trade as raw material for beads are the Sinai Peninsula, Central Asia and China. Because of its high value, in certain cases its colour has been imitated by other natural or artificial materials.

The turquoise beads from the prehistoric (Neolithic to Chalcolithic) site of Orlovo (Haskovo District) are considered as the first and earliest report of this gemmological material in Southeast Europe (Kostov *et al.* 2007). In Western Europe, mainly variscite prehistoric beads of a similar colour are known from many Neolithic sites in Iberia (Spain and Portugal) and Brittany (France). The finds at Orlovo of a polished bead and perforated bead blanks of turquoise (Plate 5i–k; Plate 6w) suggest a local prehistoric bead workshop for this prestigious material. The most reliable source for the raw material is the Spahievo ore field South West of Haskovo, where turquoise mineralization has been found both during underground mining and at the surface as small veinlets. Together with the Chalcolithic workshop at the village of Sedlare in the Eastern Rhodopes, the Orlovo finds document a second prehistoric workshop in this area utilising rich local mineral resources of gemmological value (cf. a third, recent discovery of a turquoise workshop at Vrhari (Boyadzhiev *et al.* 2010).

Organic matter (coal)

The coal bead (Plate 6s: Inv. 2766) is supposedly related to the coal-bearing local strata of the Paleogene coal-bearing formation (see above, p. 14).

Animal materials and fired clay

Apart from a small number of bone fragments, that are indeterminable to species, two classes of animal remains have been identified in the Orlovo ornament assemblage.

The **wild boar incisor** is a well-known material for the making of ornaments, with its large size, impressive colour and sheen and its associations with a ferocious wild beast. It is probable that hunting of wild boar was staged in local woodland.

The **red deer canine** is also well-known for the perforations which transform the tooth into an ornament. Only the stag has canines and then only two per animal. This gives a high prestige value to the red deer canine, over lengthy periods of prehistory – Upper Palaeolithic and Mesolithic (Newell *et al.* 1990: 104 and Table 74) and in the Neolithic and Chalcolithic of Central and South East Europe (Choyke 1997). This rarity cachet has led to the imitation of the red deer canine

using bone or other teeth (Choyke 1997). It is probable that hunting of red deer was practised in local woodland.

The use of **fired clay** for ornament-making is also dependent upon a common local resource. The site of Orlovo lies above the flood-plain of the Harmanlijska reka (Fig. 1.2), with its abundant sources of clay.

In summary, the characteristics and distribution of the resources used in the making of ornaments that were deposited at Orlovo show a varied selection of those parts of the natural world that were given a cultural value by the local inhabitants and also by those living further afield. Materials derived from all of three main zones constituting the prehistoric world – the Familiar, the Other and the Foreign (Chapman 2007; see above, p. 6). The Familiar zone produced animal parts and clay, as well as freshwater snails and gastropods such as *Melanoides* and *Theodoxus*; it may also have produced up to 20% of the raw materials for making stone ornaments and up to 80% of the stone for tool-making. The Other zone – the Northern part of the Rhodope foothills and the plains to the North of the site – yielded many of the rocks for ornaments, including marble, jasper, picrolite and turquoise. The Foreign zone – here perhaps best conceptualised as the far side of the Rhodope Mountains – was the source of the vast majority of the marine shells used for ornaments. Current sourcing data suggest a strong preference for the Other Zone for stone and the Foreign Zone for shells, expressed as an inverse relationship between proximity and popularity (Fig. 3.2).

The question of the contemporary availability of marine molluscs from the Black Sea and/or the Aegean continues to be a matter of debate (Todorova 1995a; Shackleton and Elderfield 1990). Here, we can propose the high probability that both *Spondylus gaederopus*, *Glycymeris sp.* and *Dentalium sp.* derived from the Aegean and not the Black Sea but that the majority of other species – including *Cerastoderma edule, Cyclope neritea* and *Ostrea edulis* were found in both bodies of water.

Exchange or Procurement?

There is such a variety of raw materials, deriving from seemingly rather different places, that reached the Orlovo community that several mechanisms are necessarily invoked to explain this concentration. Local collection can be assumed for materials in the Familiar Zone, whether from walks along the floodplain of the Harmanlijska reka to collect clay, snails and gastropods or hunting expeditions in the gallery forests for the wild boar incisors and the red deer canines (one animal each). It is hard to determine whether the volcanic stones used for ornaments were collected in the Familiar Zone or from further afield, in the Northern Rhodopes. Equally, walks of less than one day along the river valley would have led to the procurement of turquoise,

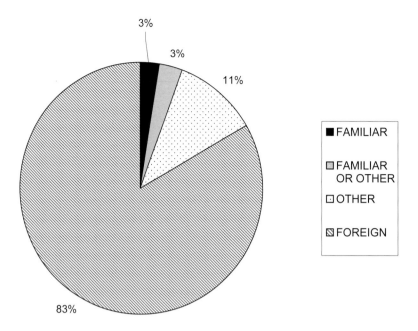

Figure 3.2. Proximity of source vs. abundance in raw materials deposited at Orlovo

while hikes of 20–30 km into the North Rhodopean foothills would have led to the main material sought – marble – as well as sources for serpentinite, jasper and picrolite.

The most interesting questions concern the persons collecting Aegean and/or Black Sea shells and bringing them 120 km (over the Rhodopes) or 200 km (from the Black Sea coast South of Burgas) to Orlovo, as finished ornaments, as half-finished objects or as unworked materials. A minimalist view would identify a single round trip by one or more long-distance specialists (*pace* Helms 1993) to collect the complete range of objects, weighing less than 5 kg, in one or two skin bags and bring them home to their community. This model requires the existence of coastal communities exploiting a wide range of molluscan species for their own ornament-making. Chronological support for this model (see below, pp. 103–4) would require a tight dating in one phase for all datable parallels for the Orlovo ornaments. There is no necessarily strong support for the assumption that the variety of *chaînes opératoires* for different shell species correlates to different mechanisms of exchange or procurement. The opposite extreme would be a long-term consolidated, directional exchange across or around the Rhodopes to settlements such as Orlovo. This model would require a very different chronological pattern of cross-dating, viz. good datable parallels for the Orlovo ornaments in several phases. In each case, the expectation is that a certain number of exotic materials from Orlovo's Familiar and Other Zones would reach the shores of the Black and/or Aegean seas, either as bartered objects by long-distance specialists or as prestige objects exchanged by

regular partners. As the reader may expect, there is a range of additional alternatives between these two extremes. The identification of the precise mechanism(s) is laden with theoretical and methodological difficulties (Chapman 2008). We shall return to this discussion after the collection and assessment of all other relevant data.

Chaînes opératoires

One way to approach the study of the manufacture of prehistoric things consists of the establishment of a *chaîne opératoire* – the sequence of making in successive stages from raw material to finished object and beyond (see above, p. 7). As an initial step, we have identified four stages (the term in the Catalogue is 'Classes'):

1. Unworked raw material
2. Partially worked, unfinished objects or the débitage from working
3. Complete artifacts
4. Fragmentary artifacts (viz., complete artifacts that have subsequently been broken)

A preliminary stage of analysis used seven general groups of raw materials to give an overall impression of the stages present at Orlovo: *Spondylus*, *Dentalium*, *Cyclope*, Other Shell, Marble, Other Stone and Bone + Antler + Teeth (Table 3.3 and Fig. 3.3). Only two general material groups (GenMat) showed all four stages of the *chaîne opératoire* – *Spondylus* and Other Shell (Fig. 3.4). However, over 90% of *Spondylus* objects were either complete or fragmentary

Table 3.3. Chaîne opératoire *stages by General Raw Material Groups*

	Stage 1	*Stage 2*	*Stage 3*	*Stage 4*
Spondylus	100	100	100	100
Cyclope	100	100	100	0
Marble	0	0	100	100
Dentalium	100	0	100	0
Other Stone	0	42	67	16
Other Shell	88	38	75	12
B+A+T	0	33	100	33
All Shells	90	45	81	22
All Stones	0	45	63	33

Key: percentages refer to the proportion of individual species with each specific stage represented; B + A + T = Bone + Antler + Teeth

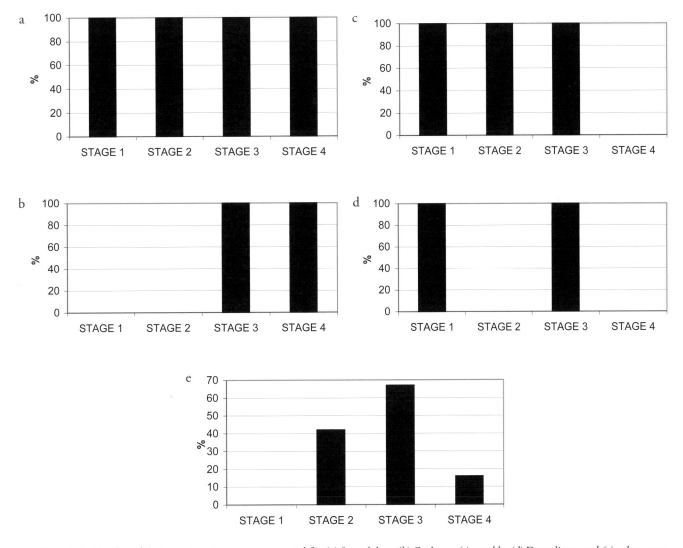

Figure 3.3. Number of chaîne opératoire *stages represented for (a)* Spondylus; *(b)* Cyclope; *(c) marble; (d)* Dentalium *and (e) other stone*

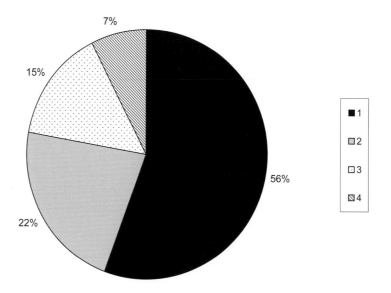

Figure 3.4. Number of chaînes opératoires *for all raw material classes*

artifacts and only one 'Other Shell' species (*Cerithium*) revealed all four stages. All *Dentalium* objects except one artifact consisted of Stage 1 unworked shells. The Other Shell group, comprising many different species, showed peaks in Stage 1 and Stage 3, suggesting collection of raw materials as well as ornament deposition. All of the Marble objects were either finished or finished and broken artifacts (Stages 3 and 4), while Other Stone and Bone/Antler/Teeth objects included more artifacts (Stages 3 and 4) than half-finished Stage 2 objects. These results suggest that on-site working was going on for all of the GenMat groups except marble.

This impression was confirmed by an analysis of the *chaîne opératoire* for each individual Raw Material (n = 27; Table 3.4). There is an inverse relationship between the number of stages and the number of raw materials represented by those stages, with over half of the 27 raw materials represented in only one stage (Fig. 3.5). There are as many as ten different combinations of Stages for 27 raw material classes (Fig. 3.5). This finding is consonant with an incomplete, surface collection but nonetheless gives an impression of considerable diversity of ornament biographies.

In terms of the molluscan remains, *Spondylus* and *Cerithium* production left remains of all four Stages, while *Cyclope*, *Glycymeris* and *Melanoides* species included remains from the first three stages of production. Ten species of shells were present as raw material (Stage 1), four of them with partial working. No molluscan species was found with Stage 2 partial working without evidence for the unmodified raw material Stage. While three species (*Cerastoderma*,

Conus and *Dentalium*) included remains from Stage 3 as well as Stage 1, the *Ostrea* species was the sole example of a molluscan species occurring as only a finished (Stage 3) artifact. Deposition has occurred of artifacts, either whole or fragmentary, made from a total of nine of the twelve molluscan species present.

In comparison with the shell remains, the stone ornaments have a stronger representation of complete or fragmentary objects, with no examples of unworked stone at all. Indeed, there are only five examples of stone raw material types with signs of half-finished working – an unidentified black stone, jasper-like material, limestone, turquoise and volcanic tuff. It is particularly interesting that, despite the large number of marble ornaments, there is no sign of on-site working of marble. The preponderance of stone ornaments occurred as Stage-3 finished objects, as represented by ¾ of the stone raw material types (n = 9/12). Among these stone types, only turquoise occurred as half-finished and finished artifacts, only marble was represented by complete as well as fragmentary ornaments, while volcanic tuff occurred in all three Stages (2–4). In addition, a single fragmentary object (Stage 4) was the sole example of the raw material identified as coal.

The Stage 2 fired clay and bone ornaments could have been made using local animal remains and clay. There are also Stage-3 red deer canine and boar's tusk ornaments – the latter with a Stage 4 fragment as well – made from local animal resources.

Where there are positive signs of Stage 2 objects, these results are a convincing demonstration of on-site working of a range of raw materials, including five molluscan species

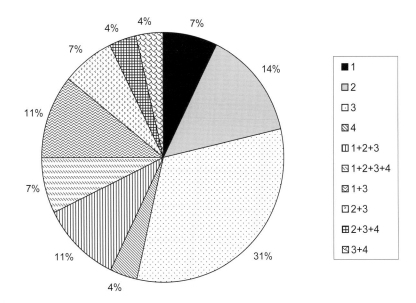

Figure 3.5. Number of chaîne opératoire combinatons for all raw material classes

Table 3.4. Chaîne opératoire stages by raw materials

	Stage 1	Stage 2	Stage 3	Stage 4	Total
Amphibolite	0	0	1	0	1
Coal	0	0	0	1	1
Serpentinite	0	0	1	0	1
Picrolite	0	0	1	0	1
Black Stone	0	1	0	0	1
Jasper-Like	0	1	0	0	1
Limestone	0	1	0	0	1
Marble	0	0	1	1	2
Turquoise	0	1	1	0	2
Volcanic Rock	0	0	1	0	1
Volcanic Tuff	0	1	1	1	3
Boar Incisor	0	0	1	0	1
Red Deer Canine	0	0	1	1	1
Bone	0	1	1	0	2
Fired Clay	0	1	0	0	1
Cardium	1	0	1	0	2
Glycymeris	1	1	1	0	3
Ostrea	0	0	1	0	1
Spondylus	1	1	1	1	4
Cerithium	1	1	1	1	4
Conus	1	0	1	0	2
Theodoxus	1	0	0	0	1
Cyclope	1	1	1	0	3
Dentalium	1	0	1	0	2
Marginella	1	0	0	0	1
Melanoides	1	1	1	0	3

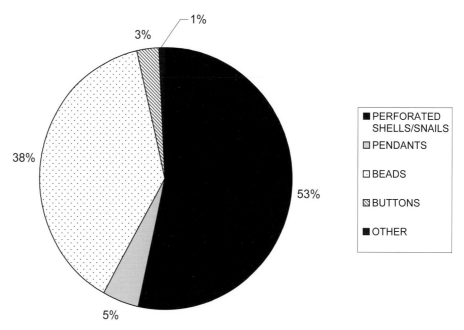

Figure 3.6. Total number of ornaments by general type

and five types of stone, as well as bone and fired clay. The discovery of on-site working evidence for as many as 12 raw material classes indicates the importance of the Orlovo ornament assemblage. However, the opposite inference is not so reliable: in the absence of excavation, the absence of Stage 2 objects for certain raw material classes data cannot necessarily be taken to mean an absence of on-site working of these materials. Nonetheless, in the case of marble, the probability of on-site working must remain rather low.

Ornament types

The distribution of ornaments by type indicates the predominance of beads, followed by fragmentary rings, pendants (including fragmentary pendants), buttons (incl. fragmentary buttons) and fragmentary pins. Other types include an appliqué, axe-pendants, a bird, a burnisher, a toggle and various horned objects (Fig. 3.6). The raw material distribution shows a predominance of *Spondylus* and *Cyclope*, with *Dentalium* and marble far less widely represented (Fig. 3.7).

Turning to the relationship between raw materials and ornament types (Fig. 3.8), bead-making was dominated by *Spondylus* and marble, with a wide range of sub-types. Fragmentary rings, pendants, buttons and one pin were also made predominantly of *Spondylus* shell but with Other Shells important too. The only artifact type not predominantly of *Spondylus* shell was the fragmentary ear-ring, made of *Cerithium*. The dominance of *Spondylus* is partly, but not

wholly, related to its numerical preponderance, while marble was used for a narrow range of artifacts – almost entirely beads. It is also clear that *Spondylus* was used for a wider range of artifact types than all other GenMat classes and, indeed, than any individual raw material (Fig. 3.9). While this point is partly related to the high absolute number of *Spondylus* shell items, there is some variability in the number of raw materials vs. the number of artifact types (Fig. 3.9). This result emphasises the use of marble for a narrow range of types – almost all beads – in comparison to Other Shells, which, with the same number of items, were made into many artifact types. A consideration of the different raw materials comprising the Other Shells group showed a rather generalised choice of shell species for artifacts, with the occurrence of very little specialised selection of one shell species for a specific ornament type.

A more detailed consideration of the rare raw materials shows a rather generalised choice of raw material for artifact types (Fig. 3.9), with pendants made from four materials (*Spondylus*, marble, other stone and bone), beads and buttons made from three materials (*Spondylus*, marble and bone in both cases), fragmentary beads and fragmentary pendants rings from two materials (respectively *Spondylus* and Other Stone and *Spondylus* and marble) and the remainder from one material. The reverse relationship (Fig. 3.8) indicates *Spondylus* was used for making nine different artifact types (including complete and fragmentary variants for beads and pendants), marble and Other Stone used for four types, Other Shell for three types, Bone + Antler + Teeth for two

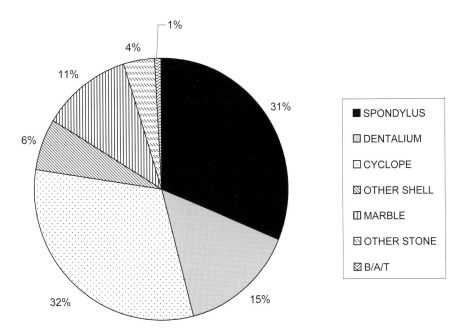

Figure 3.7. Proportions of ornaments by general raw material type

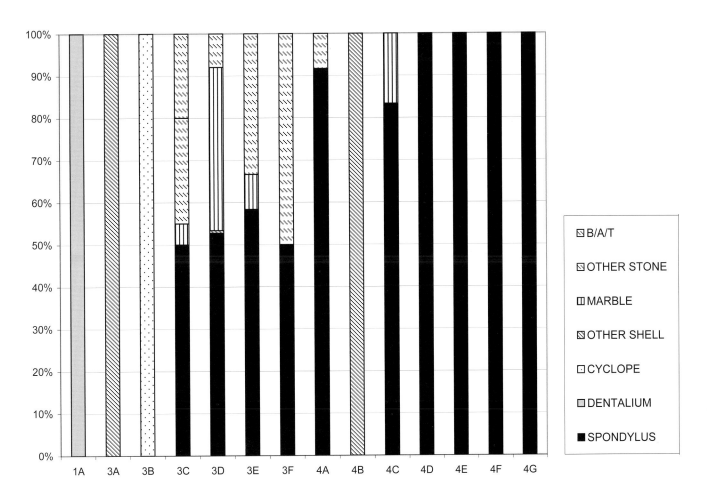

Figure 3.8. Ornament types by raw materials

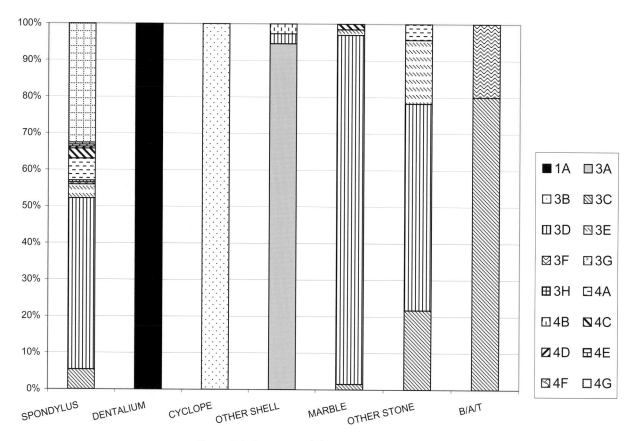

Figure 3.9. Raw materials by ornament types

types and *Dentalium* and *Cyclope* used very specifically for one type only. Aspects of *Spondylus gaederopus* that would have led to such a generalised ornament production must include its size and shape, as well as potential variations in its colour and brilliance (Chapman and Gaydarska 2006).

The chaîne opératoire *of raw materials for ornament-making*

In this section, we present the more specific evidence for each Stage of the *chaîne opératoire* as found in the Orlovo assemblage.

Class 1: unworked pieces

General type 1A: unworked shell
A total of 101 pieces of shell may be characterised as unworked items, with an overwhelming predominance of *Dentalium* shells (84%)(Plate 5b). The Size plot of the *Dentalium* shells shows a preference for medium-size shells, 6–10mm in length (Fig. 3.10). The only other shell found in more than two cases was *Glycymeris* (Plate 5c). Eight shell raw materials appeared once or twice, including *Cardium* (Plate 5d), *Cerithium, Conus, Marginella, Melanoides* and

Spondylus (Plate 5a). These data suggest an interest in, and collection of, a wide range of molluscan species, with a distinct preference for *Dentalium*.

General type 1B: unworked shells of snails
Nine examples of unworked snail shells have been found – all but one *Cyclope* and the other the sole example of *Theodoxus* found on the site. The predominance of *Cyclope* (Plate 5e) matches the strong preference for this species for perforation for use in ornaments.

Class 2: half-finished pieces

General type 2A: half-finished shells
A total of 21 pieces occurs, comprising nine *Spondylus* pieces, seven *Cerithium*, two each of *Glycymeris* and *Melanoides* and one *Conus* Two classes of half-finished pieces can be differentiated: shells with working towards an unidentified type of ornament and unfinished ornaments of a recognisable type. The former predominates, with eleven pieces showing signs of removal of the surface by cutting (Plate 5g) (three with additional perforation(s)) and three pieces with grinding (Fig. 3.11i, k and l). Three fragments of

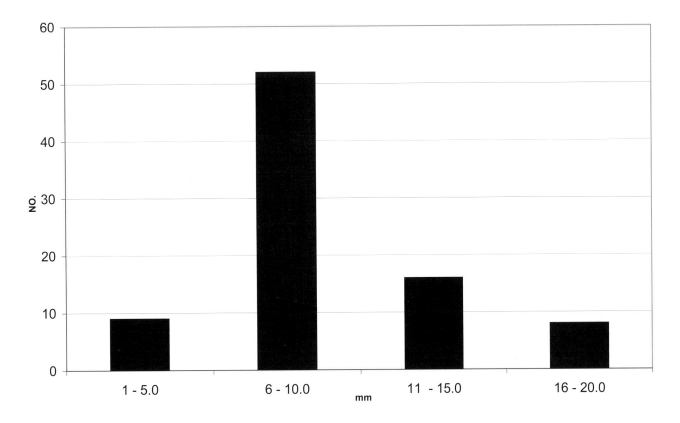

Figure 3.10. Length of Dentalium shells

Cerithium have possible perforations. The *Glycymeris* piece is sub-rectangular with two perforations and signs of grinding (Fig. 3.11k). Two parts of *Spondylus* rings occur – one that seems to have been broken during manufacture (Plate 5g: Inv. 3350/3), the other broken and re-used to make a pendant but with half-finished perforations (Inv. 3316/7). A circular piece 9 mm in diameter has been removed from the medial part of a third *Spondylus* piece, probably to make a bead or button blank (Plate 5h: Inv. 2991/1). This shows that bead blanks were made from not only broken rings or pendants but from raw shells. These examples betoken on-site working of five marine shell species, including at least three exotic species, probably mostly from the Aegean.

General type 2B: bead blanks
Nineteen bead blanks have been found for the making of one form of bead only – the disc bead. The largest number is made from volcanic tuff (n = 7) (Plate 5f and m; Fig. 3.11o; Fig. 3.12l), with five examples of *Spondylus* (Plate 5 l; Fig. 3.11m), three turquoise (Plate 5j) and one each of limestone (Fig. 3.11q), a jasper-like rock, an unidentified black stone and fired clay (Fig. 3.11r). The turquoise examples are the first bead blanks to be discovered in the Balkan Neolithic/

Eneolithic (Kostov *et al.* 2007). The maximum size of the bead blanks is 20 × 15mm, with a tendency for smaller sizes (Fig. 3.14). Most of the bead blanks have already been perforated, with straight perforations being twice as common as hour-glass forms. Both forms of perforation were used in each raw material, except for the straight form in volcanic tuff. The bead blanks represent various stages of completion. The sole limestone example is sub-rectangular and unperforated (Fig. 3.11q: Inv. 3379/37). Most blanks (n = 15) have perforations, smooth upper and lower surfaces but unfinished edges; two of these derived from broken *Spondylus* pendants or rings (Plate 5l: Inv. 2781/3). Two examples are the products of the re-use of chipped stone-working in volcanic tuff. The first is a core rejuvenation flake with a half-finished perforation ((Fig. 3.12a: Inv. 3050/26), while the other is made from a struck flake and has unfinished sides and an upper surface (Fig. 3.12l: Inv. 3862/1). These data indicate on-site ornament production in a variety of materials, mostly stone but also *Spondylus* and fired clay, with materials from broken or utilised artifacts as well as natural sources. The extended life histories of these bead blanks is a point of major significance that will be explored later (see below, pp. 107–8).

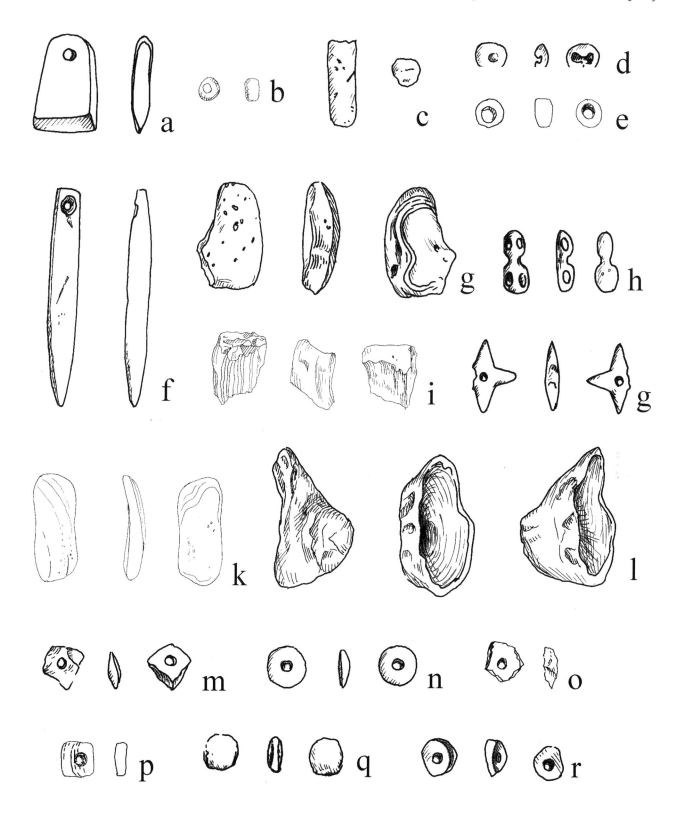

Figure 3.11. Ornaments 1: a. serpentinite axe-pendant: Inv. 3858/1; b. Spondylus disc bead: Inv. 3316/22; c. fragmentary Spondylus pin: Inv. 3350/17; d. Spondylus button: Inv. 3350/37; e. Spondylus disc bead: Inv. 3360/9; f. bone pin: Inv. 3351; g. fragmentary Spondylus plaque: Inv. 3350/1; h. Spondylus toggle: Inv. 3379/18; i. half-finished Spondylus: Inv. 3316/6; j. marble star-shaped pendant: Inv. 3379/19; k. ground-down and perforated Glycymeris: Inv. 3316/2; l. ground-down Melanoides: Inv. 3350/26; m. Spondylus bead blank: Inv. 3379/16; n. marble disc bead: Inv. 3379/32; o. volcanic tuff bead blank: Inv. 3505/15; p. Spondylus applique: Inv. 3360/35; q. limestone bead blank: Inv. 3379/37; r. fired clay bead blank: Inv. 3379/36; (drawn by Elena Georgieva).

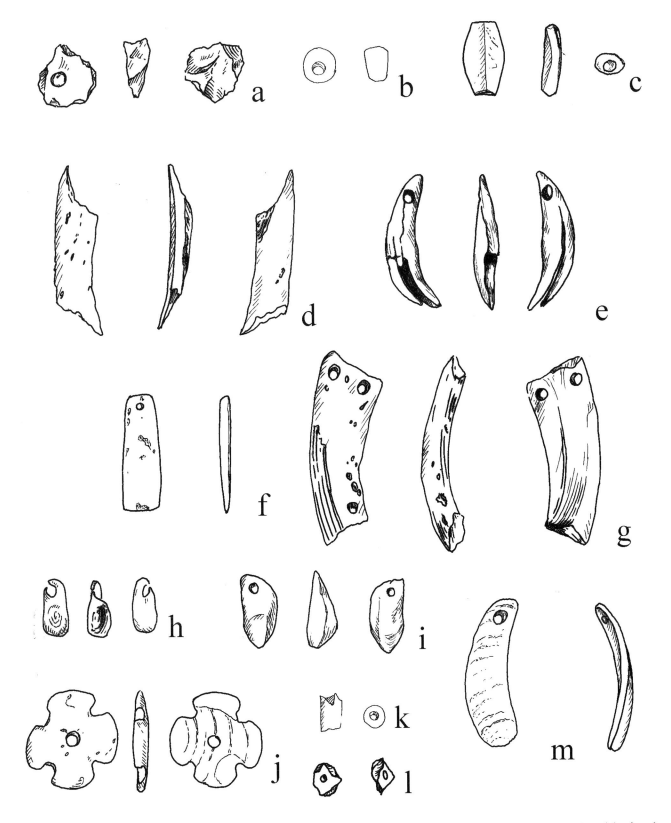

Figure 3.12. Ornaments 2: a. volcanic tuff flake re-worked into bead blank: Inv. 3050/26; b. marble disc bead: Inv. 3360/10; c. Spondylus barrel bead: Inv. 2764/1; d. fragmentary Spondylus ring: Inv. 3224/13; e. boar's incisor pendant: Inv. 3243/26; f. picrolite stone pendant: Inv. 3859/1; g. fragmentary Spondylus pendant: Inv. 3224/26; h. imitation red deer canine pendant: Inv. 3243/25; i. genuine red deer canine pendant: Inv. 3243/24; j. Spondylus clover-leaf pendant: Inv. 3243/31; k. fragmentary Spondylus cylindrical bead: Inv. 3360/4; l. volcanic tuff bead blank: Inv. 3862/1; m. Spondylus pendant: Inv. 3860/1; (drawn by Elena Georgieva).

General type 2C: débitage
A small number of pieces (n = 7) occurs which represent the discard from bone and shell-working. Four bone splinters are found, the half-finished perforation on one of which suggests breakage during making. Two *Spondylus* chunks appear to be débitage from ring-making (Fig. 3.11i: Inv. 3316/6; Plate 6a: Inv. 3350/9), as does a ventral fragment made of *Melanoides*. As with the bead blanks, these pieces provide convincing evidence for on-site ornament making.

General type 2D: half-finished shells of snails
There are 28 examples of *Cyclope* with parts of the surface missing in the course of ornament making. Most of these involve removal of the posterior part by cutting, although examples are known which miss either anterior, ventral or ventral-and -dorsal parts. One example has traces of grinding, while another has a break across decoration. These examples indicate local, on-site working of land snails (Plate 6d).

Class 3: complete artifacts

General type3A: perforated shell
A group of 45 perforated shells indicates minimal working, mostly though a single perforation through the dorsal surface, to produce an ornament that could be used as part of a necklace. Rare examples include two or three perforations, perforations through the ventral surface and one example of perforations through both ventral and dorsal. A wide range of six molluscan species has been used in this practice: 26 *Glycymeris* (Plate 6i–j), seven *Cardium* (Plate 6b), five *Melanoides*, four *Cerithium* (Plate 6c), two *Conus* (Plate 6f) and the only *Ostrea* on the site (Plate 6h). Although there is no direct evidence that such perforations were made on site, the diversity of other working practices and the simplicity of making such holes suggests that this was probably the case.

General type 3B: perforated shells of snails
A large number of perforated snails, all *Cyclope*, has been discovered (n = 184), representing the single most frequent ornament type (Plate 6e). Both types of shell – the possibly worked and the perforated – share the same preferred length of 12–13mm (Fig. 3.15). The snails have been subject to one or several perforations to facilitate stringing in a necklace. Fully ¾ of the snails have been perforated once, while a single example has been perforated five times (Fig. 3.16).

General type 3C: pendants
A total of 20 pendants has been found, made from nine materials – 10 *Spondylus* pieces, 2 examples each of red deer canine and boar's incisor and one each of amphibolite, marble, picrolite, serpentinite, a volcanic rock and volcanic tuff. The variety of raw materials is fully matched by the

diversity of pendant forms, of which there are eight. The commonest (n = 10) is a sub-rectangular form with one or two hour-glass perforations at either end and a distinct curvature, made from a fragment of a *Spondylus* ring (Fig. 3.12m: Inv. 3860/1). Three examples were made from ring terminals, six from mid-sections (Plate 6k: Inv. 3050/11) while one is unclear. There are four examples of polished stone axe-pendants (see below, Chapter 4), two of which were made from miniature trapezoidal axes (Fig. 3.11a: Inv. 3858/1) and two from a more elongated form (Plate 6m: Inv. 2779). In comparison with the dimensions (Length vs. Width) of the total sample, (Fig. 3.17A), both the axe-pendants (Fig. 3.17B) and the pendants made from *Spondylus* shell (Fig. 3.17C) have a tendency for longer and wider sizes. Both hour-glass and straight perforations were used. Four pendants were made from wild animal teeth. A genuine red deer canine pendant with a straight perforation (Fig. 3.12i: Inv. 3243/24) can be contrasted with a 'fake' red deer canine pendant actually made from another tooth, probably a pre-molar (Fig. 3.12h: Inv. 3243/25). While such 'fakes' have been found in Late Neolithic mortuary contexts in Hungary (Choyke 1997) and Moldova (Dergachev 1998), the Orlovo 'fake' is believed to be the first example identified in Bulgaria. Two boar's incisor pendants have been found – the first a complete, worn pendant with signs of burning, that has led to splitting (Fig. 3.12e: Inv. 3243/26), the other a fragment of a polished pendant with a straight perforation (Plate 6n: Inv. 3050/23). Four *Spondylus* pendants in three other forms are known – two clover-leaf pendants, one with a straight perforation, the other with a flake detached from the dorsal surface through use (Fig. 3.12j: Inv. 3243/31; Plate 6l: 3050/9), one star-shaped pendant with an hour-glass perforation (Fig. 3.11j: Inv. 3379/19) and one partially-polished T-shaped pendant (Plate 6t: Inv. 3350/29). The final pendant is made from amphibolite in the form of an irregular trapeze, with an hour-glass perforation (Plate 6o: Inv. 3360/44). The widest range of pendant forms is associated with the most frequent raw material (*Spondylus*: e.g. Plate 6u). Conversely, each pendant form is represented here by only one raw material. There is no evidence as to the place of making of the complete stone pendants but the assumption could be made that the pendants made from wild animal teeth were of local origin. The existence of all stages in the *Spondylus chaîne opératoire*, as well as on-site examples of fragmentary shell rings, makes it probable that the shell pendants were made locally.

General type 3D: beads
A total of 165 complete beads has been discovered at Orlovo – the second most frequent artifact type. The beads comprise six forms and an unknown category, being made from a wide range of materials – stone (4 materials), shell (two materials), bone and fired clay. The commonest form of bead is the disc bead, a circular bead with a diameter far in excess of its

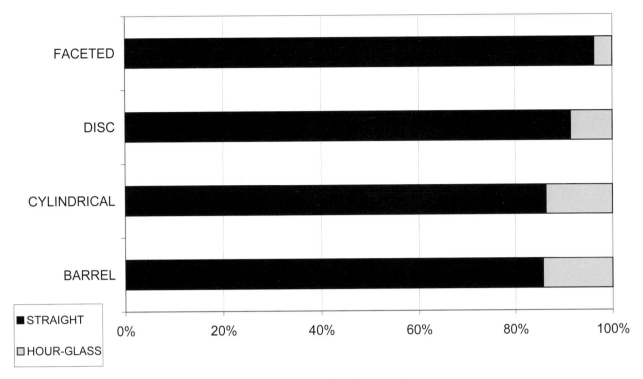

Figure 3.13. Type of perforation vs. bead types

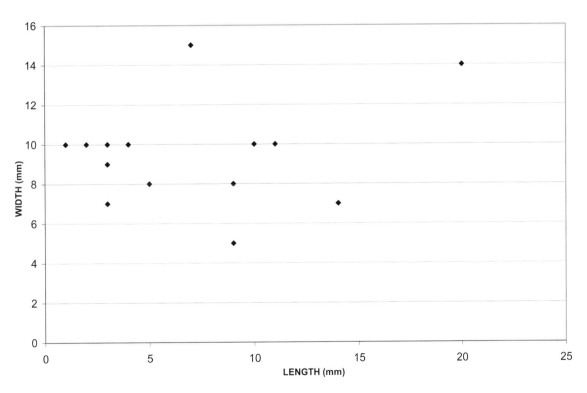

Figure 3.14. Size of bead blanks

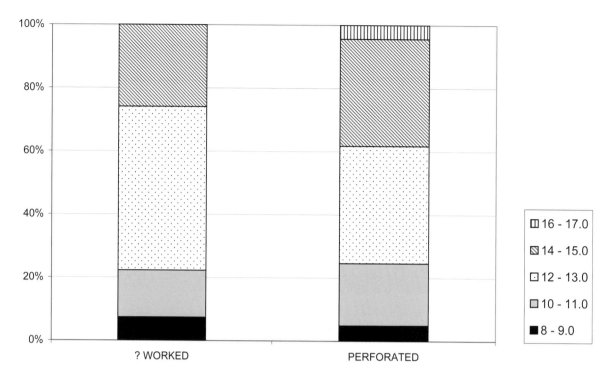

Figure 3.15. Length of worked vs. perforated Cyclope *(mm)*

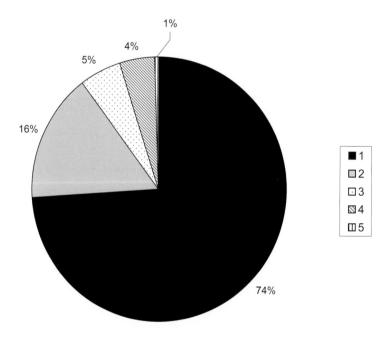

Figure 3.16. Number of perforations in Cyclope

thickness (Fig. 3.11e: Inv. 3360/9; Fig. 3.11n: Inv. 3379/32; Fig. 3.12b: Inv. 3360/10; Plate 5k: 3316/60; Fig. 3.11b: Inv. 3316/22). This is the only type of bead for which there is good evidence for local, on-site making in the form of bead blanks (see above, p. 51). Cylindrical beads have a tubular

shape with a single, symmetrical, longitudinal perforation (Plate 6p: Inv. 3360/42; Plate 6q: Inv. 3316/18; Plate 6w: Inv. 2991/4), whereas barrel-shaped beads have a medial swelling (Plate 6y, cc; Fig. 3.12c: Inv. 2764/1). Both of these forms of beads occasionally have longitudinal facets – a making

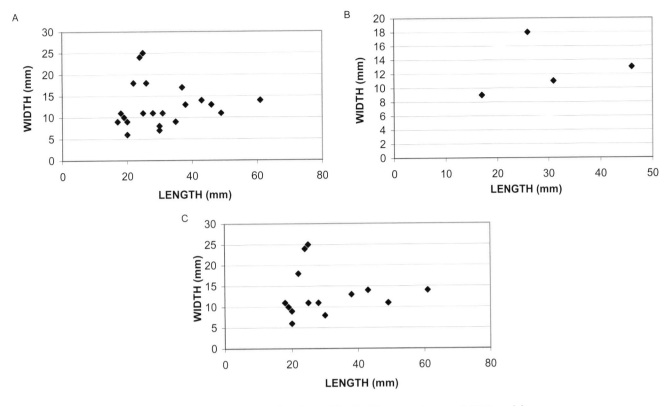

Figure 3.17. Dimensions of pendants: (A) all; (B) axe-pendants; and (C) Spondylus

technique recently discussed by one of the authors in the light of his mineralogical and gemmological expertise (Kostov 2007: 73–77). The number of facets varies from four to six to eight (Plate 6y and dd), with rare combinations of facets and natural garland decoration. There are rare examples in both types of unpolished and partly polished beads, sometimes so as not to obscure or remove the fine natural decorative lines (Plate 6q: Inv. 3316/18). There is one example of a sub-rectangular bead with a large round perforation (Plate 6r: Inv. 3360/37), as well as one bead blank in such a form (Plate 5i: Inv. 3316/55). The preferred method of bead perforation for each of the types is the straight perforation, with fewer than 20% hour-glass perforations in all types.

There is much overlap in the dimensions (length vs. diameter) of the various bead sub-types in comparison with the overall sizes (Fig. 3.18 a–e). The length of beads varies from 3 mm to 37 mm, while the diameter varies from 9mm–12 mm (Fig. 3.19a–c). The diameters are the most standardised for all sub-types – 1–8 mm for disc beads (though with a peak at the smallest size: Fig. 3.19c), 5–12 mm for barrel beads, 5–11 mm for faceted beads and 4–9 mm for cylindrical beads. The length of cylindrical, barrel and faceted beads peaks at a similar range of 7–9 mm (Fig. 3.19a–b), although cylindrical forms can reach four times that length (Fig. 3.19 b).

Each type of bead is made in several different raw materials, with both strong and weak preferences as to material (Fig. 3.20). The strong preferences concern barrel and cylindrical beads, both predominantly of *Spondylus*. The weak preferences concern faceted beads and disc beads, each made of broadly similar frequencies of marble and *Spondylus* (Fig. 3.20). The two predominant materials used in bead making are *Spondylus* (51%) and marble (38%)(Fig. 3.21). All known types of bead are made from each of these materials, marble is used to make 4 types, turquoise and greenstone are used for two types and the less common materials are used to make a single bead type. There are few signs of selection in the making of beads from specific raw materials.

With the exception of disc beads, we are not in a position to support the proposal of local, on-site bead making at Orlovo, despite the occasional occurrence of unpolished or partly polished beads. Since the total weight of the Orlovo bead collection hardly surpasses 1 kg, the exchange of several strings of necklaces onto the site is a feasible alternative to local making.

General type 3E: buttons

The total number of complete buttons at Orlovo amounts a dozen – in four types and made of three or four materials (Fig. 3.11d and Plate 6x: Inv. 3350/37;). Most buttons are

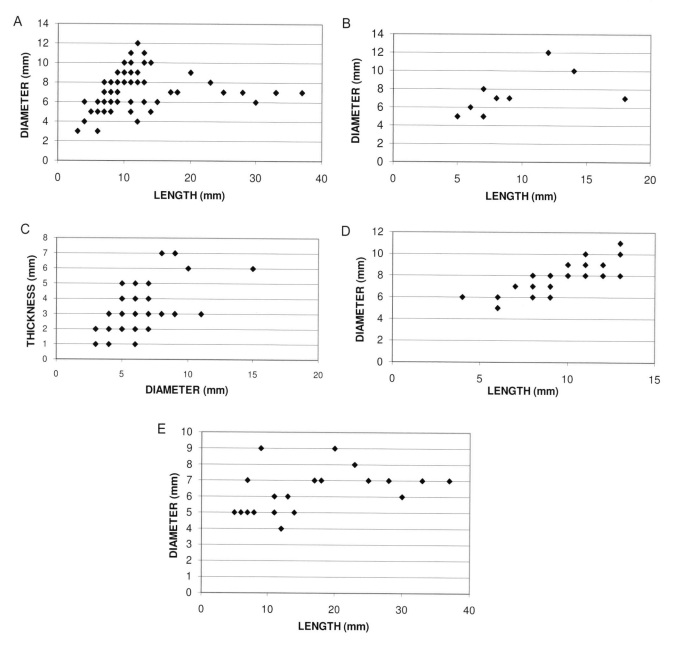

Figure 3.18. Sizes of bead types: (A) all beads; (B) disc beads; (C) barrel beads; (D) faceted beads; (E) cylindrical beads

circular (n = 8), with two oval, one pyramidal and one sub-rectangular type. The buttons range from 3–12 mm in length to 7–12 mm in width (Fig. 3.22). There is no evidence that they are not buttons but dress-weights, as Iakovidis (1977) has argued for Mycenean '*conuli*'. Seven of the buttons, including most of the circular type, are made of *Spondylus*, while volcanic tuff is used for three examples and either volcanic tuff / greenstone and marble for only one. All but one of the buttons has straight perforations, with a single V-perforation comparable to those common in West European Beaker graves, Irish and British Food Vessel contexts and

bog deposits (Harbison 1976, 14–21 and Plates 21–24/A–Y). Most of the *Spondylus* buttons are decorated with natural lines, with one such button remaining unpolished to reveal the linear patterning (Inv. 3360/2). There is only one piece of evidence supporting the local, on-site making of buttons – the *Spondylus* débitage from a possible button (or bead) blank (Plate 5h). Otherwise, the buttons may have been made elsewhere and brought onto the site in a small textile bag (cf. the so-called '*nécessaire*' bags at Durankulak (Gurova 2002: 252: 2005).

The remaining three artifact types occur in such small

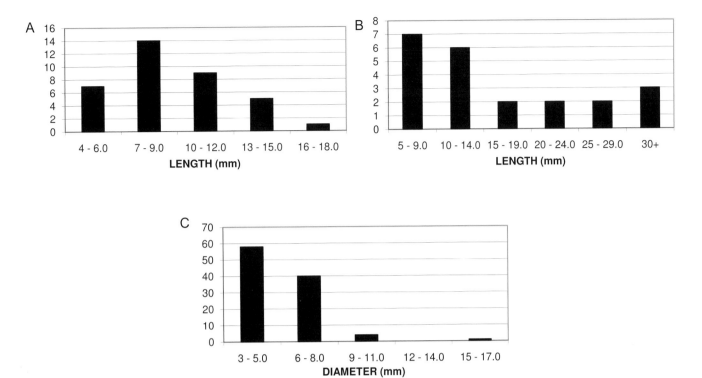

Figure 3.19. Bead dimensions: (A) length of barrel and faceted beads; (B) length of cylindrical beads; (C) diameter of disc beads

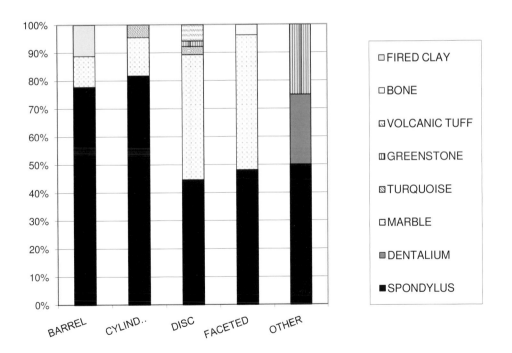

Figure 3.20. Beads by raw material and form

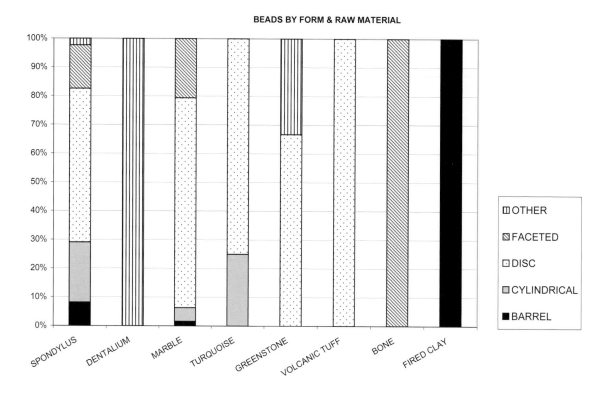

Figure 3.21. Beads by form and raw material

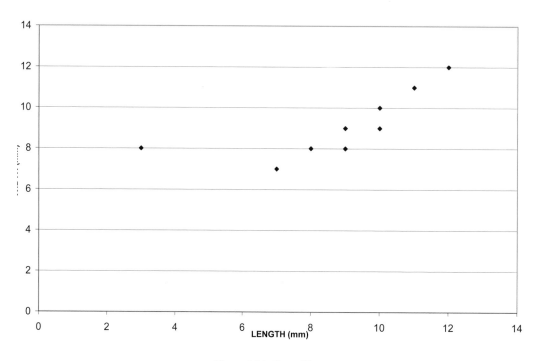

Figure 3.22. Size of buttons

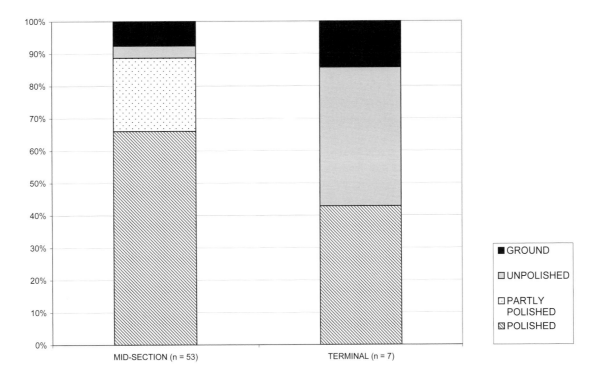

Figure 3.23. Polish and wear on Orlovo Spondylus rings

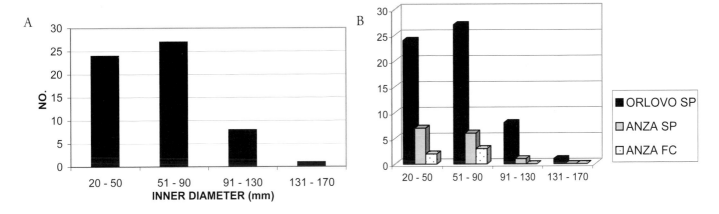

Figure 3.24. Inner diameter of Spondylus rings: (A) Orlovo; (B) Orlovo and Anza. Key SP = Spondylus; FC = fired clay

numbers (viz., one example of each!) as to make it doubtful that they represent 'types' in a statistical sense, since you cannot make a 'type' from one example. Yet each of them has a distinctive visual appearance and should be considered as a rare but important example of the Orlovo material culture.

General type 3F: applique
a rectangular Spondylus applique with a hour-glass perforation (Fig. 3.11p: Inv. 3360/35).

General type 3G: bone pin
a bone pin with an hour-glass perforation at the top (Fig. 3.11f: Inv. 3351).

General type 3H: toggle
a Spondylus figure-of-eight toggle with two straight perforations (Fig. 3.11h: Inv. 3379/18).

Class 4: fragmented artifacts

General type 4A: fragmentary beads
With one exception, the 15 fragmentary beads consist of the same types found in complete state – barrel, cylindrical, disc and faceted barrel beads. The sole exception is the unusual broken fish-shaped bead made of coal (Plate 6s: Inv. 2766). Despite the more easily fragmented disc beads, the commonest broken bead is the cylindrical type, with seven *Spondylus* (Fig. 3.12k: Inv. 3360/4) and two volcanic tuff examples. Each of the sole examples of barrel and faceted beads is made of *Spondylus*, as is one of the disc beads – the other is of volcanic tuff. All of the perforations except two are straight perforations – the hour-glass perforations through a polished cylindrical bead and a faceted barrel bead. Four of the cylindrical beads have remained unpolished to highlight the natural decorative lines.

General type 4B: fragmentary ear-ring
The sole example of an annulet so small in diameter as to be termed an 'ear-ring' is made of polished, perforated *Cerithium* which has subsequently been broken (Plate 6v: Inv. 3316/52).

General type 4C: fragmentary pendants
Six fragmentary pendants have been found – one made from marble and five made of *Spondylus*. They comprise: a marble T-shaped pendant, with an hour-glass perforation and a broken shaft (Plate 6t: Inv. 3350/29); a fragment of *Spondylus* pendant of unclear shape but natural decorative lines (Inv. 3350/15); and a second *Spondylus* pendant fragment broken across an hour-glass perforation (Inv. 3379/15). There are three examples of fragments of former *Spondylus* rings, in which the hinge holes have been expanded to form perforations for pendants (Fig. 3.12g: Inv. 3224/26). Discrimination between accidental and deliberate fragmentation of these pendants is extremely difficult.

General type 4D: fragmentary perforated shell
The hinge perforation of a sole *Spondylus* shell has been expanded and subsequently broken (Inv. No. 3379/6).

General type 4E: fragmentary pin
The single example of a broken pin is made of *Spondylus* and comprises the mid-section of the shank with a single groove (Fig. 3.11c: Inv. 3350/17).

General type 4F: fragmentary plaque
The single example of a fragmentary plaque (Fig. 3.11g: Inv. 3350/1) was part of a sub-rectangular plaque made of *Spondylus*, decorated with natural garlands.

General type 4G: fragmentary rings
A total of 60 fragmentary rings has been found – all made of *Spondylus* shell (Fig. 3.12d: Inv. 3224/13; Fig. 3.12g: Inv. 3224/26). The vast majority (88%) was made from the mid-section of a ring fragment rather than the terminal but the choice of polish on the rings was quite varied (Fig. 3.23). While most of the ring fragments were polished, there were numerous examples of partly polished, unpolished and only ground pieces, some with facets, others with perforations and yet others with fine natural decoration. Measurement of the inner diameter of the ring fragments was possible in 60 cases (Fig. 3.24A). As is often the case with *Spondylus* rings (cf. Anza rings: Fig. 3.24B; for discussion, see Chapman and Gaydarska 2006: 169), few of the rings – in this assemblage fewer than 10 – were large enough to be worn by an adult male or female of average wrist size. The largest inner diameter was 160 mm, the smallest 20 mm and the mean 67 mm. All of the examples cited here could have formed the basis for further transformations in *Spondylus* ornament-making, whether into buttons, beads or plaques.

Production techniques

Although much attention has been paid to the *chaînes opératoires* for each ornament class, the general techniques used to produce ornaments has not been outlined for the whole collection. It transpires that a suite of five similar techniques have been used for most of the raw material classes used for making ornaments: cutting away; grinding; polishing; perforation; and faceting (cf. Kostov 2007: 73). Many ornaments show signs of the application of several of these stages on the same object.

Cutting away

Although there are very few examples of removals prior to the stage of the stone ornament blank, they are common in shell ornaments. There are two examples of struck flakes used as bead blanks – both of volcanic tuff (Fig. 3.12a: Inv. 3050/26; Fig. 3.12l: Inv. 3862/1). Most of the stone ornaments have passed through two stages – grinding and polishing – which removed the traces of prior flaking. There is one example of a volcanic tuff bead blank (Plate 5f: Inv. No. 3243/22) which requires further flaking to produce a symmetrical shape. For the shell ornaments, four species show evidence of cutting away part of the shell to leave an ornament pre-form or blank. One *Spondylus* fragment had a 9 mm section cut away medially to leave a button or bead blank (Plate 5h: Inv. 2991/1); another comprised the ventral part and the umbo, with the rest cut away (Inv. 3316/5). Two *Glycymeris* shells had all of their sides cut away (Inv. 3316/46 and 3379/2). The ventral part of a *Melanoides* shell had the rest cut away (Inv. 3379/5). The final example is a *Cyclope* shell with most of the dorsal and ventral cut away (Inv. 3350/53). Although no use-wear analysis has been attempted on any of the Orlovo lithics, it is probable that the cutting away of shell was completed using a flint blade (cf. Tsuneki 1989; Miller, M. 2003).

Grinding

The Orlovo collection is not rich in grindstones but these would have been a vital part of the site toolkit in ornament production. There is also very little chance, even in an excavation, to discover the abrasives necessary for any grinding, but especially grinding of fine objects. Kostov (2007: 75) discusses the possible mechanisms for some of the finest gemmological products found at the Varna cemetery. The use of alluvial sand as an abrasive is attested in other cultural contexts and validated experimentally (Coles 1973:113–118).

Although polishing ornaments would have removed most traces of grinding, some unfinished objects show grinding traces, such as the *Cerithium* shell (Inv. 3350/28), the *Glycymeris* shell perhaps destined to form a pendant (Fig. 3.11k: Inv. 3316/2) and a partly ground *Melanoides* shell (Fig. 3.11l: Inv. 3350/26). No such traces occur on the two unpolished *Spondylus* beads (Inv. 3316/21 and 3360/43) and not at all on stone ornaments.

Polishing

The vast majority of complete and fragmentary objects have been polished with the aims of bringing out additional richness in the colour of the object, as well as creating an aesthetically pleasing sheen. The polishing process requires a graded series of increasingly fine abrasives, as discussed above.

Perforation

This activity is one of the most visible on the Orlovo ornaments, as a feature characteristic of beads and pendants. Successful perforations required fine, highly-skilled workmanship and the use of abrasives and probably flint drills, as has been demonstrated in later-period Bronze Age workshops in Afghanistan and India (Bulgarelli 1981; Kenoyer 1991; Lechevallier, M. and Quivron, G. 1981; cf. Coles 1973, 117–118).

Both of the typical forms of perforation – straight and hour-glass – have been used on most raw materials, whether shells or stone. Seven species of shell have been perforated – *Spondylus*, *Glycymeris*, *Ostrea*, *Cardium*, *Conus*, *Melanoides* and *Cerithium*, while six rock types – marble, jasper-like stone, limestone, volcanic tuff, turquoise and picrolite – comprise the perforated stone types. All three organic materials – boar's incisors, red deer canines and bones – have been perforated, with one example of a half-finished perforation on a bone splinter (Inv. 3243/79).

The only reliable statistics on the form of perforation comes from the beads (Fig. 3.13). The popularity of straight perforations in all but one bead class (sub-rectangular) cannot be considered a sign of sample size, but rather a genuine preference for a technique with which it is harder to achieve results than with the hour-glass method, with its less precise specifications.

Faceting

One of the major surprises of the analysis of Late Copper Age beads from the Durankulak and Varna cemeteries has been the recognition of carnelian beads with multiple facets on each tapering half (Kostov *et al.* 2004; Kostov 2007: 66–77). While the majority of faceted beads have 32 facets, the maximum number totals 39 (Kostov 2007: 66–67, 71). Although this technical feat is not paralleled at Orlovo, it is important to note the occurrence of faceted *Spondylus* and marble beads, as well as one example of bone beads. At Orlovo, the maximum number of facets present is eight. As far as we are aware, this is the first occurrence of faceted stone and shell beads outside major Late Copper Age cemeteries. There is also one example of an axe-pendant made of volcanic rock, with side facets and an hour-glass perforation (Plate 6m: Inv. 2779).

The existence of all five major techniques for the making of ornaments is a sign that similar sequences of ornament production were practised both at Orlovo (especially for shell ornaments) and in other places (especially for stone ornaments). The co-existence of all five techniques in use for both shell *and* stone ornaments may indicate similar craft skills shared between groups of related craft specialists, living in South East Bulgaria, and who could work in a range of raw materials.

Colour and brilliance

Two important visual aspects of personal ornaments were their colour and their brilliance. We have seen in the previous section how the vast majority of ornaments were polished at a late stage of the *chaîne opératoire*; here, we examine the colours selected by the producers and the wearers of the ornaments.

Whether colour is investigated by the number of raw material types (Fig. 3.25) or by the number of objects (Fig. 3.26), the result is similar – there has been an overwhelming preference for white ornaments. All of the shells species except one – the *Glycymeris*, which ranges from off-white to puce, are white and all of the bones, antler and teeth made into ornaments are also white. There are internal colours in both *Spondylus* and *Glycymeris* ornaments that have, but only rarely, been revealed: zones of red, pink, orange and brown in the former, red, pink and orange lines in the latter. It is in the categories of stone raw materials where more colour variability is expressed. Various shades of green are encountered, ranging from the light green of turquoise to the green with black lines of picrolite. Also, dark grey jasper-like rocks and a hitherto unidentified black stone present the darkest colours of the entire ornament group (Plate 7f).

Once the number of objects is taken into consideration, there is an even stronger emphasis on white – reaching close to 90% of all ornaments (Fig. 3.27). The very low total of two dark-grey – black objects indicates the minimal

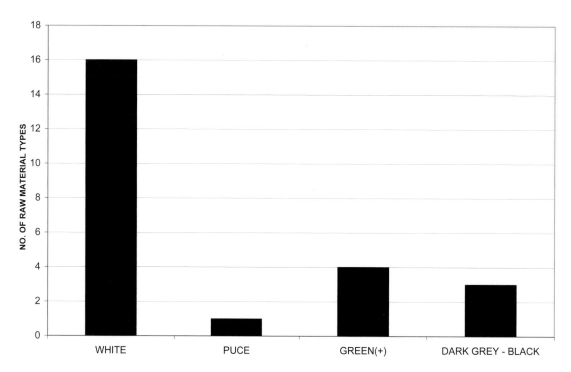

Figure 3.25. Colour of Orlovo ornaments by raw material types

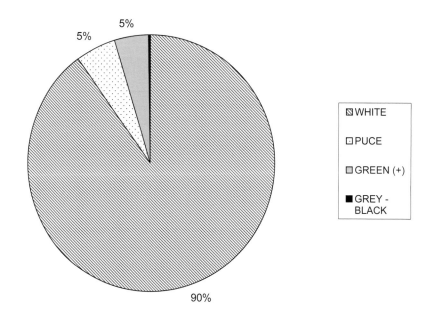

Figure 3.26. Colour of Orlovo ornaments by number of objects

significance for these colours in ornament production. In his survey of Balkan prehistoric ornaments, Kostov (2007) highlights the significance of the colour 'green' yet, in the Orlovo collection, only 5% of the objects in four raw material classes comprise this elsewhere favoured colour.

In terms of the relationships between object colour and raw material general classes, the shell objects favour only two colours – white and puce (Fig. 3.28) – while whites, greens and dark colours are used for the stone objects and only white colours for the bone/antler/teeth. Only the colour white was used for shell, stone and bone/antler/teeth objects; all other colours were restricted to a single class of

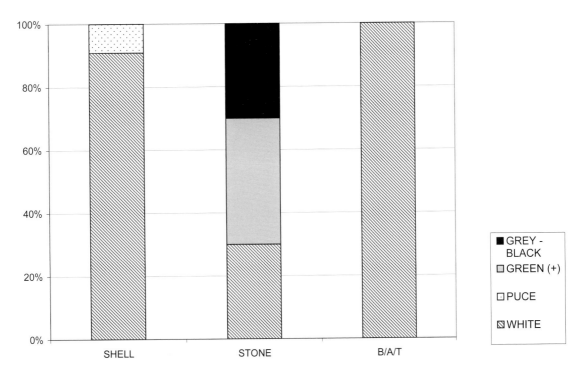

Figure 3.27. Raw material type by object colour, Orlovo ornaments. Key: B/A/T = bone/antler/teeth

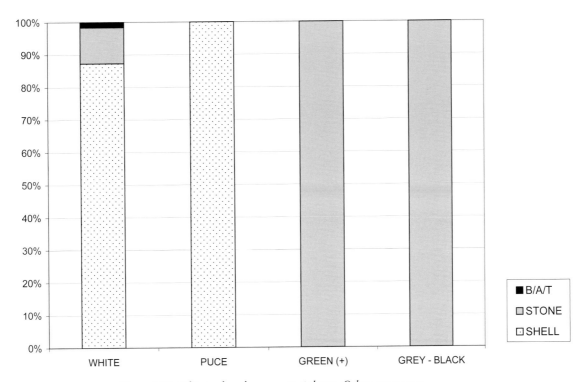

Figure 3.28. Object colour by raw material type, Orlovo ornaments

raw material: puce for shells, green and grey – black for stone objects. This suggests that, in parallel to the predominance of white, there is a rather specific suite of symbolic associations for particular kinds of raw materials.

Inter-site comparisons

The comparative study of the Orlovo ornaments was conducted according to the principles defined above (see pp. 11–12). Of fundamental importance for the comparison of Copper Age ornaments was Todorova and Vajsov's (2001) pioneering study *"Der kupferzeitliche Schmuck Bulgariens"*. Likewise, Nikolaidou's systematic publication of all ornaments from the Sitagroi tell, N. Greece, permitted a more fine-grained diachronic analysis than from any other single site (Nikolaidou 2003; Elster and Renfrew 2003). The sites with dated parallels for the Orlovo objects are shown below by half-millennium Cal BC (Table 3.5).

A final point concerns the classes of fragmentary artifacts

(Type 4A–G). Since all but the *Spondylus* rings (Type 4G) have been discussed with reference to their complete versions, the space-time discussions are not repeated for the incomplete objects.

Type 1A (Table 3.6) Unworked shells are a widespread object in later Balkan prehistory, with a diachronic span of three millennia (late 7th–early 4th millennia Cal BC) and a spatial distribution spanning North Greece to Eastern Hungary (North–South) and the North West Pontic and Moldavia to Western Hungary (East–West). Unworked shells have been deposited at settlements as much as in graves, while there is one occurrence in a hoard, deposited in Early Neolithic Galabnik. The settlement finds, whether on tells or flat sites, cover the full chronological range, the mortuary finds a shorter interval (5500–3500 Cal BC). The occurrence of unmodified *Ostrea, Cerastoderma, Unio* and *Columbella* shells in the chronologically uncertain culture level (LCA or EBA) at Strashimirovo, on the shore of the Varna Lake, has

Table 3.5. Chronological framework for sites with ornament parallels (calibrated ^{14}C dates BC)

Late 7th M	Early 6th M	Late 6th M	Early 5th M	Late 5th M	Early 4th M	Late 4th M
Achilleion EN	Maluk Preslavets	Ezero MN	G. Delchevo I–VIII	G. Delchevo IX–XV		
	Anza I–III	Anza IV	Varna I and II	Vinitsa I–III	Traian (Cuc AB)	
	Galabnik	Durankulak Hamangia I–IV	Durankulak LCA	Zimnicea	Ariuşd (Cuc AB)	
	Gura Baciului	Sitagroi I	Sitagroi I	Sitagroi II	Sitagroi III	Sitagroi IV–V
	Divostin I	Limanu cemetery	Ovcharovo II–VII	Ovcharovo VIII–XII		
	Karanovo I–II	Karanovo III	Karanovo IV–V	Karanovo VI	Pusztaistvánháza	
	Azmak I–II	Azmak III	Azmak V	Azmak VI	Tiszavalk-Kenderföld	
	Ecsegfalva 23 (main)	Ecsegfalva 23 (late burial)	Tiszapolgár-Basatanya ECA	Tiszapolgár-Basatanya E/MCA	Tiszapolgár-Basatanya MCA	
	Slatino Horizon 2	Ceamurlia de Jos	Slatino Horizon 6	Krivodol		
	Malo Pole	Agigea	Cernica cemetery	Hârşova		
	Kovachevo	Cernavoda	Čoka tell	Zavets tell		
	Endrőd 119		Vészto tell	Draguşeni		
			Zengővárkony	Brad hoard		
			Obre II	Hăbăşeşti		
			Vlădisceasca	Karbuna hoard		
			Podhájska	Smilčić		
			Liubcova-Orniţa	Devnja cemetery		
			Tartăriă	Sadievo tell		
			Kökénydomb	Dolnoslav Horizon C		
			Rast	Gradeshnitsa		
			Mórágy	Devetaki Cave		
			Vaksevo	Tell Ruse		
			Andolina	Giurgiuleşti		
			Polgár-Csőszhalom-dűlő	Targovishte cemetery		

been used to argue for a md-Holocene marine incursion into the lake rather than as shell collection (Margos 1961). As at Orlovo, the commonest molluscan species used without modification is the *Dentalium*, with mussel shells (*Unio* sp. – NB, NOT found so far at Orlovo) more frequent than *Spondylus*, *Cardium* and *Ostrea* (one dated occurrence of

each). The dated finds for this type cover both the local Neolithic and Copper Age periods at Orlovo.

Type 1B (Table 3.7) There is only one well-dated parallel for the use of unworked snails – the placing of snails in the Ritual Pit Γ at Traian, Moldavia, dated to the early 4th millennium

Table 3.6. Parallels for Type 1A unworked shells

Site	Phase	Period	Comments
Achilleion	Phase Ia	EN	unworked *Spondylus*
Maluk Preslavets		EN	river shells in 5 graves
Ezero–Dipsiska mogila	8.80m depth	MN	river shells in baby's grave
Anza	IV	MN	5 unworked *Dentalium* shells
Durankulak cemetery	Hamangia I–II	LN	4 graves + *Dentalium* shells (up to 31)
Durankulak cemetery	Hamangia III–IV	ECA–MCA	12 graves + *Dentalium* (up to 491 per grave; *Dentalium* shroud in Gr. 609)
Durankulak cemetery	Hamangia III–IV	ECA–MCA	7 graves + *Unio* shells
Durankulak cemetery	Varna I–III	LCA	1 grave + unworked shells
Durankulak lakeside settlement	Hamangia I–II	LN	*Unio* shells used to impress pottery decoration
Durankulak Big Island tell	Hamangia IV	MCA	*Cardium* shells used to impress pottery decoration
Goljamo Delchevo tell	Horizon XII	LCA	4 shells (1 mussel, 2 *Cardium* and 1 ??)
Vinitsa tell	Horizons I–III	LCA	7 contexts + *Unio* or ? *Unio* shells
Slatino	Level 6	ECA	hoard of 35 mussels (+ 36 *Spondylus* ring fragments)
Sitagroi	II	LN	*Dentalium* beads
Sitagroi	III	CA	*Dentalium* beads
Sitagroi	IV	EBA	*Dentalium* beads
Karanovo	IV	LN	3 mussels in a vessel + other 'household tools'
Azmaska mogila	V	MCA	1 complete *Spondylus* shell
Galabnik hoard		EN	*Dentalium* beads
Mórágy-Tűzkődomb	Lengyel	ECA	*Dentalium* beads
Giurgiuleşti		LCA	*Unio* shells used to impress pottery decoration
Tiszapolgár–Basatanya	Tiszapolgár	ECA	unworked shell
Tiszapolgár–Basatanya	Bodrogkeresztúr	MCA	unworked shell
Andolina	Boian	LN	*Dentalium* beads
Cernavoda cemetery	Hamangia	LN	freshwater shells in several graves
Traian Pit Γ	Cucuteni AB	LCA	shells in middle pit-fill
Vésztő–magóri halom	Tisza	LN	shells in several graves
Čoka	Tisza/Vinča	LN	graves + *Dentalium* beads
Gura Baciului	Criş	EN	1 grave + bed of stones, sherds, bones and freshwater shells
Cernica cemetery	Boian I	MN	1 grave + *Ostrea* shells; 3 graves with *Ostrea* pendants and 1 grave with both
Limanu cemetery	Hamangia	LN	necklace of 40 *Dentalium* beads
Zimnicea	Gumelniţa	LCA	necklace of shell and *Dentalium* beads
Zengővárkony	Lengyel	ECA	*Dentalium* beads and unworked shells
Cernica cemetery	Boian I	MN	2 graves
Varna I cemetery	Varna I–III	LCA	thousands of *Dentalium* shells (large accumulations in certain graves)
Strashimirovo	?	LCA or EBA	*Ostrea*, *Cardium*, *Unio* and *Columbella* in cultural layer (? natural occurrence)
Yasa tepe	K. III	MN	4 shells (? *Glycymeris* and *Cardium*)

Table 3.7. Parallels for Type 1A unworked snails

Site	Phase	Period	Comments
Traian Pit Γ	Cucuteni AB	LCA	snails in middle pit-fill and in several vessels
Varna II cemetery	Varna	MCA	necklace of *Dentalium* in Grave 3

Table 3.8. Parallels for Type 2A shell pre-forms

Site	Phase	Period	Comments
Cernica cemetery	Boian I	MN	1 grave
Sitagroi	II	LN	*Spondylus* ring and pendant pre-forms
Sitagroi	III	CA	*Spondylus* ring and pendant pre-forms; *Glycymeris* ring pre-forms
Sitagroi	V	EBA	*Spondylus* ring pre-forms

Table 3.9. Parallels for Type 2B bead blanks

Site	Phase	Period	Comments
Anza	I	EN	3 unperforated blanks
Obre II		LN	2 bone ring blanks
Goljamo Delchevo tell	Horizons XI and XIII	LCA	possible sub-rectangular and circular blanks
Krivodol		LCA	described as 'irregular, unperforated schist beads'

Cal. BC (Dumitrescu, H. 1958). This is a very useful and specific time-range for Type 1B. The dated parallel for this type covers the local Copper Age period at Orlovo.

Type 2A (Table 3.8) Shell pre-forms (half-finished shell objects) are a comparative rarity in later Balkan prehistory. There are only two well-dated sites with such finds – the Cernica cemetery (shells not identified to species) and the Sitagroi tell, where *Spondylus* pre-forms for rings and pendants and *Glycymeris* pre-forms for rings indicate local ornament production (Nikolaidou 2003; Miller, M. 2003; Shackleton N. 2003). The mortuary finds occur in the early 5th millennium Cal. BC, while the settlement finds span over a millennium (late 5th–late 4th millennia Cal. BC). The dated finds for this type cover both the local Neolithic and Copper Age periods at Orlovo.

Type 2B (Table 3.9) All of the few known cases of bead blanks in later Balkan prehistory derive from settlement contexts, dating from the early 6th–late 5th millennia Cal. BC. The geographical range of these sites covers FYROM to Bosnia (North–South) and North East Bulgaria–Bosnia (East–West). No workshops for bead production have been yet claimed since the debitage from the *chaîne opératoire* stages is scanty and no specialist tools such as micro-borers have been recovered, as in the much later, 4th millennium BC bead workshops from Mundigak and Mehrgarh, in South Asia (Bulgarelli 1981; Lechevallier and Quivron

1981). The dated finds for this type cover both the local Neolithic and Copper Age periods at Orlovo.

Type 2C No datable analogies for the debitage from ornament-making have yet been published from elsewhere.

Type 2D No datable analogies for partly-completed ornaments made from snails have yet been published from elsewhere.

Type 3A (Table 3.10) The majority of perforated shells have been found in settlement contexts, concentrating in the 6th and early 5th millennia Cal. BC except at Sitagroi, where the finds continue into the late 4th millennium Cal. BC. The only cemeteries with such finds occur in the West and North West Pontic zones in the 5th millennium Cal. BC. Unperforated shells are also found in two hoards, both dating to the early 5th millennium Cal. BC, in Hungary and South Romania respectively. The dated finds for this type cover both the local Neolithic and Copper Age periods at Orlovo but with a higher probability of a Late Neolithic / Early Copper Age date.

Type 3B (Table 3.11) Perforated snails are not as common in later Balkan prehistory as perforated shells and there are few well-dated examples. Todorova and Vajsov (2001) quote five Bulgarian Copper Age tells with individual snails or necklaces of perforated snails but without further details; the

Table 3.10. Parallels for Type 3A perforated shells

Site	Phase	Period	Comments
Vinitsa cemetery		LCA	Grave 10 + 1 perforated shell
Goljamo Delchevo tell	Horizon XV	LCA	perforated *Cardium* shell
Goljamo Delchevo tell	Horizon X	LCA	perforated *Spondylus* pendant
Anza	IV	MN	perforated bivalve (?? species)
Hârşova	Gumelniţa A2	LCA	necklace of 5 perforated *Cardium* shells
Krivodol		LCA	most ornaments of *Cardium*
Sitagroi	I	MN	*Glycymeris*
Sitagroi	II	LN	*Glycymeris, Mytilus, Cardium, Columbella*
Sitagroi	III	CA	*Glycymeris, Cardium, Columbella, Murex, Neritea, Unio*
Sitagroi	IV	EBA	*Glycymeris, Cardium, Cypraea*
Sitagroi	V	EBA	*Glycymeris*
Divostin	I	EN	shell pendant
Karanovo	??	??	perforated shells
Čoka hoard	Tisza/Vinča	LN	perforated *Cardium* shells
Vlădiceasca hoard	Gumelniţa A1	LCA	526 *Lithospermum* beads
Giurgiuleşti		LCA	*Unio* shell pendants in 1 grave
Hódmezővásárhely–Kökénydomb	Tisza	LN	2 graves + perforated *Ostrea* bead necklaces
Ovcharovo	??	CA	single find of perforated *Cardium* shell
Durankulak cemetery	Tisza/Vinča	LN	Grave 224 + 2 *Spondylus* pendants + 1 main perforation and lots of small impressions
Ruse	??	LCA	shell pendant (no ID to sp.) in area + graves on tell
Yasa tepe	K. III	MN	one perforated *Cerithium*
Chavdar	Levels VI and V	EN	3 perforated *Cardium* shells

Table 3.11. Parallels for Type 3B perforated snails

Site	Phase	Period	Comments
Karanovo	11.2m depth; Kara. II	EN	adult male burial + 7 perforated snailshells
Zengővárkony	Lengyel	ECA	snailshell beads
Varna I cemetery	Varna I–III	LCA	Grave 97 + necklace of *Cyclope* snails
Ovcharovo tell		CA	perforated snails or snail necklaces
Poljanica tell		CA	perforated snails or snail necklaces
Radingrad tell		CA	perforated snails or snail necklaces
Sava tell		CA	perforated snails or snail necklaces
Pernik–Krakra		CA	marble imitation of perforated *Melanoides* (? *Cerithium*)
Goljamo Delchevo tell		CA	perforated snails or snail necklaces

most likely date for these examples is the 5th millennium Cal. BC. Mortuary finds fall in the early 6th and the early 5th millennia Cal. BC, in Western Hungary as well as the West Pontic zone. The dated finds for this type cover both the local Neolithic and Copper Age periods at Orlovo.

Type 3C (Tables 3.12–3.14) There are analogies for four of the pendant sub-types in the Orlovo assemblage, each with rather different dating: red deer canine pendants, boar's incisor

pendants, sub-rectangular pendants and axe-pendants.

Red deer canine pendants (Table 3.12) have a predominantly North Balkan–Carpathian distribution, with regional clusters in settlements and hoards in Moldavia–Moldova–E Transylvania in the late 5th millennium Cal. BC and outliers in the Alföld in the early 4th millennium Cal. BC. The cemetery distribution is rather different, with early 5th millennium tell and flat site burials in Eastern Hungary in contrast to the late 6th–late 5th millennia Cal. BC focus in

Table 3.12. Parallels for Type 3C red deer canine pendants

Site	Phase	Period	Comments
Durankulak cemetery	Hamangia I–II	LN	8 graves (up to 27 per grave)
Durankulak cemetery	Hamania III–IV	ECA–MCA	7 graves (up to 44 per grave)
Varna II cemetery	Varna	MCA	Grave 3 + perforated red deer canine
Zavets tell		LCA	necklace of perforated red deer canines
Sava tell	Varna	LCA	> cemetery area + necklace of perforated Red deer canines
Ariuşd hoard	Cucuteni AB	LCA	10 examples
Draguşeni	Cucuteni A4	LCA	11 fired clay imitations of red deer canines
Brad hoard	Cucuteni A	LCA	190 red deer canines (incl. fakes)
Hăbăşeşti hoard	Cucuteni A	LCA	22 red deer canines
Karbuna hoard	Cucuteni ??	LCA	124 red deer canines
Giurgiuleşti		LCA	3 graves + 1 each
Tiszavalk–Kenderföld	Bodrogkeresztúr	MCA	
Cernica cemetery	Boian I	MN	6 graves
Karanovo	??	??	animal tooth pendant
Polgár-Csőszhalom-dűlő	Herpály	LN	found in graves of both males and females

Table 3.13. Parallels for Type 3C boar's incisor pendants

Site	Phase	Period	Comments
Ariuşd hoard	Cucuteni AB	LCA	3 fragmentary examples
Dolnoslav	Horizon C	LCA	Several examples
Malo Pole		EN	unperforated example
Sitagroi	III	CA	2 perforated boar's tusks
Čoka hoard		LN	unperforated boar's tusk plate
Giurgiuleşti		LCA	1 grave + several
Tiszapolgár–Basatanya	Tiszapolgár	ECA	
Tiszapolgár–Basatanya	Bodrogkeresztúr	MCA	
Zengővárkony	Lengyel	ECA	boar's tusk ornaments
Cernica cemetery	Boian I	MN	5 graves
Polgár-Csőszhalom-dűlő	Herpály	LN	Only in richest male graves

West Pontic and Southern Romanian cemeteries. There are no other published examples of red deer canine pendants from Southern Bulgaria. The dated finds for this type cover both the local Neolithic and Copper Age periods at Orlovo.

Boar's incisor pendants (Table 3.13) have been deposited in settlements, graves and hoards, over a period of two millennia (early 6th–early 4th) and from North Greece to Hungary (North–South) and the North West Pontic to Western Hungary (East–West). The settlement deposits begin earlier, in the early 6th millennium Cal. BC but, from the early 5th millennium Cal. BC, such pendants occur in all three contexts. The dated finds for this type cover both the local Neolithic and Copper Age periods at Orlovo.

Sub-rectangular pendants (Table 3.14) are, generally, as frequent as boar's incisor pendants, found in the same three contexts but with a narrower temporal and spatial range: 5th and early 4th millennia Cal. BC and an East Balkan

distribution (no further West than South West Romania. The dated finds for this type cover the local Copper Age period at Orlovo.

We have been unable to find any published analogies for the axe-pendants in later Balkan prehistory, although miniature fired clay axes imitating shaft-hole copper axes are known from the Cucuteni A4 settlement of Draguşeni, in Moldavia (Marinescu-Bîlcu 2000, Fig. 178/45–46).

Type 3D (Tables 3.15–3.17) The range of beads in later Balkan prehistory is wider than for all other ornament types – and this is also the case, in microcosm at Orlovo. There are six bead sub-types with well-dated analogies: cylindrical, disc, barrel, faceted, sub-rectangular and plate beads.

The simplest form – the cylindrical – is also the most widespread in time and space (Table 3.15). Settlement finds, which form the most frequent context, cover three millennia

Table 3.14. Parallels for Type 3C sub-rectangular pendants

Site	Phase	Period	Comments
Rast		MN	perforated pendant made from a *Spondylus* ring
Sitagroi	II–III	LN	Several
Durankulak cemetery	Hamangia III–IV	ECA–MCA	12 graves (up to 10 per grave)
Durankulak cemetery	Varna I–III	LCA	31 graves (up to 40 per grave)
Ariuşd hoard	Cucuteni AB	LCA	29 + 1 or 2 perforations
Dolnoslav	Horizon C	LCA	1 example
Vratsa sites (Gradeshnitsa)		LCA	4 examples
Vinitsa cemetery		LCA	Grave 10 + 1 example
Sitagroi	III	CA	Several

Table 3.15. Parallels for Type 3D cylindrical beads

Site	Phase	Period	Comments
Slatino	2nd B. Horizon	EN	*Spondylus* bead
Durankulak cemetery	Hamangia I–II	LN	10 graves + *Spondylus* beads (up to 9 per grave)
Durankulak cemetery	Hamangia III–IV	ECA–MCA	34 graves + *Spondylus* beads (up to 25 per grave)
Durankulak cemetery	Varna I–III	LCA	22 graves + *Spondylus* beads (up to 14 per grave)
Anza	I	EN	2 *Spondylus* examples
Anza	II–III	EN	1 fragmentary *Spondylus* example
Anza	IV	MN	2 *Spondylus* examples
Vinitsa cemetery		LCA	6 graves + *Spondylus* beads (up to 14 per grave)
Ariuşd hoard	Cucuteni AB	LCA	40 examples (*Spondylus*, bone, antler, polished stone, and marble)
Sitagroi	I	MN	shell, marble
Sitagroi	II	LN	shell, stone, fired clay
Sitagroi	III	CA	shell, stone, marble, *Spondylus*, copper
Sitagroi	IV	EBA	shell, stone, fired clay
Sitagroi	V	EBA	shell
Tiszapolgár–Basatanya	Tiszapolgár	ECA	limestone beads
Hódmezővásárhely–Kökénydomb	Tisza	LN	grave + marble and *Spondylus* beads
Cernica cemetery	Boian I	MN	28 graves(shell)
Devetaki Cave		CA	large marble bead + incomplete perforated; marble curved bead
Ruse tell		LCA	3 *Spondylus* bead, 2 from area + burials (but not in grave)
Ruse tell		LCA	necklace of fired clay beads (best parallel for FC barrel bead)
Ovcharovo tell	VI	LCA	curved *Spondylus* bead
Ovcharovo tell	IX	LCA	necklace of fired clay beads (best parallel for FC barrel bead)

(early 6th–late 4th), with finds distributed from North Greece to Hungary (North–South) and from North East Bulgaria to Eastern Hungary (East–West). There is an overlapping time-scale distribution for cylindrical beads in mortuary contexts, found only in the late 6th and 5th millennia Cal. BC and from the Pontic to Hungary North of the Danube valley. The only case of cylindrical beads in a hoard attests to the widest variety of raw materials used – *Spondylus*, bone, antler, marble and another polished stone are used in the Cucuteni AB Ariuşd hoard (Sztáncsuj 2005), dated to the early 4th millennium Cal. BC. There is also variation in the distribution of raw materials used for these beads. The most widespread is *Spondylus*, extended over the full temporal and

spatial range. Marble beads are moderately common, with a narrower time range and fewer regional foci. The cylindrical beads made from limestone, bone, antler or fired clay have a late temporal range (late 5th–early 4th millennia Cal. BC) and a predominantly East Balkan distribution. The cylindrical fired clay beads from the Ovcharovo tell are the closest parallels for the fired clay barrel beads at Orlovo. Thus, the dated finds for *Spondylus* and marble forms of this type cover both the local Neolithic and Copper Age periods at Orlovo. No analogies for the cylindrical turquoise beads have yet been found in Hungary and the Balkans.

Disc beads (Table 3.16) are also a relatively common ornament form in later Balkan prehistory, with a 3

Table 3.16. Parallels for Type 3D disc beads

Site	Phase	Period	Comments
Gradeshnitsa		EN	child burial + 25 'mineral' beads
Durankulak cemetery	Hamangia III–IV	ECA–MCA	14 graves + *Spondylus* beads (up to 60 per grave)
Durankulak cemetery	Varna I–III	LCA	3 graves + *Spondylus* beads (up to 3 per grave)
Anza	I	EN	11 *Spondylus* beads
Anza	IV	MN	5 *Spondylus* beads
Vinitsa cemetery		LCA	Grave 36 + 25 *Spondylus* beads
Goljamo Delchevo tell	Horizons XI–XVII	LCA	Polished stone, *Spondylus* and ? Fired Clay examples
Ariuşd hoard	Cucuteni AB	LCA	5 *Unio* beads
Krivodol		LCA	schist beads
Sitagroi	I	MN	Fired clay and stone
Sitagroi	II	LN	stone, *Spondylus*, shell, copper
Sitagroi	III	CA	stone, *Spondylus*, shell, copper, fired clay, mother-of-pearl, gold
Sitagroi	IV	EBA	stone, fired clay
Sitagroi	V	EBA	shell, marble
Draguşeni	Cucuteni A4	LCA	1 fired clay bead
Tiszapolgár–Basatanya	Tiszapolgár	ECA	limestone disc beads
Tiszapolgár–Basatanya	Bodrogkeresztúr	MCA	marble disc beads
Pusztaistvánháza	Bodrogkeresztúr	MCA	over 1000 marble beads in 1 grave
Hódmezővásárhely–Kökénydomb	Tisza	LN	grave + marble and *Spondylus* beads
Cernica cemetery	Boian I	MN	24 graves (shell)
Devnja cemetery	Varna	LCA	Grave 18 + malachite and agate disc beads

millennium-long distribution (early 6th–late 4th) and findspots in an area stretching from North Greece to Hungary (North–South) and from Moldavia to Eastern Hungary (East–West). Disc beads are rare in hoards (only one – the Ariuşd hoard) but are represented at similar numbers of settlements and cemeteries but the quantity of disc beads in some cemeteries is extraordinarily high (e.g. more than 1,000 marble beads in a Bodrogkeresztúr grave in the Pusztaistvánháza cemetery, Eastern Hungary: Hillebrand 1929, 26, 33). The mortuary distribution is a Northern Balkan one, reaching North and West from the Lower Danube valley; settlements with disc beads have the full range of distribution. As with cylindrical beads, there is considerable variety with disc beads' raw materials. Again, *Spondylus beads* are found at more sites, and over a wider temporal range, than beads of other materials. Fired clay and polished stone variants are limited to the 5th and early 4th millennia Cal. BC, while other materials fall mostly in the late 5th and early 4th millennia Cal. BC (e.g. *Unio*, schist, mother-of-pearl, marble and agate). For these reasons, the dated finds for *Spondylus* forms of this type cover both the local Neolithic and Copper Age periods at Orlovo, while disc beads of other materials are more likely to be coeval with the local Copper Age at Orlovo.

Barrel beads, with their distinctive carinated form, are by no means as common as cylindrical or disc beads but share a similar temporal distribution (early 6th–late 4th millennia Cal. BC) (Table 3.17). However, the spatial spread diverges, with a settlement cluster in Northern Greece, FYROM and Southern Bulgaria (covering the full temporal range) and a mortuary cluster in the West Pontic, North East Bulgaria and South East Romania, but limited to the 5th millennium Cal. BC. There are no known examples of barrel beads deposited with hoards. *Spondylus* examples exhibit a wide temporal range but barrel beads made of other materials (carnelian, marble, shell and fired clay) have a much patchier spatio-temporal distribution. Given the proximity of Orlovo to the Southern settlement focus, it seems probable that the settlement dates for barrel beads are more applicable: thus, the dated finds for this type cover both the local Neolithic and Copper Age periods at Orlovo.

The special case of faceted beads – rare in itself at Orlovo – is also very rare in later Balkan prehistory. It is a sign of the significance of the Orlovo bead forms that the only analogies for this sub-type derive from the Late Copper Age Varna I and Durankulak cemeteries (cf. Kostov 2007). These data are significant in demonstrating, beyond reasonable doubt, that there were deposition activities at Orlovo in the Late Copper Age (viz., the 5th millennium Cal. BC). The technical skills required to make these tiny shell facets were

Table 3.17. Parallels for Type 3D barrel beads

Site	Phase	Period	Comments
Anza	I	EN	1 *Spondylus* example
Kardzhali		EN	tiny carnelian bead
Anza	IV	MN	3 *Spondylus* examples
Cernica cemetery	Boian I	MN	12 graves (shell)
Hódmezővásárhely–Kökénydomb	Tisza	LN	grave + marble and *Spondylus* beads
Sitagroi	II	LN	Fired clay
Durankulak cemetery	Hamangia I–II	LN	1 grave + 2 *Spondylus* beads
Goljamo Delchevo tell	Horizon II	ECA	1 shell example
Durankulak cemetery	Hamangia III–IV	ECA–MCA	9 graves + *Spondylus* beads (up to 13 per grave)
Durankulak cemetery	Varna I–III	LCA	14 graves + *Spondylus* beads (up to 17 per grave)
Vinitsa cemetery		LCA	4 graves + *Spondylus* beads (up to 4 per grave)
Goljamo Delchevo cemetery		LCA	1 grave + shell bead (? *Spondylus*)
Sitagroi	III	CA	fired clay, *Spondylus*, shell
Sitagroi	V	EBA	*Spondylus*

Table 3.18. Parallels for Type 3E buttons

Site	Phase	Period	Comments
Karanovo	??	??	*Spondylus* button
Durankulak cemetery	Varna I–III	LCA	Grave 616 + 1 *Spondylus* example
Sitagroi	III	CA	*Spondylus* + V-perforation
Durankulak cemetery	Hamangia III–IV	ECA–MCA	Grave 527 + 1 *Spondylus* example
Čoka hoard	Tisza	LN	shell (including *Cardium*) and marble buttons + V-perforation
Čoka	Tisza	LN	shell button + V-perforation in grave
Hódmezővásárhely–Kökénydomb	Tisza	LN	shell button + V-perforation in grave
Varna II cemetery		LCA	Grave 3 + round *Spondylus* button
Goljamo Delchevo tell	II	LCA	round button (? part of diadem)
Ecsegfalva 23	Körös	EN	stone button + V-perforation
Ecsegfalva 23	AVK	MN	stone button + V-perforation

matched only by the aesthetic appreciation of the brilliance that the facets produced.

Of the two remaining rare bead sub-types, the sub-rectangular form has only one parallel – beads of both marble and *Spondylus* in an intra-mural grave at the Tisza site of the Kökénydomb, Eastern Hungary (Banner 1930), dated to the early 5th millennium Cal. BC. Similarly, the plate bead has a single analogy, in the Boian I cemetery at Cernica, Southern Romania (Comşa and Cantacuzino 2001), dated to the same period as the Kökénydomb. These data too provide two diagnostic temporal markers for ornament deposition at Orlovo in the 5th millennium Cal. BC – probably the early part of that millennium at that.

Type 3E (Table 3.18) Polished buttons have a thin but wide

distribution in Hungary and the Balkans, with few clusters in any context – whether settlement, mortuary or hoard. The temporal spread covers two millennia (early 6th–early 4th), with findspots from North Greece to Hungary (North–South) and from the West Pontic to Hungary (East–West). While the settlement examples cover the full chronological range, all of the mortuary and hoard finds cluster in the 5th millennium Cal. BC. Only the stone examples from the Körös and AVK phases at Ecsegfalva 23, Hungary (Starnini *et al.* 2007), date to the 6th millennium Cal. BC, while the buttons from most other raw materials (*Spondylus*, *Cardium*, marble and unidentified shell) were deposited in the succeeding millennium. Thus, the dated finds for this type cover both the local Neolithic and Copper Age periods at Orlovo.

Type 3F No precise parallels have been published, to date, for the *Spondylus* applique at Orlovo.

Type 3G Bone pins are a relatively common feature of later Balkan prehistory but the specific type found at Orlovo is rarely paralleled in specific detail. The closest analogies derive from early 6th and 5th millennia contexts in Northern Greece and Bulgaria, suggesting that the dated finds for this type cover both the local Neolithic and Copper Age periods at Orlovo.

Type 3H The only close parallel for the Orlovo *Spondylus* toggle derives from the early 5th millennium Boian I cemetery at Cernica (Comşa and Cantacuzino 2001), where this type is found in as many as 18 graves.

Type 4G (Table 3.19) In view of the well-established significance of *Spondylus* rings in the European Neolithic and Copper Age (Séfériadès 2000: 2003; Todorova 1995; Chapman and Gaydarska, in press), it is perhaps not surprising that this type is well represented in many sites

Table 3.19. Parallels for Type 4G fragmentary Spondylus *rings*

Site	Phase	Period	Comments
Vinitsa tell	all Horizons	LCA	examples from Houses 10, 11, 13, 15 and 21 and from cultural levels
Goljamo Delchevo tell	Horizons IV, X and XII	MCA–LCA	3 examples (1 from each Horizon)
Anza	I	EN	1 example
Anza	II–III	EN	8 examples
Anza	IV	MN	10 examples
Slatino	Level 6	ECA	hoard of 36 examples (+ 35 mussel shells)
Malo Pole		EN	1 example
Kovachevo	I	EN	1 example
Kolena		CA	fragments of *Spondylus* rings
Sitagroi	II	LN	*Spondylus* + *Glycymeris* rings
Sitagroi	III	CA	*Spondylus* + *Glycymeris* rings
Sitagroi	IV-V	EBA	*Spondylus* + *Glycymeris* rings
Obre II	Butmir	LN	3 fragments
Karanovo	??	??	*Spondylus* fragments
Hârşova	Gumelniţa A2	LCA	19 fragmentary bracelets
Ceamurlia de Jos	Hamangia	LN	1 fragmentary ring
Endrőd 119 Pit 12	Körös	EN	2 fragmentary rings
Gura Baciului	Criş	EN	1 fragmentary ring
Liubcova–Orniţa	Early Vinča	MN	2 fragmentary rings
Sadievo tell	Karanovo VI	LCA	complete *Spondylus* ring
Čoka hoard	Tisza	LN	complete and fragmentary *Spondylus* rings
Galabnik hoard	WBPW	EN	complete *Spondylus* ring
Mórágy-Tűzkődomb	Lengyel	ECA	complete *Spondylus* rings
Tărtaria	Early Vinča	MN	complete *Spondylus* ring
Podhájska	Lengyel	ECA	complete *Spondylus* ring
Cernavoda cemetery	Hamangia	LN	complete *Spondylus* rings
Smilčić	Danilo	MN	complete *Spondylus* ring
Hódmezővásárhely–Kökénydomb	Tisza	LN	complete bracelet in 1 grave
Limanu cemetery	Hamangia	LN	complete bracelet in 1 grave
Agigea cemetery	Hamangia	LN	2 complete bracelets in 1 grave
Cernica cemetery	Boian I	MN	6 graves
Targovishte cemetery		LCA	Grave 9 + complete bracelet
Provadia tell		CA	hoard of 5 complete bracelets
Omurtag Tell		LCA	hoard of 19 fragmentary bracelets

in these regions. Rings, whether complete or fragmentary, occur over three millennia (early 6th–late 4th) and in many regions, from Northern Greece to Hungary (North–South) and from Moldova to the Adriatic coast (East–West). While the most spectacular finds and quantities of *Spondylus* ring deposition occur in the mortuary context (e.g. the Varna I cemetery), with dates ranging from the early 6th to the 5th millennia Cal. BC, there is a wide range of settlements in which small numbers of shell rings occur. The settlement finds cover the complete spatio-temporal range of ring deposition. The hoards containing *Spondylus* rings are few in number, but range widely in time and space. Thus, the dated finds for this type cover both the local Neolithic and Copper Age periods at Orlovo.

Let us try to summarise this complex picture – this mosaic of ornament preferences and rejections. There are two forms of further analysis of the data that have been presented. The first is an examination of the clustering of types in particular time slices; the second concerns the identification of types with specific parallels in a restricted time range. The data have been summarised below (Table 3.20). These analyses do not take into account the certainty of spatial variation in the rate of adoption of innovative ornament types (cf. pottery styles in the Vinča culture: Chapman 1981). However, the use of a coarse-grained time frame of 500–year time slices represents the best compromise between gross error and exaggerated precision.

In the first approach, the key periods of frequent ornament use, leading to external analogies for the Orlovo ornaments, are the early 5th and the late 5th millennium Cal. BC, with a few examples in the 6th and the early 4th millennia Cal. BC. There is an element of circularity in the argument that most of the Orlovo ornaments date to the 5th millennium because this is when most ornaments were produced in the period 6500–3000 Cal. BC, so this is when

most analogies present themselves for the Orlovo assemblage. There is no obvious way around this circularity, which is also an objective fact – the peak of ornament production is indeed the 5th millennium.

The second approach supports the conclusions of the first analysis while suggesting something different: there are four ornament types which have analogies only in the early 5th millennium, while this is the case with only one type for the late 5th and the early 4th millennia respectively. The combined conclusions indicate that, with a fairly high probability, the majority of the Orlovo ornaments date to the 5th millennium Cal. BC but it is impossible to rule out the occurrence of earlier and/or later ornament deposition. Since we have already defined the local transition between the Late Neolithic and the Copper Age in South East Bulgaria at 4750 Cal. BC, this means that some ornaments deposited in the early 5th millennium may be classed as 'Neolithic' objects, while others may be 'Copper Age' artifacts.

Despite this ambiguity, the inter-site comparison of ornaments from later Hungarian and Balkan prehistory provides a general time frame for the Orlovo ornament assemblage. We would maintain that deposition occurred in at least several phases through the 5th millennium and on into the early 4th millennium Cal. BC, with the possibility of earlier deposition in the 6th millennium.

There is much spatial data within the chronological parallels, always bearing in mind the bias towards the tells and cemeteries of North East Bulgaria, which are far more extensively published than any other regional suite of finds (Fig. 3.29). The two data sets comprise the number of parallels for each ornament type / sub-type by region (Fig. 3.30) and the number of individual site parallels by region (Fig. 3.31). Four interesting conclusions emerge from these data. The first point is the breadth of inter-regional networks emerging from the ornament parallels, which

Table 3.20. Comparative dating of ornament types found at Orlovo

Type	Early Neo	Middle–Late Neo	Early–Middle Copper Age	Late Copper Age	Early Bronze Age
Unworked	xxxx		xxxxxx		
½ Finished		xxxxx	xxxxxx		xxxxx
Bead Blanks					
Debitage					
Perforated		xxxxx	xxxxxx	xxxxx	xxxxx
Sub-Rect. Pendant		xxxxx			
Disc Beads	xxxx	xxxxx	xxxxxx	xxxxx	xxxxx
Cylindrical Beads	xxxx	xxxxx	xxxxxx	xxxxx	xxxxx
Barrel Beads	xxxx	xxxxx	xxxxxx	xxxxx	xxxxx
Plate Beads		xxxxx			
Sub-Rect. Button			xxxxxx	xxxxx	
Round Button		xxxxx			
Toggle		xxxxx			
Fragm. Ring	xxxx	xxxxx	xxxxxx	xxxxx	xxxxx
Complete Ring	xxxx	xxxxx	xxxxxx	xxxxx	xxxxx

Key: each X signifies one site parallel

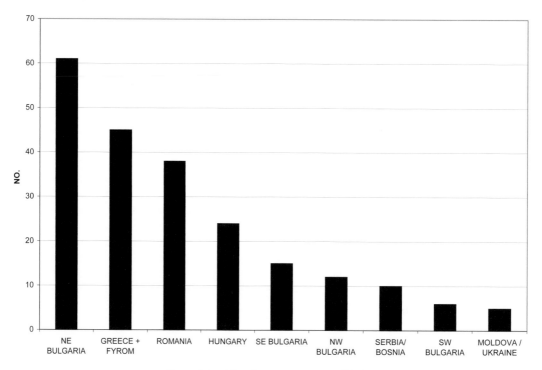

Figure 3.29. No. of site ornament parallels by region

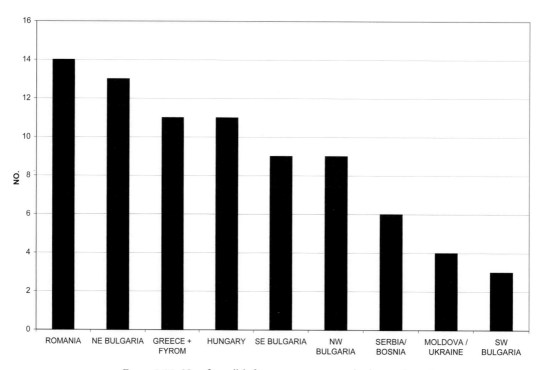

Figure 3.30. No. of parallels for ornament types and sub-types by region

shows that communities across much of the Balkans, with strong connections to Romania, moderately strong links to Hungary and less intensive relations with Serbia/ Bosnia. One of the key axes of the network is from Orlovo to North East Bulgaria, on into Romania and fading out as far away as Ukraine. There is little evidence that South West Bulgaria is included in the network linking the Orlovo area with Greece and FYROM, rather that there is a direct and strong link across the Rhodopes. Finally, while there are local ornament parallels in Orlovo's home region of South

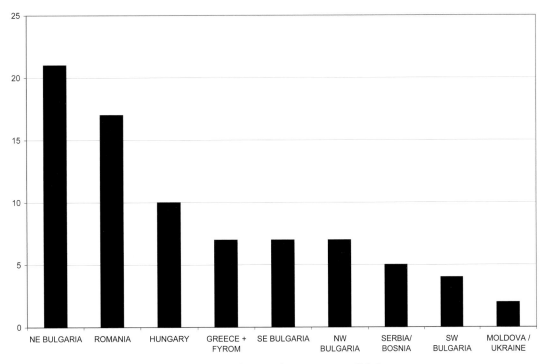

Figure 3.31. No. of sites with ornament parallels by region

East Bulgaria, these links are relatively weak in comparison with other aspects of the social network.

The final aspect of the ornament analogies concerns the contexts of discovery of the similar objects, here divided into settlement, cemetery and hoard (Fig. 3.32). There is a clear relationship between the three regions with important mortuary contexts – North East Bulgaria, Romania and Hungary + Slovakia – and the high frequencies of parallels in those areas. The negative relation is also documented in those regions with no mortuary contexts and low frequencies of parallels – South East, South West and North West Bulgaria and Serbia + Bosnia. However, the exception to these trends is Greece + FYROM, with no cemeteries but a large number of settlement parallels. The wide variety of finds contexts with parallels for the Orlovo ornaments simply underscores the significance of the site in Balkan prehistory.

Discussion

The collection of almost 700 ornaments deposited at Orlovo raises important questions concerning the time-space relations with other communities across the Balkans, as much as about the object biographies created by Neolithic and Chalcolithic groups in these regions.

The comparative study underlines the long period of time – perhaps approaching as much as two millennia – during which settlement deposition probably occurred at Orlovo. There is no sense of a continuous occupation from 5500 to 3500 BC – rather a series of punctuated phases when

the place at Orlovo became 'active' again after a phase of 'passivity' or abandonment. There is currently no means (i.e., without excavation) by which we can identify the duration of these 'active' phases but the ornament comparisons are clustered primarily in the 5th millennium BC, with groups of specific parallels in both the early 5th and the late 5th millennium, as well as some less intensive analogies in the late 6th and the early 4th millennia BC. The scenario of punctuated deposition militates against the minimalist model of ornament procurement in a single journey, since there is no reason to suppose that ornament deposition was of significance to the local community in only one occupation phase. While the overall peak of ornament production and deposition in the Balkans was the fifth millennium BC, it is still highly probable that some deposition took place both earlier and later.

The principal social implication of the spatial patterning of ornament parallels is that, like other sites in South East Bulgaria, the Orlovo community was tied into a wide-ranging network criss-crossing Greece, the Balkans and the Pannonian Basin. This open, permeable network consisted of persons who would have recognised some or many of the ornaments deposited at Orlovo as objects which would have held some (minimal) meaning – as not only a stylistic combination of features made in a common or related material but also as a way of communicating a social message and embodying a personal or communal identity. The key feature here is the materiality of the ornaments, which presenced a large number of absent people and places. Only

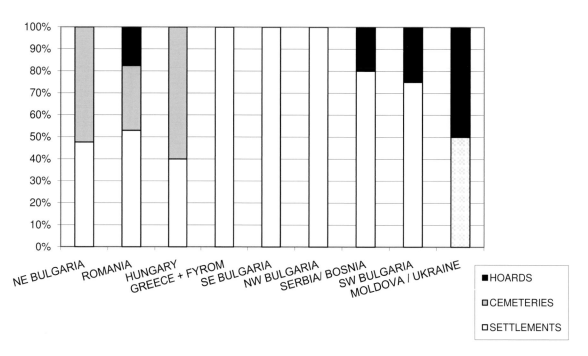

Figure 3.32. Types of site with ornament parallels by region

a spatially much wider investigation, not considered feasible at his stage, would be able to define the precise limits of such a network; for example, one obvious North Western extension of the network concerns the use of *Spondylus* ornaments as far away from Orlovo as the Paris Basin and Southern Scandinavia (Müller 1997; Müller *et al.* 1996). But the distances covered in this network suggest social ties covering 150 km to the South West, 300 km to the North and 370 km to the North West. The fall-off in the intensity of shared analogies with distance is particularly marked to the North East, where Ukrainian parallels are far fewer than those in the Cucuteni area, which in turn are exceeded by those in North East Bulgaria. But such a fall-off with distance is reversed to the North West, in the case of the analogies with Hungary, which are more common than with those in Serbia and Bosnia, in turn more frequent than those in South West Bulgaria. There are clearly social factors at work as well as spatial variables which need further explanation.

There is good evidence for the development of an aesthetic of colour and brilliance that permeates the Balkan Neolithic and Chalcolithic (Chapman 2006: 2007: 2007a). The ornaments deposited at Orlovo support this principle, in which the principal colour is white and a proportion of the ornaments are either naturally shining or artificially polished. While almost all of the shell ornaments, and a majority of the stone objects, are white, the only material portraying darker shades and green tones is stone. A colour

contrast is thus expressed in the chosen materials, though not an absolute distinction between shell things and stone objects. Perhaps part of this symbolic contrast refers to the source of the shells – whether marine or riverine – in water, while the more varied stone colours refer to the terrestrial, mainly rocky, sources of the stones used for ornaments.

A much stronger contrasts between shell and stone ornaments relates to the stages in the *chaînes opératoires* represented at Orlovo. Whereas ten out of the twelve molluscan species show signs of raw material or local, on-site working, stone ornaments are represented mostly by complete or fragmentary artifacts. Only five stone types – not including the most frequent type, marble – attest on-site working and there is no sign of the deposition of any stone raw material at Orlovo. When the disparity in distance from the raw material sources is taken into account, the contrast between shells and stones becomes even stronger; most of the shells were brought from far further than the stones – between 120 and 200 km rather than 5–25 km. This would suggest transport of shell raw materials to Orlovo, either directly or through trans-Rhodopean exchange networks, with other upland sites producing stone ornaments for use and deposition in liminal settlements such as Orlovo, before possible further exchange into the Thracian valley. Since all of the on-site working of stone materials is dedicated to the production of disc beads, the implication is that all other bead sub-types, including the very unusual faceted marble beads, as well as the stone buttons, were produced off-site. With the possible exception of Late Copper Age Sedlare (Raduntcheva 1997), and a recent new discovery, these upland 'workshop' sites remain to be identified, as do their social and spatial relationships to the stone sources (? quarry sites).

There is a multi-faceted relationship between the selection of raw materials and the form of the ornaments, which is not at first sight at all obvious. The greatest contrast lies between the beads, most of which are made from either marble or *Spondylus*, and all other artifact types, almost all made of shell. Otherwise, there is a generalised choice of raw materials for any particular ornament type, as with the suite of nine raw materials used in the making of 20 pendants or the use of several different materials to make each bead sub-type. Conversely, while almost all of the marble was used to make beads, *Spondylus* shell was used to make a total of nine ornament types, including every single ring fragment. It is possible that these conclusions have no chronological implication at all but it is tempting to speculate that a single episode of deposition of objects not curated for lengthy periods would have yielded a more consistent set of relationships between raw materials and ornament types. What can be stated more positively is that, for the most part, the Orlovo collection shows the signs of generalised raw material selection, with an emphasis on the exotic, the colourful and the shiny.

Thus far, emphasis has been placed on the contrasts between shell things and stone objects but there is one area in which the two materials share far more than hitherto. We can identify five production techniques – cutting, grinding, polishing, perforating and faceting – which are common to stone and shell ornaments. If a high probability could be demonstrated that stone ornaments were made on site, this finding would suggest that the same group of craft workers were using identical techniques to make ornaments from rather different raw materials. However, the conclusion that most shell ornaments were made on site whilst the majority of stone ornaments were made elsewhere suggests a wider knowledge of embodied techniques of ornament-making, shared between several communities in the peri-Rhodopean and Rhodopean zone. It should be underlined that the faceting of stone and bone beads has hitherto been recognised at very few sites – namely the Late Copper Age cemeteries of Varna and Durankulak (Kostov 2007) – making the Orlovo finds of considerable interest. Another rare occurrence at Orlovo is the deposition of not only an authentic red deer canine pendant but also a red deer canine pendant fake made from the tooth of another species! The presence of a fake pendant simply underscores the importance of the authentic object, with its symbolism of the hunt, the killing of the mighty stag and the careful perforation of one of its twin canines for an ornament to be worn close to the neck of a prestigious human.

The red deer canine pendant raises the question of object biographies – in one sense, central to the study of the Orlovo ornaments. Each different material presences a single source or several potential sources far from or close to Orlovo. This network of presencing maps onto parts of the spatial network of ornament parallels extending in all directions from Orlovo. It is interesting to note that the regions from which the raw materials were derived – the South and the East, the Aegean, the Rhodopes and the Black Sea coast – are two of the directions with the strongest ornament analogies. The personal contacts in these networks which enabled the gathering of the raw materials produced concomitant visual contacts that stimulated imitation of differing ornament styles and personal or group identities.

The other dimension of object biographies is the temporal. There is one limitation on understanding the temporality of a surface collection – the information retrievable on ornament curation – the deliberate keeping of an antique object worn first by a great grand-parent and passed on hand to hand over the generations. While we can discern variations in the extent of polishing in the fragmentary *Spondylus* rings, from none to partial to completely polished – distinguishing recent from ancient wear on rings and beads is much harder. While the paucity of wear on even stone ornaments suggests that these objects were perhaps deposited relatively soon after making or kept carefully for a longer period, the same cannot be confidently asserted for shell objects.

Nonetheless, there are several examples of objects with an extended biography in the Orlovo collection. The volcanic tuff bead blanks that constitute débitage from the flaking process – the *Spondylus* beads made from fragmented rings – the axe-pendants ground and polished into new life from an old broken axe – these are all excellent examples of the way that different persons contributed to a biography of a thing by interventions at different stages in its life. This is even more true of the collection of shells from underwater, such as the *Spondylus* shell stuck hard onto rocks at depths of up to 15 m, for divers were personally responsible for the retrieval of each shell (for further details on the biography of shell rings, see Chapman and Gaydarska 2006: Chapter 7). But it is also true of those who collected stone materials from a quarry face or a low rock exposure and brought them to a production site, where someone else may have continued the making process. In this way, the Orlovo collection represents a library of object biographies, which render present nearby and remote people and places, linking them by exchange, or procurement, or stylistic resemblances to the people living in the valley of the Harmanlijska reka.

4. The Polished Stone Tools

Introduction

One of the primary characteristics of the Orlovo site is a high intensity of discard of polished stone tools – something that has either been neglected in past site investigations or is not so common elsewhere. Whatever the reason, the Orlovo collection presents an excellent opportunity to describe, analyse and interpret a medium-sized polished stone tool collection from the South East Balkans. The way that this chapter is structured seeks to mirror the artifact biographical approach that we utilise in the entire book, beginning with the evidence for local production, moving to primary traits such as tool size, morphology, raw materials and their movement, and colour, before investigating tool use and the (inevitably poor) data on deposition. The study concludes with an inter-regional comparison to situate the Orlovo collection in its wider space – time context.

Evidence for local production

The nature of the assemblage as a museum collection rather than an excavation collection with a clearly defined recovery method makes it very difficult to characterise the stages of the *chaîne opératoire* (Mauss 1936; Leroi-Gourhan 1964). What we can do is to note the existence of several production techniques, which may be helpful in explaining how polished stone (mostly display) axes were made in this part of prehistoric Bulgaria.

We can define four standard techniques and one rare technique from the remains left on the axes deposited at Orlovo. The common techniques comprise flaking, grinding, polishing and faceting; the rare technique, found in only one case, is perforation using an hour-glass technique from both sides (Fig. 4.1a: Inv. 3228). As yet, there is no evidence for the sawing of pre-forms from rocks, as at Divostin II (Prinz 1988). The final two stages in making many axes contrasts polishing with faceting. A X^2 test of the stages of polishing plotted against the incidence of faceting shows a highly significant difference in association at the 0.001% probability (Table 4.1). The predominance of fully polished axes with multiple facets is offset by the occurrence of all stages of polishing in association with each form of faceting;

there is even one case of an unpolished axe with multiple facets, suggesting that there is no specific sequence of using these two techniques.

However, more than one-third of the tools (n = 26) have some particularities that make them candidates for possible local production (Fig. 4.1; Colour Figs. 7–8). The most numerous (n = 11) are the examples of ground tools and tools with partial or selective polish. A fair question is – are these artifacts really half-finished tools made locally or are they finished tools with grinding and polishing on the edge only? A comparison of polished stone axe assemblages from other Balkan Neolithic and Chalcolithic sites shows the rarity of partly-polished axes. At Obre I and II, all axes were fully polished (Sterud and Sterud 1974: 229), as were the axes from Early Neolithic Ecsegfalva 23 (Starnini *et al.* 2007) and those in all phases of Sitagroi (Elster 2003). Although many of the porcellanite axes from Divostin showed signs of flaking, there were no examples of edge-ground flaked axes (Prinz 1988). Thus, in the absence of a tradition of edge-ground tools which are nonetheless mostly unpolished, the examples of Orlovo are more likely to present unfinished tools. The first argument to support this conclusion is the desirability of shiny, brilliant surfaces on everyday objects. A second argument rests on the four examples of partial or selective polish where polish is not entirely excluded but probably rather not yet finished. In addition, there is a single example (Plate 7j: Inv. 2755/1) of polish over blade damage – which is representative for the re-worked group of tools in the assemblage. The latter consists of tools either made of previous (maybe larger) tools or presents a practice of tool repair. There are three

Table 4.1. Polishing vs. faceting, Orlovo stone tools

	Unpolished or partly polished	Polished
No facets	5	1
Facets	8	11
Multiple facets	5	41

X^2 = 48.428 with 2 degrees of freedom (p = <0.0001)

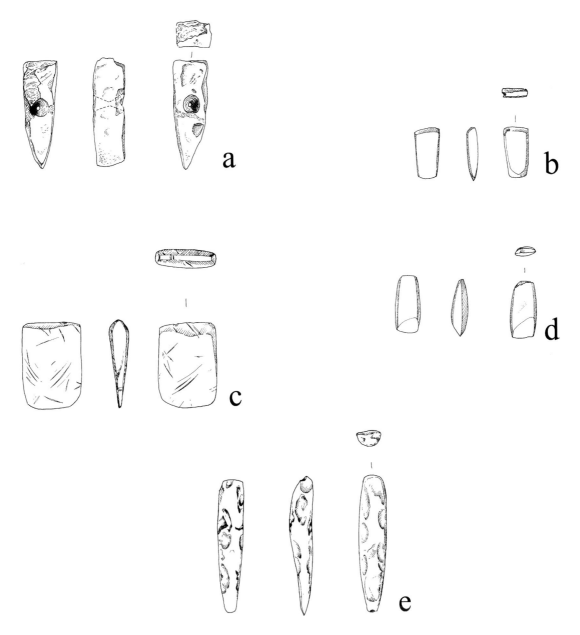

Figure 4.1. Polished stone tools 1: a. Inv. 3228; b. Inv. 2782/1; c. Inv. 3263; d. Inv. 2753/3; e. Inv. 3337/2 (drawn by Elena Georgieva)

examples where the butt curvature suggests that the tools are made from a much larger axe (e.g. Inv. 3006/1 Plate 7i). Another two have an asymmetric thickness of their sides, pointing to a specific shape of the raw material that might have been the pre-existing, constraining shape of another tool (Fig. 4.1d: Inv. 2753/3; Inv.2754/2). An interesting case is Inv. 2783/1 (Plate 7e), which has a facet on the present butt that was designed to be the blade but, for some reason, such an aim was abandoned and a new blade was made. The only example of a reversed trapezoidal shape present a similar biography – the butt has started as a blade but, after the blade was damaged, the two ends of

the tool have been reversed (Inv. 2782/1). Another group of possibly unfinished tools are the four examples with poorly developed faceting (Inv. 3193/6; 3193/8; 3193/9; Plate 7f: 3358/1). In two of them, this is probably due to the early stages of polishing, while the other two exhibit a poor faceting technique, indicating an inexperienced maker who is still learning and developing his/her skills. There is only one example of a very thick, blunt blade that probably suggests a tool awaiting sharpening (Inv. 3193/12: Plate 7b). And finally, Inv. 3337/2 (Fig. 4.1e) is an almost finished axe rough-out, with thinning flakes detached from all faces and with unfinished facets on each side.

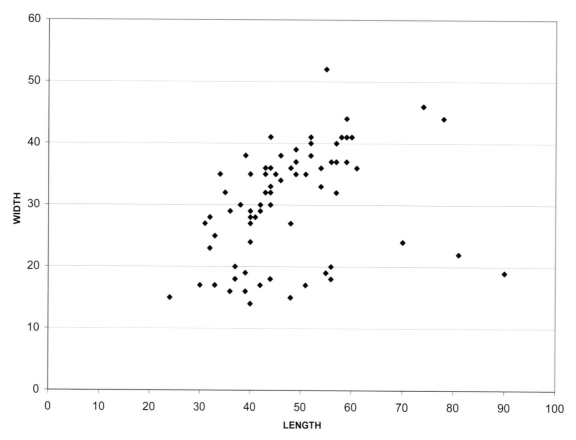

Figure 4.2. Dimensions (length vs. width) of Orlovo axes

Most commentators on small-size tools have suggested that they have been produced from once big artefacts after they have been worn and/or damaged (Prinz 1988). From the above discussion, it is clear that this is certainly the case in Orlovo. It is possible that all the discussed examples have been processed to their current state at some other sites and were subsequently brought to Orlovo. However, such a scenario is not very likely, since the value of unfinished tools (e.g. lack of shine or amorphous shape, etc.) would be lower than shining, finished objects in gift exchange, enchainment or any other social interaction. Another possibility is that the tools may have travelled from some distance with their owner/producer. However, apart from the flat axe Inv. 3263 (Plate 7g), the assemblage from Orlovo shows a high degree of internal integrity of raw material preference, shape and size that makes the identification of potential "outsider" tools very difficult, if not impossible. Therefore, given the limitations of the assemblage, one can conclude that there is some evidence for local polished stone production at the site of Orlovo. The axe rough-out provides a very strong case for local, on-site working in the form of a late stage in the *chaîne opératoire*. This would help to make sense of the site location, which lies close to secondary sources of

volcanic and other rocks, and only 25 km from the rich axe rock sources in the East Rhodopean foothills.

Size

There is a tendency in Balkan axe studies to make a distinction between "miniature" and "normal" axes, with a further, often implicit, implication that the former are symbolic with social connotations, while the latter are working tools with functional connotations. However, few studies have deconstructed the meaning of this division and sought to understand if it is a real division in terms of a site polished stone tool assemblage. Here, the size of the stone tools is considered as a primary variable and examined in comparison with two other sites with a comparable level of recorded detail.

There are but few excavation reports which deal with polished stone tools in sufficient detail to facilitate a detailed comparison with the Orlovo material. The two sites selected for such a comparison are Divostin, an open site with Early Starčevo and Late Vinča components in Central Serbia (Prinz 1988) and Sitagroi, a Neolithic, Copper Age and Early Bronze Age tell in Northern Greece (Elster 2003).

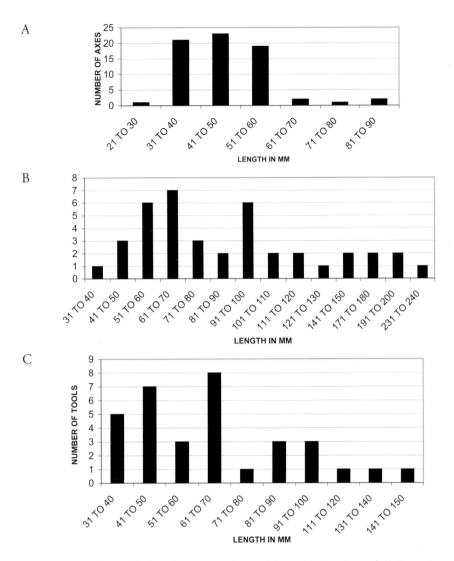

Figure 4.3. Length of stone tools: (a) Orlovo; (b) Divostin; and (c) Sitagroi

The most striking overall point arising from the comparisons is that the Orlovo stone tools present much smaller examples (Fig. 4.2). The Divostin and Sitagroi tools indicate greater diversity in length, especially bearing in mind the smaller samples of complete tools – 40 in Divostin and 33 in Sitagroi (Fig. 4.3). There is some degree of similarity between the tool lengths at Sitagroi and Orlovo; the first distributional peak in Sitagroi is at 41 to 50 mm, which is the dominant length range in Orlovo. The axes between 41 and 50 mm in length form 21% of the Sitagroi sample, while they represent 32% of the axes at Orlovo. However, there is a second peak in Sitagroi, with examples up to 150 mm long, which is not represented at Orlovo. Therefore, the initial impression of the Orlovo assemblage as consisting mainly of small tools is confirmed.

Looking at the width of the tools from the three sites,

a similar conclusion can be drawn. It is possible that the bigger sample from Divostin, including fragmentary as well as complete axes (n = 133), produces a bimodal pattern of distribution, while the similar sample sizes from Sitagroi and Orlovo show distributions that are close to normal (Fig. 4.4). This suggests that the width of the tools in both sites was deliberately targeted. While the distribution of tools with the most popular width (between 31 and 40 mm) is similar at both sites (36% in Sitagroi and 42% in Orlovo), the presence of a relatively high number of wider axes in Sitagroi (33% are more than 40 mm wide) confirms once again the generally small size of axes in Orlovo (9% are more than 40 mm wide).

Moreover, the thickness of the tools from the three sites shows a set of patterns that are close to normal distributions (Fig. 4.5). Divostin presents the thickest tools and the

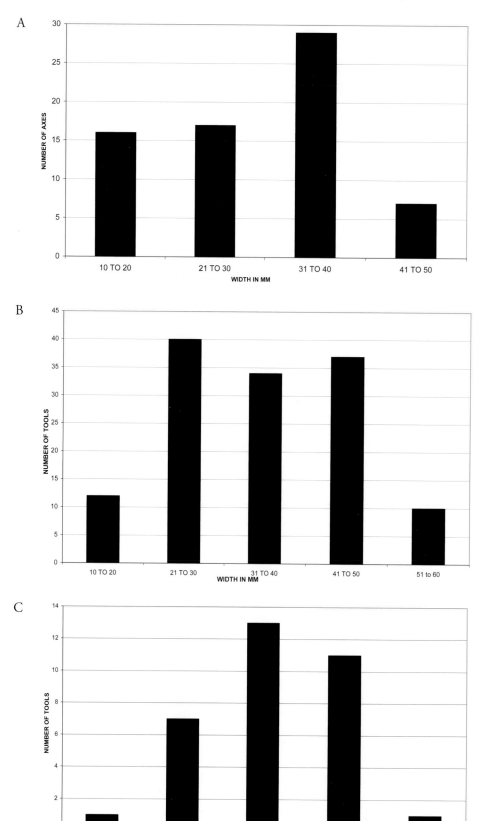

Figure 4.4. Width of stone tools: (a) Orlovo; (b) Divostin; and (c) Sitagroi

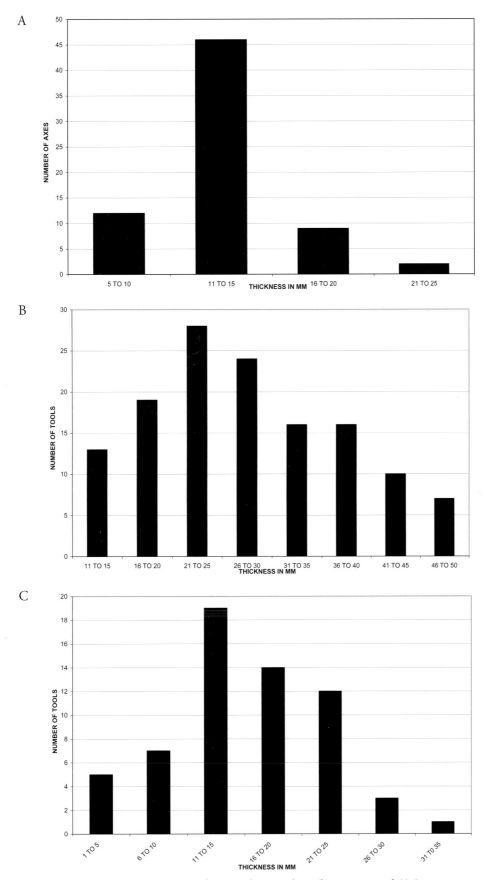

Figure 4.5. Thickness of stone tools: (a) Orlovo; (b) Divostin; and (c) Sitagroi

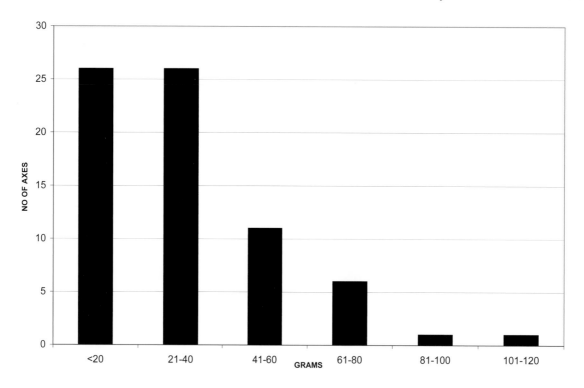

Figure 4.6. Weight of polished stone tools at Orlovo

greatest variety of thicknesses – from 11 to 50 mm, with its peak at 21 to 25 mm – the largest thickness category at Orlovo. The diversity of sizes and the presence of very thick axes at Divostin is maybe due to the large sample size, which again includes fragmentary axes. The peak at both Sitagroi and Orlovo is defined by tools between 11 and 15 mm thick but, while these axes reach 31% at Sitagroi, with its additional diversity in thickness, in Orlovo the peak represents 2/3rds of all the axes.

A final proxy measure of size is the weight of the stone tools (Fig. 4.6). While the total range of object weights covers 10 g to 110 g, the heaviest object is a pounder and the heaviest 'axe' weighs in at 90 g. The peak of weights for Orlovo is 10–40 g, with three specimens weighing as little as ca. 10 g. The weight results support the inference from the size data that the Orlovo assemblage as a whole would seem to consist of generally small examples, more suited to display than to heavy use.

Form and 'typology'

The polished stone tools discarded at Orlovo comprise a total of 69 objects. For the preliminary report on this collection (Chapman *et al.*, n.d.), a preliminary functional identification was made as follows: 37 trapezoidal axes, 16 miniature tools, 10 chisels, 14 other axes, two pounders, one shaft hole axe and one fragmented axe. We noted the important point that

the proportion of complete axes was remarkably high in comparison with many other sites. But, at the beginning of the interpretative study of the axes, one of the authors felt what probably most of the colleagues that have ever tried to make sense of a polished stone assemblage have felt – all the axes look similar but at the same time are different in subtle or obvious ways, thus making any conventional typology almost impossible – otherwise, we could end up with 2–3 axes in a type or, worse still, only two types for 69 axes.

During the recording process, a 'common-sense' typology was developed based on the visual characteristics of the tool with reference to widely accepted terms in petro-archaeology. Thus, two main types – 'chisels' and 'axes' – were defined, each with internal variation of form and size. In the next stage of the study, the primary typology was not followed up (although there are references to it: see below, pp. 87–90), since it was felt that such an artificial structure reflects more the convenience of the researcher rather than the initial choices of the makers (Todorova *et al.* 1975; Todorova *et al.* 1983). Instead a more perceptual strategy was adopted that nonetheless led to an objective form of analysis. We accept that the initial choice of how a certain tool should look like is based on previous experience of the available raw materials and the shape of the tools made from them. This would lead to a set of pragmatic guidelines for tool production concerning how long, thick and wide the tool should be with regards to the available raw material. Repeated experience of making

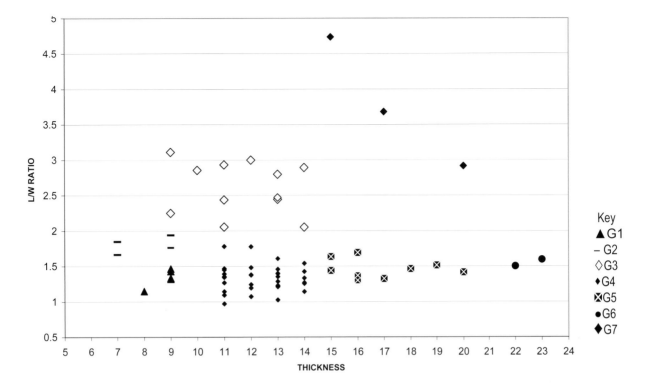

Figure 4.7. Length/width ratio vs. thickness of polished stone tools

similar tools would lead to the development of embodied skills that would facilitate future production.

The first stage in the new approach to the data was the establishment of three parameters – the ratio between the length and the width of each tool, the ratio between the length and the thickness of each tool and the ratio between the width and the thickness of each tool. Then each of the ratios was plotted against the corresponding dimension, e.g. the length: width ratio versus the thickness, etc. A series of scattergrams was produced and on each of them a definition of different groups was tried based on their differential distribution. The most productive scattergram in terms of both the production process and the formal typological results appeared to be the scattergram of the length: width ratio plotted against the thickness (Fig. 4.7). After several attempts to define different groups, the current division into seven groups was accepted. Because it is difficult to make the most objective determinations of boundaries between groups on visual inspection of the scattergrams, the final definition of groups in this classification was based not only upon the visual groupings but also on the repetitive clustering of certain tools on the other scattergrams (Figs. 4.8–4.9). In this sense, although the interrelations between the other dimensions (e.g. the width: thickness ratio versus the length) were not a leading factor in the current division, they are very important in the process of refining the present seven groups of tools. In addition, the visual characteristics

of the stone assemblage confirm such a general division, insofar as all of the 'chisels' fell within a single group, as did all of the 'long thin axes'.

Length/Width ratio vs. Thickness (Fig. 4.7)

From the viewpoint of embodied skills, it would not be a problem for an experienced tool-maker to produce a tool that is long as twice as wide or as long as wide or indeed any other combination. Such ability is considered to be intentional and is reflected in the L/W ratio. Similarly, the thickness of a certain tool can be a consequence of intentional choice – starting with the proportions of the tool blank and finishing with the grinding of the end-product. The series of choices that the tool-maker makes may result in a small axe as wide as it is long or in a long, narrow chisel. Such tools would appear at the opposite ends of a L/W ratio vs. thickness scattergram (as they indeed do!). This is what makes it clear that the L/W ratio vs. thickness scattergram is a reliable indication of identifying the choices made in tool production. The diagram helps in the preliminary grouping of the polished stone tools into seven groups.

Group 1

This Group consists of 5 tools, four of which according to our primary typology were determined as miniature axes

(Plate 7f). Their length is up to one and half times greater than their width and they are 8 or 9 mm thick (Fig. 4.7). Three of them have an asymmetric trapezoidal shape, one is symmetrically trapezoidal and one is only slightly trapezoidal. Three are made of volcanic rock, the remaining two of volcanic tuff that explains the difference in colour – grey to black for the volcanic specimens and light and greenish for the others. The tools have suffered little damage and no or very little wear, pointing to careful or limited use and curation. Only one specimen bears traces of medium damage, suggesting a more complicated artefact biography.

Group 2

It consists of four tools that can be determined as miniature tools. The difference from group 1 is that they are narrower, thus increasing the L/W ratio and making them look longer (Fig. 4.7). The thickness varies between 7 and 9 mm. There is a greater variation of shapes – two are asymmetrically trapezoidal, one is symmetrically trapezoidal, with the only example in the assemblage of reversed asymmetrically trapezoidal shape (Fig. 4.1b). Three of the tools are made of jasper-like rock, while the remaining one is of volcanic tuff. Despite the different raw materials, the colour range of all examples is similar – generally dark, from grey to black. Only one of the tools has traces of little wear that, in combination with the lack or paucity of damage for three out of the four tools suggests that the tools were discarded soon after production and/or were prepared for purposes of display. Such a hypothesis is not contradicted by the only example of medium damage, since the tool lacks any traces of wear. The damage may have been accidental or the consequence of a long life.

Group 3

The group includes 12 tools (Plate 7e) that, according to our primary typology, were classed as 11 chisels and 1 axe fragment. The tools are more than twice as long as they are wide and with variations of thickness from 9 to 14 mm that affects the degree of their plumpness (Fig. 4.1d). The uniformity of this group, despite its dispersion across the scattergram (Fig. 4.7), is confirmed by the overall similarities in shape – six tools of cylindrical shape, four of rectangular shape, one elongated trapezoidal shape and a trapezoidal axe fragment. The choice of raw material is similarly varied – four tools are made of respectively altered volcanic rock and volcanic tuff, three are made of other volcanic rock and one is made of jasper-like rock. Since all of them are made of hard volcanic rock, it would appear that it was not the physical property of rock that was as important for the choice of raw material as the different colour of these rocks. Group 3 has the most diverse colour range, bearing in mind its relatively large sample size (n = 12). It starts from white and beige,

through yellow-green and grey-green to dark-brown, dark grey and black. An interesting wear pattern shows that, of the four tools made of altered volcanic rock that seems an easily worn material, three of them (Inv. 3282/1: Plate 7a) are worn but the fourth tool is not particularly worn. This fact once again suggests the discard of relatively "new" tools. As a general pattern, group 3 contains examples of little or no wear but with more visible traces of damage (only three tools are not damaged), thus extending the possible uses of stone tools to a variety of social practices during which flaking or similar damage may occur.

Group 4

Group 4 is the most numerous group, comprising 34 tools (Fig. 4.7). What unifies them in a single group is that they are up to twice as long as they are wide and their thickness is between 11 and 14 mm (Plate 7b–d and j). Depending on the actual dimensions of the tools, the Group could theoretically be sub-divided into a group of small axes and a group of large axes. However, for the sake of simplicity, such a subdivision is avoided and priority is given to the proportions of all the specimens that appeared to be quite similar. In addition, 21 axes (62%) share the same asymmetrically trapezoidal shape that points to a preferred combination of shape and proportion. The differences within this general asymmetrically trapezoidal shape are in the butt and blade treatment, the degree of "trapezoidality", the presence of facets, etc. Such differences are related to the available raw material blank and/or the possible use of the tool but most of them are probably related to the personal preferences of the tool-maker. Therefore, we accept group 4 as a single type with internal variations that are responsive to different shaping choices. The diversity of shapes of this type is completed by seven axes with a symmetrically trapezoidal shape, three with slightly trapezoidal shape and one of rectangular shape with rounded corners, one of symmetrical sub-rectangular shape and finally, one of cylindrical shape. The rectangular axe with rounded corners (Fig. 4.1c and Plate 7g: Inv. 3263) is not typical for the Balkan Neolithic and Copper Age and it may be dated post-Copper Age on account of its possible similarity to metal wedges. The closest parallel for this form of axe known to us derives from the Cucuteni A4 site of Drăguşeni, in Moldavia (Marinescu-Bîlcu 2000, Fig. 45/15). The relatively large sample size (n = 34) provides the greatest diversity of raw materials of the whole assemblage. Again, there is a certain preference for volcanic rocks (13 tools are made of volcanic tuffs, 12 of other volcanic rock) but other rock types are also present – six tools are made of jasper-like rock, two of serpentinite, one of schist. In the light range of colours are the beige, green and grey axes but the majority are in the dark range – dark brown, dark grey and black. Especially visually affective are the two black and green examples made of volcanic tuff and the only dark-speckled

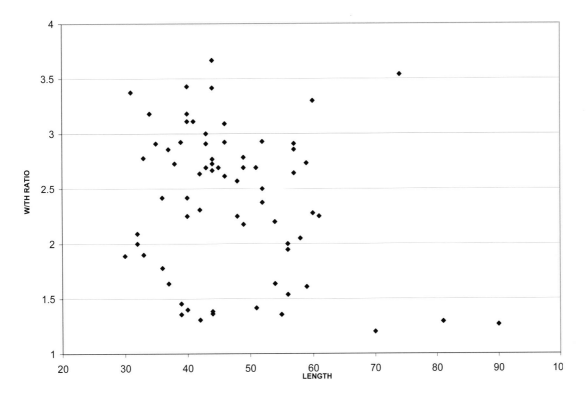

Figure 4.8. Width/thickness ratio vs. length of polished stone tools

example of the whole assemblage made of porphyry. The sample size can explain the mixed pattern of combinations of wear and damage. There are examples with no or little wear and no and little damage, in addition to examples of medium and heavy wear plus medium and heavy damage. As a general pattern, however, slightly more than a half of the tools have no or little damage, leaving the remaining 44% with medium and heavy wear. Almost equal is the number of tools with no and little wear and the tools with medium and heavy wear. Having in mind that this is the most numerous group, it would be expected that it would be representative for the entire assemblage. Indeed, it contains tools that are relatively "new", as in group 2, as well as heavily used tools, as in group 5. Some of the tools are at the beginning of their lifetime, while others bear signs of a long and/or complicated artefact biography, either by careful curation or by multiple manipulations in various sets of social practices.

Group 5

This group consists of nine tools, whose L/W ratio is not more than 1.7 (very similar to Group 4) but they are thicker than the group 4 examples (Fig. 4.7) and therefore look much plumper (Plate 7i). There is some tendency to produce symmetrically trapezoidal axes with such dimensions, since there are four axes of such shape,

plus one axe having a slightly symmetrical and trapezoidal form. Two axes have an asymmetrically trapezoidal shape, while one is slightly asymmetric and trapezoidal. The last example has a rectangular shape, which is generally rare in this assemblage. The colour range is dominated by dark tones of grey, brown and black and the lightest colour is green. It would appear that the tools from that group were the most utilised examples in the whole assemblage. With very few exceptions, they exhibit medium wear and damage, suggesting balanced but intensive use.

Group 6

The tendency toward increased plumpness mentioned for the previous group is reinforced by the only two examples of group 6 (Fig. 4.7), which are the thickest tools in the whole assemblage (Plate 7h). Both are made of a beige sandstone but their small number is inconclusive for the possible relationship of type – raw material – colour. The size of the group does not allow general conclusions for damage and wear (for details, see the catalogue, pp. 152 and 154).

Group 7

This is the "miscellaneous" group of three outliers not included in any of the previous groups (Fig. 4.1e). However,

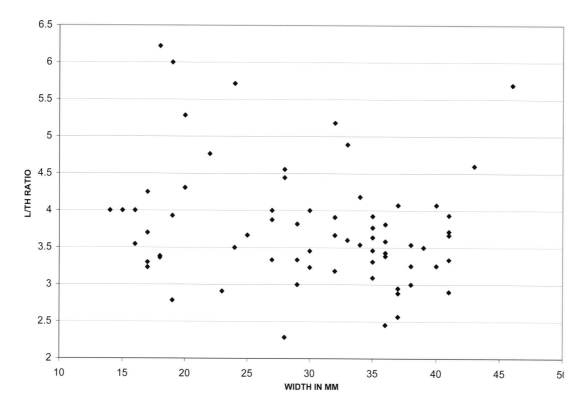

Figure 4.9. Length/thickness ratio vs.width of polished stone tools

although not a "real " cluster as compared to the other groups, the three examples of group 7 show internal consistency. All are exceptionally long for this assemblage and relatively narrow for such a length (Fig. 4.7). These dimensions make the two un-perforated examples look like the 'chisels' of our primary classification; these two tools are not included in group 3, since they are much longer than the Group 3 tools. The third example is the only shaft-hole axe of the assemblage (Fig. 4.1a: Inv. 3228). The size of the group does not allow general conclusions for damage and wear (for details, see the catalogue, p. 154, Inv. 3228).

Width/Thickness vs. Length (Fig. 4.8)

The lower range of this relationship shows a good match between our initial type determination and the actual proportions of the tools. Two-thirds of the tools whose Width/Thickness ratio is equal to or less than 1.5 (i.e. their width is up to one and a half times greater than their thickness) corresponds to our primary type of 'chisel'. The only example in the assemblage with a shaft-hole also appears in the lower end of this cluster, since its shape is indeed thin and elongated. An axe fragment also appears there. Four examples classified as 'chisels' do not appear in the lower end of the cluster – which means that the formal

shape of the tools may resemble a 'chisel' but the actual proportions of each specimen is different from the most common proportion for this assemblage – i.e. up to one and a half times wider than thick. The 'chisels' vary in length. The 12 tools located in the lower range of the scattergram include the entire group 7 and nine out of 12 tools from group 3, which is a good confirmation of the definition of the above Groups – based as it is on repetitive clustering for more than one proportional relationship.

The next cluster is characterised by widths up to twice as great as their thickness (Width/Thickness ratio between 1.6 and 2). The cluster comprises nine tools, including the remaining 4 'chisels', the entire group 6 and three other tools. The common morphological feature of these otherwise very different tools is their oval cross-section, which makes them look plump. The most numerous are the examples (n = 37) that are from two to three times wider than their thickness (Width/Thickness ratio between 2.1 and 3) – a variable discriminating well-proportioned 'axes'/'adzes' from 'chisels'. There is a great length variation in this group – from 33 mm to 61 mm. This may suggest a divergence between 'axes' and 'miniature' axes. This division is generally confirmed by the comparative study, where most of the Orlovo examples were smaller than the types in the comparative sample. The last 11 tools are more than 3 times as wide as they are

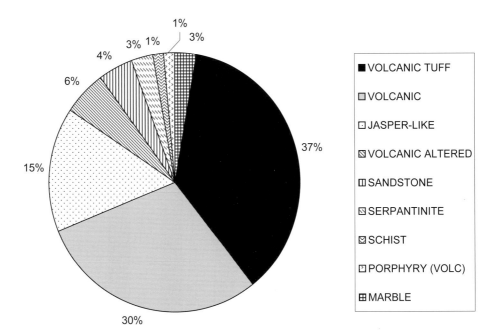

Figure 4.10. Raw materials used for polished stone tools

Table 4.2. List of sites with polished stone tool comparanda

Site Name	Zone	Timespan	Type of Excavation
Chavdar	NW	EN	Totally excavated tell
Ohoden	NW	EN	Partially excavated open site
Gorna Beshovitsa	NW	EN	Partially excavated open site
Tsakonitsa	NW	EN	Partially excavated open site
Altimir	NW	MN	Partially excavated open site
Krivodol	NW	LCA	Sonda on open settlement
Maluk Preslavets	NE	EN	Excavated cemetery
Samovodene	NE	EN–LN	Partially excavated tell
Goliamo Delchevo	NE	EN, ECA–LCA	Totally excavated tell
Durankulak	NE	LN–LCA	Excavated cemetery; partially excavated tell
Ovcharovo	NE	ECA–LCA	Totally excavated tell
Vinitsa	NE	ECA–LCA	Totally excavated tell
Omurtag	NE	LCA	Partially excavated tell
Krumovgrad	SE	EN	Partially excavated open site
Rakitovo	SE	EN	Totally excavated open site
Muldava	SE	MN	Partially excavated open site
Kapitan Dimitrievo	SE	MN–LN, LCA	Partially excavated tell
Draginova tell	SE	LN–LCA	Partially excavated tell
Drama	SE	LCA	Partially excavated tell
Kolena	SE	CA	Partially excavated tell or flat site
Krainitsi	SW	EN	Partially excavated open site
Sofia–Slatina	SW	EN	Partially excavated open site
Slatino	SW	ECA–LCA	Partially excavated open site

thick, indicating broad and thin forms. This form resembles 'adzes' that, again, could be divided into 'miniature adzes' and 'adzes' on the basis of size.

In summary, the ratio/dimensional analysis of the Orlovo polished stone tools has provided an objective typology with room for the archaeologist's judgment in interpreting the three principal scattergrams. Variables such as colour and use have already received comments in the discussion of each Group. The resultant seven Groups will next be used to consider another key aspect of the assemblage, namely raw materials.

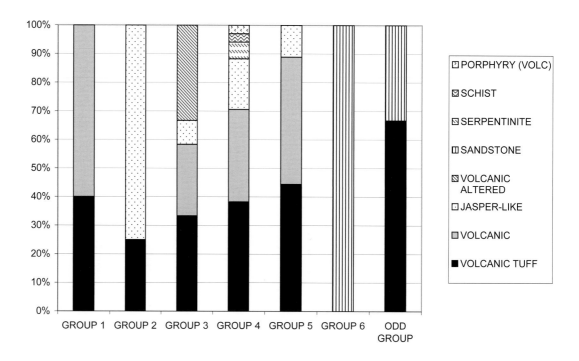

Figure 4.11. Stone tool groups by raw materials

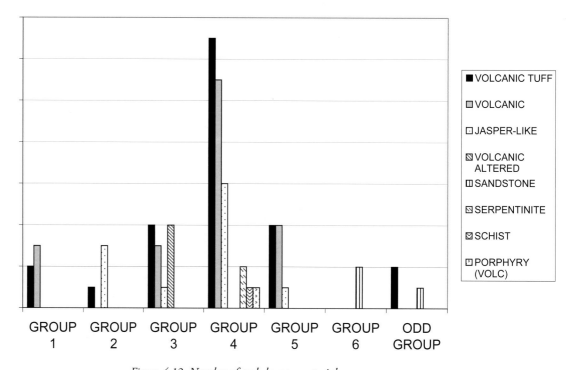

Figure 4.12. Number of tools by raw material

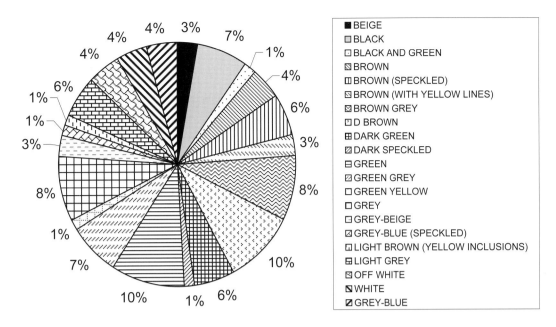

Figure 4.13. List of rock colours used for polished stone tools

Raw materials, production and exchange

If there is a single strong characteristic of the type of raw material from which the Orlovo axes are made, this is the striking preference for volcanic rocks (Fig. 4.10). Over one-third of the tools are made of volcanic tuffs (Plate 7j), similar to the number of tools made from other volcanic rocks (30% – volcanic (Plate 7i), 4% – volcanic altered (Plate 7a) and 1% porphyry volcanic (Plate 7d). The remaining 28% are dominated by jasper-like tools (Plate 7e), a few examples of sandstone (Plate 7h), marble (only the two pounders) and serpentinite (Plate 7b), as well as a single tool made of schist (Plate 7c). The paucity of sandstone and schist tools is probably due to the possible function of the objects, which are more like personal belongings and adornments rather than working tools. However, little use is made of serpentinite rocks, which is in common use at other prehistoric sites (Kostov 2007). The main rock and mineral types among the artifacts are represented in Table 4.2. (for details of lithic sources, see above, pp. 14–16).

A possible explanation of such a repetitive choice is the widespread availability of such volcanic rocks in the Northern foothills of the Eastern Rhodopes, and found also as pieces of pebbles along the rivers or in the conglomerate strata near the site. In addition, it is probably not so much the hardness of the raw material as its high reception to polishing, clearly expressed by the high percentage (n = 55, or 78%) of polished axes from the whole assemblage. However, despite their common origins, the rocks are of different colours, introducing another important aspect in the raw material procurement – colour alongside physical properties as hardness and shine.

Morphological groups

The distribution of raw material in the morphological groups shows an interesting pattern (for overall percentages: Fig. 4.11; for numbers: Fig. 4.12). All groups but one have tools made from volcanic tuffs, while the next most popular raw material is other volcanic rocks, found in 4 out of 7 groups. The same is the distribution of jasper-like rocks, which, in view of their lower frequency (15% of all tools), poses in interesting question about a possible strategy of diversifying the relationship between raw materials and shape. In addition to the well-established volcanic rocks, it would appear that a new raw material is tested for different shapes. Support for this hypothesis comes from the pattern of two groups having only one tool made of jasper-like rocks. The general distribution of raw materials corresponds to the distribution pattern in each group – e.g. the most common volcanic tuffs (37%) are found in each group but one. Only one group (Group 6) has axes made of the same material but its small sample size prevents the inference of any further conclusions. Similarly, the small sample size of groups 1, 2 and 7 hinders the general issue of whether we are faced with a genuine choice of only two types of raw material to produce particular tools or whether such a pattern is a function of the sample size. Groups 3 and 5 present a similar preference for volcanic tuffs and other volcanic rocks, with occasional jasper-like tools. It is interesting that the four examples made of altered volcanic rocks are all in group 3, i.e. there is a weak tendency to produce some tools from a certain type of raw material. The most numerous group (Group 4) is the only one in which six out of the eight possible rock types are used.

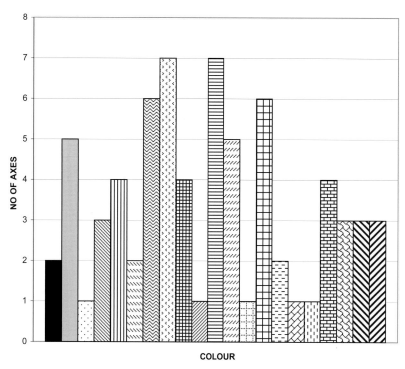

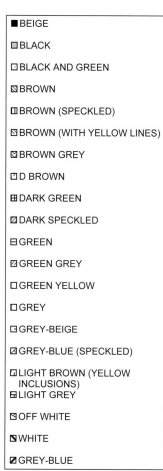

Figure 4.14. Abundance of rock colours

In summary, there is little evidence for specialised selection of rock types for particular axe shapes but, rather, a generalised attitude that leads to many shapes being made from the same rock types. This conclusion may relate more to the diversity of persons bringing stone tools to Orlovo for discard or to the wide range of polished stone toolmakers existing at or near to the site.

Colour

Visual inspection of the colour of the stone tools has led to the definition of 21 different colours (Fig. 4.14). The most common appeared to be the green and dark brown colours – 10% each (Fig. 4.13). For the sake of simplicity, five groups of unified colours were defined – light (incl. white (Plate 7a) off white (Plate 7h) and beige); dark (incl. black (Plate 7f) and black and green); brown (incl. brown, brown-speckled, brown with yellow lines, brown-grey, light brown and dark brown (Plate 7g)); green (incl. green, dark green (Plate 7j), dark-speckled (Plate 7d), green-grey (Plate 7e), green-yellow) and grey (incl. grey (Plate 7i), grey-beige (Plate 7c), grey-blue (Plate 7b), grey-blue-speckled, light grey). There is a clear prevalence of brown axes, followed by green and grey colour in comparable amount (respectively 25% and 23%), light 11% and dark 8%. Such a pattern

is probably easier to understand if we look at the relation between colour and raw materials (Figs. 4.15 and 4.16). If we exclude the single specimens because of their low statistical value, then it is clear that the brown axes are made almost entirely of volcanic rocks and volcanic tuffs, with the occasional serpentinite and jasper-like rocks. Volcanic tuffs are also the major source for the grey axes but the decreased amount of volcanic rocks is compensated by jasper-like rocks and again with occasional serpentinites and schists. The green axes seem to derive from the same three major rock types – volcanic, volcanic tuff and jasper-like but the larger number of jasper-like tools (in comparison to the brown and grey tools) may explain the relatively small number of green axes in the collection. The green jasper-like sources may not have been as abundant or as close as the brown and grey volcanic and the volcanic tuff sources. Alternately, if the sources of all the three major rocks were equally available, a certain preference was expressed for volcanic rocks and volcanic tuffs either owing to their hardness and/or to their colour – brown rather than grey or green. Noteworthy is the presence of lightly coloured tools comprising marble and sandstone but also volcanic altered rocks (Fig. 4.16). Their relatively high percentage among the prestige items (see below) suggest that one reason for exploitation of lightly coloured minerals may have been its symbolic connotations.

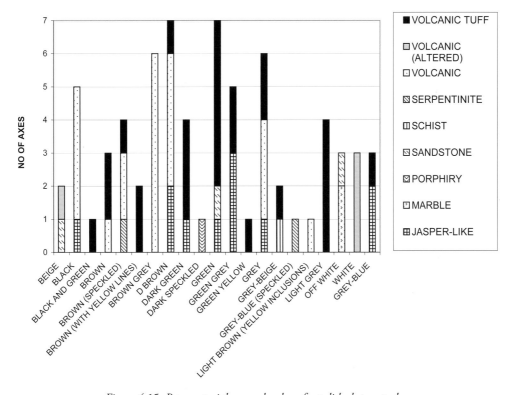

Figure 4.15. Raw materials vs. rock colour for polished stone tools

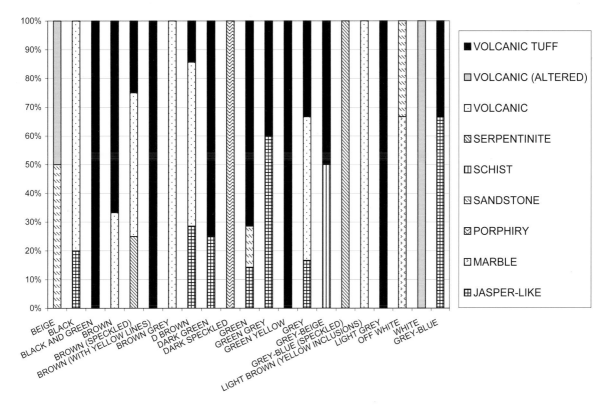

Figure 4.16. Raw materials vs. colour for polished stone tools

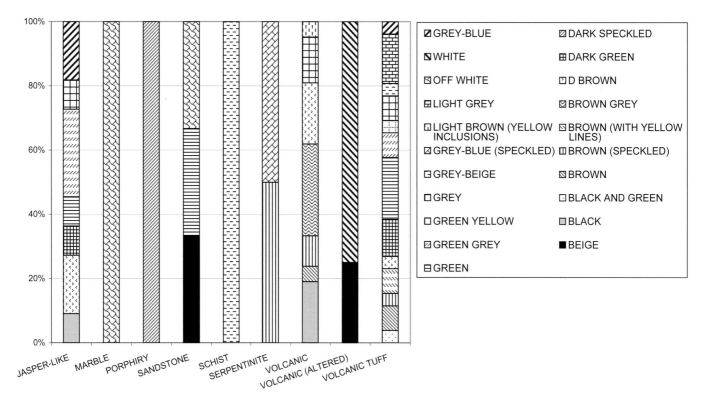

Figure 4.17. Raw materials vs. polished stone axe colours

There is a strong tendency for the association of specific colours with artefacts made of similar colours (Keates 2002), places where such colours proliferate (Diáz-Andreu 2001) or seasons with a predominance of certain colours (e.g. autumn reds: Borić 2002). After removing from study those colour groups comprising only one tool, there is a weak tendency at Orlovo for the relationship of a particular colour to only one type of raw material (only 4 out of 16 colours, Fig. 4.16). The majority (n = 8) are related to two types of rocks and, in four cases, one colour can come from three different types of rocks. Therefore the availability of raw materials was not an aesthetic constraint but, on the contrary, an aesthetic stimulant for people to choose a certain colour first and then to choose from two or three different rocks. If we look at the reverse relationship, then only three minerals appeared to be statistically significant – jasper-like, volcanic rocks and volcanic tuff (Fig. 4.18). The first two are available in seven different colours, each thus undisputedly suggesting that colour diversity was sought and appreciated by the Orlovo inhabitants. An even stronger reminder that the physical properties of the rocks – often considered as a primary factor in the choice of raw material – should not be divorced from the importance of colour are the tools made of volcanic tuffs in 13 different colours. One may suggest that such a choice was predetermined by the actual availability of rocks as exposures, from which collection was possible, but,

until analytical sourcing studies are conducted, we prefer to give credit to human agency and the deliberate choice of different colours. We do this because there are studies on the aesthetics of colour that build a strong case for the role and appreciation of colour in the past in combination with a well-exploited seam of symbolic practices (Jones and MacGregor 2002).

Use, wear and damage

Unfortunately, it was not possible to perform a formal, microscope-based use-wear analysis. However, general observations on the state of the tools were recorded, based on visual inspection and the use of a hand lens. The traces of wear and damage may have been a result of purposeful use but whether such activities were necessarily connected to a use as working tools is difficult to assess. In terms of the difference between use-wear and damage caused by other activities, in the following section the term 'wear' is understood as use-related, while 'damage' is related to non-working causes and reasons. It is important to note that there is no sign of plough-damage on any of the stone tools.

Almost 2/3 of the tools have little or no wear (Fig. 4.19; e.g. Fig. 4.1c; Plate 7e), which means that either they are used as personal adornments/belongings rather than as everyday tools, or that the axes are at the beginning of

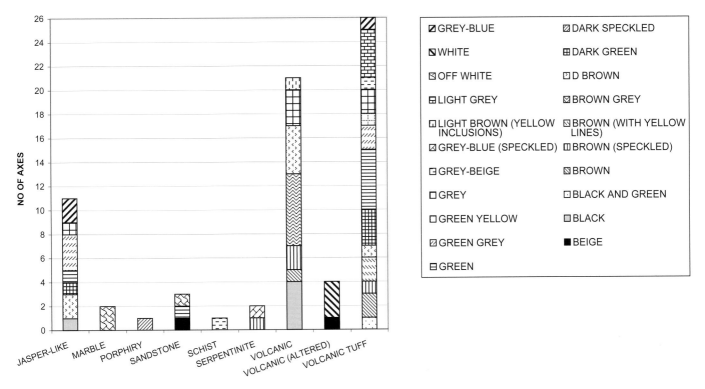

Figure 4.18. Polished stone axe colours vs. raw materials, Orlovo

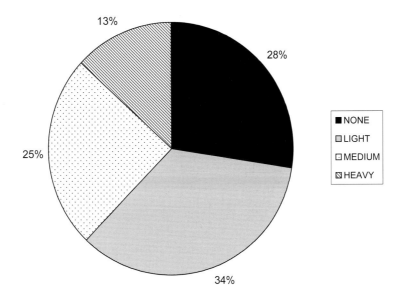

Figure 4.19. Degree of wear

their "life-history", and therefore, they are not yet worn by intensive use. The range of damage on tools ranges from none to heavy (Fig. 4.20). However, the relationship between blade wear and damage is not simple or direct; Fig. 4.21 shows that there is a number of tools with no or light blade wear that have suffered different degrees of damage (e.g. Fig. 4.1a). In other words, there are indeed some tools that have either been discarded very soon after production or were carefully curated, resulting in no or little wear and damage. A much larger percentage of tools show

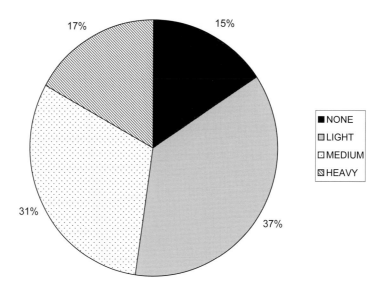

Figure 4.20. Degree of damage

little working evidence but considerable damage (Fig. 4.21; e.g. Plate 7a). Such a pattern suggests that the tools from Orlovo were not necessarily perceived as working objects but rather as objects of visual display, perhaps prestige, that embodied different properties (shine, colour, etc.).

The remaining 38% of the tools have medium to heavy wear (Fig. 4.21; e.g. Plate 7i). It is interesting that three of them have no traces of any damage, thus suggesting that despite the fact that they are heavily used (to achieve such a blade wear), they are very carefully kept from any other damage. Such objects may be personal tools for different tasks kept by their owners with them all the time. The remainder of the tools with different degrees of damage in addition to their blade wear indicates objects with a long and/or intensive life history during which the tools have undergone several transformations, perhaps including symbolic changes, as a consequence of accidental and/or deliberate use-wear and damage (e.g. Plate 7j).

If we look at the relationship between wear and damage from the point of view of damage (Fig. 4.22), more than half of the tools have no or light damage, suggesting the presence of a few "new" tools and careful curation of the rest. However, 48% of the assemblage has medium to heavy damage not related to working. Although accidental damage should not be excluded, it is difficult to imagine what type of accidents may have contributed to such a substantial figure. It is also possible that the damage may have been caused by (numerous) later interventions or exposure to natural conditions. It will be unwise, however, to exclude the possibility of damage (not necessarily willingly) during some practices that involved manipulation with stone tools.

Comparative study, dating and regional trends

Here, we turn to the main methodology that is used to place Orlovo in its broad time-space context – a wide-ranging comparison of the collection with sites in Bulgaria dating from the Early Neolithic to the Early Bronze Age (for the constraints on this approach, see above, p. 13). A total of 23 sites were chosen from a wide range of published reports as the most meaningful reference points available for comparison with the Orlovo assemblage, in order to place the latter in its broader chronological and spatial context. The choice of sites reflects coverage of the Neolithic and Chalcolithic periods, as well as the widest geographical area (Table 4.2). The sites are generally assigned to one of four areas in Bulgaria (NE, SE, NW, SW), although sometimes their current allocation does not necessarily coincide with a strict geographical affiliation – e.g. the tell Kapitan Dimitrievo is situated in Southwest Bulgaria but the long-term tradition of the site links it more closely to the material culture of Southeast Bulgaria, and therefore this particular tell is assigned to the SE area for the purposes of the current study.

Most of the tools (60%) have parallels with shapes dated to both the Neolithic and Copper Age. Six examples showed no similarity with any of the tools from the 23 selected sites (Table 4.2). One of them (Inv. 3263) resembles a metal wedge and may therefore date to the Bronze Age, while it is surprising that the only example of a shaft-hole perforated axe from the Orlovo assemblage had no parallels at all. One possible reason for such a lack of similarity is probably the state of the existing publications of ground stone tools in Bulgaria (see above, p. 13). The same explanation is valid for the remaining two specimens with no obvious

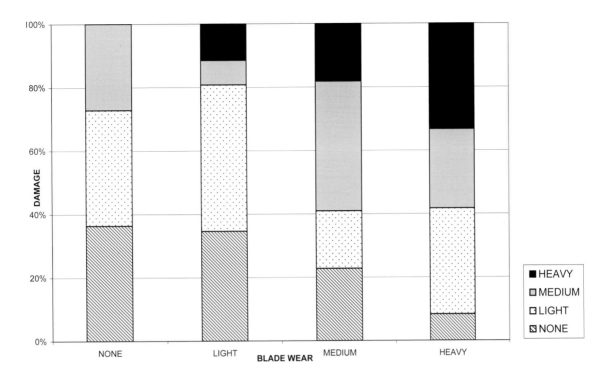

Figure 4.21. Blade wear vs. damage

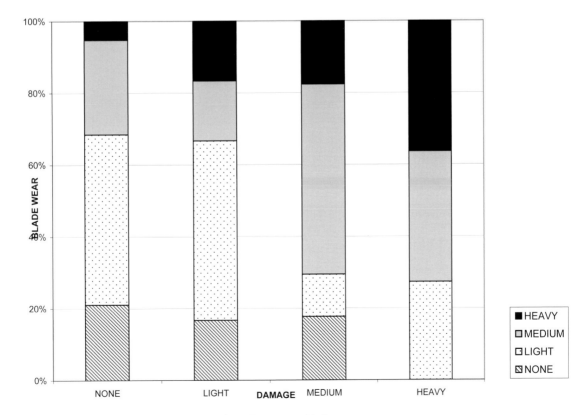

Figure 4.22. Damage vs. blade wear

Table 4.3. List of polished stone tools with close analogies in dated sites

Phase	No of Tools + Analogies	Phase	No of Tools + Analogies	Phase	No of Tools + Analogies
Early Neolithic	2	Early Copper Age	2	Neolithic and Copper Age	42
Middle Neolithic	1	Middle Copper Age	1	Bronze Age	23
Late Neolithic	-	Late Copper Age	5	No Analogies	6
		Copper Age	12		
Total	3		20		

Table 4.4. List of polished stone tools with close analogies in geographical areas

NW	NE	SE	SW	No. of Tools
xx				1
	xx			23
		xx		1
xx	xx			5
	xx	xx		16
	xx		xx	3
xx	xx	xx		1
	xx	xx	xx	12
xx	xx	xx	xx	3

Key: XX – shows areas with close stone tool analogies; each line shows the combination of areas with analogies

analogues – a miniature chisel (Fig. 4.1d: Inv. 2753/3) and a trapezoidal axe (Inv. 3193/6). For two other tools, broadly identified as pounders, parallel with published materials were not sought, since the shape of such artifacts varies enormously. In addition, this category of tools seems to suffer severely from non-publication. Less than 20% of all tools can be related generally to the Copper Age, while a further 11% can be related more specifically (Table 4.3). Altogether, this comprises a total of 28% of all tools from Orlovo with solely Copper Age analogies. There are only three examples (i.e., 4%) with only Neolithic parallels. Bearing in mind the above-mentioned disadvantages of the published ground stone tools from Bulgaria, the results of the comparative analysis shown in Table 4.3 show the presence of some Neolithic and some Copper Age tools but the largest group of stone tools are artifacts with a stable morphology that is equally common for both the Neolithic and the Copper Age.

At first sight, the spatial distribution of the parallels of the Orlovo tools shows a strong tendency towards the Northeast. Not only does 34% of the Orlovo assemblage have analogues entirely in sites in the Northeastern area, but a further 62% of the tools find parallels in the Northeast, together with other areas as well (Table 4.4). Such a distributional bias is caused by the uneven and selective excavation and publication of most Bulgarian prehistoric sites that is inevitably reflected in the sample sites for comparison. The only so far fully excavated tells that provide several series of published artifacts derive from Northeast Bulgaria. The sites

and therefore the artifacts from the rest of the country are known from trench excavations of tells or investigations of short-lived occupations (Table 4.2). In this respect, given that there is a problem with the representativity of the comparative sample, the pattern in Table 4.4 should be interpreted as suggesting that, apart from two specimens, there is no territorial preference of the tools from Orlovo. In other words, there is no demonstrable link between a certain type of tool and a certain area. This suggests either broadly shared knowledge, skill and technology across much of Bulgaria and/or wide-ranging exchange networks linking a large group of communities (Fig. 4.23). The notion that Neolithic / Chalcolithic communities are in constant contact with each other and exert a degree of mutual influence on each other is not at present widely recognised, owing to the over-reliance on an outdated cultural-historical mode of explanation (Nikolov, V. 1997: 2004).

Discussion

It is not quite clear why polished stone tools have attracted so little attention in the Balkans. The most obvious explanation is that archaeologists have overlooked their interpretative potential. The following paragraphs should be viewed as an attempt to overcome this research neglect and the general negative attitude exhibited towards polished stone tools.

The relatively small size of Orlovo tools have pointed towards three possible ways through which the polished artefacts may have been engaged in people's lives in the past. They may have been used as personal tools, worn as amulets or newly produced/almost finished tools ready for display or distribution. The lack of contextual data makes it very difficult to evaluate any of the above hypotheses but should not stop the exploration of all three possibilities.

Probably the most favourite explanation for Bulgarian archaeologists, with their functionalist preoccupations, would be their use as personal tools. And indeed, the Orlovo tools were small and handy, could easily have been tucked in clothes or pockets and were always available for small jobs or ad hoc situations. Such usage was prone to damage and wear and one would expect medium to heavy damage and comparable wear. The number of tools with a damage and

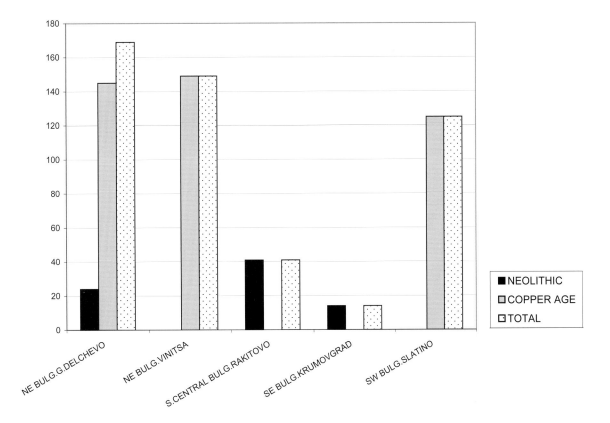

Figure 4.23. Parallels for Orlovo polished stone tools by period and area

wear pattern related to some kind of active use amounts to only 20 – 7 out of 9 tools from Group 5, 10 from Group 4, single examples from Groups 3 and 7 and one pounder. It should be immediately pointed out that the emphasis here is not on the possible *use* but on the *personal* engagement with this particular type of material culture. It is the small size of the tools that probably initiates the relations with people (it is difficult to imagine one carrying around heavy axes) that is later perpetuated by common experience and hence the mutual attachment that the person and the object developed. In any case, the present way of looking at tools as types and functions may help archaeologists to put order in their studies but does not bring us any closer to an understanding of the people that have used these tools. That is why, if we accept a functionalist interpretation for the 20 tools with damage and wear, it is preferable to see these tools as personal tools – extensions of persons – rather than utilitarian. We are assisted in such a view by the small size of the tools but this not to say that bigger tools did not have such personal relation with their users. A favourite heavy axe for tree-felling – used and re-used to cut up many trees – may well have held a special place in the emotions (and tool-kit) of a forester.

At the other end of the damage-and-use spectrum are the tools that have no or little evidence for such activity. These are the most likely candidates for newly-produced or nearly-finished tools ready to be exchanged, given as a gift or kept for display. There are 29 such examples from Orlovo, some of which were made from rocks probably acquired locally (volcanic rocks and tuffs), other coming from further afield. Tools from all groups form this most numerous and diverse set of accumulated potential waiting for (re-)distribution.

Last but not least are the remaining 22 polished tools with different combinations of damage and wear that can be broadly interpreted as prestige objects and more specifically in the case of Orlovo because of their small size as amulets. While axe-amulets (or axe-pendants) are more common in Western and Mediterranean Europe (Skeates 1995; Childe 1957; Bradley 1990), such objects are virtually unknown in the Balkans. In his excellent study of axe-amulets from the Central Mediterranean, Robin Skeates discusses mainly perforated examples but does mention that there are un-perforated axes also reported (1995: 279–280). Following that evidence we are tempted to suggest that at least 22 tools from Orlovo (more than half of them less than 45 mm long) may have been used as amulets. They come mostly from Groups 4 (12 examples) and 3 (5 examples), with single examples in five other Groups. Prestige goods bearing a close resemblance to their utilitarian/functional counterparts does not constitute a new concept in archaeology (Bradley and Edmonds 1993) but such a subversive thought is still to be acknowledged in the Balkans. This comes as a surprise, bearing in mind the recognition of non-functional super-blades in the Varna and Durankulak cemeteries (Manolakakis 2005; Sirakov 2002, Gurova 2007; cf. Nikolov, V. 2005 for a highly derivative account of Western social anthropological theory). The rationale behind the creation of artifacts that look like heavily utilised tools is that they embody the same physical properties but probably the former have stronger symbolic connotations than the latter. In the case of the axe-amulets, the miniature tools encapsulate the properties of the "real" axes that are strong and hard tools, that can break many things, can till the soil, can be used in warfare, etc. (Skeates 1995). The interpretation of the axe-pendants varies from objects of cult to speculations for magical powers to protect and cure (for details, see Skeates 1995: 283). The understanding of their role as animate objects has been aided, in popular culture, in the example of the Lord of the Rings: like the rings, the amulets are believed to have activated the people that have worn them. Such axe-amulets can be identified in the archaeological record by an exploration of their size,

context of deposition and traces of microstratigraphy – all of which can lead to a better understanding of their biography. Needless to say, evidence for such artefacts is scarce at the moment in the Balkans, with only one more or less secure example of a miniature axe found in a hoard at a tell in North East Bulgaria (Gaydarska *et al.* 2004). It has been suggested that the green colour was deliberately targeted as the colour of prestige objects (Kostov 2007). However, only one axe (or two if we accept the dark speckled example as generally in the green tonality) is green in this group of suggested prestige objects that diversifies the colour range of the potential high-status artefacts – 36% in brown tonality, 23% of each grey and light nuance and 9% of green and dark colours (Fig. 4.15). Even if such a colour range was not an initial choice for prestige items, the life history of the axes, involving long-term participation as a symbol in different ceremonies or processes of enchainment, made them important for the Orlovo population, which ultimately categorised them as highly valued objects. It is possible that the personal tools discussed above may also have become amulets, especially in view of the pre-existing close relations between the person and the tool.

5. Interpreting the Site and the Objects

The reader will recall that, in this book, we have a single aim and two principal objectives. Our primary aim is to shed light on the worlds of the Neolithic and Chalcolithic communities of the Balkans through the prism of a single site with its remarkable assemblage of surface artifacts, while our two objectives are the re-evaluation of these three finds categories in terms of their relation to social practices and the characterisation of a coherent methodology for assemblages such as Orlovo. We can now start to move towards the fulfilment of our aim and objectives through a comparison of the results for each type of object in a single framework. We begin with an assessment of the periods of occupation at the site, before moving on to an extended discussion of the kind of site represented at Orlovo.

Chronology of site occupation

A brief account of the time of the occupation of Orlovo is needed, since these conclusions underpin all of our other analyses. There are two chronological questions that we seek to answer: the general phase of occupation at Orlovo and the kind of occupation – whether more or less continuous or more punctuated.

As to the first question, the three finds categories have all produced differing indications of the date of deposition (Fig. 5.1). The least specific are the stone tools, with parallels for most examples in both the Neolithic and the Copper Age. The greater chronological specificity of the ornaments and the figurines produces an intriguing contrast – figurine usage begins in the 6th millennium BC and peaks in the 5th, the latter also being the dominant period for wearing ornaments. We cannot dismiss the clear indication of an Early Neolithic presence at the site, as documented by figurine and some ornament analogies. The second phase of occupation seemed to have started in the late 6th/beginning of the 5th millennium BC, with the first figurine and ornament peaks coming in the early 5th millennium BC: this is equivalent to both the Late Neolithic *and* the Early Copper Age. There is an uncertainty over the presence of a Middle Copper Age occupation phase at Orlovo, mainly because this phase

– although potentially an important transitional phase for later social formations (Todorova 1995) – is represented by few sites in Bulgaria. The third, and major, phase – dated to the Late Copper Age – is shown by the intensification of figurine and ornament discard in the late 5th millennium BC. There is some evidence from ornaments and stone tools for early 4th millennium BC occupation which, together with the traces of Iron Age habitation, and the impressive barrow of presumed Thracian date, shows that Orlovo is one of the best examples of place-value – a site to which people return over and over again and whose value as an ancestral home increases with each visit.

The second chronological question is necessarily much harder to answer, in view of the absence of excavations; even with excavations, genuine continuity through time is difficult to assess (cf. 'continuity' in multi-community zones in North East Hungary: Chapman *et al.* 2003). The number of objects datable exclusively to the Early Neolithic is quite small, suggesting two possible ways in which they came to be found at Orlovo. The first concerns discard during a small-scale occupation during the Early Neolithic – the initial occupation of the site. Alternatively, the first settlers arrived later, in the early 5th millennium BC, bringing with them a small number of carefully curated objects of ritual significance that had been transmitted via generations as heirlooms. The patterns of use-wear on the figurines are not conclusive either way in this argument, since careful curation would have reduced such wear in order to maintain the sacrality of the objects.

The many analogies for figurines, ornaments and stone tools from the late 6th to the late 5th millennia BC prompt the question of whether the occupations at Orlovo during this millennium took the form of one or two major phases, with long gaps with little or no dwelling, or rather punctuated occupation with more but shorter dwelling and many hiatūs. The open-ended answer is suggested by the existence of such great variability in each of the finds categories (morphology in figurines, relationships between form and raw materials for ornaments and stone tools) that it is hard to imagine the use and deposition of the complete range of materials in only two phases of settlement. Rather than one or two major expeditions for raw materials in the Rhodopes, we could envisage the establishment of long-lasting social networks leading to preferential gift exchange relations with certain upland communities that endured over many human generations, perhaps surviving breaks in the occupation at Orlovo itself.

Site type

What were the main social practices that characterised the multiple occupations at Orlovo site? Throughout this book, we have emphasised the sheer quantity of ornaments and stone tools in mint condition – some of them surely of non-local origin. Since this quantity of finely finished objects is more typical for large/rich graveyards such as Varna and Durankulak rather than for settlements, can we be sure that the surface finds at Orlovo have not been ploughed up from a long-lasting prehistoric cemetery? After all, prestige goods and personal ornaments, of which there are many in Orlovo, have long been associated with processes of social negation during burial practices (Binford 1971) and, indeed, their so far relative paucity on Balkan settlement sites supports such a claim. Therefore, an assessment of whether we are presented with material coming from a settlement or a cemetery leads us to the other two types of artifacts deriving from Orlovo – figurines and utilised stone tools. Figurines are typically related to settlement contexts, with very few exceptions (Bánffy 1990/1), which clearly points to at least some dwelling practices at Orlovo. While polished stone tools in general are equally common for both settlements and cemeteries, worn and/or damaged tools are as rare in mortuary contexts as non-utilised stone tools are in settlement contexts.

The unconfirmed information that the axes, the figurines and the ornaments derived from three different areas within the Orlovo site may be indicative of spatially distinct zones for settlement and burial. However, there are two reasons why we think that burials did not take place at Orlovo. The first, and probably the most obvious, is a taphonomic point, viz., the degree of recovery of different types of artifacts – some organic objects as small as 2mm in diameter – suggests that the presence of human bones would have been recorded either by the local collectors or by the archaeologists. The issue of preservation can be addressed by the good preservation of bone artefacts, while the possibility of cremation, that cannot be lightly dismissed, can be answered by the rarity of such a form of body treatment in the Neolithic and Chalcolithic in Bulgaria (Bacvarov 2003; Chapman 1983).

The second reason concerns our current knowledge of mortuary practices in Bulgaria. Neolithic burials in Thrace are known mainly from tells, featuring incomplete skeletons with few or no grave goods (Bacvarov 2003).

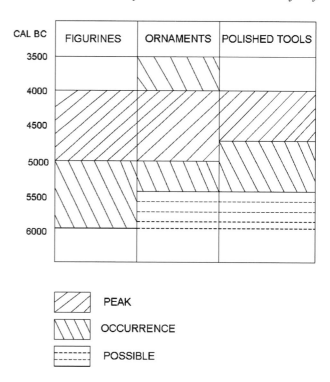

Figure 5.1. Summary of dating analogies for all finds, Orlovo

Artifact-rich cemeteries, spatially separate from settlements and containing local and exotic material such as *Spondylus* ornaments, flint super-blades and ornament sets, appeared in the Middle/Late Copper Age and more importantly, with a concentration in Northeast Bulgaria. So far, only four Copper Age graves have been reported from Thrace, near the large tell of Bereketska (Kalchev 1996). Thus, the social and taphonomic factors make it very difficult to support the tempting idea of a potential cemetery at Orlovo. Bearing in mind that the site may have been both a settlement and a cemetery, it seems on balance that our initial response to the Orlovo collection was justifiable – an unusually rich and diverse set of objects denoting primarily settlement remains. But what kind of settlement ?

Site definition, and hence site terminology, has never been a strong point in Bulgarian prehistory (Gaydarska 2007, p. 13, 26–27) and terms like 'tell', 'settlement mound', 'multilayer settlement', 'flat settlement' and 'open-air settlement' are in common use but without any formal definition and therefore theoretical or practical differentiation between them (but for a exception pertaining to the Late Copper Age, see Raduncheva 2003, Ch. 1). The current picture suggests that multilayer and flat (called open-air) settlements were dominant in Western Bulgaria, while tells and occasional flat sites are characteristic for the Eastern part of the country in most periods (Todorova 1986; Todorova and Vajsov 1993). Such a pattern is in itself interesting, despite the terminological inexactitudes of authors such as Nikolov V. (1996, 134–5), who confuses the size of flat sites with their depth of stratigraphy, does not take palaeo-environmental change into account in discussing large flat sites with deep stratigraphies and fails to transcend functionalist explanations for the growth of settlement mounds. This pattern suggests a settlement dynamic that is currently poorly understood in Bulgarian prehistory. One vector of dwelling concerns the frequency of repeated occupations on such flat sites.

Flat sites dated to a single phase are not unknown in Balkan prehistory – indeed they were once thought to typify the Karanovo IV phase of off-tell settlement in Thrace (e.g. Hlebozavoda: Kunchev and Kuncheva 1988). We can now recognise considerable variations in the size of such settlements, from 0.15 ha (e.g. Golio rid and Lisiiska chuka, both near the village of Buchino: Grebska-Kulova 2004, 134) to 60 ha (e.g. Usoe: Todorova and Vajsov 1993, 155). Analogies for such flat and enclosed sites are also known from adjacent regions, such as the enclosed site of Makriyalos, dating to the Late Neolithic in Northern Greece (Pappa and Besios 1999). But the category of the multi-period flat site is poorly recognised in Bulgaria, if not in other regions (viz., the mean number of six phases of dwelling on prehistoric sites in the Polgár Block of the Upper Tisza Project, in North East Hungary: Chapman *et al.* 2003).

As it happens, the site of Orlovo has multi-period, non-tell occupations, falling neatly in the middle of this poorly understood settlement pattern in prehistoric Bulgaria, with a location in the Southeast and its best parallels for site type and the chronology of occupation at the site of Vaksevo in Southwest Bulgaria. The latter has well-documented building horizons from the Early Neolithic, Middle Neolithic, Late Neolithic, Late Copper Age and Early Bronze Age, with evidence for Early Copper Age occupation 200 m Southwest of the major habitation area (Chohadziev 2001). There are several other candidates with similar settlement features (e.g. Balgarchevo and Kovachevo: Pernicheva 1995; Drenkovo-Ploshteko: Grebska-Kulova 2004) but the current approach to the publication and interpretation of settlements hinders further comparative study.

The fact that recurrent occupation failed to produce an impressive silhouette of a settlement mound or a tell is due to a complex of factors – site taphonomy, intensity of habitation and more diffuse relations with the ancestors. What sustained tell formation for Sherratt (1983) was a combination of three factors:

- spatial concentration – (as documented on tells by the continuous overlaying of dwelling structures: Bailey 1991)
- building in mud (mud-brick or wattle-and-daub)
- intensive occupation (cf. Nanoglou (2008)'s distinction

that tells have 'intensive' occupation but 'flat' sites have 'extensive' occupation).

Absence of any one or more criteria meant that tells did not develop. Chapman (1989) has maintained that tell sites imply a strict adherence to the principle of ancestral settlement – that you live directly above your ancestors – while flat sites in some way embody the weakening of this principle (contrast the tell with the 'flat' parts of the Sesklo settlement: Kotsakis 1999). But it is unwise to define 'flat' settlements in a negative sense, by the absence of something 'tell-like'; we do not wish to suggest that tells have some formal priority over flat sites. Rather, we suggest that all tells started off as flat sites and, in many cases, the dwelling practices on a settlement continued to lead in a different direction from mound formation. What was once characterised as the limits to social practices on tells (Chapman 1989) can just as readily be identified as the positive aspects of living on a flat site: the additional space between houses allows the creation of gardens for intensive cultivation, the keeping of domestic animals in pens, possibilities for outdoor practices as varied as dances, sacred rituals, high-temperature pyrotechnology (pottery, metallurgy), cooking and feasting (for an example, see the development of the Selevac site: Chapman 1990). The maintenance of a space between houses also avoids the formalisation of socio-spatial relations involved with high-density housing, as well as practical problems of privacy, inter-house audibility and problematic neighbours (cf. Halstead 1999). But perhaps the two most important aspects of inter-house separation involved the creation of a different form of relationship between, first, household and community and, secondly, humans and animals. In the first case, there arose a more distinct identity for each household than on the tell, with a greater possibility for difference, whether in the size, decoration and internal fitting of the house itself or the social practices permissible for household members. In the second place, the creation of space close to the house for animal-keeping meant a closer and more personal incorporation of animals into these communities than was possible for tells, perhaps leading to the kind of ontological differences in the significance of animals that Nanoglou (2008a) discusses for variations in animal and human representations in the Early Neolithic of Thessaly and the Central Balkans.

It can thus be seen that the choices to stay in exactly the same place for generation after generation was far from being a 'natural' or inevitable judgment or series of decisions but involved an active and long-term displacement of a relatively wide range of often important practices from in or near the household to somewhere else. Paradoxically, this displacement of practices unsuitable for the tell living space necessarily diffuses the tight tell-based focus on houses to include other areas off the tell, to which the tell-dwellers were intimately related. Important ontological differences may have co-arisen out of these contrasting uses of social space.

There are two ways in which the distinction between 'tell' and 'non-tell' is rendered less absolute. The first is the development of off-tell settlement areas, in which it is supposed that many of these activities took place, even if we know less than we need to about these intriguing dwelling areas (but cf. Bailey *et al.* 1998; Chapman *et al.* 2005). The second is the choice of continued dwelling on a 'flat' site but through the use of horizontal displacement to avoid the direct superposition of houses. This is what we take to mean by the term 'multi-layer' settlement of the kind that exists at Orlovo. Settlers at such a site maintained a weaker adherence to the ancestral principle than on tells but gained the advantages of a nexus of more varied social practices around the more separate domestic place called 'home' – paradoxically, a closer spatial focus of shared household practices than was possible on the tell. In summary, the occupational 'pulsations' at Orlovo, suggested by the discussion of the chronology (see above, pp. 103–4), should not only not surprise us but, on the contrary, should be viewed as one of the examples of hitherto scarcely recognised but typical dwelling practices in prehistoric Bulgaria – dwelling practices that have been recognised at other flat sites such as Yabulkovo (Leshtakov 2006) and Ljubimets (Nikolov, V. 2002; Nikolov, V. and Petrova 2008).

If we can establish that Orlovo was indeed a multi-layer settlement, what was the range of non-tell social practices that typified the various occupation phases? We shall begin to answer this question through the artifact biographies of the Orlovo figurines, ornaments and stone tools before considering the political economy of the region as well as wider spatial relations.

Artifact biographies

The time when the making, using and discarding of artifacts were viewed as different and unrelated processes is long past; this approach has been replaced by the links between all phases of an object's 'life' through a biographical approach (Kopytoff 1986; Skeates 1995). Current studies of artifact biographies have used the detailed observation and recording of each individual object to learn the maximum about each stage of an object's life-history.

Figurines

It is most unfortunate that we cannot be sure whether the figurines deposited at Orlovo were also made at Orlovo. The techniques of production – from a single ball of clay or in two or many parts, with an occasional clay coating, are known during both the Balkan Neolithic and Copper Age

and from a wide range of settlements. Fragmentation studies of the large Late Copper Age figurine assemblage at tell Dolnoslav showed that many parts of the mostly incomplete figurines were missing from the almost totally-excavated site, with the strong suggestion of off-site movement of figurine fragments (Gaydarska *et al.* 2007). Therefore, it is possible that figurines were made and fragmented locally or brought in as fragments from other sites, and most probably both. In the former case, the maker(s) created different shapes and decorations emphasising specific features or, on the contrary, created shapes (and decorations) full of uncertainty and ambiguity.

The surface colour of the figurines was mostly in the earthy range (yellow, orange, red and brown) leaving light and dark colours as a choice for other types of material culture (white predominates among the ornaments, dark nuances are preferred in stone tool production). Sometimes the desired colour is achieved by clay coating and the contrast between the core and the surface colour is indicative that the latter may have been deliberately created. It is a general assumption that potting clay (including non-utilitarian objects) is procured locally – in this case, from the alluvial zone of the Harmankijska reka or from the clay belt to the South (for a scientific exception, see Spataro 2007). If so, an unwanted local clay colour may have been masked by adding a clay coating (possibly non-local?) to produce the desired colour. The other factor vital to achieving the desired surface colour is the method of firing. The earth colour range and the presence of second colours and smudges and the difference in core and surface colours suggests a relatively low temperature, with accidental contact with other objects or fuel and the presence of oxygen readily associated with bonfire rather than kiln firing. Therefore, control over the surface colour of figurines was relatively easy to achieve (one could remove the figurine or stop the fire) though prone to changes in the weather. Both red and white colours are used to emphasize eyes, while red predominates for crusting and white for incrustation. Although it is difficult to claim with certainty at Orlovo, previous experience with figurine assemblages suggests that, while incrustation contributed largely to the making of a figurine, crusting may have been a part of the 'mid-life' of a figurine. In certain practices, red (usually associated with blood) may have been applied to a figurine, although such associations could also have occurred in the process of making.

The different size of the figurines suggests that their own future environment was borne in mind during the making; e.g. a sitting female should not have been too big for her clay bench or a standing unsexed figure should not have been too small for the corner of their public building. If figurines were brought to Orlovo, then there was an obvious selection for particular types and sizes of effigies. Few of the practices in which figurines participated left archaeological traces, among which we can identify repeated holding, rubbing, wearing and breaking. The figurines from Orlovo are highly fragmented and deposited at different stages of the fragmentation chain (cf. Chapman and Gaydarska 2006). At first sight, such a statement is contradictory but what it means is the fragments are small, not that they have many breaks. This has important implications – if you make a small figurine (e.g. up to 8 cm long), the potential for fragmentation is less because it is harder to break and has smaller body parts. Therefore size comprises an additional factor, apart from the weak points of a figurine's shape, for its fragmentation potential. The smaller fragments at Orlovo had mostly one or two breaks, while the 'bigger' fragments had mostly three and more breaks. It is tempting to suggest that the fragments with more breaks possessed a richer biography through the display of more enchained links. It is important to point out that, despite the preference for heads (with little fragmentation potential) and upper bodies (with great fragmentation potential) and the very small number of legs (with moderate fragmentation potential), the overall fragmentation pattern at Orlovo does not differ from the one registered for Dolnoslav (Gaydarska *et al.* 2007, 120). Such a result suggests that figurine fragments were *not* only and solely used in fragment enchainment but in various and changing social practices. Thus, for example, an ambiguous anthropomorphic terminal may not have been treasured for its unknown other part but for the fact of the ambiguity itself. Similarly, a non-characteristic base or stand may have been kept for recycling that consequently would have made the resultant product/s more valuable and part of enchainment (e.g. our non-characteristic fragment is crushed for a vessel's filler, thus linking it to the previous clay object). Ultimately, a leg with three breaks is valued for its enchained relations and may be kept for a future break and a new enchained relation. The nature of the collection from Orlovo does not allow more conclusive claims about the role of the figurines at the site but the surface treatment of the figurines suggests that they were treasured and, although intensively used (seen through breakage and wear), they were curated, with their shine and brilliance still cared for. Hence it would be reasonable to conclude that the figurines, in their whole or fragmentary state, formed an important part of the social life of the site, contributing to household and possibly other rituals and the sustaining of inter-personal relations through enchainment.

Ornaments

The preference for ornament types at Orlovo follows an intuitive consumption pattern based upon the numbers expected in a person's costume: a large number of beads for necklaces, between one and four rings and pendants for an individual (for burial data, see Todorova *et al.* 2002) and a small number of pins and buttons per person. The potential future use of the different type of ornaments (around a neck, on a wrist or ankle, etc.) and their possible association with other ornaments (beads in a necklace, beads and pendants in a necklace, stone and shell necklaces, etc.) did not affect the choice of raw material – there is little evidence for specialised selection of raw materials for ornament types. The inverse relationship is slightly more complex. Marble tends to be used mostly for bead production, while the *Spondylus* shell is used for the widest range of types, with the other raw materials between the two. One way of explaining such a differential choice lies in the varying aesthetic potentials of raw materials. *Spondylus* has a higher potential for revelation of its many colours, while turquoise has striking properties of the blue-green colour that is so rare in prehistoric material culture. Another aesthetic criterion is the technological potential of the stone and its suitability for faceting, and more importantly, the effects of the faceting. The evidence from Orlovo – an overwhelming preference for white ornaments and the faceting on many *Spondylus* beads – argues against such a simplistic either/or approach and add two further possible reasons for this particular choice of ornament/raw material relationship – (a) the colour symbolism of the material, and (b) the relationship of the ornament to the sources of its raw materials (water, rocks, earth). For the first, there was an overwhelming preference for white ornaments – especially shells – although the stone ornaments have a wider colour variability, including a wide range of greens, dark grey/black. Perhaps the community at Orlovo symbolised the sea through the whiteness of its shells. The second reason relates to the degree of exoticity that a material possesses, in turn a function of absolute and/or cognitive distance from Orlovo and the place-values set on the source area and places on the route to home. In summary, the choice of raw material for a certain ornament is a complex and not always obvious preference for shine, colour or other intrinsic properties, as well as external properties such as social and symbolic value.

The similar techniques used for making both shell and stone ornaments present us with two possibilities – they were all produced at Orlovo or, if produced and used on different sites, there is a remarkable uniformity in ornament production at the regional level. In favour of the former are the ten raw materials with evidence for on-site working (five shell, five stone) and the great diversity of ornament biographies (10 combinations of the four stages in the simplified *chaîne opératoire*). However, all the on-site stone production evidence consists of Stage 2 rough-outs for making disc beads, while there is no extant evidence for on-site making of faceted beads and buttons. The question of whether or not *all* the ornaments were made at Orlovo, although reasonable, is in danger of reducing the debate to little more than production choices. While most certainly some of the ornaments at Orlovo were worn, others were (re-)worked and a third group were ready for exchange. Support for such a claim is provided by the major difference between shell ornaments, with many Stage 1 and 2 examples, and stone ornaments, with mostly Stage 3 artifacts and some Stage 2 products. The portability of the raw material might explain the presence of Stage 1 shell ornaments – there is a limit to the number of pebbles easily carried over the landscape! The paucity of Stage 3 shell ornaments may point to export, while the Stage 3 stone ornaments may point to local consumption.

Fragmentation is a crucial stage in most *chaînes opératoires*. All the *Spondylus* rings from Orlovo are fragmented, while there are fragments of six other ornament types. There is no need to repeat the arguments for deliberate fragmentation as a basic enchainment practice in Balkan prehistory (Chapman 2000) and it is important to point out that the fragments represent the last stage of the currently suggested operational chain. While it is unwise to deny any production mishaps, the polish on more than 60% of the rings suggests that they were not broken during manufacture. Therefore, some of the fragments from Orlovo were either deliberately broken at the site or brought to the site as fragments. In any case, this is a strong indication for fragment enchainment and points at Orlovo as a consumption site, as well as a re-distribution site. Even if part of the fragments were meant for re-working, their continuing biography makes them more valuable for any future exchange and enchainment practice – certainly more valuable than production 'waste'.

The fascination of the Orlovo collection is that one can identify and follow aesthetic and technological choices at work (rough-outs/half-finished/ready products) and get a closer insight of how the shared appreciation of colour and brilliance may have been achieved. However, the lack of context for the Orlovo ornaments hinders the identification of one of the most revealing relationships between the size of beads and the number of beads in a given type of complete costume set. If there are limits on the size or number of beads per set, the assumption is that small beads would mean more beads per set and hence a wider potential range of enchained relations, while big beads are more rare, and therefore, more prestigious and shiny. If we accept Chapman's (1996) conclusions for Balkan Late Copper Age societies, then we may see a chronological difference in the use of the two types of ornaments – the former more appreciated in the earlier periods when enchainment seemed to be a major practice, the latter preferred in a later time when social power was achieved, *inter alia*, by the accumulation of prestige objects. Of course, the evidence from the Varna cemetery suggest that both ornament types (many small beads in one set; a few big beads/pendants in one set) were in contemporary use but in many senses Varna is a fusion of tradition and innovation. In the case of Orlovo, with its considerable time depth of occupation, we are tempted to suggest that we are witnessing the process of change from ornaments that symbolise multiple relations to ornaments that symbolise the increased importance of visible individual identities.

This not to say that enchained relationships have lost their meaning but rather that the sources of social power have diversified towards the end of the Copper Age. One possible mechanism of re-conceptualising the meaning of ornaments to integrate two different directions – multiple relations on the one hand, individual prestige on the other – is the great diversity of ornament biographies (see above, p. 106). If a bead/pendant/appliqué was initially worn as single ornament or in combination and then it was later given/exchanged and or re-worked several times, it has already acquired a rich biography and hence enchained personal value. Even if the people were not aware of the number of times that a bead was used in different necklaces, they must have been aware of the enchainment potential of even single beads, pendants or appliqués as one of their intrinsic properties. And while, in the earlier periods such intrinsic properties were reinforced by multiplication (many beads in a necklace), in the later periods other intrinsic properties of the same object became more important. This is not necessarily obvious from Orlovo but from what we know for the social processes concerning personhood and artifact biography in prehistoric Bulgaria and its supporting archaeological evidence.

In any case, the multiplicity of personal ornaments at Orlovo must have animated a wide variety of persons in all of the periods of occupation. Whether in private experience or public performance, ornaments had the capacity to add to, and transform, the social *persona* of the wearer, giving a new layer of meaning to their identities.

Polished stone tools

The life of many polished stone tools started with the raw material making a trip from the mountain to the site vicinity, with either people or rivers carrying it to the Familiar zone. Here, it was reduced to easy-to-carry rough-outs and blanks. The proximity of the river suggests that sand and water for abrasion, grinding and polishing were not an issue but the lack of contextual data hinders the possible location of stone tool production.

Four areas of great variability characterise the Orlovo assemblage:- morphological types, tool size, rock types and colours. This variability cannot be reduced to functional considerations, although task differentiation is indeed suggested by shape/size variations. The seven morphological types of stone tool suggest a wide variety of tasks with which the axes exploited the embodied skills of their owners. The small size of the axes is indicative of a preference for display axes, which would, for example, reduce the number of possible utilitarian activities.

The relationship of axe size and morphology to raw material is complex, with the use of volcanic tuffs in six out of seven groups and other volcanic rocks in four out of the seven groups suggesting a standard value for the symbolic and physical value of hard rocks. Moreover, it seems that jasper-like rocks were tested for several shapes, thus reinforcing the variable relation between the particular type of rock and a particular shape. This would not seem to be an expected result for a functionally-oriented explanation of variability. The same is true for the relationship between rock type and rock colour, owing to the dominance of mostly dark colours in the Orlovo assemblage and the weak tendency for colour to relate to one single rock type or a group (e.g. jasper-like rocks were available in 7 different colours, with volcanic tuffs found in 13 different colours).

While a tool may have been made for a specific job, different types of axe also indicate multiple relations to the makers in which their personal biography is inscribed and communicated. It should immediately be pointed out that we do not separate the utilitarian function of an axe from the personal biography of its maker. Thus, a tool can be made for hide-scraping, while its shape and colour could at the same time be associated with the life and enchained relations of its maker and previous owners. The notion of making an axe for an individual could lead to the embodiment of inter-personal differences in the axe, just as images of different persons, or categories of persons, could lead to variable types of figurines.

Naturally, at Orlovo, we see axes at different stages of their life-history. There is reasonably strong evidence for local stone tool production on up to $\frac{1}{3}$ of the axes (e.g. lack of polish and one rough-out), in addition to the sharing of four out of the five production techniques used for both ornaments and axes. Moreover, all the seven groups have at least one candidate for local production. The differential polish pattern may be interpreted as a deliberate choice not to polish the tools and therefore the axes may have been made at another site. The lack of shine reduces the aesthetic (and maybe symbolic) value of a tool and gives prominence to its physical properties. However, it does not affect the narratives connected to a given tool, which most certainly would have been the case with objects such as the flat axe (Plate 7g: Inv. 3263), which derived from the Foreign zone.

The clear preference for small size suggests a possibility that small tools were made from larger tools, as is seen on some of the Orlovo axes. Recycling is not unknown on Bulgarian prehistoric sites but, again, it is heavily burdened with functional/utilitarian connotations. In terms of artifact biographies, this is a new stage in the life of the axe, maybe related to its owner/user's life or to the life of the object itself. If, for whatever reason, an artefact had fulfilled or exhausted its current potential, there is always the conceptual difficulty of how to dispose of it (the problem of matter out of place: Douglas 1966). One solution among many is a change of size and shape, giving a new life and meaning to what had become a conceptually dangerous artifact.

It is always very difficult to assess whether the absence or paucity of wear – which constitutes 2/3 of the tools from Orlovo – means newly-made or carefully-used tools.

Comparison with the data for damage (less than ½ tools with no or little damage), however, presents a complex but paradoxically clearer pattern. Some of the Orlovo tools were display axes or were deposited soon after making, while others had a long use life, which, for some, included curation. There are three possible uses for the small tools – as personal tools, as amulets suspended round the neck, or as display tools. Their convenient size – fitting in the hand or the pocket – makes them as portable as the people moving around, adding to the intimacy of the inalienable link between person and tool. Hence, the use of small axes as personal tools for everyday tasks enables their use as metaphors, substitutes or symbols for their owner/users and (maybe) vice versa.

The same inalienable link is valid for the amulets and their owners but the symbolic potential of the axe-amulets is somewhat stronger. Amulets animate people, they also protect and cure, and ultimately give their owners a pleasing appearance. Such display tools are prestigious objects with commonly recognized social power that can be used in various social practices or disputes. The display tools may also have been inalienable objects whose ancestral power and magic is potentially transferred during exchange. Annette Weiner's (1985) sense of 'keeping-while-giving' means that any person holding a stock of inalienable objects will try to keep the maximum of ancestral power as embodied in the object, while exchanging less endowed objects. It is intriguing that green – often considered as a prestigious colour – is not so common for display axes at Orlovo. It is possible that, if tools were made from previously working tools with a different colour, the prestigious element (the value) of the newly made axe came from the associations (links and symbolism) of the once bigger tool, rather than from its colour alone. The value of larger tools would have been based upon persistence and survivorship as much as size, colour and their personal attachment to owners; there may well have been relatively few axes which kept their original size and shape through use, without the need for a biographical transformation into a smaller tool.

The polished stone tools from Orlovo went through a double 'domestication' by their incorporation into the dwelling practices of the occupants. First, their places of origin (and the persons concerned with this exploitation) were linked to a narrative of the site and place-values were created to relate these distant places to the centre of the world – Orlovo. Secondly, a more personal 'domestication' occurred through the establishment of enchained relations between the owner of an axe that had reached Orlovo, its subsequent inalienable exchange and its movement away from the site. The accumulation of so many axes in mint condition, as well as axes with the well-borne scars of an appropriately interesting biography, demonstrates the significance of the site of Orlovo, as a place where 'keeping-while-giving' had its own distinctive place.

Now that we have examined the object biographies of the figurines, ornaments and tools at Orlovo, we turn to the human counterpart – the issue of how personhood was developed in the periods of site occupation.

Personhood at Orlovo

Personhood in archaeology has been related to a new wave of dynamic approaches to material culture, targeting burials (Fowler 2004), architecture (Jones 2005), ornaments and figurines (Chapman and Gaydarska 2006; in prep.). The essence of the approach is that, although primarily a mental concept, people's awareness of themselves and others was necessarily communicated through material culture. At moments of social negotiation and especially with the emergence of new type of persons (e.g. herders, copper smelters, figurine-knappers, etc.), the materialisation of personhood became particularly crucial. It is very important to note Fowler's (2004) demonstration that the contemporary Western tradition of individual personhood is *not* the only way of defining people and person(hood) (cf. Brück 2001; Whittle 1998; 2001; 2003; Chapman and Gaydarska 2006, Chapter 2). Thus, Melanesian persons metaphorically exchange parts of themselves through enchainment of material gifts to others, while the crucial exchanges for South Indian persons focus on the symbolism of bodily fluids. Research on the Balkan Neolithic and Copper Age has demonstrated specifically prehistoric ways of creating personhood, with the exchange of object fragments playing a central role in these strategies (Chapman and Gaydarska 2006). For example, the fragmentation of a complete androgynous Hamangia figurine into two or more parts creates a loss of one gender for each part, enabling the negotiation of gendered relations using gendered figurine fragments (Chapman and Gaydarska 2006, Chapter 2; see above, p. 6).

Previous studies have demonstrated that figurines were one of the most direct ways of communicating personhood through the representation of different stages in the life-course by different figurine parts (Chapman 2000; Chapman and Gaydarska 2006, 182–184). Changing perceptions of people, both of themselves and their relation to others, leads to new methods and strategies of human representation, as is shown by a comparison of the narrow range of types and figurines found in the Neolithic and the huge diversity of types and vast number of images in the Late Copper Age.

One limitation of the Orlovo collection is the lack of differentiated dating for most figurines. Its absence prevents us from developing a more dynamic picture of personhood, especially through the prism of the changing diachronic relationship between lowlands and uplands, one of whose principal characteristics would have been differences in relationships between humans, domestic and wild animals and birds. What we can suggest is that the formation of Neolithic/Chalcolithic personhood, as seen from the Orlovo figurines, was a dynamic, complex and open process of integration of origin myths, changing social relations and shifting views of the outside world. The lack of fine chronological resolution at Orlovo unfortunately hinders the identification of the development of the personhood concept through time.

If there are two specific features in the Orlovo figurine collection, they are the ambiguity and the hybridity of the images – characteristics not unique for Balkan figurine assemblages (for a comparison of sexual ambiguities in Andalusian carnivals and prehistoric figurines, see Bailey 2005, 190–195) but often overlooked or misinterpreted (e.g. Gimbutas' notion of the "Bird Goddess": Gimbutas 1974). The interwoven identities of anthropomorphic, zoomorphic and ornithomorphic images pose questions about the boundaries of the body and its permeability, as well as the origins of humanity and the relations between people and the outside world. If Nanoglou (2008a) is correct in arguing that different figurine forms sustain and empower different worlds and experiences through the different practices which they enable, the Orlovo assemblage indicates perhaps profound differences from those of other communities whose figurines are based upon less ambiguous, or less hybrid, categories. Nanoglou (2008a, 10) has distinguished the anthropocentric discourse framing Early Neolithic lifeways in Thessaly from the ways in which both humans and animals form reference points for people's lives in the Early Neolithic of the Central Balkans. He mentions 'mixed' ontological categories without expanding the discussion, adding that there is little detail shown of body parts in Balkan Early Neolithic figurines (2008a, 5, 9). It is this ambiguity inherent in unspecified identities that allows multiple interpretations of such figurines, which are also common at Orlovo. But the Orlovo assemblage takes Nanoglou's difference between Thessaly and the Central Balkans further in highlighting the hybridity of many of the images. This development goes further than the incorporation of new members – viz., domestic animals – into the human community; it also goes further than Mullan and Marvin's (1987, 3) observation that "in an important sense, animals are human constructions" (cf. also Bailey 2005). Instead, the makers of the Orlovo figurines created radically different ontological categories that have no basis in zoological facts – in 'real life' – but were clearly grounded in their own cultural experience of categorisation processes and their relationship to social power relations.

In her groundbreaking research on Celtic art, Miranda Aldhouse-Green (2001; 2004) has discussed the power of the unusual and atypical, contrasting the norms of single-sex, single-species representations with the transgressive subversion of ambiguous, ambivalent and hybrid images. She defines these terms as follows (Green 1997, 898–905): while ambiguous images show the blurring of edges and a confusion of identity (an either/or identity, such as a youthful bearded face), ambivalent images stand for the duality of symbolic power (a both/and, as in hermaphrodites) and hybrids portray at once a multi-functional image separate from reality and a denial of harmony – in Green's telling phrase "the dissonance of equivalence". Each of these types of image provides space for thinking about the paradox of the similarities and differences between humans and animals/ birds.

While single-sex, single-species images are frequent at Orlovo, there are several examples of ambiguous and hybrid types (for a discussion of ambivalent, hermaphrodite figurines, see Chapman and Gaydarska 2006, Chapter 3). The most frequent ambiguous types present heads or vessel terminals that could be either (a) human or animal or (b) anthropomorphic or ornithomorphic. The absence of examples of human heads on zoomorphic or ornithomorphic bodies, or indeed a bird-head on a zoomorphic body, is largely a function of the high fragmentation rate of the assemblage. The incompleteness of many heads prevents an identification of hybridity, since the ambiguous heads had been broken from their body. But we cannot eliminate the possibility of the transformation through breakage of a hybrid 'monster' into two different parts: an ambiguous head and an unambiguous body(!). The power relations involved in such a transformation of a figurine's biography would have considerable ritual and cognitive significance.

Four kinds of hybrid images occur, portraying (1) zoomorphs with otherwise human coiffure; (2) typically anthropomorphic eye decoration on ornithomorphs; (3) the use of similar styles of decoration, including ornate, textile-based clothing, on anthropomorphic, zoomorphic, ornithomorphic and also on ambiguous figurines; and (4) the modelling of four- and six-toed feet on otherwise human figurines (cf. Chokadzhiev's (2004) study of three-fingered shamans in Balkan prehistory). These images from Orlovo transgressed as many categorical boundaries as have been created, opening up spaces for thinking about liminality and the permeability of boundaries. Moreover, the use of masks is well known in Balkan figurines (especially in the Vinča group: Gimbutas 1974, Chapter 4), as a means of transforming identities in specific contexts of change or boundary-maintenance. The Orlovo figurines show a surprising capacity for evoking dissonance and transcending normally accepted categories.

By contrast, coiffure, tattooing and clothing are all signs of personal appearance, marking deliberate acts of the shared construction of identity. The depiction of such particularities can be either a materialisation of a certain type of person, who imposed or sanctioned the particular fashion or style, or the communication of an already accepted shared personal identity. Inter-site comparisons of large assemblages of figurines would be the key in pursuing this issue. An additional point concerns the only bodily feature emphasized

by decoration – the eyes painted in both red and white. It is possible that, at certain moments, the attribution of specific features/forces to the eyes – whether good or evil – rendered their depiction a necessity for both humans and animals. An alternative is the emphasis on 'vision' in the prehistoric past as the key sense in apprehending the explosion in visual culture that is a hallmark of the Neolithic and Chalcolithic.

The opposite trend to the ambiguity of figurine types is shown by the high percentage of figurines with a clear gender identity, whether female or male but not androgynous. At Orlovo, gender ambiguity was not sought, in contrast to the androgyny of typical Hamangia figurines, or the profusion of unsexed figurines in most Bulgarian Neolithic/Chalcolithic cultural groupings (Chapman and Gaydarska 2006). If the pattern of the surface figurines at Orlovo reflects the total assemblage, then we may suggest that, on habitation sites such as Orlovo, gender identities were actively and constantly negotiated, producing a slowly accumulating assemblage of images, in use until dwelling ceased, while, on depositional sites, such as Dolnoslav and Medgidia – Cocoaşe (Haşotti 1985), representation of *all* gender identities – including the ambiguous unsexed – is more important than gender tensions because the images were deposited in their final resting place and could not have been re-used. This is the difference between a series of fleeting images that materialised specific, short-term statements about gender relations – images that may have been combined and re-combined in various ways – and a summary of these short statements, a resolution, for at least a period of time, of ongoing gendered negotiations through the act of major, public deposition to which many persons contributed *their own* figurine and which would have taken its place in local cultural memory.

The linking of figurines with ornaments and stone tools is not straightforward but two ways are possible at Orlovo – figurine perforations and the depiction of ornaments. The perforation of the figurine for suspension is not a very common feature on Balkan figurines (Hansen 2007). The presence of several examples at Orlovo (e.g. Plate 3c and g) points to an intimacy between image and wearer, perhaps to animate or protect the person but, in any case, to demonstrate publicly the association between absent ritual practices and persons and the wearer. This practice echoes the perforation of shells for suspension as parts of ornament sets, as well as the perforation of re-shaped axe-amulets.

The second way depends on the depiction of ornaments on figurines. There is only one possible exception of a bracelet shown by incised lines on the wrist (Fig. 2.1 g). The Orlovo evidence is generally consistent with the rare occurrences of figurines with decoration depicting jewellery and possibly ritual signs. A good example comes from Late Copper Age Durankulak, in the cenotaph grave No. 453, where an ornithomorphic head on a female body wore a copper bracelet on the left arm (Vajsov 2002, 263 and Abb. 256/7). Similar scenes are found in the Vinča group (e.g. the medallion suspended from the neck of the 'Lady of Predionica': Galović 1959, and at the Gumelniţa site of Pietrele, where a bone figurine wore a neckalce of copper beads and anklets of copper beads: Zidarov 2008, fig. 2). Given that most persons wore richly-ornamented costumes on special occasions, there is a marked discrepancy in the reluctance to portray the ornaments on figurines compared to the willingness to represent the costumes themselves. One possible reason for this discrepancy is that the tendency of ornaments to form individual more than corporate identity is the reverse of costumes, with their stronger links to group differentiation, whether based on age, gender, household or lineage.

If ornaments do not only enhance the individual but actually constitute them, what kinds of constituents have been added to the persons living at Orlovo? The juxtaposition of one's own skin and the incisor of a fierce wild boar, or the canine of a mighty red deer, portrays another facet of the relationship between humans and wild animals – the metaphor of a great and successful hunter who has brought the dangerous prey home from the forest. In similar vein, the combination of stone beads into a bright, shining necklace also presences the uplands, acting as a metaphor for seasonal visits to high peaks, encounters with wild creatures and a safe return home.

Equally, wearing marine shell ornaments not only symbolises the conquest of distance in the search for the exotic but also the metaphor of the deep-sea diver, lungs bursting as she detaches the shell from the submarine reef. If each single ornament from each different shell species or rock type conveys a range of contextually differentiated messages, the metaphorical power of each individual object is increased by the combination of multiple shell species or rock types that a person wears. There is also the sense of successful relations within a widespread social network that were necessary to acquire such prized objects.

This sense of the multiplication of dramatic effects caused by wearing ornaments from a diversity of places would have been increased still further by the concentration of the sum total of diversity of stones and shells worn by all the Orlovo residents. This spectacle would have been played out only at the principal seasonal festivals for all the communities of the Harmanlijska valley and acted as both a show of corporate identity and a mapping of political relations across the Balkan Peninsula. This complex presencing of a community's allies and exchange partners, the places where its members had travelled and acquired gifts and the other objects that had been kept-but-not-given created the space for a library of narratives defining the place and ancestry of both the individuals at Orlovo and their community. The likelihood that other communities in Southeast Bulgaria had chosen different ways of defining their personhood

and corporate identity from those characterising Orlovo is suggested by the weakness of the parallels with the Orlovo ornaments.

However, if the communities in the Harmanlijska valley selected distinctive material ways of presenting themselves to the outside world, the widespread distribution of parallels for the Orlovo ornaments, stretching to the Middle Danube Basin and Northeast Romania, is indicative of a wide network of persons recognising the same general framework of meanings of the messages carried by the style, raw materials and combinations of the Orlovo ornaments – what the ornaments meant in terms of personal, group and wider identities. The diversity of local meanings within this meta-narrative has been demonstrated by the strongly contrasting age and gender affiliations shown for identical material culture categories by the three Late Copper Age communities of Vinitsa, Devnja and Ovcharovo in Northeast Bulgaria (Chapman 1996). While many communities shared the same material culture as found at Orlovo, what they made of such "raw material" differed according to local traditions and ancestries and the social structure of the groups. The principle of the diversity of practice within a material cultural tradition is of widespread applicability in the Balkan Neolithic and Chalcolithic, if not further afield.

Turning to polished stone tools, there is a basic distinction between tools that were used in work, sometimes so heavily that re-shaping was necessary, and tools that were carefully curated and used only in display. It is reasonable to assume that, at a particular stage of the object biography, the current user of the tool regarded it as a personal tool, which, when used, activated the body, leading to the mobilisation of embodied skills relevant to the tasks of display or work. This was perhaps the most significant way in which stone tools contributed to individual personhood. We can extend the notion of Weiner (1985) that the fame of *kula* partners was totally inter-linked with the fame of those very *kula* rings they exchanged, and vice versa, to suggest that the previous history of a stone tool (meaning also a person), together with their point of origin, their aesthetic qualities and their fitness for work purpose, defined the framework for personal choice, with the axe finding the appropriate person as much as vice versa. This matching process hinged on the construction of narratives of ancestry for both objects and persons, with the origin point of the stone an important metaphor for the social relations and breadth of contacts of the new owner of the stone tool. It should be noted, however, that polished stone tools have often proved to be exceptions to the Balkan prehistoric practice of fragment enchainment, insofar as the vast majority appears to have been enchained as complete objects (Chapman 2000). This custom increased the importance of curating complete tools, perhaps in hoards in settlement contexts such as Orlovo. An additional way in which stone tools could contribute to a person's identity was through the conversion of the stone tool into a personal ornament – i.e., the re-fashioning into an axe-amulet.

As a final general point, it is expected that the differentiation of personhood, especially at the onset of farming and the early stages of the Late Copper Age, led to an increase in the number and diversity of objects, most of which stimulated new kinds of embodied skills in Balkan communities. There is a high probability that those people who were in the state of 'becoming' new kinds of persons would have sought to materialise their newly emergent identities by association with new types of object, whether stone tools, ornaments or figurines. This would not have been so necessary within the community as when individuals met others from different communities through social networks. The qualities of those objects which could best symbolise the new categories of persons would be colour and brightness, exoticity and ancestry – a classic combination of intrinsic properties and interesting biographies. We have seen that many of the objects found at Orlovo match these criteria very well.

The political economy of Orlovo

The combination of the evidence for the artifact biographies of figurines, ornaments and stone tools and its implications for personhood shows how the Orlovo site could have made a contribution to a wider political economy, necessarily considered at the regional scale in terms of production, distribution and consumption.

Production

The possibility that production practices may have played a significant role at Orlovo would be of great significance in Balkan prehistory, since production sites are not readily recognizable in the Balkans and especially in Bulgaria. A rare exception conveys the kind of archaeological evidence for production that could well be related to the archaeological assemblage considered in this book. At Late Copper Age Sedlare, near Momchilgrad in the Eastern Rhodopes, production foci have been discovered in all three occupation horizons (Raduntcheva 1997). In the poorly preserved Horizon 1, lithic production is concentrated on a large cobbled surface, with some shaping and re-sharpening of axes and adzes. In Horizon 2, production is located inside small rooms (annexes) attached to houses and in pits on the edge of the settlement. The annexes have grindstones and abrasives for grinding tools. It is in this Horizon that the vast majority of the 30,000 pieces of jasper and agate débitage was discarded. In Horizon 3, there is evidence for production in all the houses, including one pottery workshop, houses in the Northern part of the site with bone and antler working debris and lithic production in the other houses. In summary, both the scale and the spatial

locus of production activities varied throughout the site's long occupation. Moreover, the disjunction between 30,000 waste flakes and 200 finished tools, only 20 of which having use-wear, suggests that the jasper and agate blades were produced only partly for local consumption and mostly for export (Raduntcheva 1997). The production evidence summarised here would suggest that the community of Sedlare included potters, bone and antler-tool makers, axe-makers, flint-knappers and probably traders.

The lack of excavations at Orlovo makes it impossible to determine whether or not Orlovo was a self-sustaining mixed farming settlement or whether the site relied on exploitation of its key location at the junction of the uplands and lowlands to develop specialist seasonal transhumance to the Rhodopes. Although arable and pastoral production cannot be documented, there is solid evidence for Orlovo as a craft production site, with inhabitants making part of the shell and stone ornaments in up to a dozen different raw materials, as well as some of the ground and polished stone tools, with the additional possibility of making some or all of the fired clay figurines. The production evidence at Orlovo refers to the possibility of workshop activities on this multi-layer settlement, though not necessarily specialist craftspeople. At first sight, this reading of the Orlovo data is in concordance with Bailey's (2000) notion that tells were centres for cereal storage rather than production sites, with the latter preferentially found on flat sites. However, it is increasingly difficult to support, either at a theoretical or an empirical level, a separation between settlement / dwelling activities and activities centred on production, for the simple reason that they are co-terminous.

As with many other themes in Bulgarian/Balkan prehistory, production is under-theorised, with the presumption that it is an activity designed to achieve self-sufficiency for the inhabitants of an average site. This is an idea rooted in Gordon Childe's notion of the self-sufficiency of the Neolithic (Childe 1935) – an idea that has been overtaken by developments in exchange theory and the relationships between people and things. Instead, we can begin by embedding production in the everyday life of a community, with persons objectified by the production of things (Miller, D. 1987) and social relations objectified through the movement of people and things between households (Skourtopoulou n.d.). These processes also occurred at a wider spatial scale with the objectification of economic and social values in exotic exchange, embedded in inter-cultural contact (Skourtopoulou 2006) (see below, pp. 114–120). Skourtopoulou's key point is to see artifacts as "material metaphors of inter-personal relations" at various socio-spatial scales. The presence of personal tools, some of the ornaments and, in particular, the figurines are features generally associated with settlement sites in the Neolithic and Chalcolithic. They point to everyday and/ or cyclical subsistence activities like scraping and cutting (the tools);

to everyday and/or cyclical manifestations of personhood and identity (the ornaments); and to everyday and/or cyclical negotiations of social relations through ceremonies and practices (the figurines). Naturally, there was no rigid division between the types of the material culture and their role and participation in people's life; a personal tool may have been equally important for one's identity as was a *Spondylus* ornament or a figurine may have been a crucial participant in ceremony related to a certain subsistence practice. In myriad quotidian ways, the material culture of a site such as Orlovo made its distinctive, cumulative contribution to the emergence of social orders at the personal, household, community and network scales.

Distribution, acquisition and re-distribution

It is impossible at Orlovo to make a conceptual separation between production and distribution, since the former practice relies on the successful acquisition of either raw materials or half-finished objects from one or more of the three social zones surrounding Orlovo – the Familiar, the Other and the Foreign.

The popularity of Bulgarian studies in prehistoric exchange of goods and trade (Todorova 1995a) stems from the 'economic' bias usually assumed, so that trade goods have an unashamedly practical function, whether involving livestock, other organic products, raw material or finished goods. One important item rarely mentioned concerns the exploitation and exchange of salt in prehistory (but see Raduntcheva 1986; Gaydarska 2004; Chapman and Gaydarska 2004; Nikolov, V. 2008). While the economic aspect should not be overlooked, especially given the importance of complementary upland – lowland resources, the significance of exchange and acquisition for building and maintaining social relations is also a vital part of prehistoric lifeways. We have mentioned the objectification of economic and social values created in the exchange of exotic material culture, whether through enchained relations or less directly personal relations of acquisition (Chapman 2008). These relations were inextricably linked with another key resource which is not usually considered in this way – the cultural heritage of the Orlovo region and its wider inter-connected worlds – those specific forms of knowledge and meaning that animated objects just as much as objects animated people. It was the sharing and transfer of such knowledge that enabled the creation and maintenance of a tradition, into which every newly-established settlement fitted in some way or other. In this way, not only objects but also cultural knowledge overcame the friction of distance in bringing the shared understanding of contextual meanings to different communities. In the next section, we shall seek to integrate data on exchange with information about the wider cultural relations embodied by the Orlovo assemblage.

The Familiar

The Familiar Zone has been defined as the settlement itself with its surrounding Community Area – occupied by a closely knit group of people related by kinship and co-residential ties (Neustupný 1998, 65). The conventional 5 km radius of maximum economic distance for key subsistence tasks (Higgs and Vita-Finzi 1970) is used to define the permeable boundaries of the Familiar Zone, which incorporates an intensively interacting network of people with close relations to most of the others moving within this zone. This may be an exaggeration for Orlovo, whose nearest neighbour settlement – the Konush tell to the West – lies exactly 5 km from the site.

While microregional links within the Familiar Zone must have been the strongest for things as much as for people and places, the evidence for the use of local sources at Orlovo is decidedly ambiguous for all types of material culture. Coal, limestone and sandstone from local geological formations, snails (*Theodoxus* and *Melanoides*) from the local meadow and teeth / tusks from local red deer and wild boar were all locally available within a few km of the site and were presumably used, if rarely, for ornament and stone tool production. If we assume local making of figurines, there is one source of suitable clay. – the alluvial clay from the Harmanlijska reka – adjacent to the site. The most problematic issue concerns the origins of the stone for axes and ornaments. Although the primary sources of volcanic tuffs, volcanic rocks, schist, amphibolite and jasper are located in the Eastern Rhodopes, in the Other Zone, secondary pebble sources of all of these rocks occur in accessible, eroded parts of local geological formations and may have been exploited by the Orlovo community. Resolution of this dilemma would require an extensive programme of geological source sampling and thin-sectioning of ornaments and tools, without a guarantee of success, since it is often hard to distinguish the mineralogical components of primary and secondary sources of the 'same' rock type. The resulting uncertainty is summarised below (Fig. 5.2a–d). The range of ornaments from possible Familiar Zone sources ranges from 2%–22%, while this range increases to 3%–56% for stone tools! The only tentative conclusion that can be drawn at this juncture is that sources from both the Familiar *and* the Other Zones were most probably utilised in the production of ornaments and tools but the ratio of Zones cannot be determined. What is also apparent is that the combination of evidence for possible local sources shows a varied pattern for the three types of material culture.

The Other

The Other Zone has been characterised as the Zone occupied by people from different communities from the relevant site but sharing similar material culture (Neustupný 1998, 65–66). However, this definition creates a significant problem

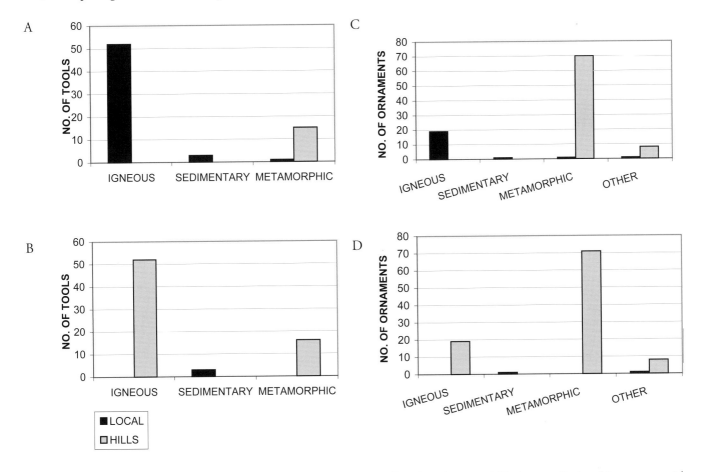

Figure 5.2. Possible stone sources: (a) tools with maximal local collection; (b) tools with maximal Rhodopean collection; (c) ornaments with maximal local collection; (d) ornaments with maximal Rhodopean collection

because of the dramatic spatial variations through time in the material cultural links between Orlovo and the wider world, ranging from the whole of the Balkans and Hungary in the Early Neolithic (the so-called 'First Temperate Neolithic according to John Nandris (1970)), much of the East Balkans in the Late Copper Age (the so-called Karanovo VI–Gumelniţa–Kodzadermen network linkage: Sherratt 1972), to Southern Bulgaria with Northern Greece in the Late Neolithic (Keightley 1986). The alternative to the 'cultural' criterion is the use of a geographical definition of the boundaries, such as a day's journey to a given destination point and a day's return trip – or a radius of 15–20 km. Such an area coincides broadly with the Southern part of the Thracian Plain and the Northern hills of the Eastern Rhodopes and in a broader sense with SE Bulgaria. Thus, the Other Zone constitutes a social network including significant parts of both the uplands and the lowlands, with the local Harmanlijska valley as the first area of interest but with lower intensities of interaction than in the Familiar Zone.

The settlement background to the Other Zone of the Orlovo inhabitants is formed by the sites in the East–West-running Harmanlijska reka. During the early stages of the Neolithic, several flat settlements are known in the valley, one of which may well have been Orlovo. The latter was not, however, a founder site, since it never developed into a tell, as did the sites near Konush and Dinevo. The importance of Orlovo seems to have increased during the late stages of the Neolithic, probably at the time of the mature development of the Konush and Dinevo 1 tells. The scarce Early Copper Age evidence from Orlovo, as well as the absence of Middle Copper Age occupation, is part of a valley-wide pattern of settlement discontinuity, in which only two of the earlier sites were re-settled and two new settlements emerged. The attraction of ancestral Orlovo led to re-settlement as a flat site, at a time when other settlements were developing into Late Copper Age tells. This trend for re-occupation was continued during the Bronze Age when one tell and two flat sites in the valley were settled again and hence may correspond to the weak occupational evidence at Orlovo.

Two points can be made about the pattern of valley settlement: first, the long-term existence (Late Neolithic–Early Bronze Age) of two different modes and ideologies of dwelling – the tell and the non-tell; and, secondly, the long-term characteristic of relatively large spacings between most settlements. If there were differences in the *habitus* – the regular, quotidian social practices – between tell and non-tell communities, these could have been noted and utilised in identity-formation, perhaps leading to small-scale self-reinforcing differences between people and their settlements. The repeated settlement of most sites shows long-term attachments to places, whether as flat sites or tells, grounding the identities of inhabitants in the place where they were born.

Moreover, the spacing between these communities was not conducive to frequent contacts, with only one site (the Konush tell) within a 5-km walk from Orlovo and the other Neolithic–Chalcolithic sites 11 and 13 km away respectively, or further. While the inhabitants of Konush and Orlovo may well have seen each other in the course of farming work or on hunting/fishing trips, the main structured interaction would have been in seasonal agglomerations of feasting, ritual and the exchange of marriage partners. It was at such performative occasions, perhaps more so than in occasional 'local' meetings, that the principal confirmation of social relations between sites along the whole valley would have taken place – that bonding that maintained the identities of the four or five communities at the level of the valley as much as within a wider cultural unit. It is a drawback of the regional coverage in this valley that only surface identifications have been carried out at the other Harmanlijska valley sites, preventing any comparative study of their finds with those of Orlovo.

There are three main stages in the social networks connecting Orlovo to the plains communities to the North and the upland communities to the South. In the Early Neolithic, there is an extensive network of settlements in the Eastern Rhodopes which are linked to sites in the Harmanlijska reka such as Orlovo and also, possibly, to the North Aegean coast. In the Middle and Late Neolithic and the Early–Middle Copper Age, the archaeologically visible lowland network of plains sites is de-coupled from the upland zone, which shows little or no evidence of deposition in these periods. There is a dramatic resurgence of lowland–upland links in the Late Copper Age, defined partly by the 'sudden' emergence of upland depositional places (sanctuaries), as a sign of a changed perception of the memorialisation or monumentalisation of certain encounters through material deposition in the Late Copper Age but with the roots for the development of such intimate knowledge and special relations in the preceding periods.

Turning to the spatial vectors of cultural knowledge in the Other Zone, paradoxically, the material links with the Other are much more visible than for the Familiar Zone for all three types of material culture (Fig. 5.3). What appear to be common for the entire Other zone are close similarities in figurines and polished stone tools. The paucity of preferential

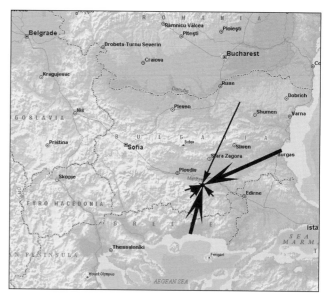

Figure 5.3. Spatial links in cultural knowledge between Orlovo and the Other and Foreign Zones. Key: thickness of arrow betokens strength of connection

regional links for the latter (e.g. the Vrhari turquoise workshop near Sedlare: Boyadzhiev *et al.* 2010) suggests widely shared, embodied technological knowledge and skills across the Other Zone and beyond (see below, pp. 118–19). The figurine pattern does, however, show distinctly closer links for Southeast Bulgaria than for other areas – presumably the result of their customary usage in the domestic context and the prevalence of local enchained links rather than long-distance exchange of such ritual objects. An unexpected finding was the lack of links in ornaments between Orlovo and other sites in the Other Zone. This finding is only partly caused by the absence of comparable sites – whether cemeteries or settlements – in Southeast Bulgaria. One possible explanation is the relatively 'low' exoticity value, at other sites, for ornaments locally made at Orlovo or acquired from the Eastern Rhodopes. If personhood and/or group identity is predicated on the possession of bright, highly coloured exotic objects, perhaps copper objects from the West Balkans or honey-coloured flint from Northeast Bulgaria would have been more attractive than ornaments made at Orlovo or its upland periphery.

We have already discussed the dilemma of accurate sourcing of the stones used for the making of tools and ornaments (see above, p. 114). There is a likelihood that some of the stone objects were derived from the Eastern Rhodopes but the proportion of non-Familiar Zone objects made of volcanic tuffs, volcanic rocks, schist, amphibolite, and jasper is not determinable. What is more clear is that there is a good source of Tertiary clays in a zone stretching from Most Eastwards to Dubovets, some 12 km South of Orlovo. It is also clear that turquoise, marble, serpentinite

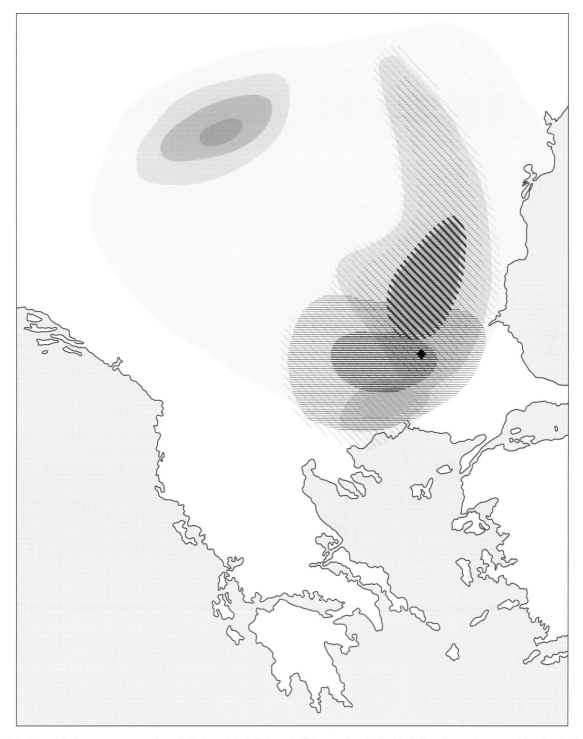

Figure 5.4. Spatial links in raw materials with Orlovo: (a) shell (tones); (b) stone (hatched); (c) shell and stone (tones and hatching); diamond – Orlovo. Drawn by Yvonne Beadnell

and picrolite were not available as secondary deposits in the Familiar Zone of Orlovo but had to be transported to the site from a distance (Fig. 5.4). The most probable source of the turquoise has been identified at Spahievo (Kostov *et al.* 2007), some 18 km West (upstream) of Orlovo, while the other rocks are found in primary outcrops in the East Rhodopes. The Other Zone also acted as a transit zone for the movement of shells or shell products from the Foreign Zone, either across a network of Rhodopean settlements or via the lowland Maritsa route (Fig. 5.4).

In the two periods of strong lowland–upland connections, it would seem more probable that the primary resources for volcanic rocks and other stones would have been used, perhaps through exchange, while, in the intermediate period of the de-coupling of lowland from upland networks, there may well have been a preference for secondary stone sources in the Familiar Zone. This interpretation may well suggest that the periods when Rhodopean marble, serpentinite and picrolite from the Other Zone were preferred may have been the Early Neolithic or the Late Copper Age – but we should recall the dangers of a circular argument here.

The Foreign

The Foreign Zone has been defined in relative terms as that Zone beyond the Other Zone with which there is relatively little contact for those dwelling in the Familiar Zone (Neustupný 1998, 65). In terms of our study, the Foreign Zone extends far in all directions, reaching Northern Greece to the South, the Black Sea to the East, Moldavia to the North and Western Hungary to the West. Each of the areas included in the Foreign Zone has its own sequence of settlement dynamics, with two principal communalities: wide-ranging material links amongst the earliest farming communities, and a climax in settlement and social complexity in the mid 5th–early 4th millennia BC (Late Neolithic in the West Balkans, Copper Age in the East Balkans) (Chapman 2000).

The strongest links within this extended area for all three types of material culture are between Orlovo and Northeast Bulgaria (Fig. 5.3). They tend to continue across the Danube into Romania and fade away towards Moldavia, where only figurines indicate possible relations. There are also strong if not consistent links with Northern Greece, more for ornaments than for figurines and tools, that must have taken place across the Rhodopes rather than via Southwest Bulgaria, where ornament parallels are lacking and figurine similarities are very weak (Fig. 5.4). The paucity of similar ornaments in Southwest Bulgaria is indicative of an exchange system in which Greece is the starting point and Orlovo appears to be one of the secondary production and re-distribution points for further exchange beyond the Stara Planina into Northeast Bulgaria and Romania. This pattern is also confirmed by the weak ornament distribution in Southeast Bulgaria. Such an exchange network would have included many other things and concepts, thus leaving weak, though visible, similarities in figurine and polished stone tools between Greek and Bulgarian sites.

The overwhelming stylistic similarities between Orlovo objects and those in Northeast Bulgaria, and even North of the Danube, attest not only to a long-term sustainable exchange network but also to a shared social understanding in which figurines, tools and ornaments (and perhaps other objects) had a comparable, commonly accepted framework of value that facilitated communication, negotiation and enchainment, despite major differences in ceramic traditions. Why this is not the case with the other neighbouring areas cannot be explained simply by lack of comparable investigations or indeed by the presence of different ceramic traditions. Moreover, the only places known so far with faceted stone beads of the type found at Orlovo are the artifact-rich Late Copper Age cemeteries of Varna and Durankulak, suggesting a specific social and chronological context for the deposition of these special beads.

The evidence from Orlovo is unambiguous that both ornaments and figurines have links with artifact traditions in the West Balkans and Central Europe, including a series of strong ornament analogies with the Lengyel cemeteries of Western Hungary (Fig. 5.4). Such a pattern suggests sustainable though sporadic contacts between remote communities, of a kind with few modern or recent analogies. There would seem to be two possibilities. First, the services of long-distance specialists, *sensu* Helms (1993), who would negotiate for the acquisition of those prestige goods which were most desirable for their home community. Secondly, overlapping networks of exchange could have helped to maintain the shared cultural values underpining the networks, within which goods and raw materials would have been passed and exchanged from community to community in regular acts of goodwill, display, social negations and enchainment – all of which are crucial for successful social and biological reproduction. Since the long distances involved in such networks call the logistical practicalities of long-distance specialists into question, it may be that the explanation of dense, well-connected exchange networks carrying a high density of cultural information as well as exchange objects may be preferable.

Last but not least are the polished stone tools with their seemingly unhelpful undifferentiated distribution. The absence of a long-term programme of archaeo-petrological investigations (cf. the British and Irish Neolithic stone axe programmes: Clough 1988; Clough and Cummins 1979; Cooney and Mandal 1998; Sheridan *et al.* 1992) makes it hard to contextualise the Orlovo results. Two Late Copper Age examples, from the Durankulak and Varna cemeteries, provide analogies biased towards the mortuary domain. At Durankulak, two-thirds of the sample of analysed polished stone tools derived from volcanic rocks with no local sources in the Dobrudzha, most probably from the Burgas area and the Strandzha Mountains (Dimitrov, K. 2002: 208–9). Similar results derive from the analysis of over 100 polished stone tools from the Varna cemetery, where 90% of the polished stone tools were made from non-local rocks, mostly volcanic tuffs (60%), (Kostov 2007, 86), with the remainder of local limestone and quartz. While noting the probable similarities in the reliance on non-local stones at Orlovo and the two cemeteries, there is a contrast between the Orlovo stone tool pattern, with evidence for local stone tool production, morphological parallels everywhere in the Balkans but with no shape characteristic for a specific place, and those at Varna and Durankulak, where the absence of evidence for local production of stone tools using exotic rocks, even in nearby settlements (the Durankulak tell on the Big Island: Chapman *et al.* 2006), suggests exchange in finished stone tools from distant sources. One is tempted to suggest that, in addition to the existence of wide-ranging exchange networks, there were widely shared, embodied technological knowledge and skills among prehistoric societies in Bulgaria whose operational principles are yet to be identified.

In addition to those aspects of cultural knowledge and tradition that are clearly very widely shared across the Neolithic and Copper Age of the Balkans and Central Europe, we can pinpoint one specific flint type and a range of shell resources that can confidently ascribed to sources in the Foreign Zone (Fig. 5.4). The high-quality honey-coloured flint objects found in the 2006 surface collection at Orlovo are typical of the Razgrad flint outcrops of Northeast Bulgaria (Manolakakis 2005). It is possible that the strong artefact-based links between Orlovo and Northeast Bulgaria were partly mediated through the exchange of flint to the South.

There are no exclusively Black Sea sources for any of the Orlovo shell species, while there are exclusively Aegean sources for *Dentalium*, *Spondylus* and *Glycymeris* shells. At present, there is no possible analytical separation between Black Sea and Aegean sources of *Cerastoderma* (*Cardium*), *Cerithium*, *Conus*, *Cyclope*, *Marginella* and *Ostrea*, indicating that either were potential sources for those particular Orlovo shells. The Pontic shells could potentially have been derived from any point on the Black Sea coast, or from many points, from Istanbul to Constanța. The strength of the links between Varna, Durankulak and Orlovo suggest that the exchange of shells could have further consolidated the already complex exchange network linking Northeast to Southeast Bulgaria (for the links between these areas in copper exchange, see Chapman 2008 and Fig. 5.5 below).

There are also competing routes for the movement of Aegean shells to Orlovo. One route traverses the Rhodopes via transit sites in the Momchilgrad, Kardzhali and Krumovgrad basins. A second possibility is the longer but less steep route via the Maritsa valley, which skirts the Eastern end of the Rhodopes near modern Edirne. However, a strong argument against the Maritsa route in the Late Copper Age is the perhaps surprising paucity of Karanovo VI settlements in Turkish Thrace (Erdogu 2004). Since the Orlovo community knew the shorter mountain route network from their regular trips for resources, such a preference was more probable, except for those periods (Karanovo III–V) when there was a de-coupling of the lowland–upland network.

Orlovo as a gateway community?

It is difficult to assess whether the exotic objects were meant for further exchange or whether Orlovo was their final destination. Given their overwhelming number, a cautionary note can be made for the presence of some kind of *exchange centre*, reflecting Orlovo's key location at the upland/lowland junction. It would be unwise to claim that *all* exotic objects were stored for future exchange, since the maintenance of daily relations necessitated an element of local material consumption, whether as gifts to the gods, statements of social categorisation, metaphors of inter-household links or personal enchained relations. Given the prevalence of fragment dispersion (Chapman and Gaydarska 2006), there is a case to be made that broken *Spondylus* rings, with long life-histories acquired through a process of fragment enchainment and valued for the places and people they symbolise, would have been just as attractive for re-exchange as unworn, complete axes and ornaments in mint condition. Is there a wider socio-spatial framework in which to embed the question of re-distribution?

A useful concept first mooted in the late 1970s is the model of a gateway community, suggested as an effective means of explaining the emergence of market centres in the context of early inter-regional exchange networks in Formative Mesoamerica societies (Hirth 1978). Sites such as Chalcatzingo developed in the context of overall increases in regional population, internal social ranking and the demand for increased resources. Located in sparsely populated upland/lowland frontier areas that were marginal to the main social centres, gateway communities succeeded insofar as they controlled the production or movement of scarce resources; they went into decline following economic decline or the loss of their exchange hinterland (Hirth 1978).

While the Balkan example does not fit entirely with its classical American counterpart, not least in terms of the lower level of social complexity and density of exchange in the Balkans, Orlovo certainly has some of the traits of a gateway community – its strategic location at the lowland–upland interface, its potential to channel the complementary resources from both zones and the evidence for local production of scarce resources. Gateway communities are, in fact, a classic example of the dynamic nominalist theory, in which new categories emerge together with their perceived need. In the early part of its site biography, Orlovo was just one of a handful of Neolithic settlements in the Harmanlijska valley, at the junction of the lowlands and the uplands. The Neolithic inhabitants would have gained experience in both the acquisition of raw materials, some from the Rhodopes and some from the Foreign Zone, as well as in object production. Even though there was reduced site occupation in the Early Copper Age, and none in the Middle Copper Age, the cultural memory and social relations linking the valley communities to the

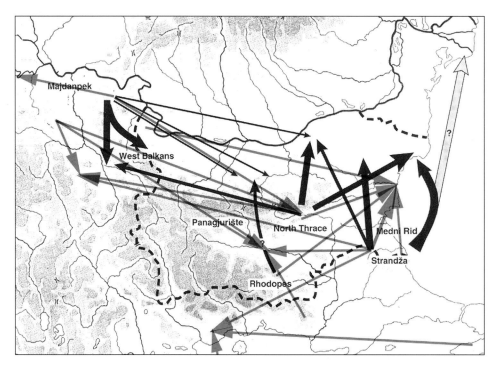

Figure 5.5. Copper exchange networks in the Late Copper Age of the Balkans (source: Chapman 2008, Fig. 7.3). Key: black lines – data from Pernicka et al. *1997; grey lines – data from Gale* et al. *2000*

uplands would have persisted, seemingly at another site.

We have already identified the Late Copper Age as a time of intensification of raw material procurement and consumption closely related to the differentiation of both site types and new categories of people. The number of Late Copper Age settlements reached a peak for most parts of the East Balkans. Not only was there an expansion in the quantities of traditional materials in exchange (lithics, shells, ceramics) but new materials such as copper and gold were transforming the domain of consumption (Fig. 5.5). Moreover, there is a strong case that processes of social differentiation were kick-started by the consumption practices of cemeteries such as Varna and Durankulak, the former now dated to the very beginning of the Late Copper Age (4750–4550 BC: Higham *et al.* 2007; Chapman *et al.* 2006). It is exactly this period when the external parallels for the Orlovo objects reach a peak for all three forms of material culture, indicating an important occupation in the Late Copper Age. It is suggested here that Orlovo's interface location and possibly previous tradition and experience in exchange and enchainment practices was an obvious candidate for a gateway community in this period, bringing exotic resources into the plains in exchange for North East Bulgarian lithics and shells. Whether or not Orlovo was the most important, or even the sole, gateway community in the Late Copper Age is open to further investigation of other sites along the Harmanlijska valley. But the research of the principal investigator of the Haskovo region – Dimcho Aladzhov – has not revealed anything remotely resembling the

wealth and diversity of the Orlovo surface collection on any other site as yet – rather, the standard surface pottery, lithics and daub with an occasional worn figurine (Aladzhov 1997).

We have seen how the period of half a millennium between the end of the Early Neolithic and the start of the Late Copper Age was characterised by the de-coupling of the lowland – upland network. This is another way of stating that the Orlovo site lost part of its exchange hinterland that formerly brought upland resources to the valley. The same phenomenon occurred at the end of the Late Copper Age, when the widespread and multiplex networks were transformed into much more directional exchange routes carrying far fewer materials. In both periods, the role of Orlovo as a linking site between lowland and upland fell into decline, with a consequent reduction in settlement practices and on-site deposition. One of the dynamics of occupation at Orlovo may well have depended upon the extent to which the intensity of on-site deposition was a reflection of the success, or failure, of the gateway community role of successive communities at Orlovo. On this reading, there were phases of fluctuating success and failure at Orlovo consonant with the growth and diminution of on- and off-site material consumption.

Deposition

It may come as a surprise that deposition is discussed when the lack of contextual information at Orlovo has been repeatedly underlined. But in harmony with the second objective of this book, we are trying to establish a methodology that overcomes the limitations of unprovenanced surface/museum collections by looking at the objects themselves. And one of the most obvious characteristics of the Orlovo collection repeated over and over again is large amount of objects, usually more readily associated with the excavation of burial sites or complex settlements. On such sites, deposition was either deliberate or *de facto* but, in any case followed the concentration principle – namely, that prehistoric persons deposited as much of their material culture as possible in the same place where the objects were made and lived their lives. This is, we believe, the case with Orlovo too and is a part of the explanation for the unusually large number of objects at Orlovo. We have sought to demonstrate in previous sections and in Chapters 2–4 that some objects were made and stored at Orlovo, others were used there, and a third group was deposited and/or curated there.

The lack of plough damage on all three types of objects suggests a reasonably good level of site and object preservation. The relatively little wear on figurines and the consequent survival of crusted and incrusted decoration are indicative of depositional conditions that would, in most cases, protect the objects from the weather and mechanical damage. Such contexts may have included those buildings whose collapsed walls protected the objects, as well as pits, in which the objects were formally deposited and thus protected from outside effects. However, there are artifacts that suffered post-depositional damage either in the past or closer to their discovery in the 20th century. While, for figurines and ornaments, it is difficult to distinguish the criteria for damage caused by people's use from unintentional post-depositional damages, the criteria for polished stone tools are less demanding. The combination of wear by use and damage caused by any other reason proved to be a useful indicator for allowing the separation of newly made tools, heavily used tools, carefully curated tools, and ultimately tools with post-depositional damage (few in number).

Without pushing the evidence too far, one cannot omit the fact that there is an obvious difference in figurine deposition between Orlovo and the Dolnoslav tell. The majority of heads at Orlovo, as opposed to the majority of legs at Dolnoslav, was suggested to related to a concentration of heads on production sites, legs in middens. The difference in gender deposition was also attributed to differences of type of occupation: active with some formal deposits at Orlovo, more formal than active at Dolnoslav. However, the patterns of fragmentation of figurines at both sites seem to be very similar, suggesting that fragmentation as a social practice was equally important for habitational and formal deposition sites. This conclusion supports a previous finding in relation to *Spondylus* ring breakage, found equally in cemeteries and settlements albeit with different re-fitting trends (Chapman and Gaydarska 2006, Chapter 6).

Traditionally ornaments and ornament sets are usually more related to formal deposits such as graves and hoards and not so much to settlement deposits, as is confirmed by the evidence from prehistoric Bulgaria (Todorova and Vajsov 2001). Insofar as the evidence from Orlovo indicates local production, it constitutes a rare case of large amount of ornaments seemingly related to a settlement/production site. The stone ornaments show little use-wear or damage, suggesting deposition soon after making – a finding that cannot be confirmed for shell ornaments. The ornaments find their closest and most numerous analogies in areas with important mortuary and hoard contexts (NE Bulgaria, Romania and Hungary), in contrast to the paucity of analogies in areas with few hoards/mortuary contexts (the rest of Bulgaria, Serbia and Bosnia). This finding suggests that there is a particular trend towards a formal consumption of ornaments – many of which are the types found at Orlovo. The cultural rules shared between the communities of NE Bulgaria and the Orlovo community on the basis of close material culture similarities do not rule out the formal deposition of ornaments or their sets in hoards rather than graves, alongside ornament production. After all, the deposition of hoards in settlement contexts had a long tradition in Balkan prehistory, starting with the Early Neolithic, and with the same proportion of hoards in settlements or houses in the Neolithic as in the Copper Age (Chapman 2000, 112–3). Intriguingly, however, only a very low percentage of East Balkan tells (Karanovo VI–Gumelniţa–Kodzhadermen) and Cucuteni–Tripoye settlements contained hoards (2000: 113). The key contrast in hoards was the selection of a far wider variety of raw materials in settlement hoards than in extra-mural hoards (2000: 115–6). This characteristic of settlement hoards is also found at Orlovo, constituting an important social resource – a library of object biographies – which could be drawn upon for future giving or keeping. It is therefore difficult to separate out the twin strands of the settlement hoard – the past-oriented accumulation of enchained people, things and places and the future-oriented resource for further enchained exchange (re-distribution).

In summary, the interpretation of the surface collection at Orlovo is particularly challenging when our concern is to outline the social practices characterising the varied communities living there over two millennia or more. The total length of time over which Orlovo attracted dwelling in the Neolithic and Chalcolithic covers up to 60 human generations. There is therefore an inevitable sense of dynamic change and transformation that is particularly hard to seize in the study of an 'undated' surface collection. Nonetheless, the methodologies used have produced some reasonably convincing links between the site of Orlovo and the well-documented long-term changes occurring in the wider worlds of South East Europe. The principal conclusions of this tacking to and fro, from site to region, will be re-stated in the final chapter.

6. Conclusions

The starting point for our study was a village collector who visited the Archaeological Museum at Haskovo and sold the museum some prehistoric objects from a site in his village territory. Some 30 years later, this book is published and the name of 'Orlovo' becomes more widely known in European prehistory than the collector could ever possibly have imagined at the time of his first collecting activity all those years ago. Starting on a group of ploughed fields, the research spread out to involve two universities (Durham University (UK) and the Sv. Ivan Rilski University of Mining and Geology, Sofia, Bulgaria), three museums (the Regional Historical Museum of Haskovo, the Natural History Museum, London and the Hancock Museum, Newcastle upon Tyne) and consultations with colleagues in one Asian and several European countries.

What have we learnt about Orlovo during our recent study? Have we been successful in our primary aim and our two main objectives? Have we managed to shed light on the worlds of the Neolithic and Chalcolithic communities of the Balkans through the prism of a single site? What has our re-evaluation of the three finds categories told us in terms of their relation to on-site social practices? And can we define a coherent methodology for artifact-rich surface collections such as Orlovo? Let us tackle these three questions in order, beginning with the perspective on the Balkans as viewed from Orlovo.

What can Orlovo do for Balkan prehistory?

We wish to highlight six important advances that we suggest can be made on the basis of our study of the Orlovo assemblage.

(1) Our discussion of site types raises general issues of the definition and characterisation of site residues in terms of meaningful site categories that can be used cross-culturally and with some clear sense of formation processes. At a level removed from the primary division between tells and flat sites is the secondary distinction between one-phase flat sites and multi-period flat sites. The latter type relies on the creation and maintenance of place-value that is intermediate in strength between that of the tell, with its highly focussed core of dwelling, and the single-phase settlement where place-value necessarily had a shallow ancestry. The low ratio of built: unbuilt space on such sites enabled a diversity of outdoor practices close to the house, including gardening, high-temperature pyro-technology, animal-keeping and outdoor ceremonies – all of which provided a socio-spatial identity for the house that was paradoxically stronger than the identity formed for houses on a tell, since there were such strong constraints on what could be done outdoors on tells. While the potential for different social practices was high inside houses on tells, the opportunity for a wide variety of outdoor practices as well as indoor diversification created greater potential variability in dwelling on multi-period flat sites. Moreover, the mobility of dwelling foci on multi-period flat sites meant that it was the house rather than a particular space which featured in negotiations over power and identity. In areas with both tells and multi-period flat sites, this led to tensions between the dominant social units on which identities were focussed – the community level on the tell, the household on the flat site. This suggested differentiation is not meant to imply that there were neither communities on flat sites nor households on tells – rather that the tensions between larger corporate groups and households which were necessarily a feature of all Neolithic and Chalcolithic settlements took different forms in settlements with contrasting dominant social structures. Moreover, interactions between persons coming from settlements with these different social structures would themselves have encountered diverse forms of *habitus*, leading to inter-village misunderstandings, if not tensions. These inter-settlement variations were probably on the same level as the different uses to which villages put categorisations of the same material culture (Chapman 1996).

(2) Much has already been written about artifact biographies and their relations to personal objectification. But the notion of artifacts as 'material metaphors of inter-personal relations' (Skourtopoulou 2006), together with its more specific variant – enchained social relations – open up conceptual panoramas for the artifact-rich communities

of the Balkan Neolithic and Chalcolithic. The key aspect of this notion, which has so far been but rarely worked through with prehistoric artifact assemblages (but see Makriyalos, Greece), is its applicability to both the unique and prestigious object, such as the great gold-painted dish from grave 36 in the Varna cemetery (Eluère and Raub 1991) as much as to the quotidian and supposedly unspectacular unretouched lithic tools discarded in dwelling contexts. It is the socio-spatial scale of the inter-personal relations, not the principle of the material metaphor, which varies with the objects under discussion. In a Neolithic/Chalcolithic whose dedication to object typologies and typo-chronologies could readily be lampooned, the implementation of this approach would immediately re-connect the people and their things, the households and their neighbourhood relations, the communal cemeteries and their extended hinterlands peopled by kinsfolk, friends and enemies.

(3) The third advance, we suggest, is the borrowing from Mesoamerican processualism of Kenneth Hirth's idea of the 'gateway community'. This form of site derives from a classification of site function that cross-cuts the site typology mentioned in (1) above. The gateway community both channels exotic resources from one suite of environments, and produces exchangeable objects, with the aim of further exchange (re-distribution) to a different environmental zone. The complex topography of the Balkan Peninsula and the Pannonian Basin means that the conditions were ripe for the development of such sites, located at the interface of the lowland and upland zones, with their complementary resources (Sherratt 1972). Indeed, it is surprising that such gateway sites have not yet been identified as such.

Obvious candidates include the Late Neolithic combined tell and flat site of Polgár-Czőszhalom (Raczky *et al.* 2002; 2007) and the flat site of the same period at Sárazsadány (Kutzian 1966). Both sites are located near the junction of the Northern Mountains and the Alföld Plain. Excavations at both parts of the Czőszhalom site indicate wide-ranging connections in all directions and a large quantity of lithics for export, leading Raczky to pinpoint a major exchange role for the tell and communities in the plain. Although excavations at Sárazsadány have been limited, gridded surface collection and magnetometry by the Upper Tisza Project (Chapman *et al.* 1993) revealed a massive collection of lithic raw materials, mostly limnoquartzite and obsidian from the Zemplén Mountains, ready for onward trade into the plain. Two gateway communities can be considered for the extensive Vinča exchange networks – the Vinča–Belo Brdo tell and the group of settlements near Vršac (Chapman 1981). The Vinča tell is located on the fringe of the Pannonian Basin and at the Northern corner of the rolling Šumadija hills; copper, marble, alabaster and lithics were collected from the South for re-distribution into the plain. Located at the Western edge of the inner Western Carpathians and the

border of the Pannonian Basin, the Vršac group channelled *Spondylus* shells from the Iron Gates gorge, as well as lithics from their upland hinterland, for exchange with the plains communities. A final candidate is the Late Copper Age settlement network on the Varna Lakes (Ivanov and Bozhilova 1986), acting as a gateway for maritime Black Sea exchange routes and the products of the exploitation of local salt and inland copper. Many other candidates for this site type could well be identified with careful analysis in the coming years.

(4) The fourth, by now obvious, result concerns the quantity and diversity of production practices on a so-called 'settlement site'. The complete *chaîne opératoire* for *Spondylus* ornaments is the only such example currently known from the Neolithic and Chalcolithic of the East Balkans. This assemblage represents not only exchange of raw shells from the Aegean coast some 100 km to the South across the Rhodopes as the crow flies (160 km via the Maritsa/Meriç valley) but also local on-site ornament-making. But it is not only *Spondylus* shells whose production has been identified but also a wide range of other shell species and rock types used for ornaments, many of which with evidence of on-site making. The list includes the first known evidence for on-site making of turquoise ornaments. Such a set of production practices is consistent with the local manufacturing of a gateway community.

(5) Polished stone tools have been the object of unjustifiable neglect for far too long in Balkan prehistory – the poor relations of Neolithic material culture, even though they once, in the AD 19th century, defined what it meant to be 'Neolithic' (Lubbock 1865). There are several factors causing this situation, among them the difficulties of making straightforward typologies (Prinz 1988), the perception that the slow rate of change in the design of polished stone tools made them chronologically undiagnostic objects, and the slow development of petro-archaeology (but NB Cotoi 2000; Schléder *et al.* 2002; Szakmány and Starnini 2002; Kostov 2007). Underlying all these factors, however, is the fundamental functionalism of most Balkan prehistorians, which limits the significance of polished stone tools to shafted and mounted hand tools used to cut and scrape, whittle and gouge. The identification of a polished stone assemblage of mostly small tools, often with little wear or damage, suggests a rather different picture – the production of mainly display items with close links to the persons who made them and carried them. The notion of prestige axes is hardly new to European prehistory (Whittle 1995; Bradley and Edmonds 1993) and should not come as a surprise to Balkan prehistorians familiar with the Varna cemetery, where over 10% of the graves contained miniature trapezoidal polished stone axes similar to the Orlovo examples. What is important at Varna, Orlovo and other sites is the enchained link between artifacts, persons and their conjoined biographies.

(6) The plethora of images, mostly of fired clay and predominantly of anthropomorphs, is a defining characteristic of the Balkan Neolithic and Chalcolithic and, as such, merits further discussion. The distinctive contribution of the Orlovo figurines concerns their hybridity – the combinations of humans and animals, humans and birds and animals and birds, as well as the use of 'human' styles of decoration on animals and birds. This aspect of figurines has been downplayed in recent years, perhaps because of the way that their over-interpretation as deities swelled Marija Gimbutas' prehistoric pantheon to bursting point (Gimbutas 1974). These ambiguous and hybrid images are not only novel, utterly cultural ontological categories – without any basis in the 'natural' world – but also make available to their makers and users the transgressive power of images which cross-cut normative categories (Aldhouse-Green, M. 2004). The uncertainty that stems from the mixed categories – is it a bird or a human? – is linked to several other cultural practices – the frequent ambiguity in species represented in Early Neolithic zoomorphs – is it a bull or a ram? – and the Early Neolithic penchant for species, such as amphibians, who can colonise both earth and water (e.g. the Kardzhali and Eleshnitsa nephrite frogs: Kostov 2007). We shall return to this question in a wider reprise of the relationships between human, animals and their images (see below, p. 128). But, for now, it is worth noting the parallelism between mixed categories of the images and the varied, perhaps unique, forms of person which are particularly distinctive in the Late Copper Age. These persons were not simply farmers or herders, carpenters or copper miners but often combined skills in diverse fields to create potentially unique individuals – viz., persons with a suite of bodily skills that no-one else in the community possessed. Following the logic of materially-refracted relations of enchainment, each person with their own special set of skills and talents would have developed contrasting links to objects related to these skills, as well as to other persons with inalienable interests in such objects.

We now reverse the direction of flow, moving from a presentation of those contributions from the Orlovo assemblage to the wider horizons of the Balkan Neolithic and Chalcolithic to a discussion of the light shed on the three parts of the Orlovo assemblage by our general understanding of the Balkan Neo/Chalcolithic. This section will begin at the widest spatial scale before gradually focussing in on South East Bulgaria and the Harmanlijska valley.

The wider contexts of Orlovo

The most interesting result is the vast spatial scale over which analogies for the Orlovo objects have been identified. Complex and specific parallels have been identified in a zone stretching from the Ukraine in the East to Western Hungary in the West, Northern Greece in the South and

Northeast Hungary in the North (Fig. 5.3). The existence of such a network of interactions, which connects material culture not just from the mortuary domain but also from the settlement domain, lends credence to the very notion of a specifically 'Balkan' Neolithic – Chalcolithic phenomenon, as distinct from the Neolithic of any other part of Eurasia. When Nandris identified a 'First Temperate Neolithic' for the Early Neolithic (Nandris 1972), and Gimbutas spoke of an entity called 'Old Europe' (Gimbutas 1974), both authors were seeking to characterise this zone in terms of the shared internal similarities and contrasts to external differences. The recognition of parallels for over 50 artifact types over overlapping parts of this whole zone indicates a shared cultural tradition at a very general level, as part of the *habitus* of a very large number of individual settlements, whether farmsteads, hamlets, villages or Tripolye mega-sites (with sizes of up to 450 ha., the largest known sites in 4th millennium Europe: Videiko 2004). In terms of social practices, this finding means that a group of long-distance specialists from Western Hungary who by chance arrived at a Rhodopean village during commemorative funeral rites would not feel totally out of place in terms of the materialisation of the deceased person's social relationships.

However, the sharing of multiple strands of material culture, though impressive and significant, does not necessarily confirm the possession of similar cultural meanings for these objects. The analysis of the age/gender categories associated with identical object categories from three Late Copper Age village cemeteries from Northeast Bulgaria (Chapman 1996) showed that each village had developed different age-gender associations for each of the tool types, each of the ornament types, each of the copper objects and most of the ceramic types. Indeed, there was only one object category in over 50 types which symbolised enchained links with the same (all) age-gender categories in all three cemeteries – the carinated bowl, perhaps to be interpreted as a symbol of being human. What this result means is that communities drew upon widely shared material culture to create their own local spectrum of values and metaphors, not so much because there was no social power great enough to compel uniformity of practice but also because the differentiation of community identity had, by the Late Copper Age, become a significant issue in social networks of increasingly dense traffic. This point may help to explain, for example, the lack of analogies for the Orlovo figurines in other settlements in Southeast Bulgaria.

It is worth devoting some thought on a particularly special ornament type deposited at Orlovo – the faceted marble or shell bead. The only parallels for the Orlovo finds come from the two rich Late Copper Age cemeteries of Varna and Durankulak. At the former, alongside the hugely varied sets of gold, copper and shell ornaments, as well as tools and weapons, there is a small collection of carnelian beads, and an even smaller group of agate beads, that were buried in a restricted number of graves – 134 in Grave 43, 71 in Cenotaph Grave 4, 66 in Grave 41, 60 in Grave 35, 13 in Grave 97 (including 12 large faceted beads), eight in Grave 26, six in Graves 49, 143 and 154, four in Grave 254 and one in Grave 190 (Kostov 2007, 70–71). Carnelian beads have also been found in some 18 graves at the large Neolithic and Chalcolithic cemetery of Durankulak (Todorova 2002a; Kostov 2007, 68). There is a high correlation between the presence of carnelian beads and graves with a large number and great variety of grave goods – for burials of what Chapman *et al.* (2007) have termed 'paramounts'.

The Bulgarian gemmologist, Ruslan Kostov, has made a special study of the small group of faceted carnelian and agate barrel beads, using a gemmologist's lens to detect the fine facets that have minutely altered the shape of the barrel – facets which no previous investigator had noticed (Kostov 2007, 66–77). Varying numbers of facets have been produced on the two tapering halves of the barrel beads – 12 facets on beads from Grave 97, 16 on each half of the beads from Graves 4 and 43, as well as on carnelian beads from Durankulak (2007, fig. 26). Each of the facets has a width no greater than 3 mm and their regularity under the lens is extraordinary.

There is no evidence for a Balkan source of carnelian, nor for any kind of carnelian bead-making in this region. There are therefore at least two possibilities. First, the faceted beads may have been exchanged into the Western Black Sea region from points East, reaching the wide-ranging exchange networks connecting Varna West to Serbia, North to Moldavia, South to the Aegean, if not the Cyclades and East to Anatolia. Secondly, small lumps of carnelian may have been exchanged by the same network for production of beads by local specialists.

Evidence for local bead-making is scanty in the Greek and Balkan Neolithic and Chalcolithic, being restricted to four sites. Unfinished beads made of *Spondylus*, *Cerastoderma edule* shell and stone are known from Sitagroi (Miller, M. 2004); the complete *chaîne opératoire* for Spondylus beads has been found at Late Neolithic Dimini, Central Greece (Tsuneki 1989); bead blanks for disc beads are known from Orlovo; and there is a possible *Spondylus* shell bead workshop on the Hârşova tell, in South East Romania (Galbenu 1963; but see Chapman 2000 for another view). However, the Orlovo surface collection includes marble and *Spondylus* beads of two shapes – cylindrical and barrel – both of which have facets. The number of facets varies from four to six to eight, with rare combinations of facets and natural garland decoration. The Orlovo marble derived from local sources in the Eastern Rhodopes, not more than 25–30 km distant, while the *Spondylus* shells were brought from further afield, probably the North Aegean coastline. Thus, there is one case of the local, viz. Balkan, production of faceted beads.

Although the individual objects comprising the Orlovo surface collection are themselves undated, the complete absence of faceted beads from all prehistoric periods except the Late Chalcolithic makes a strong chronological argument for dating part of the Orlovo site to this period, even though this technological link with the faceted carnelian beads becomes somewhat circular!

Does the technological information embodied in the carnelian beads offer any solutions to the origins of the beads? The *chaîne opératoire* for carnelian beads must involve at least six stages: (1) acquisition of the raw material in the form of a roughly cylindrical lump; (2) grinding of the bead blank into a final barrel shape; (3) polishing of the barrel pre-form; (4) longitudinal perforation; (5) marking up the barrel bead for facetting; and (6) final grinding and polishing of the facets (based on Kostov 2007, 73, with modifications). Kostov's observations of the wear traces on these beads indicate that two or three different kinds of abrasive were needed – a hard abrasive for the bow-drill to make an hour-glass perforation along the long axis of the bead, a medium abrasive for the initial grinding of the raw material and pre-form, and a very fine abrasive for making the facets. Kostov (2007, 73) insists that the unidirectional traces of grinding along the edges of the facets could not have been made by manual grinding, raising the possibility of the use of some kind of simple rotary or lap wheel – something rather more complex than the rotary motion of the traditional bow-drill. The hint of rotary, lap-wheel technology perhaps strengthens the case for the import of such beads into the Varna region.

The current evidence does not allow us to differentiate between the two ideas of local vs. exotic making of faceted carnelian beads. Whichever is the case, the precision necessary for this ultimate transformation of nature into cultural order is matched only by the eyesight and hand–eye co-ordination necessary to produce the facets. The making of faceted carnelian beads surely indicates a craft specialist whose powers of creation may well have given him / her a supernatural dimension linked to brilliance; for the *only* reason for the creation of fine facets on a bead is to make the bead shine even more brightly than it does after Stage 3 polishing (Gell 1992). The issue is whether the craftsperson of supernatural skills worked in a workshop on an Oriental tell, in which case the amazing visual results are what impressed people at a dozen funerals at Varna and more at Durankulak; or whether the craft specialist was a local East Balkan resident, whose transformational skills, dexterity with bow-drill and lap-wheel were on view for his / her local community in addition to the results of their magical talents (cf. Apel 2001 for Danish Late Neolithic bifacial points).

Let us now return to the long-term aspects of the Orlovo site. It is the diachronic development of the social networks in this part of the East Balkans that helps us to understand

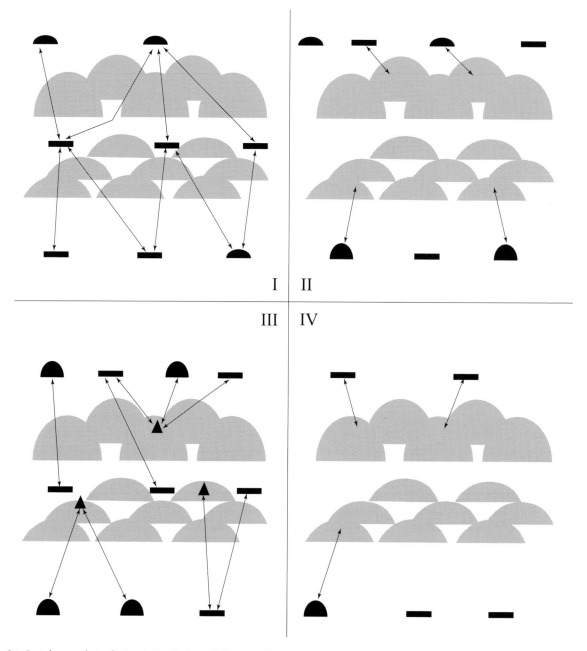

Figure 6.1. Social networks in the South East Balkans: I.Karanovo I–II; II.Karanovo III–IV–V; III. Karanovo VI; IV. post-Karanovo VI. Key: grey shapes: hills; black rectangles: flat sites; black semi-circles of varying sizes: tells; black triangle: peak sanctuaries. Drawn by Yvonne Beadnell

another dimension to the context in which Orlovo can be set (Fig. 6.1). The settlement data from the Eastern Rhodopes demonstrate the four phases of interaction between lowlands and uplands. An initial phase of widespread settlement in the Early Neolithic confirms an extensive social network criss-crossing the Eastern Rhodopes, linking Turkish and Aegean Thrace to the Upper Thracian valley across the mountains in the period 6250–5250 BC (Fig. 6.1/I). The key focus of this early extensive network for settlers in the Rhodopes and the Maritsa valley was the maintenance of

links to the ancestral settlement areas further to the South and South East. The absence of material discard from the Karanovo III, IV and V periods at any known Eastern Rhodopean site suggests a de-coupling of the lowland–upland network, with direct procurement of Rhodopean rocks for stone tools and ornaments the most probable method of acquisition in the period 5250–4750 BC (Fig. 6.1/II). The implication of this radical break was that the linkages with ancestral settlements were no longer necessary in view of the long-term tells established in South Bulgaria.

Renewed connectivity between lowland and upland is supported by Late Copper Age settlement and/or discard at a number of Eastern Rhodopean sites, including some of the peak sanctuaries such as Perperikon and Tatul. This strong and extensive social network, dated 4750–4000 BC (Fig. 6.1/III), would have been critical in the exchange of both upland and lowland objects across much of the East Balkans, including copper, marble, serpentinite, nephrite and honey-coloured flint, and possibly also graphite for pot-painting (Lestakov, P. 2004; 2006). In the fourth stage, dated to the 4th millennium BC, a second de-coupling of the lowland–upland network is seen in the Eastern Rhodopes (although not in the Central Rhodopes as at Yagodinska peshtera and Haramijska dupka: Boyadzhiev 1995). This discontinuity in inter-regional interactions can be seen in the drastic narrowing of the range of exchanged materials and objects in this millennium (Fig. 6.1/IV).

What was the impact of these four contrasting periods of interaction on the communities who occupied Orlovo? The caveat to be introduced at this stage is that the emphasis on the important role of Orlovo in phases 1 and 3, in contrast to its minimal discard in phases 2 and 4, could turn out to be a circular argument, simply confirming what is known at a much larger socio-spatial scale. However, the chronological evidence for periods of dwelling at Orlovo does not provide an exact or neat fit with this picture of exchange dynamics. There is relatively little discard – mostly figurines – that can be incontrovertibly dated to the Early Neolithic, while there are more objects with close analogies in the Karanovo IV period than in the Early Neolithic, the Karanovo III or V periods. What is clear from Orlovo is that the period with the widest number of reliable parallels is the Karanovo VI or Late Copper Age – the period of maximum exchange network connectivity across the Eastern Rhodopes. These conclusions point to the variable importance of Orlovo in the group of Harmanlijska valley sites that could each have acted as nodes in the lowland – upland network. The key period when there is a strong probability that Orlovo became a gateway community for the Eastern Rhodopes was the Late Copper Age. The community used their traditional knowledge of the upland sources of hard rocks for tools and ornaments, consolidated in the Karanovo IV period of direct procurement, as well as any links to upland settlements that had remained in the cultural memory for several centuries. The extent of Late Copper Age discard of tools, ornaments and figurines suggests a period of peak material engagement which was presumably related to the success of the gateway exchange practices. We can hardly underestimate the importance of the discovery of faceted beads made from both marble and *Spondylus* at Orlovo, whose sole parallels known to date derive from the Varna and Durankulak cemeteries. The makers would have required a graded series of abrasives and huge technical skill, as well as unusually precise near-sight, to make the tiny shell facets

on the *Spondylus* beads. The fact that these embodied skills were in very short supply explains why these enhanced exotic objects were deposited at so few sites. The greatly reduced discard dating to the 4th millennium BC at Orlovo matches the decline in lowland–upland networks though an assessment of whether as cause or effect is currently out of reach.

It is in the sense of fluctuating network participation and material discard that Orlovo may be related to another widespread phenomenon in Balkan prehistory – the presence and absence of concentrations of artifact-rich discard in certain times/places. These variations have often been related to contextual differences: thus, the absence of copper in Western Hungary in the Early Lengyel phase has been connected to the absence of extramural cemeteries and metalwork hoards, its presence in the Late Lengyel related to the presence of these two contexts of discovery and preservation (Bánffy 1995). The same may be said of the discrepancies between the large quantities of copper objects in the Late Copper Age of Northeast Bulgaria, with its rich cemeteries, and the far smaller quantities of copper in Southern Bulgaria, where burials are hardly known (for one exception, note the Dolnoslav tell: Gale *et al.* 2000). There is, however, an interesting recursive relationship between the presence of both display contexts and display objects, whereby those communities who attract differential concentrations of multiply enchained prestige goods were likely to encounter contradictions over traditional and novel forms of personhood, which may indeed require new socio-spatial domains (mortuary, agrios) for an attempt to resolve such contradictions. Conversely, the absence of display objects may have implied less of a challenge to traditional modes of value, denying the need for differentiated domains for the defusing of social tensions. If our current perspective is accepted on the significance of highly coloured and brightly shining exotica for social reproduction in all Balkan Neolithic and Chalcolithic societies (Chapman 2006; 2007; 2007a), successful participation in long-distance exchange networks was fundamental to status differentiation. But whereas some communities managed to acquire such prestige goods, many others did not, leaving a patchwork of settlements with a wider or narrower range of status differentials. In those periods in which artifact-poor discard was typical but in which there were always exceptions (e.g. Karanovo III, IV and possibly V), occasional precocious concentrations of ornaments or metalwork would signify short-term advances in production or exchange networking (e.g. Promachon–Topolnica, in the Struma valley, with its remarkably early copper finds: Koukouli-Chryssanthaki *et al.* 2007). In this sense, it is likely that the Orlovo settlement in the Early, Middle and Late Neolithic, as well as the Early Chalcolithic, provided small quantities of upland exotica to other plains communities but did not develop this exchange capacity until the Late Copper Age, when local production and upland exchange combined to bring a wide range of prestige exotica to the site – some for further exchange and some for local consumption.

But there was more to lowland–upland relations at Orlovo than relatively small numbers of shiny exotic objects. The ecological contrasts between the Familiar and the Other zones betokened differences in the likely attitudes of the inhabitants to domestic and wild animals and birds – all encountered as material representations at Orlovo. In the Early Neolithic, the use of social space at the flat site encouraged the close proximity of domestic animals and humans within a pattern of dispersed houses with much inter-house space for animal pens and gardens. The inclusion of domestic animals into Neolithic households may well be related to their depiction as zoomorphs. The wide spacing of Early Neolithic settlements in the Harmanlijska valley has a different significance – the availability of large zones for potential hunting and fishing trips between the handful of settlements. The wider pattern of Early Neolithic artifact discard in the East Balkans connects domestic dwelling to wild animals in two ways – the making of bone spoons from the metapodial of usually the aurochs (Nandris 1972a) but sometimes domestic cattle (Choyke 2007) and the use of wild boar bristle as a paintbrush to paint the fine (< 1 mm in thickness) white lines on red slipped and burnished ware surfaces. These objects would have carried the symbolism of the successful hunter from the *agrios* back into the domestic domain. The occasional hunting of aurochs, deer, boar and possibly jaguar (if that is the species shown by the felid figurine from Early Neolithic Eleshnitsa: Nikolov V. and Maslarov 1987) would have augmented the material-based 'domestication' of these large and dangerous species through the consumption of venison, wild boar or beef steak – meats of dark colour and special flavour which would have created a taste for the cuisine of the wildwood. Exchange links into the upland zone would have provided additional access to wild animals and birds living at (usually) safe distances from Early Neolithic settlements. The pleasure and prestige of upland hunting expeditions would have combined with the acquisition of exotica, and even possibly transhumance involving domestic animals, to create a highly satisfying time away from the settlement.

These practices would no doubt have continued into the Middle and Late Neolithic and the Early Copper Age but without the sociability of meeting with kinsfolk or friends from upland settlements. Such social links would have been renewed in the Late Copper Age, when a new kind of relations with wild animals began – the making of personal ornaments, worn around the neck or on costume, from red deer canines and wild boar incisors. It is currently not clear whether or not any part of the aurochs was used for personal ornaments. Nevertheless, the symbolism of the hunt and the successful hunter was materialised in these ornaments, whose discovery at Orlovo marks the first instance in prehistoric Bulgaria. The discovery of a panther figurine, as well as lion bones, at Goljamo Delchevo (Ivanov S. and Vasilev 1975, 284; Ninov 1999; cf. for the Pannonian Basin: Vörös 1987), underlines the ferocity of some of the wild animals in the Late Copper Age fauna in the East Balkans. The importance of maintaining a clear categorical division between wild from domestic must have become increasingly evident throughout the Copper Age. It is, after all, in this period when the increasing use of secondary animal products would probably have led to new aspects of human relations with domestic cattle, sheep and goats, some of which may have been materialised as zoomorphs.

This last section underlines how new kinds of relations between humans, animals and birds were just as important to the development of Neo/Chalcolithic lifeways as was the creation of different relations between people and places, as well as people and objects. The emergence of such relations can be glimpsed at Orlovo, with the assistance of insights gained from other sites and other areas in the Balkans.

Methodological advances

The nature of the circumstances of collection at Orlovo has been constantly emphasised: the surface collection targeted on special finds – axes, figurines and ornaments – to the detriment of everyday finds, such as pottery, daub and chipped stone. The strict Bulgarian rules about fieldwork involving other nationals, strictly applied by a former Director of the Institute of Archaeology, has meant that the obvious way of dating the site and understanding its spatial structure – gridded fieldwalking with total pick-up and analysis – has not been possible. This lack of basic information has turned our methodological necessities into virtues. The previous experience of two of the authors (JCC, BG) with artifact biographies and their *chaînes opératoires* confirmed the importance of close observation of each object with the aim of extracting the maximum information about all stages of the biography. Fortunately, a third author (AR) had vast experience of the two fields of study where those two authors had less experience – artifact typology and relative dating. This combined approach led to a greater depth of comparative analysis of objects from other sites, regions and countries than is perhaps normal for a post-fieldwork report. For each of the three main groups of objects, systematic comparisons were made with cognate material from all over the Balkans and the Carpathian Basin, recording the level of similarity, as well as the site location of the *comparandum* and the relevant time-range. The latter was achieved through visual estimations of calibrated ^{14}C years rather than Bayesian modelling and thus is potentially inaccurate. This led to the identification of spatial concentrations and chronological peaks in close analogies, which we used to define the chronology of the occupations at Orlovo and the range of social networks with which Orlovo was connected. We paid particular attention to those artifact types whose *comparanda* had a narrow chronological range – the equivalent of '*fossiles directrices*'.

The study of the figurines was derived from the methods developed for the equally fragmented anthropomorphic figurine assemblage from the Dolnoslav tell (Gaydarska *et al.* 2007), with the addition of the categories of zoomorphs, ornithomorphs and hybrid types and the omission of procedures for fragment re-fitting and the detailed recording of figurine breaks. Since there was only one complete figurine at Orlovo, the typological basis for the study comprised the body part. The artifact biographical approach required the recording of all the details of each object's production (size and presence of body parts, surface and core colours, surface treatment and decoration), mid-life (breaks, wear, damage and overlapping decoration) and death.

The large number of small personal ornaments perhaps suffered most from the loss of contextual information, since there was no idea of the *sets* that must have constituted the primary context for each individual ornament. We were immediately faced with this fragmentation of evidence, with no obvious mean of recovery. We were informed that the re-stringing of collections of ornaments into sets for display had no spatial or contextual basis. Thus, all of the comparative study of the ornaments relied upon data collection for each ornament type, with no possibilities of matching specific material, colour or morphological combinations. The artifact biographical approach provided the framework for the interpretation of the ornaments in terms of their production, exchange, local consumption and re-distribution.

The principal limitation to our study remains the lack of a detailed thin-sectioning programme of stone ornaments (the same applies to tools) and their potential sources. Because this major investment in time and funding could, in the end, unfortunately not be justified for a surface collection, the information that we have is limited to visual approximations to a rock type for each stone ornament (and tool) but a suite of possibilities for their origin – often a local secondary source of rocks as well as a primary outcrop in the Eastern Rhodopes.

For polished stone tools, we have developed a multi-pronged approach which seeks to integrate intrinsic aspects of the tool – its geological source, hardness, colour and capacity to shine – with those attributes of cultural choice that produced one form or a series of ever-smaller shapes – size, shape, faceting, perforation and finishing procedures. The use of absolute dimensions plotted against ratio measurements provides the opportunity to combine measures of shape and size in the same graph. This technique provides a useful way of creating an intuitive typology.

Before this project, we were well aware of the value of close and detailed observation, description and recording of each single artifact. What this project has taught at least two of the authors (JCC and BG) is the considerable value of a detailed, exhaustive comparison of the maximum range of site assemblages from as wide an area as possible. In summary, we believe that the methodologies which we have used in the investigation of an artifact-rich surface collection are widely applicable in sites of such a type, which can only be improved with detailed information on finds provenance. It could hardly be emphasised more that the potential of this collection makes excavation at the Orlovo site a high priority.

Appendix 1: Catalogue of Finds

The Figurines

Fired clay

Anthropomorphic Figurines

ARM

Inv. No. 3061/6. H: 35 mm; W: 34 mm; Th: 22 mm. Solid arm with no gender information; fragment with 2 breaks; vertical perforation through lower arm; red burnished surface with light grey core and pebble filler; no decoration.

BASE

Inv. No. 3346/7. H: 37 mm; W: 30 mm; Th: 26mm. Solid and hollow base with no gender information; fragment with 2./5 breaks; grey smoothed surface with grey core and coarse sand filler; incised and white incrusted decoration with motif 19, looks like animal's paw.

Inv. No. 3346/8. H: 19 mm; W: 40 mm; Th: 42 mm. Hollow base with no gender information; fragment with 2./4 breaks; brown to dark-grey smoothed surface with grey core with pebbles filler; no decoration; looks like clover leaf base with groove (?) possibly created post-depositionally.

Inv. No. 3346/11. H: 38 mm; W: 26 mm; Th: 26 mm. Solid base with no gender information; fragment with 2 breaks; dark-grey and red rough surface with grey core and coarse sand filler; no decoration; looks like square bottom of base; worn.

BASE/STAMP

Inv. No. 3346/10. H: 27 mm; W: 25 mm; Th: 19 mm. Solid base/stamp with no gender information; fragment with 1 break; dark-grey smoothed surface with grey core with fine sand filler; incised decoration with motif 20 on base; could be stamp, base or hat.

FOOT

Inv. No. 3061/7. H: 57 mm; W: 41 mm; Th: 35 mm. Hollow foot with no gender information; right fragment with 2 breaks; dark-grey and brown burnished surface with grey core and pebbles filler; 4 incised toes; hollow from ankle.

Inv. No. 3346/5. H: 40 mm; W: 31 mm; Th: 25 mm. Solid foot with no gender information; fragment of ankle with 1 break; grey and red rough surface with dark-grey core and pebble filler; no decoration; very worn foot.

Inv. No. 3346/9 (Plate 4g). H: 35 mm; W: 28 mm; Th: 14 mm. Solid foot with no gender information; fragment of base with 2 breaks; orange and brown burnished surface with grey core and coarse sand filler; 5 incised toes or fingers; could be anthropomorphic or zoomorphic.

Inv. No. 3346/12. H: 34 mm; W: 27 mm; Th: 35 mm. Solid foot with no gender information; fragment of lower leg and foot with 2 breaks; red partly burnished surface with brown core and fine sand filler; incised and white incrusted decoration with motif 21 on lower leg; modelled toes.

Inv. No. 3313/3. H: 34 mm; W: 18 mm; Th: 27 mm. Solid foot with no gender information; right foot and lower leg with 3 breaks; grey smoothed surface with grey core and coarse sand filler; incised decoration with motif 54 on lower leg (Fig. 2.8); probably made in two parts; worn toes that may have been incised.

Inv. No. 3279/2. H: 29 mm; W: 27 mm; Th: 27 mm. Solid foot with no gender information; foot and lower leg with 5 breaks; dark grey smoothed surface with light grey core and fine sand filler; incised decoration with motif 48 on lower leg (Fig. 2.8); vertical incised lines between legs and bottom.

Inv. No. 3279/1. H: 38 mm; W: 20 mm; Th: 29 mm. Solid foot with no gender information; foot and lower left leg with 2 breaks; dark grey smoothed surface with light grey core and coarse sand filler; incised decoration with motif 47 on outer leg (Fig. 2.8); broken along division of legs therefore made in two parts; worn around and on base of foot.

Inv. No. 3313/2. H: 38 mm; W: 20 mm; Th: 29 mm. Solid foot with no gender information; foot and lower left leg with 2 breaks; red and dark grey smoothed surface with grey core and coarse sand filler; made in two parts; four incised lines result in five toes.

Inv. No. 3279/3. H: 37 mm; W: 28 mm; Th: 35 mm. Solid foot with no gender information; foot and lower left leg with 2 breaks; red smoothed surface with grey core and coarse sand filler; incised decoration with motif 49 on back of leg (Fig. 2.8); made in two parts.

HAND

Inv. No. 3319 (Fig. 2.1a). H: 93 mm; W: 72 mm; Th: 52 mm. Hollow hand with no gender information; fragment of left fist with 2./5 breaks; red and dark-brown smoothed surface with brown core and pebble filler; incised and white incrusted decoration with motif 42 on wrist, red crusting with motif 43 on fist; 4 modelled fingers plus one thumb.

HAND/ARM

Inv. No. 3061/2 (Fig. 2.1g). H: 35 mm; W: 28 mm; Th: 17 mm. Solid hand/arm with no gender information; fragment of hand/lower arm with 1 break; brown smoothed surface with grey core and coarse sand filler; incised decoration with motif 13 on wrist; hand with 5 fingers and two bracelets incised on wrist, two perforations through hand.

HEAD

Inv. No. 2992. H: 66 mm; W: 44 mm; Th: 36 mm. Depressions representing eyes; modelled ears?; incised mouth?; modelled nose; solid head with no gender information; 20% completeness; head and neck with 3 breaks; brown and dark-grey burnished surface on back, smoothed surface on the rest, with grey core and pebble filler; the fragment probably derives from a large figure.

Inv. No. 3058/2 (Plate 4f). H: 19 mm; W: 12 mm; Th: 15 mm. Incrusted eyes; modelled nose; solid head with no gender information; head and neck with 1 break; red and brown smoothed surface with brown core and fine sand filler; incised and white incrusted decoration with motif 6 on eyes.

Inv. No. 3354/3. H: 50 mm; W: 46 mm; Th: 46 mm. Incised and white incrusted eyes; modelled ears; incised and white incrusted mouth; modelled nose; solid head with no gender information; fragment with 5 breaks; dark-grey and dark-brown burnished surface with dark-grey core and coarse sand filler; very round shape.

Inv. No. 3369/1 (Plate 4e). H: 26 mm; W: 20 mm; Th: 23 mm. Solid head with no gender information; head and neck with 2 breaks; brown rough surface with grey core and pebble filler; dotted decoration with motif 28 on top of head and neck (Fig.2.9); the dots may represent hair style, eroded face.

Inv. No. 3564. H: 30 mm; W: 18 mm; Th: 19 mm. Incised eyes; modelled nose; hollow head with no gender information; head and neck with 2 breaks; brown smoothed surface with grey core and fine sand filler; no decoration; looks like "empty" head.

Inv. No. 3520/3 (Fig. 2.1b). H: 56 mm; W: 32 mm; Th: 36 mm. Incised eyes; modelled nose; solid head with no gender information; head with 3 breaks; grey smoothed surface with grey core and coarse sand filler; incised decoration with motif 37 on hair; the hair is modelled in triangles.

Inv. No. 3307/1 (Plate 4c). H: 71 mm; W: 60 mm; Th: 42 mm. Modelled and perforated ears; modelled mouth; modelled nose; hollow head with no gender information; head with 3 breaks; grey and red smoothed surface with grey core and fine sand filler; incised diamond on top of head; mask-like head with hole at back for attachment to the body; linear wear on cheeks prevents from tracing of decoration.

Inv. No. 3262. H: 48 mm; W: 58 mm; Th: 30 mm. Incised eyes; modelled ears; incised mouth; modelled nose; solid head with no gender information; head with 3 breaks; red smoothed surface with grey core and coarse sand filler; incised and white encrusted decoration with motif 46 on cheeks; white encrusted eyes, mouth and diamonds on cheeks.

Inv. No. 3307/2 (Plate 4a). H: 45 mm; W: 38 mm; Th: 30 mm. Incised eyes; modelled and perforated ears; modelled nose; solid head with no gender information; head with 4 breaks; red smoothed surface with grey core and fine sand filler; incised and white encrusted hair line on top front of head; horizontally perforated ears; very worn back of head showing core colour.

Inv. No. 3238/2. H: 31 mm; W: 36 mm; Th: 22 mm. Plastic eyes; modelled ears; modelled nose; solid head with no gender information; head and right arm with 4 breaks; red smoothed surface with grey core and fine sand filler; incised decoration with motif 45 on right arm (Fig. 2.8); could be anthropomorphic terminal of an altar.

Inv. No. 3309 (Plate 4b). H: 43 mm; W: 34 mm; Th: 27 mm. Incised eyes; modelled ears; solid head with no gender information; head with 3 breaks; dark grey and red smoothed surface with grey core and coarse sand filler; incised decoration with motif 51 on hair (Fig. 2.9); elaborate incised coiffure.

Inv. No. 3342/7. H: 58 mm; W: 26 mm; Th: 40 mm. Modelled and incised eyes; solid head with no gender information; left fragment of head with 3 breaks; light brown smoothed surface with grey core and fine sand filler; incised and white encrusted decoration with motif 58 on face and head (Fig. 2.9); fine head with diamond eyes and incised hair line near top of head.

HEAD AND NECK

Inv. No. 3342/13. H: 30 mm; W: 18 mm; Th: 17 mm.

Incised eyes; modelled ears; modelled nose; solid head with no gender information; right side of head and neck with 2 breaks; red worn surface with grey core and coarse sand filler; no decoration; anthropomorphic head very worn all over; right side has fracture to left of nose.

Inv. No. 3280. H: 30 mm; W: 21 mm; Th: 21 mm. Modelled ears; modelled nose; solid head with no gender information; head and neck with 2 breaks; grey smoothed (now worn) surface with grey core and coarse sand filler; no decoration; small anthropomorphic head with badly worn surface, especially top of head.

Inv. No. 3342/3. H: 42 mm; W: 32 mm; Th: 23 mm. Modelled ears; modelled nose; solid head with no gender information; head and neck with 4 breaks; red and light grey smoothed surface with grey core and coarse sand filler; no decoration; very worn on top and sides.

Inv. No. 3342/1. H: 67 mm; W: 40 mm; Th: 32 mm. Incised eyes; perforated ears; vertical line as mouth; modelled nose; solid head with no gender information; head and neck with 5 breaks; dark grey and red burnished surface with grey core and coarse sand filler; incised decoration with motif 57 on hair and motif 58 under chin; very finely modelled head with good burnish.

Inv. No. 3058/3. H: 39 mm; W: 20 mm; Th: 19 mm. Modelled ears and nose; solid head with no gender information; 20% completeness; head and neck with 1 break; brown smoothed surface with grey core and coarse sand filler; no decoration; flat top of head maybe due to heavy wear.

Inv. No. 3058/5. H: 50 mm; W: 45 mm; Th: 33 mm. Solid head with no gender information; 15% completeness; head and neck with 3 breaks; brown and grey smoothed surface with grey core and fine sand filler; white incrusted right side of head; facial details erased by breakage; depression on back of head.

Inv. No. 3346/6 (Plate 4d). H: 28 mm; W: 18 mm; Th: 22 mm. Modelled nose; solid head with no gender information; head and neck with 1 break; beige smoothed surface with brown core and fine sand filler; no decoration; schematic representation like regular triangular head.

Inv. No. 3354/1. H: 35 mm; W: 45 mm; Th: 24 mm. Modelled ears and nose; solid head with no gender information; head and neck and shoulders with 2 breaks; dark-grey partly burnished surface with grey core and coarse sand filler; incised decoration with motif 24 on top of head and nose, incised and incrusted decoration with motif 25 on shoulder, red crusting with motif 26 on eyes and cheeks; could be a zoomorphic head.

Inv. No. 3354/2. H: 35 mm; W: 24 mm; Th: 29 mm. Incised eyes; modelled nose; solid head with no gender information; head and neck with 1 break; brown and dark-grey burnished surface with dark-grey core and fine sand filler; incised and white incrusted decoration with motif 27 on neck; could be a zoomorphic head or a mask.

Inv. No. 3366. H: 48 mm; W: 29 mm; Th: 47 mm. Modelled eyes and nose; modelled horns or ears; solid head with no gender information; head and neck with 4 breaks; brown burnished surface with grey core and coarse sand filler; incised and white incrusted decoration with motif 23 on neck; a finely made head.

Inv. No. 3482/2. H: 31 mm; W: 25 mm; Th: 21 mm. Modelled ears and nose; solid head with no gender information; head and neck with 1 break; brown smoothed surface with grey core and fine sand filler; incised and white incrusted decoration with motif 32 on top of head; line on top of the head may be representing a hat.

Head and torso

Inv. No. 2762. H: 78 mm; W: 48 mm; Th: 33 mm. Modelled eyes and nose; solid female head and torso; 30% completeness; head and upper torso with 7 breaks; red and brown smoothed surface with grey core and coarse sand filler; no decoration; looks like Aegean type.

Inv. No. 2999. H: 67 mm; W: 40 mm; Th: 26 mm. Modelled nose; solid head and torso with no gender information; 20% completeness; head and upper torso with 3 breaks; orange and brown burnished surface with grey core and pebble filler; no decoration; may be zoomorphic.

Inv. No. 3060. H: 41 mm; W: 26 mm; Th: 20 mm. Modelled ears and nose; pebble as mouth; solid head and torso with no gender information; 20% completeness; head and upper torso with 2 breaks; brown and red rough surface with grey core and pebble filler; no decoration; very rough surface.

Hip

Inv. No. 3482/1. H: 45 mm; W: 45 mm; Th: 33 mm. Solid hip and torso with no gender information; bottom amd legs with 3 breaks; brown burnished surface with grey core and fine sand filler; incised and white incrusted decoration with motif 31 on hip (Fig. 2.9).

Leg

Inv. No. 3346/3. H: 53 mm; W: 17 mm; Th: 20 mm. Solid leg with no gender information; right leg with 3 breaks; red and brown smoothed surface with brown core and fine sand filler; incised decoration with motif 18 all over leg (Fig. 2.8); legs made in two halves.

Inv. No. 3346/4 (Plate 4h). H: 37 mm; W: 19 mm; Th: 17 mm. Solid leg with no gender information; lower leg with 1 break; brown smoothed surface with grey core and coarse sand filler; no decoration; the base of the foot is worn; the sides of the leg are very straight, thus is difficult to say if they are made in parts.

Inv. No. 3482/3. H: 33 mm; W: 18 mm; Th: 24 mm. Solid leg with no gender information; right leg with 1 break; grey smoothed surface with grey core and fine sand filler; no decoration; vertical perforation through foot; possible reuse as pendant after fragmentation.

Inv. No. 3482/4 (Plate 3d). H: 71 mm; W: 22 mm; Th: 25 mm. Solid leg with no gender information; left leg with 3 breaks; brown smoothed surface with grey core and coarse sand filler; incised decoration with motif 33 on front and side and back of leg (Fig. 2.8); dotted decoration motif 34 on side and back of leg (Fig. 2.9).

Inv. No. 3520/7. H: 54 mm; W: 28 mm; Th: 29 mm. Solid female leg; right leg with 4 breaks; light-brown smoothed surface with grey core and fine sand filler; incised and incrusted decoration with motif 40 all over leg (Fig. 2.8); red crusted decoration motif 41 on back of leg (Fig. 2.9).

SEATED

Inv. No. 3369/3. H: 24 mm; W: 27 mm; Th: 24 mm. Solid with no gender information; torso with bottom with 4 breaks; brown smoothed surface with grey core and fine sand filler; no decoration; modelled posterior.

Inv. No. 3313/4. H: 50 mm; W: 44 mm; Th: 26 mm. Solid unsexed torso with both arms, bottom and right leg with 3 breaks; grey and light brown smoothed surface with grey core and fine sand filler; incised decoration motif 55 on torso, bottom and legs (Fig. 2.9); swollen stomach and possible pubic triangle may indicate female.

Inv. No. 3238/1 (Plate 3f). H: 43 mm; W: 39 mm; Th: 29 mm. Solid no gender information; 30% completeness; lower torso, bottom and upper legs with 4 or 5 breaks; grey and dark grey burnished/smoothed surface with grey core and coarse sand filler; incised and white incrusted decoration motif 44 on lower torso, bottom and upper legs; red crusted on bottom and upper legs (Fig. 2.9); made in two halves.

Inv. No. 3313/1. H: 36 mm; W: 33 mm; Th: 34 mm. Solid no gender information; torso with upper legs with 4 breaks; grey and brown worn surface with grey core and coarse sand filler; incised decoration motif 53 on hips and legs (Fig. 2.8); vertical line through bottom means that the figurine is made in two parts.

STANDING

Inv. No. 2743 (Fig. 2.1d). H: 75 mm; W: 43 mm; Th: 27 mm. Solid standing female; 60% completeness; torso with legs with 5 breaks; dark-grey and brown smoothed surface with grey core and pebble filler; incised decoration with motif 1 on front torso; and motif 2 on front legs, side and bottom; irregular firing.

Inv. No. 2988 (Plate 4i). H: 54 mm; W: 17 mm; Th: 12 mm. Solid standing unsexed; 80% completeness; left torso with legs with 1 break; brown smoothed surface with grey core and fine sand filler; no decoration; cf. bone figurine, modelled arms.

Inv. No. 3011/A. H: 45 mm; W: 56 mm; Th: 19 mm. Solid standing female; 30% completeness; upper torso and right arm with 5 breaks; red partly burnished surface with grey core and coarse sand filler; incised decoration with motif 10 on front torso (Fig. 2.8); heavily damaged back.

Inv. No. 3059/1. H: 43 mm; W: 45 mm; Th: 23 mm. Solid standing female; 30% completeness; torso and left arm with 3 breaks; brown smoothed surface with grey core and coarse sand filler; no decoration; half perforation in back of left arm.

Inv. No. 3059/2. H: 57 mm; W: 43 mm; Th: 25 mm. Solid standing female; 40% completeness; neck, torso and bottom with 3 breaks; brown and grey rough surface with grey core and coarse sand filler; no decoration; two perforations in each arm, pregnant belly.

Inv. No. 3061/1. H: 31 mm; W: 26 mm; Th: 26 mm. Solid standing female; 20% completeness; neck and upper torso with 4 breaks; brown and grey smoothed surface with grey core and pebble filler; no decoration; perforation in left arm.

Inv. No. 3342/4. H: 54 mm; W: 28 mm; Th: 21 mm. Solid standing with no gender information; cylindrical part (torso?) with 4 breaks; dark grey and light brown smoothed surface with grey core and coarse sand filler; no decoration; two "lugs" on either side of cylindrical leg, each has horizontal perforation (one broken).

Inv. No. 3311/1. H: 47 mm; W: 55 mm; Th: 17 mm. Solid standing female; torso with right arm with 5 breaks; dark grey smoothed surface with dark grey core and coarse sand filler; no decoration; two small breasts; horizontal perforation in each arm.

Inv. No. 3239. H: 69 mm; W: 45 mm; Th: 18 mm. Solid standing female; neck, torso and right arm with 4 breaks; dark brown and light brown burnished surface with dark brown core and coarse sand filler; no decoration; breasts and swollen stomach may indicate pregnancy.

Inv. No. 3311/3 (Plate 3c). H: 41 mm; W: 47 mm; Th: 18 mm. Solid standing female; torso with both arms with 5 breaks; grey and red smoothed surface with grey core and coarse sand filler; no decoration; both breasts broken off; under the right breast there is a hole maybe indicating an injury?; after basal torso was broken off 3 small holes were made, cf. black magic.

Inv. No. 3636. H: 48 mm; W: 36 mm; Th: 23 mm. Solid standing female; bottom and legs with 2 breaks; brown rough surface with brown core and coarse sand filler; no decoration; vertical perforation in base.

Inv. No. 3342/5. H: 32 mm; W: 24 mm; Th: 23 mm. Solid standing with no gender information; cylindrical part (torso?) with 4 breaks; light grey smoothed surface with grey core and pebble filler; no decoration; two "lugs" on either side of cylindrical leg or torso, each has horizontal perforation (one broken); one frontal projection.

Inv. No. 3310. H: 60 mm; W: 71 mm; Th: 24 mm. Solid standing female; neck, upper torso and right arm with 7 breaks; light brown burnished surface with light brown core and fine sand filler; incised decoration with motif 52 on mid torso (Fig. 2.8); very fine clay and very fine surface treatment (an exception in the collection); right breast complete, left breast broken off.

Inv. No. 3311/2. H: 38 mm; W: 54 mm; Th: 25 mm. Solid standing female; torso with both arms with 3 breaks; grey and red worn surface with grey core and coarse sand filler; no decoration; right breast complete, left breast broken off; double horizontal perforations in each arm.

Inv. No. 3313/5. H: 49 mm; W: 30 mm; Th: 26 mm. Solid standing female; right torso and right arm with 6 breaks; red and brown smoothed surface with grey core and coarse sand filler; incised decoration with motif 56 on back (Fig. 2.9); broken right breast; horizontal perforation in each arm.

Inv. No. 3261. H: 49 mm; W: 38 mm; Th: 21 mm. Solid standing female; modeled nose; head, upper torso and both arms with 2 breaks; red and dark brown smoothed surface with grey core and coarse sand filler; the head may be ornithomorphic; worn tip of nose; vertical perforation in back of head and both arms probably for suspension.

Inv. No. 3238/6. H: 61 mm; W: 28 mm; Th: 28 mm. Solid standing female; lower torso, bottom and upper legs with 3 breaks; brown and grey burnished surface with dark grey core and coarse sand filler; vertical perforation in right arm; incised and white incrusted pubic triangle; broken down middle of legs therefore made in two parts.

Inv. No. 3342/2. H: 43 mm; W: 34 mm; Th: 28 mm. Solid standing with no gender information; foot/leg; 2 breaks; dark grey and red smoothed surface with grey core and coarse sand filler; no decoration; horizontally perforated "lug" on side of foot; start of vertical incision between parts of foot.

Inv. No. 3312/2. H: 58 mm; W: 53 mm; Th: 28 mm. Solid standing unsexed; lower torso, bottom and upper legs with 3 breaks; red smoothed surface with grey core and fine sand filler; no decoration; incised line separates space between top of legs; swollen stomach maybe indicates female.

Inv. No. 3238/5. H: 40 mm; W: 43 mm; Th: 29 mm. Solid standing male with 2 breaks; dark grey and light grey smoothed surface with grey core and coarse sand filler; swelling maybe indicates penis plus beginning of a bottom.

Inv. No. 3217/2. H: 41 mm; W: 31 mm; Th: 19 mm. Solid standing female; 50% completeness; torso with 6 breaks; red smoothed surface with brown core and fine sand filler; no decoration; the neck break is very flat.

Inv. No. 3217/3 (Fig. 2.1e). H: 73 mm; W: 28 mm; Th: 31 mm. Solid standing unsexed; 35% completeness; lower left torso and left leg with 4 breaks; red rough surface with red core and coarse sand filler; incised decoration with motif 15 on lower torso (Fig. 2.9); dotted decoration motif 16 on bottom and legs.

Inv. No. 3312/1 (Plate 3a). H: 76 mm; W: 31 mm; Th: 40 mm. Solid standing unsexed; 60% completeness; torso, bottom and legs with 1 break; red and dark grey rough surface with grey core and coarse sand filler; vertical incised lines between bottom and legs; very worn and eroded surface.

Inv. No. 3344/1. H: 59 mm; W: 33 mm; Th: 18 mm. Solid standing unsexed; 60% completeness; torso with 5 breaks; dark-grey smoothed surface with brown core and coarse sand filler; no decoration.

Inv. No. 3345/1. H: 57 mm; W: 62 mm; Th: 30 mm. Solid standing female; torso and left arm with 5 breaks; red and grey smoothed surface with brown core and pebbles filler; no decoration; one vertical perforation in arm, breasts made separately.

Inv. No. 3345/2. H: 57 mm; W: 52 mm; Th: 28 mm. Solid standing unsexed; torso with bottom 5 breaks; brown and grey smoothed surface with grey core and pebble filler; incised and white incrusted decoration with motif 17 on back lower torso and bottom hips; cf. bondage on figurines, as discussed by Bailey (2006).

Inv. No. 3482/5. H: 51 mm; W: 65 mm; Th: 30 mm. Solid standing unsexed; ; upper torso and left arm with 4 breaks; brown smoothed surface with brown core and coarse sand filler; no decoration.

Inv. No. 3487. H: 52 mm; W: 45 mm; Th: 22 mm. Solid standing female; torso with legs with 3 breaks; grey smoothed surface with grey core and coarse sand filler; incised decoration with motif 35 around hips and side of leg (Fig. 2.8).

Inv. No. 3520/4. H: 35 mm; W: 43 mm; Th: 26 mm. Solid standing female; upper torso and left arm with 3 breaks; dark-grey smoothed surface with grey core and pebble filler; incised decoration with motif 38 on waist (Fig. 2.8).

Inv. No. 3520/5. H: 26 mm; W: 75 mm; Th: 26 mm. Solid/hollow standing female; upper torso with 2 breaks; brown and grey smoothed surface with dark-grey core and pebble filler; no decoration; vertical perforation in each arm.

Inv. No. 3520/6 (Plate 3g). H: 26 mm; W: 24 mm;

Th: 14 mm. Solid standing female; torso with 2 breaks; brown smoothed surface with brown core and fine sand filler; incised and white incrusted decoration with motif 39 all over torso (Figs. 2.8–9); possibly pregnant.

Inv. No. 3344/4. H: 35 mm; W: 33 mm; Th: 22 mm. Solid standing with no gender information; base with 2 breaks; brown and dark-grey burnished surface with grey core and coarse sand filler; no decoration; one vertical perforation in each arm; oblique perforation from base to stomach; standing on base like bust.

Torso
Inv. No. 2749. H: 42 mm; W: 46 mm; Th: 26 mm. Solid female torso; 30% completeness; upper torso and right arm with 3 breaks; brown smoothed surface with grey core and pebble filler; incised decoration with motif 3 on belly (Fig. 2.8).

Inv. No. 2997. H: 43 mm; W: 62 mm; Th: 20 mm. Solid female torso; 30% completeness; upper torso and upper arms with 4 breaks; red and orange smoothed surface with grey core and fine sand filler; incised decoration with motif 4 on arm.

Torso and bottom
Inv. No. 3011/C. H: 41 mm; W: 30 mm; Th: 26 mm. Solid unsexed; 20% completeness; torso and bottom with 3 breaks; grey and white rough surface with grey core and pebble filler; no decoration; prominently modelled bottom.

Torso and legs
Inv. No. 3011/B. H: 71 mm; W: 36 mm; Th: 26 mm. Solid torso with no gender information; 20% completeness; right torso and right leg with 4 breaks; grey and dark-brown smoothed surface with grey core and fine sand filler; incised decoration with motif 5 on right torso and leg (Fig. 2.9); made in two halves.

Inv. No. 3369/2. H: 22 mm; W: 14 mm; Th: 16 mm. Solid torso with no gender information; right torso and leg with 3 breaks; brown smoothed surface with brown core and coarse sand filler; incised decoration with motif 29 on hip and bottom (Fig. 2.9); dotted decoration with motif 30 on upper leg (Fig. 2.8).

Zoomorphic Figurines
Front part of a zoomorph
Inv. No. 2750 (Fig. 2.1f). H: 68 mm; W: 59 mm; Th: 53 mm. hollow with no gender information; 40% completeness; front torso, front right leg and part of neck with 3 breaks; brown smoothed surface with brown core with pebble filler; incised decoration with motif 7 on front, both sides and neck.

Head
Inv. No. 3344/3. H: 32 mm; W: 18 mm; Th: 33 mm. Solid with no gender information; fragment with 4 breaks; red and orange partly burnished surface with grey core and pebble filler; no decoration; possible zoomorphic head with upper front torso with modelled nose.

Inv. No. 3342/10. H: 37 mm; W: 18 mm; Th: 28 mm. Incised eyes; modelled ears and nose; solid with no gender information; head with 2 breaks; dark grey smoothed surface with grey core and coarse sand filler; no decoration; horns rather than ears; right horn/ear broken off.

Inv. No. 3342/12. H: 34 mm; W: 20 mm; Th: 30 mm. Modelled ears and nose; solid with no gender information; head with 2 breaks; red worn surface with red core and coarse sand filler; no decoration; horns rather than ears; very worn all over.

Inv. No. 3308/2. H: 37 mm; W: 35 mm; Th: 34 mm. Incised eyes; modelled and perforated ears; solid with no gender information; head and neck with 4 breaks; red smoothed surface with dark grey core and coarse sand filler; no decoration; vertical perforation at back of head probably for suspension.

Inv. No. 3308/1. H: 40 mm; W: 25 mm; Th: 41 mm. Modelled ears and nose; solid with no gender information; head and neck with 3 breaks; red and light grey smoothed surface with grey core and fine sand filler; incised decoration with motif 50 on top of head; scratches on both sides; horns rather than ears.

Inv. No. 3238/3. H: 30 mm; W: 21 mm; Th: 27 mm. Modelled ears and nose; solid with no gender information; head and neck with 2 breaks; light grey and red smoothed surface with grey core and fine sand filler; no decoration; antlers or horns rather than ears.

Inv. No. 3238/7. H: 48 mm; W: 30 mm; Th: 30 mm. Modelled ears and nose; solid with no gender information; head and neck with 4 breaks; brown and dark grey burnished surface with grey core and fine sand filler; no decoration; horns rather than ears.

Inv. No. 3238/4. H: 39 mm; W: 21 mm; Th: 32 mm. Modelled ears and nose; solid with no gender information; head and neck with 2 breaks; light grey and red smoothed surface with grey core and fine sand filler; no decoration; antlers or horns rather than ears.

Inv. No. 3238/8. H: 28 mm; W: 15 mm; Th: 37 mm. Modelled ears and nose; solid with no gender information; head with 2 breaks; red smoothed surface with grey core and fine sand filler; no decoration; horns rather than ears.

Hedgehog

Inv. No. 2789/2 (Fig. 2.1c). H: 21 mm; W: 29 mm; Th: 37 mm. Perforated eyes; modelled nose; solid with no gender information; head with 1 break; brown smoothed surface with grey core with pebble filler; incised decoration with motif 8 on hair on back of head; there is a hole for replacing head on body.

Ram

Inv. No. 3061/5. H: 21 mm; W: 17 mm; Th: 17 mm. Modelled ears/horns and nose; solid with no gender information; head with 2 breaks; red and brown smoothed surface with grey core with coarse sand filler; no decoration.

Inv. No. 3057 (Plate 3b). H: 73 mm; W: 22 mm; Th: 26 mm. Solid with no gender information; 80% completeness; missing are parts of all 4 legs and right ear; 5 breaks; red and brown rough surface with grey core and coarse sand filler; incised decoration with motif 11 on both sides and front.

Rabbit?

Inv. No. 3425. H: 37 mm; W: 39 mm; Th: 51 mm. Perforated eyes; modelled ears and nose; solid/hollow with no gender information; head and neck with 1 break; brown and dark-grey smoothed surface with dark-grey core with coarse sand filler; no decoration; very worn head with possible vertical incised lines.

Unidentifiable animal

Inv. No. 3061/3. H: 53 mm; W: 41 mm; Th: 43 mm. Solid with no gender information; 50% completeness; front part/neck with 4 breaks; brown and grey rough surface with grey core and coarse sand filler; no decoration; thick forelegs.

Terminal

Inv. No. 3061/4. H: 77 mm; W: 57 mm; Th: 25 mm. Modelled ears; incised mouth; modelled nose; solid with no gender information; 20% completeness; head, neck and upper torso with 2 breaks; dark-grey burnished surface with grey core and pebble filler; no decoration.

Inv. No. 3058/1. H: 38 mm; W: 32 mm; Th: 25 mm. Snapped ears; modelled nose; solid with no gender information; head and neck with 3 breaks; red smoothed surface with grey core with fine sand filler; no decoration.

Inv. No. 3058/4. H: 61 mm; W: 43 mm; Th: 42 mm. Modelled nose; solid with no gender information; head and neck with 3 breaks; light brown smoothed surface with grey core with coarse sand filler; no decoration; terminal of a large zoomorphic figurine or vessel or a head of the so-called "bird-goddess", cf. Inv. No. 3060

Inv. No. 3058/6. H: 32 mm; W: 18 mm; Th: 24 mm.

Modelled ears and nose; solid with no gender information; 20% completeness; brown smoothed surface with brown core with fine sand filler; incised decoration with motif 12 on neck; perforation through neck to body.

Inv. No. 3058/7. H: 33 mm; W: 31 mm; Th: 31 mm. Perforated eyes, modelled ears and nose; solid with no gender information; head with 2 breaks; brown and grey rough surface with grey core and coarse sand filler; no decoration; head of zoomorphic figurine or terminal of a vessel, vertical groove in back of head.

Ornithomorphic Figurine

Head and neck

Inv. No. 2789/1. H: 25 mm; W: 16 mm; Th: 31 mm. Modelled nose; solid head with no gender information; head and neck with 1 break; brown and grey partly burnished surface with brown core and fine sand filler; no decoration; perforation at back of head cf. pendant.

Inv. No. 2789/3 (Plate 3e). H: 26 mm; W: 20 mm; Th: 37 mm. depressions representing eyes; modelled ears?; modelled nose; solid head with no gender information; head and neck with 2 breaks; brown smoothed surface with brown core and pebble filler; incised decoration; perforation at back of head cf. pendant.

Inv. No. 2789/4. H: 39 mm; W: 21 mm; Th: 38 mm. Modelled ears and nose; solid head with no gender information; head and neck with 2 breaks; brown and grey burnished surface with brown core and coarse sand filler; no decoration; perforation at back of head cf. pendant.

Inv. No. 3342/6. H: 58 mm; W: 35 mm; Th: 45 mm. Modelled eyes and ears; modelled nose; hollow head with no gender information; head and neck with 4 breaks; light brown burnished surface with grey core and coarse sand filler; red crusted decoration on eyes and back of head; ? ornithomorphic terminal above rim of vessel; possible white slip under red crusting in patches.

Inv. No. 3346/1. H: 49 mm; W: 20 mm; Th: 39 mm. Perforated ears; modelled nose; solid head with no gender information; head and neck with 4 breaks; brown smoothed surface with grey core and coarse sand filler; no decoration; oblique perforation through back of head; look like the so-called "bird-goddess".

Inv. No. 3346/2. H: 34 mm; W: 15 mm; Th: 33 mm. Modelled nose; solid head with no gender information; head with 3 breaks; brown smoothed surface with grey core and coarse sand filler; no decoration.

Inv. No. 3342/9. H: 36 mm; W: 20 mm; Th: 18 mm. Incised eyes; modelled ears; modelled nose; solid head with no gender information; head and neck with 2 breaks; red worn surface with grey core and coarse sand filler; no decoration; broken back of head and worn nose.

Inv. No. 3342/11. H: 27 mm; W: 18 mm; Th: 26 mm. Modelled eyes; modelled ears; modelled nose; solid head with no gender information; head and neck with 2 breaks; red and light grey worn surface with grey core and fine sand filler; no decoration; right side broken off (removes eye, etc.); very worn all over.

Inv. No. 3342/8. H: 42 mm; W: 20 mm; Th: 22 mm. Modelled eyes; modelled nose; solid head with no gender information; head and neck with 1 break; light brown smoothed surface with red core and fine sand filler; no decoration; oblique perforation through top: back of head; horizontally perforated eyes (?? ears).

TERMINAL
Inv. No. 2998. H: 73 mm; W: 51 mm; Th: 39 mm. Modelled ears and nose; incised mouth; solid head with no gender information; 20% completeness; head, neck and upper torso with 3 breaks; brown smoothed surface with brown core and fine sand filler; no decoration; could be terminal of a pot or altar; finger impression on shoulder.

BIRD?
Inv. No. 3520/1. H: 38 mm; W: 24 mm; Th: 32 mm. Modelled ears and nose; solid with no gender information; head and neck with 4 breaks; dark-brown to light-brown partly burnished surface with grey core and coarse sand filler; no decoration; zoomorphic or ornithomorphic figurine.

Inv. No. 3520/2. H: 36 mm; W: 20 mm; Th: 32 mm. Perforated ears; modelled nose; solid with no gender information; head and neck with 4 breaks; dark-brown partly burnished surface with grey core and coarse sand filler; incised and white incrusted decoration with motif 36 on neck (Fig. 2.9); zoomorphic or ornithomorphic figurine.

Others
UNIDENTIFIABLE FRAGMENT
Inv. No. 3346/13. H: 31 mm; W: 18 mm; Th: 24 mm. Solid with no gender information; middle fragment with 3 breaks; dark-grey and red smoothed surface with grey core and pebble filler; incised and white incrusted decoration with motif 22 (Fig. 2.8).

UNIDENTIFIABLE FRAGMENT (seated anthropomorphic figurine or hind legs of zoomorphic figurine)
Inv. No. 3217/1. H: 47 mm; W: 38 mm; Th: 42 mm. Solid/hollow with no gender information; base or hind legs with 2 breaks; brown smoothed surface with grey core and coarse sand filler; incised decoration with motif 14 on ankle (Fig. 2.8).

STAND
Inv. No. 3344/2. H: 41 mm; W: 23 mm; Th: 25 mm. Solid with no gender information; base with 3 breaks; brown and dark-grey smoothed surface with grey core and pebble filler; no decoration; either 4–footed stand with unknown upper part or four-part head and neck.

Stone
Anthropomorphic Figurines
STYLIZED
Inv. No. 2731. H: 34 mm; W: 10 mm; Th: 6 mm. Green stone; eyes made by single perforation; rounded base, unsexed; complete; highly polished with facets for body parts.

Inv. No. 3353. H: 29 mm; W: 20 mm; Th: 11 mm. Limestone; rounded base, unsexed; 50% completeness; present parts: lower torso to base; lightly polished with semi-perforation for belly-button.

Inv. No. 3236. H: 43 mm; W: 12 mm; Th: 13 mm. Limestone; flat base, unsexed; 50% completeness; present parts: right side of torso and legs; straight perforation for arm hole; incised lines separate legs.

LEG
Inv. No. 3368 (Plate 8f). H: 34 mm; W: 10 mm; Th: 10 mm. Marble; polished cylindrical leg with flat base and no gender information; 20% completeness.

Inv. No. 3316/62 (Plate 8g). L: 52 mm; W: 13 mm; Th: 11 mm. Marble; oval cross-section; leg with 6 long facets; broken at hip.

Ornithomorphic Figurine
BIRD
No Inv. No.; Comes from private collection (Plate 8h). H: 130 mm; W: 89 mm; Th: 91 mm. Limestone; dimpled bird with no gender information; present parts: head and neck; very worn with brown deposit; sits off to the right; long beak cf. heron.

Shell
Anthropomorphic Figurine
STYLIZED
Inv. No. 3237. H: 33 mm; W: 12 mm; Th: 6 mm. Shell; eyes made by straight perforations; broken base, unsexed; 80% completeness; missing parts: lower left; polished with incised grooves to mark body; eyes cf. V-perforation on shell or stone button.

The Ornaments

Fired Clay

BEAD BLANK

Inv. No. 3379/36 (Fig. 3.11r). L: 3 mm; W: 9 mm; Th: 9 mm. Trapezoidal blank for disc bead with hour-glass perforation; irregular sides.

BEAD

Inv. No. 3316/54. L: 9 mm; W: 7 mm; Th: 7 mm. Irregular globular bead with straight perforation

Amphibolite

PENDANT

Inv. No. 3360/44 (Plate 6o). L: 37 mm; W: 17 mm; Th: 6mm. Irregular trapeze shape with hour-glass perforation

Black Stone (unidentified)

BEAD BLANK

Inv. No. 3050/24. L: 1 mm; W: 10 mm; Th: 10 mm. Subrectangular cross-section; irregular blank with smooth top and bottom and 5 irregular edges; straight perforation.

Coal

BEAD FRAGMENT

Inv. No. 2766 (Plate 6s). L: 19 mm; W: 15 mm; Th 7 mm. Oval cross-section; highly polished fish-shaped bead fragment with long straight perforation.

Greenstone

BEAD

Inv. No. 3050/28. L: 3 mm; W: 5 mm; Th: 5 mm. Polished disc bead with straight perforation.

Inv. No. 3379/35. L: 2 mm; W: 5 mm; Th: 5 mm. Polished disc bead with straight perforation; the greenstone may be volcanic tuff.

Inv. No. 2350/50. L: 7 mm; W: 6 mm; Th: 2 mm. Sub-rectangular bead with hour-glass perforation

BUTTON

Inv. No. 2746. L: 10 mm; W: 10 mm; Th: 5 mm. Sub-rectangular polished button with straight perforation; the greenstone may be volcanic tuff.

Jasper-like

BEAD BLANK

Inv. No. 3050/26 (Fig. 3.12a). L: 7 mm; W: 15 mm; Th: 13 mm. Trapezoidal cross-section; struck core rejuvenation flake used as bead blank with half finished perforation.

Limestone

BEAD BLANK

Inv. No. 3379/37 (Fig. 3.11q). L: 3 mm; W: 9 mm; Th: 10 mm. Sub-rectangular blank with irregular sides; not yet perforated.

Marble

BEAD

Inv. No. Private collection No 22. L: 8 mm; W: 7 mm; Th: 7 mm. Polished barrel bead with straight perforation.

Inv. No. Private collection No 1. L: 37 mm; W: 7 mm; Th: mm. Polished cylindrical bead with straight perforation.

Inv. No. Private collection No 6. L: 7 mm; W: 7 mm; Th: 7 mm. Polished cylindrical bead with straight perforation.

Inv. No. Private collection No 17. L: 36 mm; W: 6 mm; Th: 6 mm. Polished cylindrical bead with straight perforation.

Inv. No. 3316/61. L: 15 mm; W: 15 mm; Th: 6 mm. Polished ground disc bead with hour glass perforation.

Inv. No. 3316/63. L: 5 mm; W: 5 mm; Th: 5 mm. Trapezoidal kind of polished disc bead with straight perforation.

Inv. No. 3360/10 (Fig. 3.12b). L: 6 mm; W: 10 mm; Th: 10 mm. Polished disc bead with hour glass perforation.

Inv. No. 3360/38. L: 3 mm; W: 5 mm; Th: 5 mm. Lines as natural decoration; polished disc bead with straight perforation.

Inv. No. 3379/32 (Fig. 3.11n). L: 3 mm; W: 11 mm; Th: 11 mm. Polished disc bead with straight perforation.

Inv. No. Private collection No 4. L: 3 mm; W: 7 mm; Th: 7 mm. Polished disc bead with straight perforation.

Inv. No. Private collection No 5. L: 3 mm; W: 7 mm; Th: 7 mm. Polished disc bead with straight perforation.

Inv. No. Private collection No 13. L: 3 mm; W: 7 mm; Th: 7 mm. Polished disc bead with straight perforation.

Inv. No. Private collection No 14. L: 4 mm; W: 7 mm; Th: 7 mm. Polished disc bead with straight perforation.

Inv. No. Private collection No 23. L: 4 mm; W: 6 mm; Th: 6 mm. Polished disc bead with straight perforation.

Inv. No. Private collection No 24. L: 3 mm; W: 7 mm; Th: 7 mm. Polished disc bead with straight perforation.

Inv. No. Private collection No 25. L: 4 mm; W: 7 mm; Th: 7 mm. Polished disc bead with straight perforation.

Inv. No. Private collection No 26. L: 2 mm; W: 5 mm; Th: 5 mm. Polished disc bead with straight perforation.

Inv. No. Private collection No 27. L: 2 mm; W: 5 mm; Th: 5 mm. Polished disc bead with straight perforation.

Inv. No. Private collection No 28. L: 2 mm; W: 5 mm; Th: 5 mm. Polished disc bead with straight perforation.

Inv. No. Private collection No 29. L: 3 mm; W: 4 mm; Th: 4 mm. Polished disc bead with straight perforation.

Inv. No. Private collection No 30. L: 3 mm; W: 4 mm; Th: 4 mm. Polished disc bead with straight perforation.

Inv. No. Private collection No 31. L: 3 mm; W: 4 mm; Th: 4 mm. Polished disc bead with straight perforation.

Inv. No. Private collection No 34. L: 4 mm; W: 6 mm; Th: 6 mm. Polished disc bead with straight perforation.

Inv. No. Private collection No 35. L: 5 mm; W: 6 mm; Th: 6 mm. Polished disc bead with straight perforation.

Inv. No. Private collection No 36. L: 3 mm; W: 7 mm; Th: 7 mm. Polished disc bead with straight perforation.

Inv. No. Private collection No 37. L: 3 mm; W: 5 mm; Th: 5 mm. Polished disc bead with straight perforation.

Inv. No. Private collection No 38. L: 3 mm; W: 5 mm; Th: 5 mm. Polished disc bead with straight perforation.

Inv. No. Private collection No 39. L: 3 mm; W: 5 mm; Th: 5 mm. Polished disc bead with straight perforation.

Inv. No. Private collection No 41. L: 2 mm; W: 6 mm; Th: 6 mm. Polished disc bead with straight perforation.

Inv. No. Private collection No 42. L: 2 mm; W: 4 mm; Th: 4 mm. Polished disc bead with straight perforation.

Inv. No. Private collection No 43. L: 2 mm; W: 4 mm; Th: 4 mm. Polished disc bead with straight perforation.

Inv. No. Private collection No 44. L: 3 mm; W: 6 mm; Th: 6 mm. Polished disc bead with straight perforation.

Inv. No. Private collection No 46. L: 2 mm; W: 5 mm; Th: 5 mm. Polished disc bead with straight perforation.

Inv. No. Private collection No 47. L: 2 mm; W: 5 mm; Th: 5 mm. Polished disc bead with straight perforation.

Inv. No. Private collection No 48. L: 2 mm; W: 7 mm; Th: 7 mm. Polished disc bead with straight perforation.

Inv. No. Private collection No 50. L: 3 mm; W: 5 mm; Th: 5 mm. Polished disc bead with straight perforation.

Inv. No. Private collection No 51. L: 3 mm; W: 5 mm; Th: 5 mm. Polished disc bead with straight perforation.

Inv. No. Private collection No 52. L: 3 mm; W: 5 mm; Th: 5 mm. Polished disc bead with straight perforation.

Inv. No. Private collection No 53. L: 3 mm; W: 6 mm; Th: 6 mm. Polished disc bead with straight perforation.

Inv. No. Private collection No 54. L: 3 mm; W: 6 mm; Th: 6 mm. Polished disc bead with straight perforation.

Inv. No. Private collection No 55. L: 3 mm; W: 6 mm; Th: 6 mm. Polished disc bead with straight perforation.

Inv. No. Private collection No 58. L: 2 mm; W: 4 mm; Th: 4 mm. Polished disc bead with straight perforation.

Inv. No. Private collection No 59. L: 2 mm; W: 4 mm; Th: 4 mm. Polished disc bead with straight perforation.

Inv. No. Private collection No 60. L: 2 mm; W: 4 mm; Th: 4 mm. Polished disc bead with straight perforation.

Inv. No. Private collection No 61. L: 3 mm; W: 5 mm; Th: 5 mm. Polished disc bead with straight perforation.

Inv. No. Private collection No 62. L: 3 mm; W: 5 mm; Th: 5 mm. Polished disc bead with straight perforation.

Inv. No. Private collection No 63. L: 3 mm; W: 5 mm; Th: 5 mm. Polished disc bead with straight perforation.

Inv. No. Private collection No 64. L: 4 mm; W: 6 mm; Th: 6 mm. Polished disc bead with straight perforation.

Inv. No. Private collection No 65. L: 4 mm; W: 6 mm; Th: 6 mm. Polished disc bead with straight perforation.

Inv. No. Private collection No 66. L: 5 mm; W: 7 mm; Th: 7 mm. Polished disc bead with straight perforation.

Inv. No. Private collection No 3 (Plate 6cc). L: 8 mm; W: 8 mm; Th: mm. Polished faceted barrel bead with straight perforation.

Inv. No. Private collection No 8. L: 13 mm; W: 11 mm; Th: 8 mm. Polished faceted barrel bead with straight perforation.

Inv. No. Private collection No 10 (Plate 6y). L: 11 mm; W: 10 mm; Th: 10 mm. Polished faceted barrel bead with straight perforation; 8 facets on each half.

Inv. No. Private collection No 11. L: 11 mm; W: 9 mm; Th: 9 mm. Polished faceted barrel bead with straight perforation.

Inv. No. Private collection No 12. L: 10 mm; W: 9 mm; Th: 9 mm. Polished faceted barrel bead with straight perforation; 4 long facets.

Inv. No. Private collection No 15. L: 10 mm; W: 8 mm; Th: 8 mm. Polished faceted barrel bead with straight perforation; 6 facets on each half.

Inv. No. Private collection No 18 (Plate 6bb). L: 12 mm; W: 9 mm; Th: 9 mm. Polished faceted barrel bead with straight perforation.

Inv. No. Private collection No 32. L: 6 mm; W: 6 mm; Th: 6 mm. Polished faceted barrel bead with straight perforation.

Inv. No. Private collection No 33. L: 8 mm; W: 6 mm; Th: 6 mm. Polished faceted barrel bead with straight perforation.

Inv. No. Private collection No 49. L: 4 mm; W: 6 mm; Th: 6 mm. Polished faceted barrel bead with straight perforation.

Inv. No. Private collection No 57. L: 6 mm; W: 5 mm; Th: 5 mm. Polished faceted barrel bead with straight perforation; 4 facets on each side.

Inv. No. Private collection No 69. L: 12 mm; W: 9 mm; Th: 9 mm. Polished faceted barrel bead with straight perforation.

Inv. No. Private collection No 71. L: 13 mm; W: 10 mm; Th: 10 mm. Polished faceted barrel bead with straight perforation.

BUTTON
Inv. No. 3350/37 (Plate 6x). L: 12 mm; W: 12 mm; Th: 5 mm.

PENDANT
Inv. No. 3379/19 (Fig. 3.11j). L: 18 mm; W: 11 mm; Th: 3 mm. Lines as natural decoration; polished star-shaped pendant with one tip broken and central hour-glass perforation.

PENDANT FRAGMENT
Inv. No. 3350/29 (Plate 6t). L: 24 mm; W: 10 mm; Th: 4 mm. Grey deposit as natural decoration; perforated T-shaped pendant with shank broken and hour-glass perforation.

Picrolite
AXE-PENDANT
Inv. No. 3859/1 (Fig. 3.12f). L: 31 mm; W: 11 mm; Th: 3 mm. Sub-rectangular cross-section; mix of green and black as natural decoration; highly polished pendant with straight perforation, faceted sides and ends.

Serpentinite
AXE-PENDANT
Inv. No. 3858/1 (Fig. 3.11a). L: 26 mm; W: 18 mm; Th: 6 mm. Sub-rectangular cross-section; mix of green and dark-brown as natural decoration; highly polished miniature trapezoidal axe with straight perforation and facets on both sides; no wear but the edge is not sharp.

Turquoise
BEAD BLANK
Inv. No. 3316/55 (Plate 5i). L: 20 mm; W: 14 mm; Th: 4 mm. Rectangular cross-section; regular top, bottom and two edges, plus two irregular edges.

Inv. No. 3316/56. L: 14 mm; W: 7 mm; Th: 2 mm. Rectangular cross-section; regular top, bottom and two edges, plus two irregular edges; straight perforation.

Inv. No. 3316/60 (Plate 5j). L: 3 mm; W: 9 mm; Th: 9 mm. Trapezoidal cross-section; regular top and bottom and 4 irregular edges.

BEAD
Inv. No. 2991/4 (Plate 6w). L: 11 mm; W: 5 mm; Th: 5 mm. Polished cylindrical bead with straight perforation.

Inv. No. 3316/57 (Plate 5k). L: 4 mm; W: 7 mm; Th: 7 mm. Polished disc bead with straight perforation

Inv. No. 3316/58. L: 2 mm; W: 4 mm; Th: 4 mm. Polished disc bead with straight perforation.

Inv. No. 3316/59. L: 3 mm; W: 5 mm; Th: 5 mm. Unpolished disc bead with straight perforation.

Volcanic
AXE-PENDANT
Inv. No. 2779 (Plate 6m). L: 46 mm; W: 13 mm; Th: 7 mm. Plano-convex cross-section; elongated polished pendant with hour-glass perforation and side facets.

Volcanic Tuff
AXE-PENDANT
Inv. No. 2763. L: 17 mm; W: 9 mm; Th: 2 mm. Sub-rectangular cross-section; miniature trapezoidal pendant (axe-shaped) with hour-glass perforation and side facets; one chip from blade.

BEAD BLANK
Inv. No. 2781/10. L: 3 mm; W: 7 mm; Th: 7 mm. Sub-rectangular cross-section; irregular blank with smooth top and bottom and four irregular edges.

Inv. No. 3050/25. L: 3 mm; W: 7 mm; Th: 8 mm. Trapezoidal cross-section; irregular blank with smooth top and bottom and five irregular edges; straight perforation.

Inv. No. 3243/23 (Plate 5m). L: 10 mm; W: 10 mm; Th: 3 mm. Hour-glass perforation; needs thinning; unfinished sides.

Inv. No. 3243/22 (Plate 5f). L: 9 mm; W: 8 mm; Th: 4 mm. Straight perforation; more regular; unfinished sides.

Inv. No. 3243/21. L: 9 mm; W: 5 mm; Th: 3 mm. Straight perforation starting from both sides; unfinished sides.

Inv. No. 3505/15 (Fig. 3.11o). L: 3 mm; W: 10 mm; Th: 11 mm. Flat top and bottom; hour-glass perforation; unfinished sides.

Inv. No. 3862/1 (Fig. 3.12l). L: 5 mm; W: 8 mm; Th: 7 mm. Trapezoidal cross-section; struck flake; smooth base and irregular top and edges; straight perforation

BEAD

Inv. No. 2781/7. L: 3 mm; W: 8 mm; Th: 8 mm. Polished disc bead with straight perforation

Inv. No. 3243/18. L: 3 mm; W: 5 mm; Th: 5 mm. Polished disc bead with straight perforation

Inv. No. 3243/19. L: 3 mm; W: 5 mm; Th: 5 mm. Polished disc bead with straight perforation

Inv. No. 3243/20. L: 3 mm; W: 4 mm; Th: 4 mm. Polished disc bead with straight perforation

Inv. No. 3379/34. L: 2 mm; W: 5 mm; Th: 5 mm. Polished disc bead with straight perforation

Inv. No. 3862/2. L: 3 mm; W: 7 mm; Th: 7 mm. Polished disc bead with straight perforation.

BEAD FRAGMENT

Inv. No. 2781/8. L: 6 mm; W: 4 mm; Th: 4 mm. Unpolished cylindrical bead with straight perforation

Inv. No. 2781/9. L: 5 mm; W: 4 mm; Th: 4 mm. Unpolished cylindrical bead with straight perforation

Inv. No. 3050/27. L: 2 mm; W: 8 mm; Th: 4 mm. Polished disc bead with hour-glass perforation

BUTTON

Inv. No. 3243/17. L: 9 mm; W: 8 mm; Th: 8 mm. Sub-rectangular shape with straight perforation; pyramidal.

Inv. No. 3379/33. L: 3 mm; W: 8 mm; Th: 8 mm. Polished button with straight perforation

Inv. No. 3861/1. L: 7 mm; W: 7 mm; Th: 3 mm. Round polished button with straight perforation

Boar Incisor

PENDANT

Inv. No. 3050/23 (Plate 6n). L: 30 mm; W: 7 mm; Th: 5 mm. Fragment of polished pendant with straight perforation.

Inv. No. 3243/26 (Fig. 3.12e). L: 35 mm; W: 9 mm; Th: 6 mm. Dark deposit as natural decoration; worn; straight perforation; longitudinal splitting, possibly by fire.

Bone

BEAD

Inv. No. 3350/31. L: 8 mm; W: 6 mm; Th: 3 mm. Faceted bead with straight perforation; five facets.

SPLINTER

Inv. No. 3050/20. L: 16 mm.

Inv. No. 3050/21. L: 12 mm.

Inv. No. 3050/22. L: 10 mm.

Inv. No. 3243/79. L: 13 mm; W: 3 mm. Bone splinter with half perforation.

PIN

Inv. No. 3351 (Fig. 3.11f). L: 57 mm; W: 8 mm; Th: 6 mm. Oval cross-section; polished bone pin with hour-glass perforation at top.

Red Deer Canine

PENDANT

Inv. No. 3243/24 (Fig. 3.12i). L: 19 mm; W: 10 mm; Th: 7 mm. Polished pendant with straight perforation.

Inv. No. 3243/25 (Fig. 3.12h). L: 15 mm; W: 7 mm; Th: 7 mm. Fake pendant with hour-glass perforation; fine lines to indicate (pre-)molar.

Cardium

UN-WORKED SHELL

Inv. No. 3350/18 (Plate 5d). L: 31 mm.

Inv. No. 3350/19. L: 29 mm.

PERFORATED SHELL

Inv. No. 2745/1. L: 27 mm. One perforation at dorsal.

Inv. No. 2781/14. L: 28 mm. One perforation at dorsal, ventral edge broken.

Inv. No. 3243/3. L: 27 mm. One perforation at dorsal 2mm.

Inv. No. 3350/20. L: 21 mm. Grey deposit as natural decoration; one perforation at dorsal.

Inv. No. 3350/21 (Plate 6b). L: 27 mm. Grey deposit as natural decoration; one perforation at dorsal.

Inv. No. 3505/1. L: 33 mm. One perforation at dorsal.

Inv. No. 3505/2. L: 23 mm. One perforation at dorsal.

Cerithium

UN-WORKED SHELL

Inv. No. 3316/48. L: 20 mm.

HALF-FINISHED SHELL

Inv. No. 3350/27 (Plate 6c). L: 32 mm. Two irregular perforations: possibly natural.

Inv. No. 3350/28. L: 21 mm. Partly completed dorsal and ventral grinding.

Inv. No. 3505/7. L: 19 mm. Ventral remaining.

Inv. No. 3505/8. L: 20 mm. Dorsal remaining.

PERFORATED SHELL

Inv. No. 3243/14. L: 15 mm. Possible perforation

Inv. No. 3243/15. L: 15 mm. Possible perforation.

Inv. No. 3243/16. L: 13 mm. Possible perforation.

Inv. No. 2765/2. L: 19 mm. One perforation at ventral.

Inv. No. 3316/50. L: 35 mm. One perforation.

Inv. No. 3316/51. L: 40 mm. One perforation.

Inv. No. 3505/6. L: 32 mm. One perforation.

RING/EAR-RING

Inv. No. 3316/52 (Plate 6v). L: 20 mm; W: 12 mm; Th: 5 mm. Nicks and holes as natural decoration; polished object with natural shape with hole.

Conus

UN-WORKED SHELL

Inv. No. 3316/47. L: 12 mm.

Inv. No. 3316/49. L: 10 mm.

WORKED ?SHELL

Inv. No. 3379/72. L: 15 mm. Missing posterior part.

PERFORATED SHELL

Inv. No. 3224/38 (Plate 6f). L: 18 mm. Three perforations.

Inv. No. 3505/9. L: 17 mm. Ventral perforation.

Cyclope

UN-WORKED SNAIL

Inv. No. 3050/41. L: 14 mm.

Inv. No. 3316/86. L: 14 mm.

Inv. No. 3350/40. L: 15 mm.

Inv. No. 3350/41. L: 10 mm. One perforation.

Inv. No. 3350/68 (Plate 5e). L: 15 mm.

Inv. No. 3379/56. L: 11 mm.

Inv. No. 3379/57. L: 14 mm.

Inv. No. 3379/59. L: 12 mm.

WORKED ? SNAIL

Inv. No. 2991/11. L: 14 mm. Missing posterior part.

Inv. No. 2991/13. L: 14 mm. Missing posterior part.

Inv. No. 2991/14. L: 12 mm. Missing posterior part.

Inv. No. 2991/15. L: 15 mm. Missing posterior part.

Inv. No. 3050/33. L: 13 mm. Missing ventral part.

Inv. No. 3050/34. L: 13 mm. Missing ventral part.

Inv. No. 3050/36. L: 12 mm. Missing posterior part.

Inv. No. 3050/38. L: 13 mm. Missing posterior part.

Inv. No. 3050/40. L: 13 mm. Missing posterior part.

Inv. No. 3224/39. L: 11 mm. Missing posterior part.

Inv. No. 3224/49. L: 9 mm. Missing posterior part.

Inv. No. 3224/50. L: 14 mm. Missing posterior part.

Inv. No. 3316/89. L: 13 mm. Missing posterior part.

Inv. No. 3316/91. L: 13 mm. Missing posterior part.

Inv. No. 3316/93. L: 12 mm. Missing posterior part.

Inv. No. 3350/43. L: 12 mm. possibly ground.

Inv. No. 3350/47. L: 11 mm. Missing anterior part.

Inv. No. 3350/49. L: 13 mm. Possible broken decoration.

Inv. No. 3350/53. L: 13 mm. Most of dorsal and ventral removed.

Inv. No. 3350/55. L: 13 mm. Missing posterior part.

Inv. No. 3350/56. L: 11 mm. Missing ventral part.

Inv. No. 3350/57. L: 9 mm. Missing ventral part.

Inv. No. 3350/65. L: 13 mm. Missing ventral part.

Inv. No. 3350/67. L: 14 mm. Missing posterior part.

Inv. No. 3350/71. L: 15 mm. Missing anterior part.

Inv. No. 3379/63. L: 10 mm. Missing posterior part.

Inv. No. 3379/66. L: 14 mm. Missing anterior part.

HALF-FINISHED SNAIL

Inv. No. 3350/35 (Plate 6d). L: 16 mm. Posterior part is ground to produce a hole.

PERFORATED SNAIL

Inv. No. 3224/51 (Plate 6e). L: 15 mm. One perforation.

For more perforated snails, see Table A1.1 (see end of Catalogue).

Dentalium

BEAD

Inv. No. Private collection 45. L: 11 mm; W: 3 mm; Th: 3 mm.

UN-WORKED SHELL

Inv. No. 3243/51 (Plate 5b). L: 13 mm

For full list, see Table A1.2 (see end of Catalogue).

Glycymeris

UN-WORKED SHELL

Inv. No. 3224/30. L: 29 mm.

Inv. No. 3224/31. L: 16 mm.

Inv. No. 3224/28. L: 32 mm. Unworked but broken.

Inv. No. 3224/29. L: 31 mm. Unworked but broken.

Inv. No. 3243/1 (Plate 5c). L: 32 mm.

Inv. No. 3243/4. L: 13 mm.

Inv. No. 3350/22. L: 39 mm.

HALF-FINISHED SHELL

Inv. No. 3316/2 (Fig. 3.11k). L: 41 mm; W: 16 mm; Th: 5 mm. Oval cross-section; parallel lines as natural decoration; sub-rectangular working piece with round edges and some grinding and polishing (possibly for curved pendant with two perforations)

Inv. No. 3379/2. L: 26 mm; W: 22 mm; Th: 10 mm. Lines as natural decoration; perforation at dorsal; all sides cut away.

PERFORATED SHELL

Inv. No. 2765/1. L: 29 mm. Perforation at ventral.

Inv. No. 2781/11. L: 24 mm. One perforation at dorsal; ventral edge cut.

Inv. No. 2781/12. L: 22 mm. One perforation at dorsal.

Inv. No. 2781/13. L: 24 mm. One perforation at dorsal.

Inv. No. 2991/5. L: 48 mm. Lines as natural decoration; two perforations: one in dorsal, one half finished in ventral; ventral edges cut away.

Inv. No. 2991/6. L: 35 mm. One perforation at dorsal; ventral edge cut away.

Inv. No. 3050/15. L: 29 mm. One perforation at dorsal.

Inv. No. 3050/16. L: 22 mm. One perforation at dorsal.

Inv. No. 3050/17. L: 19 mm. One perforation at dorsal.

Inv. No. 3243/2. L: 18 mm. One perforation at dorsal 2mm.

Inv. No. 3316/42. L: 47 mm. Lines and pink colour as natural decoration; tiny perforation at dorsal; old sediment on inside.

Inv. No. 3316/43. L: 18 mm. Nicks and pink colour as natural decoration; one perforation at dorsal; rest of shell cut away.

Inv. No. 3316/44. L: 18 mm. Lines and pink colour as natural decoration; one perforation at dorsal.

Inv. No. 3316/45. L: 18 mm. Nicks as natural decoration; one perforation at dorsal.

Inv. No. 3316/46. L: 31 mm. Line and nicks as natural decoration; one perforation at dorsal; rest of shell cut away.

Inv. No. 3316/64. L: 46 mm. Lines, orange and red colour and grey deposit as natural decoration; one perforation at dorsal.

Inv. No. 3350/23. L: 23 mm. One perforation at dorsal.

Inv. No. 3350/24. L: 44 mm. One perforation at dorsal; broken at ventral.

Inv. No. 3350/25. L: 31 mm. Grey deposit as natural decoration; one perforation at dorsal.

Inv. No. 3379/1. L: 47 mm. Lines and parallel notches as natural decoration; one perforation at dorsal.

Inv. No. 3505/4. L: 28 mm. One perforation at dorsal.

Inv. No. 3505/5. L: 46 mm. One perforation at dorsal.

Inv. No. 3556/1 (Plate 6 i-j). L: 83 mm; weight 140gr. One partial and one complete perforation at dorsal; chipped edge at ventral.

Inv. No. 3556/2. L: 52 mm. weight 30gr. one perforation at dorsal.

Inv. No. 3556/3. L: 45 mm. One broken perforation at dorsal; chipped edge at ventral.

Inv. No. 3556/4. L: 43 mm. One perforation at dorsal.

Marginella

UN-WORKED SHELL

Inv. No. 3350/33. L: 13 mm.

Inv. No. 3350/34. L: 12 mm. Polished.

Melanoides

UN-WORKED SHELL

Inv. No. 3556/6. L: 60 mm.

HALF-FINISHED SHELL

Inv. No. 3050/18. L: 32 mm. parts of middle spiral missing.

Inv. No. 3350/26 (Fig. 3.11l). L: 42 mm; W: 26 mm; Th: 21 mm. partially ground on both anterior and posterior parts.

DEBITAGE

Inv. No. 3379/5. L: 15 mm. ventral part only; cut away.

PERFORATED SHELL

Inv. No. 2781/15. L: 31 mm; W: 26 mm; Th: 14 mm. Perforation at ventral.

Inv. No. 3050/19. L: 37 mm. One perforation at dorsal.

Inv. No. 3379/3. L: 36 mm. Two perforations.

Inv. No. 3379/4. L: 34 mm. Two perforations.

Inv. No. 3556/5. L: 45 mm. large perforation at dorsal.

Ostrea

PERFORATED SHELL

Inv. No. 3505/3 (Plate 6h). L: 26 mm. One perforation at dorsal.

Spondylus

UN-WORKED SHELL

Inv. No. 3224/1 (Plate 5a). L: 75 mm; W: 56 mm; Th: 28 mm; weight 120gr. Outer surface 70% holes and 10% lines.

HALF-FINISHED SHELL

Inv. No. 3224/2. L: 29 mm; W: 32 mm; Th: 12 mm; weight 60gr. Lines as natural decoration; outer surface 80% holes; shell cut in three ways.

Inv. No. 3224/3. L: 49 mm; W: 32 mm; Th: 11 mm. weight 60gr. Outer surface 90% holes; dorsal part with mid-section cut.

Inv. No. 3316/5. L: 32 mm; W: 24 mm; Th: 11 mm. Lines and chevrons as natural decoration; ventral part with umbo; rest of shell cut away.

Inv. No. 3316/7. L: 33 mm; W: 29 mm; Th: 5 mm. Curved cross-section; lines, holes and grey deposit as natural decoration; possibly debitage from ring reused for making pendant; perforations started from both sides but uncompleted.

Inv. No. 3316/11. L: 45 mm; W: 20 mm; Th: 14 mm. Lines, holes and garlands as natural decoration; thick dorsal part of shell with two unfinished perforations.

Inv. No. 3350/3 (Plate 5g). L: 30 mm; W: 19 mm; Th: 11 mm. Possibly half finished thick bracelet; broken in manufacture; natural cracks.

PERFORATED SHELL

Inv. No. 2991/1 (Plate 5h). L: 33 mm; W: 20 mm; Th: 9 mm. Lines, holes and cracks as natural decoration; dorsal and medial part of shell with 9 mm circular part removed from middle; hour-glass perforation through dorsal possibly to make button or bead blank.

PERFORATED SHELL FRAGMENT

Inv. No. 3379/6. L: 20 mm; W: 19 mm; Th: 6 mm. Parallel lines as natural decoration; hour-glass perforation near edge.

APPLIQUE

Inv. No. 3360/35 (Plate 6g and Fig. 3.11p). L: 9 mm; W: 9 mm; Th: 3 mm. Lines and brown deposit as natural decoration; rectangular applique with hour-glass perforation.

BEAD BLANK

Inv. No. 2781/3 (Plate 5l). L: 3 mm; W: 9 mm; Th: 10 mm. Sub-rectangular cross-section; lines, cracks, red colour and grey deposit as natural decoration; irregular blank with smooth top and bottom and four irregular edges; reused from either pendant or pendant reused from ring.

Inv. No. 2781/4. L: 2 mm; W: 10 mm; Th: 10 mm. Sub-rectangular cross-section; lines, cracks and red colour as natural decoration; irregular blank with smooth top and bottom and four irregular edges; reused from either pendant or pendant reused from ring.

Inv. No. 2991/3. L: 3 mm; W: 9 mm; Th: 9 mm. Lines, holes and grey deposit as natural decoration; irregular blank; regular top and bottom and four partly ground edges; hour-glass perforation.

Inv. No. 3243/40. L: 4 mm; W: 10 mm; Th: 10 mm. Lines as natural decoration; possibly for disc bead; straight perforation, polished; lower face smooth; edges and upper face unfinished.

Inv. No. 3379/16 (Fig. 3.11m). L: 11 mm; W: 10 mm; Th: 4 mm. Parallel lines as natural decoration; irregular half finished bead with central straight perforation and irregular edges.

BEAD

Inv. No. 2764/1 (Fig. 3.12c). L: 19 mm; W: 12 mm; Th: 6 mm. Triangular cross-section; complex lines as natural decoration; flattened polished bead with straight perforation

Inv. No. 2781/5. L: 4 mm; W: 5 mm; Th: 5 mm. Polished disc bead with straight perforation

Inv. No. 2781/6. L: 1 mm; W: 4 mm; Th: 4 mm. Polished disc bead with straight perforation.

Inv. No. 2991/2. L: 6 mm; W: 5 mm; Th: 5 mm. Lines and holes as natural decoration; polished bead with hour-glass perforation.

Inv. No. 3050/10. L: 28 mm; W: 7 mm; Th: 7 mm. Lines, holes, cracks and brown deposit as natural decoration; polished cylindrical bead with straight perforation.

Inv. No. 3050/12. L: 3 mm; W: 9 mm; Th: 9 mm. Polished disc bead with straight perforation.

Inv. No. 3050/13. L: 3 mm; W: 5 mm; Th: 5 mm. Lines and a crack as natural decoration; polished disc bead with straight perforation.

Inv. No. 3050/14. L: 1 mm; W: 6 mm; Th: 6 mm. Lines as natural decoration; polished disc bead with straight perforation.

Inv. No. 3243/28. L: 12 mm; W: 12 mm; Th: 9 mm. Garlands as natural decoration; polished barrel bead with straight perforation.

Inv. No. 3243/39. L: 5 mm; W: 5 mm; Th: 5 mm. Complex lines as natural decoration; polished barrel bead with straight perforation.

Inv. No. 3243/32. L: 20 mm; W: 9 mm; Th: 9 mm. Cylindrical bead with straight perforation; first polished, then burnt, then grey deposit.

Inv. No. 3243/33. L: 25 mm; W: 7 mm; Th: 7 mm. Lines as natural decoration; polished cylindrical bead with straight perforation.

Inv. No. 3243/34. L: 18 mm; W: 7 mm; Th: 7 mm. Polished cylindrical bead with straight perforation.

Inv. No. 3243/35. L: 17 mm; W: 7 mm; Th: 7 mm. Lines and a crack as natural decoration; polished cylindrical bead with straight perforation.

Inv. No. 3243/36. L: 7 mm; W: 5 mm; Th: 5 mm. Lines and holes as natural decoration; polished cylindrical bead with hour-glass perforation.

Inv. No. 3243/29. L: 7 mm; W: 9 mm; Th: 9 mm. Complex lines as natural decoration; polished disc bead with straight perforation.

Inv. No. 3243/41. L: 5 mm; W: 7 mm; Th: 7 mm. Polished disc bead with straight perforation.

Inv. No. 3243/42. L: 4 mm; W: 7 mm; Th: 7 mm. Lines as natural decoration; polished disc bead with straight perforation.

Inv. No. 3243/43. L: 3 mm; W: 6 mm; Th: 6 mm. Lines as natural decoration; polished disc bead with straight perforation.

Inv. No. 3243/44. L: 2 mm; W: 6 mm; Th: 6 mm. Lines as natural decoration; polished disc bead with straight perforation.

Inv. No. 3243/45. L: 2 mm; W: 5 mm; Th: 5 mm. Lines as natural decoration; polished disc bead with straight perforation.

Inv. No. 3243/46. L: 2 mm; W: 5 mm; Th: 5 mm. Polished disc bead with straight perforation.

Inv. No. 3243/47. L: 2 mm; W: 4 mm; Th: 4 mm. Lines as natural decoration; polished disc bead with straight perforation.

Inv. No. 3243/48. L: 1 mm; W: 4 mm; Th: 4 mm. Polished disc bead with straight perforation.

Inv. No. 3243/49. L: 1 mm; W: 4 mm; Th: 4 mm. Lines as natural decoration; polished disc bead with straight perforation.

Inv. No. 3243/37. L: 6 mm; W: 5 mm; Th: 5 mm. Polished faceted barrel bead with straight perforation.

Inv. No. 3243/38. L: 6 mm; W: 5 mm; Th: 5 mm. Garlands as natural decoration; polished faceted barrel bead with straight perforation; garland symmetrical to long axis.

Inv. No. 3316/17. L: 14 mm; W: 10 mm; Th: 10 mm. Lines and holes as natural decoration; polished barrel bead with hour-glass perforation.

Inv. No. 3316/22 (Fig. 3.11b). L: 7 mm; W: 8 mm; Th: 8 mm. Lines and brown deposit as natural decoration; polished disc bead with hour-glass perforation.

Inv. No. 3316/18 (Plate 6q). L: 14 mm; W: 5 mm; Th: 5 mm. Complex lines as natural decoration; unpolished cylindrical bead with straight perforation; unpolished because of fine pattern.

Inv. No. 3316/19. L: 7 mm; W: 7 mm; Th: 7 mm. Polished cylindrical bead with hour-glass perforation.

Inv. No. 3316/20. L: 12 mm; W: 4 mm; Th: 4 mm. Lines and holes as natural decoration; polished cylindrical bead with straight perforation.

Inv. No. 3316/21. L: 13 mm; W: 6 mm; Th: 6 mm. Complex lines as natural decoration; unpolished cylindrical bead with straight perforation.

Inv. No. 3316/23. L: 2 mm; W: 6 mm; Th: 5 mm. Lines as natural decoration; unpolished disc bead with hour-glass perforation.

Inv. No. 3316/24. L: 3 mm; W: 5 mm; Th: 5 mm. Trapezoidal cross-section; lines as natural decoration; unpolished disc bead with hour-glass perforation.

Inv. No. 3316/25. L: 5 mm; W: 7 mm; Th: 7 mm. Lines as natural decoration; unpolished disc bead with straight perforation.

Inv. No. 3316/26. L: 2 mm; W: 4 mm; Th: 4 mm. Polished disc bead with straight perforation.

Inv. No. 3316/27. L: 3 mm; W: 5 mm; Th: 5 mm. Lines and grey deposit as natural decoration; unpolished disc bead with straight perforation.

Inv. No. 3316/28. L: 2 mm; W: 5 mm; Th: 5 mm. Polished disc bead with hour-glass perforation.

Inv. No. 3316/29. L: 3 mm; W: 6 mm; Th: 6 mm. Lines as natural decoration; unpolished disc bead with straight perforation.

Inv. No. 3316/30. L: 2 mm; W: 4 mm; Th: 4 mm. Lines as natural decoration; unpolished disc bead with straight perforation.

Inv. No. 3316/31. L: 4 mm; W: 5 mm; Th: 5 mm. Lines and cracks as natural decoration; unpolished disc bead with hour-glass perforation.

Inv. No. 3360/9 (Fig. 3.11e). L: 7 mm; W: 5 mm; Th: 5 mm. Lines and grey deposit as natural decoration; polished disc bead with straight perforation.

Inv. No. 3360/43. L: 18 mm; W: 7 mm; Th: 7 mm. Garlands as natural decoration; unpolished bead with straight perforation.

Inv. No. 3360/4 (Fig. 3.12k). L: 8 mm; W: 5 mm; Th: 5 mm. Lines as natural decoration (on side); polished cylindrical bead with straight perforation.

Inv. No. 3360/5. L: 9 mm; W: 9 mm; Th: 9 mm. Lines and grey deposit as natural decoration; polished cylindrical bead with straight perforation.

Inv. No. 3360/6. L: 5 mm; W: 5 mm; Th: 5 mm. Lines and grey deposit as natural decoration; polished cylindrical bead with straight perforation.

Inv. No. 3360/11. L:23 mm; W: 8 mm; Th: 8 mm. Lines and grey deposit as natural decoration; partly polished cylindrical/ tubular bead with straight perforation.

Inv. No. 3360/42 (Plate 6p). L: 11 mm; W: 6 mm; Th: 6 mm. Lines as natural decoration; polished cylindrical bead with straight perforation.

Inv. No. 3360/3. L: 6 mm; W: 6 mm; Th: 3 mm. Lines as natural decoration; disc bead with hour-glass perforation.

Inv. No. 3360/7. L: 4 mm; W: 6 mm; Th: 6 mm. Lines as natural decoration; polished disc bead with straight perforation.

Inv. No. 3360/8. L: 2 mm; W: 4 mm; Th: 4 mm. Lines and grey deposit as natural decoration; polished disc bead with straight perforation.

Inv. No. 3360/12. L: 3 mm; W: 5 mm; Th:5 mm. Lines as natural decoration; polished disc bead with straight perforation.

Inv. No. 3360/32. L: 3 mm; W: 4 mm; Th: 4 mm. Lines as natural decoration; polished disc bead with straight perforation.

Inv. No. 3360/33. L: 2 mm; W: 3 mm; Th: 3 mm. Lines as natural decoration; polished disc bead with straight perforation.

Inv. No. 3360/36. L: 3 mm; W: 5 mm; Th: 5 mm. Lines as natural decoration; polished disc bead with straight perforation.

Inv. No. 3360/39. L: 2 mm; W: 3 mm; Th: 3 mm. Lines and holes as natural decoration; polished disc bead with straight perforation.

Inv. No. 3360/40. L: 5 mm; W: 7 mm; Th: 7 mm. Lines as natural decoration; polished disc bead with trapezoidal tendencies; straight perforation.

Inv. No. 3360/41. L: 2 mm; W: 4 mm; Th: 4 mm. Lines as natural decoration; polished disc bead with straight perforation.

Inv. No. 3360/37 (Plate 6r). L: 4 mm; W: 4 mm; Th: 4 mm. Lines as natural decoration; sub-rectangular bead with big round perforation.

Inv. No. 3379/22. L: 11 mm; W: 6 mm; Th: 6 mm. Lines and holes as natural decoration; polished cylindrical bead with straight perforation.

Inv. No. 3379/24. L: 3 mm; W: 7 mm; Th: 7 mm. Lines and holes as natural decoration; disc bead with straight perforation; chipped dorsally.

Inv. No. 3379/25. L: 3 mm; W: 5 mm; Th: 5 mm. Lines as natural decoration; polished disc bead with straight perforation.

Inv. No. 3379/26. L: 2 mm; W: 5 mm; Th: 5 mm. Lines as natural decoration; polished disc bead with straight perforation.

Inv. No. 3379/27. L: 3 mm; W: 6 mm; Th: 6 mm. Lines and holes as natural decoration; polished disc bead with straight perforation.

Inv. No. 3379/28. L: 2 mm; W: 5 mm; Th: 5 mm. Lines and grey deposit as natural decoration; polished disc bead with straight perforation.

Inv. No. 3379/29. L: 3 mm; W: 4 mm; Th: 4 mm. Lines as natural decoration; polished disc bead with straight perforation.

Inv. No. 3379/30. L: 1 mm; W: 4 mm; Th: 4 mm. Lines as natural decoration; polished disc bead with straight perforation.

Inv. No. 3379/31. L: 1 mm; W: 3 mm; Th: 3 mm. Polished disc bead with straight perforation.

Inv. No. 3379/21. L: 8 mm; W: 6 mm; Th: 6 mm. Holes as natural decoration; polished barrel faceted bead with hour-glass perforation.

Inv. No. 3505/13. L: 3 mm; W: 7 mm; Th: 7 mm. Lines as natural decoration; polished disc bead with straight perforation.

Inv. No. 3505/14. L: 3 mm; W: 6 mm; Th: 6 mm. Lines and dark deposit as natural decoration; disc bead with straight perforation; top half is white, bottom half is grey.

Inv. No. 3862/3. L: 3 mm; W: 7 mm; Th: 7 mm. Trapezoidal cross-section; lines and grey deposit as natural decoration; polished disc bead with straight perforation.

Inv. No. 3862/4. L: 2 mm; W: 6 mm; Th: 6 mm. Polished disc bead with hour-glass perforation

Inv. No. Private collection No. 40. L: 6 mm; W: 6 mm; Th: 6 mm. Lines and holes as natural decoration; polished barrel bead with straight perforation.

Inv. No. Private collection No. 9. L: 33 mm; W: 7 mm; Th: 7 mm. Garlands and complex lines as natural decoration; polished cylindrical bead with straight perforation.

Inv. No. Private collection No. 2. L: 13 mm; W: 8 mm; Th: 8 mm. Lines, cracks and holes as natural decoration; polished faceted barrel bead with straight perforation.

Inv. No. Private collection No. 7 (Plate 6z). L: 13 mm; W: 8 mm; Th: 8 mm. Lines and holes as natural decoration; polished faceted barrel bead with straight perforation.

Inv. No. Private collection No. 16. L: 11 mm; W: 8 mm; Th: 8 mm. Lines and holes as natural decoration; polished faceted barrel bead with straight perforation.

Inv. No. Private collection No. 19. L: 9 mm; W: 8 mm; Th: 8 mm. Lines and holes as natural decoration; partly polished faceted barrel bead with straight perforation.

Inv. No. Private collection No. 20 (Plate 6dd). L: 12 mm; W: 8 mm; Th: 8 mm. Garlands as natural decoration; polished faceted barrel bead with straight perforation; garland is asymmetrical to facet.

Inv. No. Private collection No. 21 (Plate 6aa). L: 9 mm; W: 6 mm; Th: 6 mm. Garlands as natural decoration; partly polished faceted barrel bead with straight perforation.

Inv. No. Private collection No. 56. L: 8 mm; W: 7 mm; Th: 7 mm. Lines and holes as natural decoration; polished faceted barrel bead with straight perforation.

Inv. No. Private collection No. 67. L: 9 mm; W: 7 mm; Th: 7 mm. Lines and holes as natural decoration; polished faceted barrel bead with straight perforation

Inv. No. Private collection No. 68 (Plate 6ee). L: 7 mm; W: 7 mm; Th: 7 mm. Garland as natural decoration; polished faceted barrel bead with straight perforation.

Inv. No. Private collection No. 70. L: 9 mm; W: 8 mm; Th: 8 mm. Lines and garlands as natural decoration; polished faceted barrel bead with straight perforation; garlands are symmetrical to facet.

Bead fragment

Inv. No. 3316/32. L: 7 mm; W: 8 mm; Th: 8 mm. Lines and brown deposit as natural decoration; polished barrel faceted bead with hour-glass perforation.

Inv. No. 3316/33. L: 5 mm. Lines as natural decoration; unpolished cylindrical bead.

Inv. No. 3316/34. L: 9 mm; W: 7 mm; Th: 7 mm. Lines and holes as natural decoration; polished cylindrical bead with straight perforation.

Inv. No. 3316/35. L: 7 mm; W: 6 mm; Th: 6 mm. Lines and grey deposit as natural decoration; polished cylindrical bead with hour-glass perforation.

Inv. No. 3316/36. L: 10 mm; W: 9 mm; Th: 9 mm. Lines as natural decoration; polished barrel bead with straight perforation.

Inv. No. 3316/37. L: 7 mm; W: 7 mm; Th: 7 mm. Lines as natural decoration; unpolished barrel bead with straight perforation.

Inv. No. 3316/38. L: 5 mm; W: 5 mm; Th: 5 mm. Lines as natural decoration; unpolished cylindrical bead with straight perforation.

Inv. No. 3316/39. L: 4 mm; W: 7 mm; Th: 7 mm. Lines as natural decoration; polished disc bead with straight perforation.

Inv. No. 3379/17. L: 8 mm; W: 6 mm; Th: 6 mm. Lines and a hole as natural decoration; polished cylindrical bead, possibly broken during making.

Inv. No. 3379/20. L: 21 mm; W: 6 mm; Th: 6 mm. middle fragment of polished cylindrical bead with straight perforation.

Inv. No. 3505/12. L: 9 mm; W: 8 mm; Th: 8 mm. Lines and a hole as natural decoration; polished cylindrical bead with large straight perforation.

Button

Inv. No. 3243/27. L: 11 mm; W: 11 mm; Th: 7 mm. Lines as natural decoration; polished button with straight perforation.

Inv. No. 3316/40. L: 10 mm; W: 10 mm; Th: 4 mm. Lines and grey deposit as natural decoration; round polished button with V-perforation

Inv. No. 3316/41. L: 9 mm; W: 9 mm; Th: 4 mm. Lines as natural decoration; round polished button with broken straight perforations at back.

Inv. No. 3350/38 (Fig. 3.11d). L: 8 mm; W: 8 mm; Th: 4 mm. Round polished button.

Inv. No. 3360/2. L: 10 mm; W: 9 mm; Th: 4 mm. Oval cross-section; lines and grey deposit as natural decoration; oval unpolished button.

Inv. No. 3360/34. L: 9 mm; W: 9 mm; Th: 5 mm. Lines as natural decoration; circular button with straight perforation.

Inv. No. 3379/23. L: 7 mm; W: 7 mm; Th: 3 mm. Lines as natural decoration; oval button with straight perforation.

PENDANT

Inv. No. 2781/1. L: 22 mm; W: 18 mm; Th: 4 mm. Sub-rectangular cross-section; complex lines and notches as natural decoration; middle fragment of ring, reused as pendant with straight perforation and deepening of natural notches.

Inv. No. 3050/9 (Plate 6l). L: 24 mm; W: 24 mm; Th: 3 mm. Sub-rectangular cross-section; lines, red colour and grey deposit as natural decoration; attempt at making clover leaf pendant; flake detached from one edge through hinge fracture

Inv. No. 3050/11 (Plate 6k). L: 28 mm; W: 11 mm; Th: 3 mm. Sub-rectangular cross-section; lines, red colour and grey deposit as natural decoration; middle fragment of polished ring, reused as pendant with straight perforation.

Inv. No. 3243/31 (Fig. 3.12j). L: 25 mm; W: 25 mm; Th: 4 mm. PC cross-section; lines and holes as natural decoration; four-leafed clover pendant with central straight perforation.

Inv. No. 3316/9. L: 19 mm; W: 10 mm; Th: 10 mm. Circular cross-section; complex lines, holes and grey deposit as natural decoration; terminal fragment of ring, reused as polished pendant with hour-glass perforation.

Inv. No. 3360/1. L: 120 mm; W: 9 mm; Th: 7 mm. Irregular cross-section; lines and holes as natural decoration; T-shaped pendant; possible incised nick on right edge with perforation from back; partly polished.

Inv. No. 3379/9. L: 43 mm; W: 14 mm; Th: 7 mm; inner diameter 11 mm. Faceted oval cross-section; lines, red colour and garlands as natural decoration; middle fragment of ring, reused as pendant with hour-glass perforation; grey deposit over striking red colour.

Inv. No. 3559/1. L: 61 mm; W: 14 mm; Th: 11 mm; inner diameter 5 mm. Oval cross-section; lines, holes and grey deposit as natural decoration; terminal fragment of polished bracelet, reused as pendant with two hour-glass perforations at each end.

Inv. No. 3559/2. L: 30 mm; W: 8 mm; Th: 8 mm; inner diameter 5 mm. Sub-rectangular cross-section; complex lines and grey deposit as natural decoration; terminal fragment of un-polished bracelet, reused as pendant with hour-glass perforation at dorsal.

Inv. No. 3860/1 (Fig. 3.12m). L: 38 mm; W: 13 mm; Th: 3 mm. Oval cross-section; parallel lines and brown and grey deposit as natural decoration; polished curved oval pendant, reused from a ring with hour-glass perforation at ventral.

PENDANT FRAGMENT

Inv. No. 3224/25. L: 25 mm; W:11 mm; Th: 7 mm; inner diameter 6 mm. Sub-rectangular cross-section; hinge hole, garlands and holes as natural decoration; middle fragment of polished ring; hinge holes expanded to make two perforations for pendant.

Inv. No. 3224/26 (Fig. 3.12g). L: 49 mm; W: 11 mm; Th: 7 mm; inner diameter 12 mm. Plano-convex cross-section; garlands, complex lines and holes as natural decoration; middle fragment of polished ring with two new hour-glass perforations for pendant.

Inv. No. 3224/27. L: 20 mm; W:6 mm; Th: 6 mm; inner diameter 4 mm. Sub-triangular cross-section; lines, perforations and red colour as natural decoration; middle fragment of polished ring with one new hour-glass perforation for pendant.

Inv. No. 3350/15 (Plate 6u). L: 18 mm; W:11 mm; Th: 3 mm. Sub-rectangular cross-section; lines as natural decoration; fragment of perforated pendant with indentations; probably clover-leaf pendant.

Inv. No. 3379/15. L: 14 mm; W:8 mm; Th: 4 mm. Sub-rectangular cross-section; lines as natural decoration; irregular pendant broken across hour-glass perforation.

PIN FRAGMENT

Inv. No. 3350/17 (Fig. 3.11c). L: 22 mm; W: 7 mm; Th: 7 mm. Round cross-section; lines and cracks as natural decoration; middle section of pin shank with one groove.

PLAQUE FRAGMENT

Inv. No. 3350/1 (Fig. 3.11g). L: 26 mm; W: 19 mm; Th: 7 mm. Sub-rectangular cross-section; garlands as natural decoration; polished.

RING FRAGMENT

Inv. No. 2781/2. L: 24 mm; W: 8 mm; Th: 5 mm; inner diameter 4 cm. Sub-rectangular cross-section; nicks, lines and a notch as natural decoration; middle fragment of polished ring; perforations at dorsal.

Inv. No. 3050/1. L: 22 mm; W: 22 mm; Th: 6 mm; inner diameter 4 cm. Sub-rectangular cross-section; depression, holes and a garland as natural decoration; middle fragment of partly polished ring.

Inv. No. 3050/2. L: 31 mm; W: 8 mm; Th: 6 mm; inner diameter 9 cm. Trapezoidal cross-section; lines, holes, cracks and brown deposit as natural decoration; middle fragment of partly polished ring.

Inv. No. 3050/3. L: 40 mm; W: 7 mm; Th: 3 mm; inner diameter 5 cm. Oval cross-section; parallel lines and brown deposit as natural decoration; middle fragment of polished ring; polish removed most of lines.

Inv. No. 3050/4. L: 33 mm; W: 11 mm; Th: 8 mm; inner diameter 9 cm. Sub-rectangular cross-section; complex lines, holes, cracks and grey deposit as natural decoration; middle fragment of partly polished ring.

Inv. No. 3050/5. L: 30 mm; W: 9 mm; Th: 5 mm; inner diameter 5 cm. Sub-rectangular cross-section; lines, grooves and grey deposit as natural decoration; middle fragment of partly polished ring.

Inv. No. 3050/6. L: 33 mm; W: 7 mm; Th: 7 mm; inner diameter 3 cm. Sub-rectangular cross-section; holes, lines, grooves and cracks as natural decoration; middle fragment of polished ring; full perforation of dorsal, plus one partial perforation, possibly still being worked.

Inv. No. 3050/7. L: 25 mm; W: 11 mm; Th: 5 mm; inner diameter 10 cm. Oval cross-section; lines, holes, cracks and brown deposit as natural decoration; middle fragment of partly polished ring; faceted ring.

Inv. No. 3050/8. L: 18 mm; W: 8 mm; Th: 4 mm; inner diameter 8 cm. Oval cross-section; lines, holes, cracks and brown deposit as natural decoration; middle fragment of partly polished ring.

Inv. No. 3224/4. L: 51 mm; W: 28 mm; Th: 7 mm; inner diameter 13 cm. Oval cross-section; lines and brown deposit as natural decoration; middle fragment of ring with two broken perforations on right end.

Inv. No. 3224/5. L: 40 mm; W: 11 mm; Th: 10 mm; inner diameter 4 cm. Sub-rectangular cross-section; lines, red colour and grey deposit as natural decoration; middle fragment of polished ring with three notches.

Inv. No. 3224/6. L: 51 mm; W: 8 mm; Th: 11 mm; inner diameter 7 cm. Rectangular cross-section; lines, holes and grooves as natural decoration; middle fragment of polished ring.

Inv. No. 3224/7. L: 32 mm; W: 7 mm; Th: 6 mm; inner diameter 8 cm. Sub-rectangular cross-section; lines as natural decoration; middle fragment of polished ring.

Inv. No. 3224/8. L: 38 mm; W: 10 mm; Th: 4 mm; inner diameter 16 cm. Oval cross-section; lines, red colour and garlands as natural decoration; middle fragment of faceted ring.

Inv. No. 3224/9. L: 30 mm; W: 9 mm; Th: 5 mm; inner diameter 7 cm. Oval cross-section; lines and a hole as natural decoration; middle fragment of polished ring.

Inv. No. 3224/10. L: 29 mm; W: 9 mm; Th: 4 mm; inner diameter 6 cm. Oval cross-section; complex lines and parallel notches as natural decoration; middle fragment of polished ring.

Inv. No. 3224/11. L: 31 mm; W: 8 mm; Th: 9 mm; inner diameter 9 cm. Sub-rectangular cross-section; lines and brown deposit as natural decoration; middle fragment of polished ring; one perforation on notch.

Inv. No. 3224/12. L: 38 mm; W: 9 mm; Th: 5 mm; inner diameter 6 cm. Oval cross-section; lines and a hole as natural decoration; middle fragment of polished ring.

Inv. No. 3224/13 (Fig. 3.12d). L: 42 mm; W: 12 mm; Th: 4 mm; inner diameter 7 cm. Oval cross-section; lines, cracks and red colour as natural decoration; middle fragment of polished ring; two sharp breaks.

Inv. No. 3224/14. L: 30 mm; W: 13 mm; Th: 4 mm; inner diameter 9 cm. Oval cross-section; oblique lines and white deposit as natural decoration; middle fragment of unpolished ring.

Inv. No. 3224/15. L: 32 mm; W: 8 mm; Th: 5 mm; inner diameter 4 cm. Sub-rectangular cross-section; lines and holes as natural decoration; middle fragment of polished ring with hinge fractures.

Inv. No. 3224/16. L: 30 mm; W: 7 mm; Th: 3 mm; inner diameter 5 cm. Trapezoidal cross-section; parallel lines as natural decoration; middle fragment of polished ring.

Inv. No. 3224/17. L: 32 mm; W: 7 mm; Th: 3 mm; inner diameter 4 cm. Oval cross-section; lines and brown deposit as natural decoration; middle fragment of polished ring

Inv. No. 3224/18. L: 36 mm; W: 9 mm; Th: 5 mm; inner diameter 9 cm. Sub-rectangular cross-section; lines and notches as natural decoration; middle fragment of polished ring, including dorsal hinge.

Inv. No. 3224/19. L: 43 mm; W: 11 mm; Th: 6 mm; inner diameter 9 cm. Sub-rectangular cross-section; lines, grooves and holes as natural decoration; terminal fragment of unpolished ring.

Inv. No. 3224/20. L: 24 mm; W: 9 mm; Th: 6 mm; inner diameter 6 cm. Sub-rectangular cross-section; lines as natural decoration; middle fragment of polished ring.

Inv. No. 3224/21. L: 31 mm; W: 7 mm; Th: 7 mm; inner diameter 7 cm. Sub-rectangular cross-section; lines as natural decoration; middle fragment of polished ring; including dorsal hinge.

Inv. No. 3224/22. L: 28 mm; W: 6 mm; Th: 3 mm; inner diameter 3 cm. Sub-rectangular cross-section; complex lines and holes as natural decoration; middle fragment of polished ring.

Inv. No. 3224/23. L: 37 mm; W: 9 mm; Th: 7 mm; inner diameter 7 cm. Oval cross-section; complex lines, holes and garlands as natural decoration; terminal fragment of unpolished ring; highly decorated.

Inv. No. 3224/24. L: 33 mm; W: 8 mm; Th: 7 mm; inner diameter 6 cm. Rectangular cross-section; complex lines, cracks and holes as natural decoration; middle fragment of partly polished ring.

Inv. No. 3243/30. L: 45 mm; W: 11 mm; Th: 11 mm; inner diameter 7 cm. Sub-rectangular cross-section; lines, hinge, grey deposit and holes as natural decoration; middle fragment of polished ring.

Inv. No. 3316/1. L: 40 mm; W: 58 mm; Th: 42 mm; inner diameter 9 cm. Oval cross-section; complex lines, many cracks and holes as natural decoration; middle fragment of faceted polished Hamangia-type ring.

Inv. No. 3316/3. L: 40 mm; W: 27 mm; Th: 8 mm; inner diameter 5 cm. Oval cross-section; lines, garlands and holes as natural decoration; middle fragment of ring; broken across two grooves.

Inv. No. 3316/4. L: 24 mm; W: 27 mm; Th: 7 mm. Oval cross-section; lines, depression and holes as natural decoration; short middle fragment of ring.

Inv. No. 3316/8. L: 12 mm; W: 8 mm; Th: 8 mm. Circular cross-section; lines and brown deposit as natural decoration; broken terminal of ring.

Inv. No. 3316/10. L: 22 mm; W: 30 mm; Th: 9 mm. Oval cross-section; lines as natural decoration; middle fragment of ground ring, reused as pendant with two hour-glass perforation, then broken through one perforation.

Inv. No. 3316/12. L: 37 mm; W: 17 mm; Th: 8 mm; inner diameter 4 cm. Sub-rectangular cross-section; complex lines, notches, garlands and holes as natural decoration; middle fragment of ground and faceted ring with fine pattern.

Inv. No. 3316/13. L: 52 mm; W: 8 mm; Th: 7 mm; inner diameter 7 cm. Oval cross-section; lines, holes and pink colour as natural decoration; middle fragment of ground ring with pointed breaks.

Inv. No. 3316/14. L: 33 mm; W: 7 mm; Th: 7 mm; inner diameter 6 cm. Oval cross-section; complex lines and holes as natural decoration; terminal fragment of ground and faceted ring with fine decoration.

Inv. No. 3316/15. L: 39 mm; W: 10 mm; Th: 9 mm; inner diameter 10 cm. Oval cross-section; complex lines, cracks and holes as natural decoration; middle fragment of partly ground ring at thick dorsal part of shell.

Inv. No. 3316/16. L: 23 mm; W: 8 mm; Th: 5 mm; inner diameter 7 cm. Oval cross-section; lines, nicks and brown deposit as natural decoration; middle fragment of polished ring; dorsal end with straight perforation; reused as pendant fragment.

Inv. No. 3350/2. L: 24 mm; W: 11 mm; Th: 4 mm. Sub-

rectangular cross-section; terminal fragment of polished bracelet with incised nicks.

Inv. No. 3350/4. L: 29 mm; W: 5 mm; Th: 4 mm. Triangular cross-section; orange colour as natural decoration; faceted terminal.

Inv. No. 3350/5. L: 29 mm; W: 9 mm; Th: 4 mm; inner diameter 5 cm. Rectangular cross-section; lines as natural decoration; middle fragment of bracelet; hinge fractures at both ends.

Inv. No. 3350/6. L: 32 mm; W: 7 mm; Th: 7 mm; inner diameter 5 cm. Oval cross-section; lines, cracks and holes as natural decoration; middle fragment of polished ring.

Inv. No. 3350/7. L: 42 mm; W: 4 mm; Th: 6 mm; inner diameter 5 cm. Trapezoidal cross-section; lines as natural decoration; middle fragment of polished and faceted ring.

Inv. No. 3350/8. L: 54 mm; W: 9 mm; Th: 8 mm; inner diameter 7 cm. Sub-rectangular cross-section; lines, garlands, tiny quantity of red colour and holes as natural decoration; middle fragment of polished and faceted ring.

Inv. No. 3350/10. L: 48 mm; W: 9 mm; Th: 8 mm; inner diameter 8 cm. Sub-rectangular cross-section; complex lines and deposit as natural decoration; middle fragment of unpolished ring; coloured both grey and white.

Inv. No. 3350/11. L: 37 mm; W: 4 mm; Th: 7 mm; inner diameter 4 cm. Triangular cross-section; lines and grey deposit as natural decoration; middle fragment of polished ring.

Inv. No. 3350/12. L: 40 mm; W: 7 mm; Th: 5 mm; inner diameter 6 cm. Triangular cross-section; middle fragment of polished ring with hinge fractures.

Inv. No. 3350/13. L: 51 mm; W: 5 mm; Th: 8 mm; inner diameter 6 cm. Triangular cross-section; lines and 80% white deposit as natural decoration; terminal fragment of unpolished ring.

Inv. No. 3350/14. L: 25 mm; W: 8 mm; Th: 5 mm; inner diameter 2 cm. Sub-triangular cross-section; lines and holes as natural decoration; middle fragment of partly polished ring.

Inv. No. 3350/16. L: 22 mm; W: 5 mm; Th: 4 mm; inner diameter 3 cm. Triangular cross-section; complex lines and deposit as natural decoration; middle fragment of partly polished ring.

Inv. No. 3379/10. L: 29 mm; W: 7 mm; Th: 6 mm; inner diameter 12 cm. Twisted cross-section; lines and many cracks as natural decoration; middle fragment of partly polished ring.

Inv. No. 3379/11. L: 29 mm; W: 6 mm; Th: 4 mm; inner

diameter 4 cm. Oval cross-section; lines and hinges as natural decoration; middle fragment of polished ring; hinge traces almost polished away.

Inv. No. 3379/12. L: 36 mm; W: 8 mm; Th: 4 mm; inner diameter 10 cm. Triangular cross-section; holes as natural decoration; middle fragment of partly polished ring; pointed breaks.

Inv. No. 3379/13. L: 25 mm; W: 6 mm; Th: 5 mm; inner diameter 3 cm. Oval cross-section; lines and hinge as natural decoration; middle fragment of polished ring; perforation through hinge.

Inv. No. 3379/14. L: 24 mm; W: 6 mm; Th: 4 mm; inner diameter 6 cm. Lines and chevrons as natural decoration; middle fragment of partly polished ring.

Inv. No. 3505/10. L: 36 mm; W: 11 mm; Th: 11 mm; inner diameter 4 cm. Lines, hinge and brown colour as natural decoration; middle fragment of polished ring.

Inv. No. 3505/11. L: 17 mm; W: 7 mm; Th: 7 mm. Sub-rectangular cross-section; lines, two holes, cracks and grey deposit as natural decoration; middle fragment of polished ring.

TOGGLE
Inv. No. 3379/18 (Fig. 3.11h). L: 17 mm; W: 7 mm; Th: 4 mm. Triangular cross-section; holes as natural decoration; double toggle, figure of 8-shaped with two straight perforations cf. bone figurines.

CUT FRAGMENT
Inv. No. 3379/7. L: 21 mm; W: 16 mm; Th: 6 mm. Lines and brown deposit as natural decoration; piece of shell ready for working; possible start of perforation.

Inv. No. 3379/8. L: 32 mm; W: 13 mm; Th: 12 mm. Complex lines, garlands and holes as natural decoration; smoothed, polished piece ready for working.

CHUNK
Inv. No. 3316/6 (Fig. 3.11i). L: 26 mm; W: 21 mm; Th: 16 mm. Complex lines, cracks and holes as natural decoration; thick chunk of shell for secondary use; possibly debitage from ring.

SHELL UMBO
Inv. No. 3350/9 (Plate 6a). L: 35 mm; W: 17 mm; Th: 21 mm. Three natural holes as natural decoration; dorsal (umbo) from which part of shell was removed; possibly debitage.

The Tools

Inv. No. 2753/1. Group 3; L: 56 mm; W: 20 mm; Th: 13 mm; Weight: 40 g. Volcanic (altered) rock; beige colour; cylindrical shape, with oval cross-section and sub-rectangular longitudinal cross-section; partly ground and polished; facets on ventral sides; flakes off butt and proximal ventral; no wear; colour contrast between dorsal and left side (polished to yellow) and ventral and right side (unpolished, with brown inclusions)

Inv. No. 2753/2. Group 3; L: 55 mm; W: 19 mm; Th: 14 mm; Weight: 40 g. Volcanic tuff; brown colour (with yellow lines); cylindrical shape, with oval cross-section and oval longitudinal cross-section; polished; facets on sides and dorsal; worn butt; chips from blade; yellow deposit on proximal dorsal and ventral.

Inv. No. 2753/3 (Fig. 4.1d). Group 3; L: 37 mm; W: 18 mm; Th: 11 mm; Weight: 20 g. Volcanic tuff; grey colour; cylindrical shape, with oval cross-section and oval longitudinal cross-section; polished; facets on sides, blade and butt; no damage; one chip on blade; slightly trapezoidal cylinder, asymmetrical thickness on sides, probably due to the shape of raw material.

Inv. No. 2754/1. Group 4; L: 48 mm; W: 36 mm; Th: 14 mm; Weight: 45 g. Volcanic rock; light brown colour (with yellow inclusions); symmetrical trapezoidal shape, with sub-rectangular cross-section and sub-rectangular longitudinal cross-section; ground; no facets, damage or wear; half finished axe with wavy blade.

Inv. No. 2754/2. Group 4; L: 43 mm; W: 36 mm; Th 12 mm; Weight: 30 g. Serpentinite; brown colour (speckled); asymmetrical trapezoidal shape, with oval cross-section and oval longitudinal cross-section; polished; facets on sides; chips from butt and right proximal dorsal; flake from right dorsal blade; asymmetrical thickness on sides, probably due to the shape of raw material.

Inv. No. 2754/3. Group 5; L: 59 mm; W: 41 mm; Th: 15 mm; Weight: 70 g. Volcanic tuff; dark green colour; symmetrical trapezoidal shape, with sub-rectangular cross-section and sub-rectangular longitudinal cross-section; polished; facets on sides and butt, flakes off butt; wear on proximal dorsal and ventral, two flakes and chips off dorsal blade; proximal wear maybe due to hafting.

Inv. No. 2754/4. Group 4; L: 49 mm; W: 39 mm; Th: 14 mm; Weight: 40 g. Volcanic tuff; light grey colour; asymmetrical trapezoidal shape, with plano-convex cross-section and plano-convex longitudinal cross-section; polished; facets on sides blade (only ventral) and butt, huge flake detached from from left dorsal; no wear; the dorsal flake is old, showing signs of axe-making.

Inv. No. 2754/5. Group 4; L: 45 mm; W: 35 mm; Th: 13 mm; Weight: 30 g. Volcanic rock; brown colour; asymmetrical trapezoidal shape, with oval cross-section and oval longitudinal cross-section; ground; facets on sides; flake off proximal left dorsal; chips and small flake from ventral blade; half-finished axe, ground to final shape but with no polish.

Inv. No. 2754/8. Group 5; L: 46 mm; W: 34 mm; Th: 13 mm; Weight: 30 g. Volcanic rock; brown-grey colour; asymmetrical trapezoidal shape, with sub-rectangular cross-section and sub-rectangular longitudinal cross-section; partly polished; facets on blade (only dorsal) and sides; flake and wear on butt, left and right sides, ventral with no ground and polished surface left; chips and one flake from dorsal blade; large curved facet for blade on dorsal, ventral with small area of ground and polished area near blade (cf. edge-ground axe), rest of ventral not ground or polished; therefore, half-finished axe.

Inv. No. 2754/7. Group 5; L: 54 mm; W: 33 mm; Th: 15 mm; Weight: 40 g. Volcanic tuff; brown colour (speckled); symmetrical trapezoidal shape, with sub-rectangular cross-section and oval longitudinal cross-section; polished; facets on sides; flakes off butt; blade chipped with one flake off right dorsal; lots of brown deposit on ventral and left edge (post-depositional).

Inv. No. 2754/10. Group 5; L: 52 mm; W: 40 mm; Th: 16 mm; Weight: 50 g. Volcanic tuff; brown colour (with yellow lines); symmetrical trapezoidal shape, with oval cross-section and oval longitudinal cross-section; polished; facets on sides and butt; wear on butt and flakes off proximal left dorsal; flakes and chips from blade (ventral and dorsal); right side with two facets.

Inv. No. 2754/9. Group 4; L: 46 mm; W: 38 mm; Th: 13 mm; Weight: 40 g. Jasper-like rock; dark brown colour; symmetrical trapezoidal shape, with sub-rectangular cross-section and sub-rectangular longitudinal cross-section; polished; facets on sides and butt; wear and flakes off butt and proximal ventral; blade with one flake on dorsal and chips on ventral; very fine-grained.

Inv. No. 2754/6. Group 4; L: 58 mm; W: 41 mm; Th: 20 mm; Weight: 90 g. Volcanic rock; brown grey colour; asymmetrical trapezoidal shape, with oval cross-section and oval longitudinal cross-section; polished; facets on sides; wear on butt and proximal left edge and proximal left ventral; one chip on blade (left dorsal); butt damaged possibly from hafting; plump axe.

Inv. No. 2755/1 (Plate 7j). Group 4; L: 74 mm; W: 46 mm; Th: 13 mm; Weight: 80 g. Volcanic tuff; dark green colour; slightly trapezoidal shape with rounded butt, with sub-rectangular cross-section and sub-rectangular longitudinal cross-section; polished; facets on blade, edges and butt;

worn butt and flakes detached from ventral, right edge with flakes, left edge with hinge fractures; blade with flakes and chips on dorsal and big flake on ventral; blade damages are polished over; ventral polishing over inclusions so it looks un-polished.

Inv. No. 2755/2 (Plate 7h). Group 6; L: 59 mm; W: 37 mm; Th: 23 mm; Weight: 70 g. Sandstone; off white colour; slightly asymmetrical trapezoidal shape, with oval cross-section and oval longitudinal cross-section; partly polished; no facets; grooves and flake from proximal ventral, wear on left and right sides and probably on butt; two chips from blade (ventral); brown deposit over distal ventral (post-depositional); lack of final polish.

Inv. No. 2755/3. Group 4; L: 74 mm; W: 46 mm; Th: 13 mm; Weight: 80 g. Volcanic tuff; green colour; asymmetrical trapezoidal shape, with sub-rectangular cross-section and sub-rectangular longitudinal cross-section; polished; facets on sides and butt; grooves and flake from butt and proximal dorsal; blade and large part of dorsal removed with flakes off remaining distal dorsal; but damaged possibly from hafting.

Inv. No. 2755/4. Group 5; L: 56 mm; W: 37 mm; Th: 19 mm; Weight: 80 g. Volcanic rock; brown grey colour; slightly asymmetrical trapezoidal shape, with oval cross-section and oval longitudinal cross-section; polished; facets on sides; worn butt with flakes, flakes off left side; blade removed with huge flakes (dorsal) and big flakes (ventral); very fine-grained rock.

Inv. No. 2755/5. Group 4; L: 40 mm; W: 29 mm; Th: 12 mm; Weight: 30 g. Volcanic tuff; dark brown colour; asymmetrical trapezoidal shape, with sub-rectangular cross-section and sub-rectangular longitudinal cross-section; polished; facets on blade (only ventral), sides and butt; long flake from distal right side and a flake from proximal left side; several large flakes from blade (ventral and dorsal); one ventral flake re-polished.

Inv. No. 2782/1 (Fig. 4.1b). Group 2; L: 40 mm; W: 24 mm; Th: 7 mm; Weight: 10 g. Jasper-like rock; dark brown colour; reveresed asymmetrical trapezoidal shape, with rectangular cross-section and sub-rectangular longitudinal cross-section; polished; facets on blade, sides and butt; large flake from proximal right side; no wear; the reversed trapezoidal shape means that the butt started as blade and when the blade was damaged, the ends changed.

Inv. No. 2782/2. Group 1; L: 31 mm; W: 27 mm; Th: 8 mm; Weight: 15 g. Volcanic tuff; grey beige colour; asymmetrical trapezoidal shape, with oval cross-section and oval longitudinal cross-section; polished; facets on sides and butt; worn butt; no wear on rest of axe.

Inv. No. 2782/3. Group 4; L: 31 mm; W: 27 mm; Th: 8 mm; Weight: 15 g. Jasper-like rock; green grey colour;

asymmetrical trapezoidal shape, with sub-rectangular cross-section and sub-rectangular longitudinal cross-section; polished; facets on sides and butt; no damage; two chips from blade; small areas with white deposit (post-depositional).

Inv. No. 2782/4. Group 2; L: 40 mm; W: 24 mm; Th: 7 mm; Weight: 15 g. Jasper-like rock; green colour; symmetrical trapezoidal shape, with sub-rectangular cross-section and sub-rectangular longitudinal cross-section; polished; facets on sides and butt; no damage or wear.

Inv. No. 2782/5 (Plate 7c). Group 4; L: 60 mm; W: 43 mm; Th: 13 mm; Weight: 50 g. Schist; grey beige colour; symmetrical trapezoidal shape, with oval cross-section and oval longitudinal cross-section; ground; facets on sides; butt with flakes; blade with flakes (dorsal and ventral); final stage of grinding.

Inv. No. 2783/1 (Plate 7e). Group 3; L: 51 mm; W: 17 mm; Th: 12 mm; Weight: 20 g. Jasper-like rock; green grey colour; cylindrical shape, with plano-convex cross-section and oval longitudinal cross-section; polished; facets on sides and butt; no damage; blade with chips off; facet made on what is now butt to make a blade; this plan was abandoned and a a new blade made.

Inv. No. 3006/1 (Plate 7i). Group 5; L: 60 mm; W 41 mm; Th: 18 mm; Weight: 70 g. Volcanic rock; grey colour; asymmetrical trapezoidal shape, with sub-rectangular cross-section and sub-rectangular longitudinal cross-section; polished; facets on sides and butt (only dorsal); butt and proximal ventral with wear and flakes; blade with one flake and chips on ventral; butt curvature suggests that it was made from a much larger tool.

Inv. No. 3006/2. Group 4; L: 36 mm; W: 29 mm; Th: 12 mm; Weight: 10 g. Jasper-like rock; grey blue colour; asymmetrical trapezoidal shape, with plano-convex cross-section and oval longitudinal cross-section; polished; facets on sides and butt; distal left dorsal and proximal right dorsal with flakes off; blade with flake (ventral) and chips (dorsal).

Inv. No. 3006/3. Group 4; L: 40 mm; W: 35 mm; Th: 11 mm; Weight: 25 g. Jasper-like rock; grey blue colour; asymmetrical trapezoidal shape, with oval cross-section and oval longitudinal cross-section; polished; facets on sides and butt (only ventral); new flake from distal right dorsal, old flake from butt; blade with chips off; butt area unpolished.

Inv. No. 3192/1. Group 1; L: 40 mm; W: 28 mm; Th: 9 mm; Weight: 20 g. Volcanic rock; black colour; asymmetrical trapezoidal shape, with sub-rectangular cross-section and sub-rectangular longitudinal cross-section; polished; facets on sides and blade; chipped butt and chips on left dorsal; no wear; oblique blade facet exaggerates asymmetry.

Inv. No. 3192/6. Group 2; L: 32 mm; W: 28 mm; Th: 14 mm; Weight: 20 g. Jasper-like rock; grey colour; asymmetrical trapezoidal shape, with plano-convex cross-section and oval longitudinal cross-section; polished; facets on sides; no damage; worn butt and lower dorsal; three chips on blade.

Inv. No. 3192/3. Group 4; L: 42 mm; W: 29 mm; Th: 11 mm; Weight: 30 g. Volcanic rock; black colour; asymmetrical trapezoidal shape, with plano-convex cross-section and oval longitudinal cross-section; polished; facets on sides and blade (ventral); no damage and wear; rounded butt; slight blade asymmetry.

Inv. No. 3192/4. Group 1; L: 41 mm; W: 28 mm; Th: 9 mm; Weight: 20 g. Volcanic tuff; green colour; symmetrical trapezoidal shape, with sub-rectangular cross-section and sub-rectangular longitudinal cross-section; polished; facets on sides and butt; chipped blade on right dorsal and left ventral; worn butt; chips on blade.

Inv. No. 3192/5 (Plate 7d). Group 4; L: 43 mm; W: 32 mm; Th: 11 mm; Weight: 35 g. Porphyry (volcanic); dark speckled colour; asymmetrical trapezoidal shape, with oval cross-section and oval longitudinal cross-section; polished; facets on sides; no damage; worn butt; three chips on blade; slight blade asymmetry.

Inv. No. 3192/2. Group 4; L: 30 mm; W: 17 mm; Th: 9 mm; Weight: 10 g. Volcanic tuff; grey colour; asymmetrical trapezoidal shape, with oval cross-section and oval longitudinal cross-section; polished; facets on sides, butt and blade (dorsal); chip off right side and butt; no wear; slight blade asymmetry; deeply curved blade facet.

Inv. No. 3193/1. Group 4; L: 57 mm; W: 37 mm; Th: 14 mm; Weight: 15 g. Volcanic rock; brown (speckled) colour; asymmetrical trapezoidal shape, with sub-rectangular cross-section and oval longitudinal cross-section; polished; facets on sides, butt and blade (dorsal); flakes from right side proximal right ventral; blade with chips off (dorsal and ventral); butt curvature suggests that it was made from a much larger tool.

Inv. No. 3193/7. Group 4; L: 61 mm; W: 36 mm; Th: 16 mm; Weight: 60 g. Volcanic tuff; light grey colour; sub-rectangular trapezoidal shape, with sub-rectangular cross-section and oval longitudinal cross-section; polished; no facets; flakes off right side and butt (dorsal and ventral); flakes from blade (dorsal and ventral); rare shape; attempt at faceting.

Inv. No. 3193/3. Group 4; L: 39 mm; W: 38 mm; Th: 13 mm; Weight: 30 g. Volcanic tuff; brown colour; asymmetrical trapezoidal shape, with oval cross-section and oval longitudinal cross-section; polished; facets on sides; flakes off butt, proximal left ventral and right ventral and left dorsal, groove from proximal dorsal; flakes from blade (dorsal and ventral); almost square axe; rare shape.

Inv. No. 3193/4. Group 6; L: 54 mm; W: 36 mm; Th: 22 mm; Weight: 50 g. Sandstone; green colour; asymmetrical trapezoidal shape, with oval cross-section and oval longitudinal cross-section; ground; no facets; flakes and wear on butt; flake on blade (dorsal); final stage of grinding.

Inv. No. 3193/5. Group 4; L: 32 mm; W: 23 mm; Th: 11 mm; Weight: 15 g. Volcanic tuff; brown colour; asymmetrical trapezoidal shape, with plano-convex cross-section and oval longitudinal cross-section; polished; facets on sides and butt (only dorsal); flake on proximal right side; flake from blade (ventral).

Inv. No. 3193/6. Group 4; L: 40 mm; W: 27 mm; Th: 12 mm; Weight: 20 g. Volcanic rock; brown (speckled) colour; asymmetrical trapezoidal shape, with oval cross-section and oval longitudinal cross-section; polished; facets on sides; worn butt; flake from blade (ventral); not fully polished, hence poorly developed facets.

Inv. No. 3193/2. Group 5; L: 48 mm; W: 27 mm; Th: 12 mm; Weight: 40 g. Volcanic tuff; light grey colour; symmetrical sub-rectangular shape, with rectangular cross-section and sub-rectangular longitudinal cross-section; polished; facets on sides and butt; flake from proximal right ventral; blade with chip; butt curvature suggests it was made from a much larger tool.

Inv. No. 3193/8. Group 4; L: 44 mm; W: 36 mm; Th: 13 mm; Weight: 30 g. Volcanic tuff; light grey colour; asymmetrical trapezoidal shape, with plano-convex cross-section and oval longitudinal cross-section; polished; facets on sides; flakes off proximal left and right ventral, right side and butt; no wear; early stage of polishing, hence poorly developed facets.

Inv. No. 3193/9. Group 4; L: 38 mm; W: 30 mm; Th: 11 mm; Weight: 20 g. Jasper-like rock; green grey colour; asymmetrical trapezoidal shape, with sub-rectangular cross-section and oval longitudinal cross-section; polished; facets on sides, blade (only dorsal) and butt (only dorsal); flake off butt, left proximal side and proximal half off ventral; blade with one flake and two chips; poor faceting technique results in irregular blade facet and two small facets on right side; very fine-grained.

Inv. No. 3193/10. Group 4; L: 35 mm; W: 32 mm; Th: 11 mm; Weight: 20 g. Volcanic tuff; grey blue (speckled) colour; asymmetrical trapezoidal shape, with oval cross-section and oval longitudinal cross-section; polished; facets on sides and blade; worn butt; blade with two flakes struck off left dorsal.

Inv. No. 3193/11. Group 4; L: 35 mm; W: 32 mm; Th: 11 mm; Weight: 20 g. Volcanic tuff; dark green colour; cylindrical shape, with oval cross-section and oval longitudinal cross-section; polished; facets on sides and butt; flake from distal left ventral; chips from blade (ventral); only one facet on each side; probably not fully polished.

Inv. No. 3193/12 (Plate 7b). Group 4; L: 42 mm; W: 30 mm; Th: 13 mm; Weight: 40 g. Serpentinite; grey blue colour; asymmetrical trapezoidal shape, with sub-rectangular cross-section and oval longitudinal cross-section; polished; facets on sides and butt; flake from distal left side; no wear; very blunt blade: 4 mm thick.

Inv. No. 3193/13. Group 4; L: 34 mm; W: 35 mm; Th: 11 mm; Weight: 15 g. Jasper-like rock; black colour; symmetrical trapezoidal shape, with sub-rectangular cross-section and sub-rectangular longitudinal cross-section; polished; facets on sides, blade (only ventral) and butt; flakes off butt and distal left side; blade with flakes (dorsal) and chips (ventral and dorsal); very fine-grained.

Inv. No. 3193/14. Group 5; L: 49 mm; W: 37 mm; Th: 17 mm; Weight: 60 g. Volcanic rock; dark brown colour; symmetrical slightly trapezoidal shape, with plano-convex cross-section and oval longitudinal cross-section; polished; facets on sides and part of butt; flakes from butt, proximal left and right ventral and proximal right dorsal; blade with big flake and chips (dorsal); plump axe.

Inv. No. 3228 (Fig. 4.1a). Group 7; L: 70 mm; W: 24 mm; Th: 20 mm; Weight: 40 g. Sandstone; beige colour; pointed triangular shape, with sub-rectangular cross-section and sub-rectangular longitudinal cross-section; shaft hole axe; perforation half finished; partly ground; facets on one side; flakes off butt and right dorsal, right side and left ventral; no wear; the unfinished hour-glass perforation and the unground areas suggest local axe making.

Inv. No. 3263 (Fig. 4.1c; Plate 7g). Group 4; L: 57 mm; W: 40 mm; Th: 14 mm; Weight: 50 g. Volcanic rock; dark brown colour; rectangular shape with rounded corners; "flat axe" with sub-rectangular cross-section and triangular/ tapering longitudinal cross-section; partly polished; facets on sides and butt; grooves on butt (dorsal and ventral); no wear; unusual shape; polished only on proximal and sides, cf. flat copper axe.

Inv. No. 3267; L: 78 mm. W: 44 mm; Th: 44 mm; Weight: 110 g. Marble; off-white colour; conical pounder with rounded end and round cross-section and tapering longitudinal cross-section; partly ground; flakes and grooves off all sides; big flakes off butt; heavy wear on pounding face.

Inv. No. 3282/1 (Plate 7a). Group 3; L: 39 mm; W 19 mm; Th: 14 mm; Weight: 15 g. Volcanic (altered) rock; white colour; axe fragment with trapezoidal shape and sub-rectangular cross-section and triangular/tapering longitudinal cross-section; polished; facets on sides; broken medially, flakes from both sides; chips off blade; the only axe fragment in collection, oblique fracture, hence worn; soft material that is easily worn.

Inv. No. 3282/2. Group 3; L: 44 mm; W: 18 mm; Th: 13 mm; Weight: 20 g. Volcanic (altered) rock; white colour; cylindrical shape with plano-convex cross-section and oval longitudinal cross-section; partly polished; facets on right side; big flakes off right side and butt; chips off left side and ventral; worn blade; very plump blade for chisel; grey deposit on ventral; soft material that is easily worn.

Inv. No. 3282/3. Group 3; L: 39 mm; W: 16 mm; Th: 11 mm; Weight: 15 g. Volcanic (altered) rock; white colour; rectangular shape with sub-rectangular cross-section and triangular/tapering longitudinal cross-section; ground and partly polished; facets sides; flakes off very worn sides and worn butt; chipped and worn blade; very plump blade for chisel; grey deposit on ventral; soft material that is easily worn.

Inv. No. 3337/1. Group 7; L: 81 mm; W: 22 mm; Th: 17 mm; Weight: 60 g. Volcanic tuff; green colour; cylindrical shape with oval cross-section and oval longitudinal cross-section; polished; facets on sides; heavily worn butt, flakes off right side and right dorsal; heavily flaked and worn blade with impact flakes ventral and dorsal cf. British Group VI Langdale axe; three facets on each side.

Inv. No. 3337/2 (Fig. 4.1e). Group 7; L: 90 mm; W: 19 mm; Th: 15 mm; Weight: 35 g. Volcanic tuff; green colour; cylindrical shape with domed cross-section and triangular/tapering longitudinal cross-section; partly polished; facets on sides; no damage and wear; cf. British Group VI Langdale axe; three quarter finished axe rough-out with thinning flakes detached on all faces; unfinished facets on each side.

Inv. No. 3357/1. Group 3; L: 42 mm; W: 17 mm; Th: 13 mm; Weight: 20 g. Volcanic rock; dark brown colour; elongated trapezoidal shape with oval cross-section and oval longitudinal cross-section; polished; facets on sides and butt; chips off butt and left side; white deposit on right side

Inv. No. 3357/2. Group 3; L: 36 mm; W: 16 mm; Th: 9 mm; Weight: 15 g. Volcanic tuff; green grey colour; rectangular shape with sub-rectangular cross-section and sub-rectangular longitudinal cross-section; polished; facets on sides and butt; flake off distal ventral; no wear.

Inv. No. 3357/3. Group 3; L: 40 mm; W: 14 mm; Th: 10 mm; Weight: 20 g. Volcanic tuff; green yellow colour; rectangular shape with plano-convex cross-section and oval longitudinal cross-section; polished; facets on sides and butt; chips off butt; chipped blade (ventral); curved blade.

Inv. No. 3357/4. Group 3; L: 44 mm; W: 15 mm; Th: 11 mm; Weight: 20 g. Volcanic rock; black colour; rectangular shape with plano-convex cross-section and oval longitudinal cross-section; polished; facets on sides and butt; flakes off proximal left side, butt and proximal ventral; no wear

Inv. No. 3358/1 (Plate 7f). Group 1; L: 33 mm; W: 25 mm; Th: 9 mm; Weight: 15 g. Volcanic rock; black colour; slightly trapezoidal shape with sub-rectangular cross-section and sub-rectangular longitudinal cross-section; polished; facets on sides and butt; wear on butt; flake off right distal side, chip off left ventral side; chips on blade; poor faceting technique on left side results in four small facets.

Inv. No. 3358/2. Group 2; L: 37 mm; W: 20 mm; Th: 7 mm; Weight: 15 g. Volcanic tuff; green grey colour; asymmetrical trapezoidal shape with sub-rectangular cross-section and sub-rectangular longitudinal cross-section; polished; facets on sides and butt; flake off right proximal edge; two chips off blade.

Inv. No. 3359/1. Group 5; L: 52 mm; W: 38 mm; Th: 16 mm; Weight: 60 g. Jasper-like rock; dark green colour; trapezoidal shape with sub-rectangular cross-section and sub-rectangular longitudinal cross-section; polished; facets on sides and butt; no damage; chips on blade.

Inv. No. 3359/2. Group 4; L: 46 mm; W: 34 mm; Th: 11 mm; Weight: 45 g. Volcanic tuff; black and green colour; symmetrical trapezoidal shape with sub-rectangular cross-section and sub-rectangular longitudinal cross-section; polished; facets on sides, blade and butt; flake off blade (dorsal); no wear.

Inv. No. 3359/3. Group 4; L: 44 mm; W: 41 mm; Th: 12 mm; Weight: 40 g. Volcanic rock; dark brown colour; asymmetrical trapezoidal shape with sub-rectangular cross-section and oval longitudinal cross-section; polished; facets on sides, blade (dorsal) and butt; worn butt, chip off left side; chips on blade.

Inv. No. 3359/4. Group 1; L: 44 mm; W: 33 mm; Th: 9 mm; Weight: 30 g. Volcanic rock; grey colour; asymmetrical trapezoidal shape with sub-rectangular cross-section and sub-rectangular longitudinal cross-section; partly polished; facets on sides and butt; wear on right ventral side, polished on blade, dorsal side and butt; no wear; very little polish in ventral, cf. Inv. 3526/3

Inv. No. 3376. L: 55 mm; W: 52 mm; Th: 29 mm; Weight: 80 g. Marble; off white colour; hemispherical pounder with domed round cross-section and domed longitudinal cross-section; ground; wear on all lower sides, chips on upper surface; heavy wear on pounding face; very different form pounder Inv. 3267.

Inv. No. 3526/4. Group 4; L: 52 mm; W: 41 mm; Th:14 mm; Weight: 40 g. Volcanic rock; brown grey colour; symmetrical trapezoidal shape with plano-convex cross-section and oval longitudinal cross-section; polished; facets on sides and butt;

worn and chipped butt and lower edges, flakes and chips off dorsal, chips off ventral; big flakes off blade (dorsal); one of the most heavily used axes in sample.

Inv. No. 3526/2. Group 4; L: 43 mm; W: 35 mm; Th:13 mm; Weight: 35 g. Volcanic rock; grey colour; symmetrical trapezoidal shape with oval cross-section and oval longitudinal cross-section; polished; facets on sides and blade (dorsal); worn proximal dorsal and butt, chips off left side; two flakes off blade; two big flakes detached close to blade on left dorsal and ventral.

Inv. No. 3526/3. Group 3; L: 56 mm; W: 18 mm; Th: 9 mm; Weight: 20 g. Volcanic rock; brown grey colour; cylindrical shape with sub-rectangular cross-section and sub-rectangular longitudinal cross-section; partly polished; facets on sides and butt; no damage; flakes off blade (ventral); ventral part is unpolished, except for the blade area; cf. Inv. 3359.

Inv. No. 3526/1. Group 4; L: 51 mm; W: 35 mm; Th: 13 mm; Weight: 40 g. Volcanic rock; brown grey colour; slightly trapezoidal shape with sub-rectangular cross-section and sub-rectangular longitudinal cross-section; polished; facets on side; wear on proximal ventral near butt; chips off blade, one big flake from blade right ventral; looks unpolished but this is caused by colour variations.

Inv. No. 3526/5. Group 4; L: 57 mm; W: 32 mm; Th: 11 mm; Weight: 45 g. Volcanic tuff; green colour; slightly trapezoidal shape with sub-rectangular cross-section and sub-rectangular longitudinal cross-section; polished; facets on blade, sides and butt; flakes off butt, dorsal near butt, big flake off dorsal and right edge, chips off left ventral; nibbles off blade; cf. British Group VI Langdale axe.

Table A1.1. Summary description of perforated Cyclope *snails*

Museum Inv.	Sub-No	L mm	Description	Museum Inv.	Sub-No	L mm	Description
2765	3	15	One perf	3243	6	13	One perf
2765	4	16	One perf	3243	7	15	4 perfs
2765	5	16	Two perf	3243	8	14	1 perf + missing ventral
2765	6	14	One perf	3243	9	14	1 perf and post missing
2781	22	14	One perf	3243	10	14	1 perf and post missing
2781	23	15	Four perf	3243	11	11	One perf
2781	24	14	One perf with ventral missing	3243	12	12	One perf
2781	25	15	Four perf	3243	13	15	One perf
2781	26	15	One perf and post missing	3316	78	12	Two perf
2781	27	9	One perf	3316	79	14	One perf
2781	28	8	One perf	3316	80	15	One perf
2781	29	11	One perf	3316	81	10	One perf+ ventral missing
2781	30	10	One perf	3316	82	14	One perf
2781	31	11	One perf with ventral missing	3316	83	15	One perf
2991	7	12	One perf and ventral missing	3316	84	14	One perf
2991	8	12	Three perf	3316	85	13	Two perf
2991	9	10	One perf	3316	87	13	One perf and missing post
2991	10	13	Three perf	3316	88	12	One perf
2991	12	14	Two perf	3316	90	13	One perf
3050	29	14	One perf	3316	92	12	One perf
3050	30	14	One perf	3350	39	12	One perforation
3050	31	13	One perf	3350	42	15	One perf in ventral
3050	32	13	Three perf	3350	44	10	perf in ventral
3050	35	13	One perf	3350	45	13	"One large, two small perf"
3050	37	12	One perf	3350	46	11	Two perfs
3050	39	12	Two perf	3350	48	11	perf in ventral; dorsal missing
3224	32	11	One perf	3350	50	12	perf in ventral
3224	33	12	One perf	3350	51	14	perf in ventral
3224	34	14	One perf	3350	52	14	perf in ventral
3224	35	15	One perf	3350	54	14	4 perfs on ant
3224	36	30	One perf	3350	58	12	2 perfs
3224	37	14	Two perf	3350	59	10	One perf
3224	40	12	One perf	3350	60	14	One perf
3224	41	11	One perf	3350	61	13	One perf
3224	42	13	Two perf	3350	62	14	3 perfs
3224	43	14	Two perf	3350	63	14	2 perfs
3224	44	14	Two perf	3350	64	10	One perf
3224	45	12	One perf	3350	66	14	One perf
3224	46	14	One perf	3350	69	14	2 perfs
3224	47	13	Two perf	3350	70	14	One perf
3224	48	11	One perf	3350	72	14	3 perfs
3224	51	15	One perf	3350	73	14	2 perfs
3224	52	15	One perf	3350	74	16	One perf
3224	53	11	One perf	3350	75	12	One perf; post missing
3224	54	12	One perf	3379	53	13	One perf+ post missing
3224	55	13	One perf+ ventral missing	3379	54	14	One perf +ventral missing
3243	5	10	One perf	3379	55	13	Two perf
3379	58	13	One perf	3505	38	12	Two perf
3379	60	12	One perf	3505	39	12	One perf with post missing
3379	61	10	One perf +ventral missing	3505	40	11	One perf with post missing
3379	62	16	One perf	3505	41	12	One perf with post missing
3379	64	14	One perf	3505	42	10	One perf
3379	65	11	Two perf	3505	43	11	One perf
3379	67	12	Four perf	3505	44	12	One perf with ant missing
3379	68	12	One perf	3505	45	13	Three perf
3379	69	13	One perf	3505	46	14	Two perf

Table A1.1. continued

Museum Inv.	Sub-No	L mm	Description	Museum Inv.	Sub-No	L mm	Description
3379	70	13	One perf	3505	47	15	One perf
3379	71	11	One perf+ post missing	3505	48	12	Three perf
3379	73	14	One perf	3505	49	13	One perf
3379	74	10	Two perf	3505	50	9	Two perf
3379	75	11	One perf	3505	51	13	One perf
3379	76	11	One perf	3505	52	14	One perf with ant missing
3379	77	10	One perf	3505	53	8	Two perf
3379	78	13	Two perf	3505	54	13	One perf
3379	79	14	One perf	3505	55	14	One perf
3379	80	13	One perf+ post missing	3505	56	14	One perf with ant missing
3379	81	11	One perf	3505	57	12	One perf
3379	82	16	One perf+ post missing	3505	58	15	One perf with post missing
3379	83	13	One perf	3505	59	9	One perf with ventral missing
3379	84	13	One perf	3505	60	9	Two perf
3505	16	14	Two perf	3505	61	11	One perf with ventral missing
3505	17	15	One perf	3505	62	8	One perf
3505	18	16	Two perf	3505	63	12	One perf with ventral missing
3505	19	13	One perf	3505	64	8	One perf with post missing
3505	20	9	One perf	3505	65	15	Four perf
3505	21	15	Four perf	3505	66	16	One perf
3505	22	15	One perf	3505	67	14	Five perf
3505	23	12	Two perf	3505	68	12	One perf
3505	24	15	Four perf	3505	69	15	One perf
3505	25	12	Two perf with ventral missing	3505	70	14	One perf with post missing
3505	26	12	One perf	3505	71	13	One perf with ventral missing
3505	27	11	One perf	3505	72	14	One perf
3505	28	12	One perf	3505	73	11	One perf
3505	29	10	One perf	3505	74	12	One perf
3505	30	11	One perf	3505	75	11	One perf
3505	31	14	One perf with post missing	3505	76	16	Three perf
3505	32	10	One perf	3505	77	15	One perf
3505	33	12	One perf	3505	78	13	One perf
3505	34	12	One perf with ventral missing	3505	79	12	One perf with ventral missing
3505	35	13	Two perf	3505	80	12	One perf
3505	36	13	One perf	3505	81	11	One perf
3505	37	13	One perf	3505	82	11	Three perf

Table A1.2. Summary description of unworked Dentalium *shells*

Museum Inv.	Sub-Number	L in mm	Museum Inv.	Sub-Number	L in mm
2781	16	16	3316	70	7
2781	17	11	3316	71	11
2781	18	12	3316	72	6
2781	19	9	3316	73	7
2781	20	11	3316	74	8
2781	21	10	3316	75	5
3224	56	10	3316	76	9
3224	57	7	3316	77	4
3243	50	9	3350	32	9
3243	51	13	3360	13	16
3243	52	9	3360	14	6
3243	53	8	3360	15	4
3243	54	8	3360	16	8
3243	55	9	3360	17	10
3243	56	10	3360	18	17
3243	57	13	3360	19	20
3243	58	10	3360	20	20
3243	59	6	3360	21	13
3243	60	14	3360	22	10
3243	61	9	3360	23	6
3243	62	17	3360	24	4
3243	63	8	3360	25	16
3243	64	9	3360	26	8
3243	65	9	3360	27	10
3243	66	11	3360	28	15
3243	67	12	3360	29	10
3243	68	10	3360	30	6
3243	69	10	3360	31	17
3243	70	10	3379	38	14
3243	71	6	3379	39	13
3243	72	7	3379	40	10
3243	73	7	3379	41	8
3243	74	11	3379	42	8
3243	75	9	3379	43	11
3243	76	6	3379	44	9
3243	77	3	3379	45	5
3243	78	8	3379	46	9
3316	65	13	3379	47	8
3316	66	4	3379	48	6
3316	67	6	3379	49	6
3316	68	9	3379	50	6
3316	69	9	3379	51	3
			3379	52	4

Appendix 2: Other Objects

It is clear that the collection of the artefacts from the ploughed fields at Orlovo was selective, with special attention paid to the figurines, ornaments and polished stone tools. The two principal classes of archaeological data – present on all Neolithic and Copper Age settlements in greater or lesser densities – comprise pottery and chipped stone. Indeed, the presence of both of these classes in quantity at Orlovska Chuka can be seen in even a short visit to the site. The systematic investigation of these finds classes could provide valuable evidence for not only the chronology of the deposition of the other finds classes (especially the pottery) but also prove informative on the exchange networks and local lithic sources of the Orlovians.

In addition to the figurines, ornaments and stone tools, the Orlovo collection includes a small number of other objects, which we wish to present here for the sake of completeness. As with the other surface finds, there is no direct chronological attribution for these interesting finds which, nonetheless, embody diachronic information. As will become evident, the collectors who presented their finds to the Haskovo Museum selected very few chipped stone pieces from what was a much larger sample.

The Finds

Fired Clay

Fragmentary footed vessel (Museum Inv. No. 2778/1) (Plate 8a)
The making of the Orlovo raised stand involved wrapping a lighter grey clay core around a stick (cf. the core-drifting technique for shaft-hole copper axes: Charles 1969; see above, p. 27, for the use of clay cores for making figurines) before the modelling of the four legs, from which the angular knees have survived. There are general parallels for vessels raised on pillars or feet in the Durankulak cemetery in the Hamangia and Varna periods on the Western Black Sea coast (Todorova 2002a, Abb. 123/1–16 (Hamangia IV) and Abb. 124/17–26 (Varna II–III)). However, none of these raised vessels has a horizontal perforation through the legs and only one Hamangia IV example (2002a, Abb. 123/10) shows a vertical perforation through the base of the raised part of the vessel.

There is a more distant analogy for this footed vessel in the Cucuteni group, where the specialised vessel form known as the 'hora' (the Romanian term for a circle dance; cf. Bulgarian 'horo') indicates a open vessel raised on pillars arranged, in the classic case, in the form of dancing anthropomorphs with bent knees. While distinctive examples are know from Frumuşica (Cucuteni A levels: Matasă 1946, fig. 249) and Izvoare (Cucuteni A levels: Vulpe 1957, fig. 150) (reproduced as Mantu, C.-M. and Dumitroaia, Gh. 1997, figs 51 and 82), unpainted examples have been found at the Cucuteni A3 site of Bereşti (Monah 1997, fig. 233/4; Dragomir 1983, 81–99). This vessel form is rarely, if ever, produced locally in the Bulgarian Neolithic or Copper Age. The Orlovo example differs from most Cucuteni and Durankulak examples except Bereşti, insofar as it has a dark grey coarse, gritty and unpainted surface. The Cucuteni horae are known from settlement contexts and tend to bear elaborate painted decoration, often in trichrome as well as bichrome style, while all of the illustrated Durankulak examples are highly decorated, often in two or more styles (Todorova 2002a, Abb. 124/26: Varna II–III). It is possible that exposure to the elements has led to the erosion of the Orlovo example's surface, together with the loss of the painted decoration.

In summary, the Orlovo footed vessel has general analogies in the Hamangia IV and Varna II–III phases on the Black Sea coast, dated conjointly by AMS dating to 4800–4600 BC (Varna II–III) (Honch *et al.* 2006), while there are possible parallels in the much more remote Cucuteni A phase, dated to the late 5th millennium Cal. BC. The proposed interpretation is that this vessel may represent a local imitation of the Cucuteni form in a local fabric.

Bone

Horned stand (Museum Inv. No. 3067) (Plate 8b)
This object has two very small horn-like protuberances (2mm in length) at the top of a tubular cut-and-polished bone stand. No published analogies have been found in Central and South East Europe.

Chipped Stone

Dark brown flint side-scraper (Museum Inv. No. 3054/1) (Fig. A2.1a).
This is a blade with side-scraper retouch along all of the right dorsal edge. There is little of chronological specificity to this tool-type, since it occurs from the Early Neolithic (e.g. in Galabnik, West Bulgaria: Gatsov 1993: Pl. I/1, 5, 13–14), in the Early Copper Age (e.g. at Vaksevo: Gurova 2001, Ris. 2/9 and 3/3) and into the post-Chalcolithic (e.g. Hotnitsa-Vodopada: Sirakov and Tsonev 1995, 246 and fig. 2/10). It is interesting to note that side-scrapers are either much less common in Bulgarian prehistory than end-scrapers, especially those of the thumb-nail variety, or they have been rarely recognised as such. There is no obvious visual clue as to the source of the flint.

Honey flint bladelet (Museum Inv. No. 3360/46) (Plate 8e)
Not a particularly diagnostic bladelet. Good parallels in the Durankulak cemetery blades (Sirakov 2002, figure 5/6–7, 6/2,3,15; 7/3,10,12; 8/8). Most of these are Early Hamangia, with a single analogy in Varna I. On visual evidence, the likely source of the flint is North East Bulgaria.

Honey flint shouldered point (Museum Inv. No. 3316/53) (Fig. A2.1b)
Cf. Fiera Cleanov point (Dudeşti sites in Muntenia and Early Vinča and Vădastra sites in Oltenia: Păunescu 1968). On visual evidence, the likely source of the flint is North East Bulgaria.

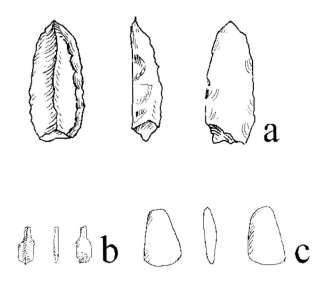

Figure A2.1. a. flint projectile point (Inv. 3054/1); b. flint shouldered point (Inv. 3316/53); c. volcanic tuff burnisher (Inv. 3360/45) (drawn by Elena Georgieva)

Ground and Polished Stone

Bird head (Private Collection) (Plate 8h)
Made of limestone, this small head is offset to the right, with dimpled eyes and a long beak. The impression is that this may represent a heron. The head is covered with a brown deposit, giving it a very worn appearance.

Of the reasonably wide variety of ornithomorphic figurines in the Balkan Neolithic and Chalcolithic, the closest resemblance comes from the Cucuteni B site of Margineni, in Moldavia (early 4th millennium Cal BC), with its finely modelled head of a duck or goose utilised as a ceramic terminal (Mantu and Dumitroaia 1997, fig. 58).

Marble leg (Museum Inv. No. 3316/62) (Plate 8g)
This small marble leg could be a part of one of three types of object:

- a seated figurine (e.g. the Late Chalcolithic example from the Gumelniţa tell (Hansen 2007, Vol. I, Abb. 135);
- a standing zoomorphic figurine (cf. the rather dissimilar fired clay examples from Orlovo: Fig. 2.1f) or the more specific parallel from Early Neolithic Lánycsók, Western Hungary (Kalicz 1990, 80 and Taf. 11/3); or, more probably,
- a lamp / altar (cf. a distinctive fired clay profile of such a leg from Early Neolithic Saidinene, Northeast Bulgaria: Nikolov, V. 2007, Tablo 3/2–3). Gaydarska (n.d.) has demonstrated that these footed vessels are one of the few artifact types that continues in use throughout the Neolithic and Copper Age. However, marble examples of each of these three types are rare, making a direct published parallel for the Orlovo leg hard to find.

Marble imitation horn (Museum Inv. No. 3368/1) (Plate 8d)
There are two aspects of this decorated marble object that are reminiscent of a caprine horn – the slight curvature of the horn and the parallel oblique grooves on one side of the horn only. No published Balkan parallels are known for such a marble horn.

Sandstone horned object (Museum Inv. No. 3068) (Plate 8c)
This small object has two horn-like protuberances of unequal size which suggest, at a very general level, the horned stands typical of the Varna group of the Western Black Sea coast. Examples that are broadly akin to the Orlovo example, if in fired clay, derive from Varna II–III graves at the Durankulak cemetery (Todorova 2002a, Abb. 124/21–26), with low-horned stands beginning in the Hamangia IV period (2002a, Abb. 123/11, 14). No published analogues in sandstone or any other stone are known.

Volcanic tuff burnisher (Museum Inv. No. 3360/45)(Fig. A2.1c)
Small pebbles can be used as burnishers for a variety of raw materials, including pottery, shell ornaments and copper.

This example is no different from the normal small size and rounded shape that fits easily into the palm of the hand. This form has no diagnostic chronological value.

Discussion

The first point to make is that the 'other' finds from Orlovo form a very disparate group of objects. Moreover, with the possible exception of the marble leg and the limestone bird head, they have little in common with the figurines, ornaments and polished stone tools from Orlovo.

The dated parallels for the items are, also, few and far between. The clearest parallel concerns the fragmentary footed vessel, with detailed similarities with the series of horae in the Cucuteni A phase in Moldavia, dated to the late 5th millennium BC. The flint bladelet and side-scraper lack a diagnostic form and can thus be paralleled in a range of lithic assemblages, from the Bulgarian Early Neolithic to the Late Copper Age. The shouldered flint point shows a more specific morphology, with resemblances to the Fiera Cleanov points of the Romanian and Serbian Middle Neolithic (Dudești, Vinča and Vădastră). This puts a date of the early 5th millennium BC for this form. The only rather general parallel for the sandstone horned object is in fired clay and concerns vessels dating to the Late Copper Age on the Black Sea coast, dated 4800–4600 BC at Varna and Durankulak. What these parallels indicate is that a date in the 5th millennium BC, with a stronger likelihood of the early rather than the late part, is the most likely date for the deposition of these probably unrelated artefacts.

Bibliography

Aladzhov, D. (1997) *Selishta, pametnitsi i nahodki ot Haskovskiya krai*. Haskovo, Atar-95.

Aldhouse-Green, M. (2001) Cosmovision and metaphor: monsters and shamans in Gallo-British cult-expression. *European Journal of Archaeology* 4/2, 203–232.

Aldhouse-Green, M. (2004) *An archaeology of images. Iconology and cosmology in Iron Age and Roman Europe*. London, Routledge.

Anastasova, E. (2008) Kamenni ansambli ot praistoricheskoto selishte Bulgarchevo: tipologicheska i funkcionalna harakteristika. In: M. Gurova (ed.) *Praistoricheski prouchvanija v Bulgaria: Novite predizvikatelstva*. Sofia, National Archaeological Institute with Museum at Bulgarian Academy of Sciences, 92–95.

Apel, J. (2001) *Daggers, knowledge and power*. Uppsala: Coast to Coast Project.

Audouze, F. (1999) New advances in French prehistory. *Antiquity* 72, 167–176.

Băčvarov, K. (2003) *Neolitni pogrebalni obredi. Intramuralni grobove ot bulgarskite zemi v konteksta na Jugoiztochna Evropa*. Sofia, Bard.

Băčvarov, K. (2005) Plastichni izobrajenia ot praistoricheskoto selishte pri Harmanli. *Arheologia* 1–4, 120–126.

Bailey, D. W. (2000) *Balkan prehistory*. London, Routledge.

Bailey, D. (2005) *Prehistoric figurines*. London, Routledge.

Bailey, D. W., Tringham, R. E., Bass, J., Stevanovic, M., Hamilton, M., Neumann, H., Angelova, I. and Raduncheva, A. (1998) Expanding the dimensions of early agricultural tells: the Podgoritsa Archaeological Project, Bulgaria. *Journal of Field Archaeology*, 25/4, 375–96.

Bánffy, E. (1990/1) Cult and archaeological context in central and south-east Europe in the Neolithic and Chalcolithic. *Antaeus* 19–20, 183–250.

Bánffy, E. (1995) Southwest Transdanubia as a mediating area. On the cultural history of the Early and Middle Chalcolithic. *Antaeus* 22, 157–196.

Banner, J. (1930) A Kőkénydombi neolithkori telep. *Dolgozatok* 6, 49–106.

Barker, G. and Lloyd, J. (1991) *Roman landscapes: archaeological survey in the Mediterranean region*. London, British School at Rome.

Bayliss, A. and Whittle, A. (eds) (2007) Histories of the dead. Building chronologies for five Southern British long barrows. *Cambridge Archaeological Journal* Supplement S1.

Bertók, G., Gáti, Cs. and Vajda, O. (2008) Preliminary report on the researdch at the Neolithic Kreisgrabanlage at Szemely-Hegyes, Baranya co., Hungary. *Archaeológiai Értesitö* 133: 85–106.

Biehl, P. (2003) *Studien zur Symbolgut des Neolithikums und der Kupferzeit in Südosteuropa*. Bonn, Habelt.

Binford, L. R. (1971) Mortuary practices: their study and their potential. In Brown J. (ed.) Approaches to the social dimensions of mortuary practices, 6–29. *Washington, D.C.: Memoir of the Society for American Archaeology 25*.

Bintliff, J. (1991) The Roman countryside in central Greece: observations and theories from the Boeotia Survey (1978–1987). In Barker, G. and Lloyd, J. *Roman landscapes: archaeological survey in the Mediterranean region*, 122–132. London, British School at Rome.

Bintliff, J. (2000) Beyond dots on the map: future directions for surface artefact survey in Greece. In Bintliff, J., Kuna, M. and Venclová, N. (eds) *The future of surface artefact survey in Europe*, 3–20. Sheffield, Sheffield Academic Press.

Bintliff, J., Howard, P. and Snodgrass, A. (eds) (2006) *Testing the hinterland: the work of the Boeotia Survey (1989–1991) in the Southern approaches to the city of Thespiai*. Cambridge, McDonald Institute for Archaeological Research.

Bintliff, J., Kuna, M. and Venclová, N. (eds) (2000) *The future of surface artefact survey in Europe*. Sheffield, Sheffield Academic Press.

Bondev, I. (1991) *Rastitelnostta na Bulgaria*. Sofia, Universitetsko Izdatelstvo Sv. Kliment Ohridski.

Bonsall, C. (2009) The use of 'Balkan flint' in the Early Neolithic of the Romanian Iron Gates. In *Abstracts, 15th Annual Meeting of the European Association of Archaeologists, Riva de Garda*, p. 148.

Boyadzhiev, Y. (1995) Chronology of prehistoric cultures in Bulgaria. In Bailey, D. and Panayotov, I. (eds) Prehistoric Bulgaria, 149–192. Madison, Wisc: Prehistory Press.

Boyadzhiev, Y. (2008) Kusnohalkolitno selishte Orlitsa. In Vaklinova, M. (ed.) *Po putishtata na vremeto. Katalog kum izlozhba 31 mart–30 april 2008*. Sofia: NAIM-BAN, 46.

Boyadzhiev, Y. and Boyadzhiev, K. (2008) Kusnohalkolitno selishte Vurhari. In Vaklinova, M. (ed.) *Po putishtata na vremeto. Katalog kum izlozhba 31 mart–30 april 2008*. Sofia: NAIM-BAN, 47.

Boyadzhiev, Y., Takorova, D. and Boyadzhiev, K. (2010) Halkolitno selishte Vrhari. *Bulgarska Arkeologia 2009*. Sofia: National Institute of Archaeology.

Boyanov, I., Kozhukharov, D., Goranov, A., Ruseva, M., Shilyafova, Zh. and Yanev, Y. (1989) *Geolozhka karta na NR Bulgaria. M1:100000. Map sheet "Haskovo"*, Sofia, BAN.

Boyanov, I., Kozhukharov, D., Goranov, A., Kozhukharova, E., Ruseva, M. and Shilyafova, Zh. (1992) *Geolozhka karta na Bulgaria. M1:100000. Karten list Haskovo. Obyasnitelna zapiska*. Sofia, BAN.

Bozhilova, E. and Beug, H. J. (1992) On the Holocene history of vegetation in SE Bulgaria (Lake Arkutino, Ropotamo region). *Vegetation History and Archaeobotany* 1, 19–32.

Bozhilova, E. and Filipova, M. (1975) Polenov analiz na kulturni plastove ot Varnenskoto ezero. *Izvestia na Narodnia muzei Varna* XI (XXVI), 19–23.

Bradley, R. (1990) Perforated stone axe-heads in the British Neolithic: their distribution and significance. *Oxford Journal of Archaeology* 9, 299–304.

Bradley, R. and Edmonds, M. (1993) *Interpreting the axe trade: production and exchange in Neolithic Britain*. Cambridge, Cambridge University Press.

Branigan, K. (1983) Archaeological survey of the Ayiofarango, Southern Crete. In Keller, D. R. and Rupp, D. W. (eds) *Archaeological survey in the Mediterranean area*, 291–294. BAR International Series 155. Oxford, Archaeopress.

Brück, J. (2001) Monuments, power and personhood in the British Neolithic. *Journal of the Royal Anthropological Institute* 7: 649–667.

Bulgarelli, G. M. (1981) Turquoise working in the Helmand civilisation. In Härtel, H. (ed.) *South Asian Archaeology* 1979, 66–69. Berlin, Dietrich Reimer.

Burkitt, I. (1999) *Bodies of thought. Embodiment, identity and modernity*. London, Sage Publications.

Chapman, J. (1981) *The Vinča culture of south east Europe. Studies in chronology, economy and society*. BAR International Series 117. Oxford, Archaeopress.

Chapman, J. (1983) Meaning and illusion in the study of burial in Balkan prehistory. In A. Poulter (ed.) *Ancient Bulgaria Volume 1*, 1–45. Nottingham, University of Nottingham Press.

Chapman, J. (1989) The early Balkan village. *Varia Archaeologica Hungarica*, 2, 33–53.

Chapman, J. (1990) The Neolithic in the Morava-Danube confluence area: a regional assessment of settlement pattern. In Tringham, R. and D. Krstić (eds) *Selevac. A Neolithic village in Yugoslavia*, 13–44, Monumenta Archaeologica 15, Los Angeles: University of California Press.

Chapman, J. (1996) Enchainment, commodification and gender in the Balkan Neolithic and Copper Age, *Journal of European Archaeology* 4, 203–242.

Chapman, J. (1997) Places as timemarks – the social construction of landscapes in Eastern Hungary. In Chapman J. and Dolukhanov, P. (eds) *Landscapes in Flux*, 137–162. Oxford, Oxbow Books.

Chapman, J. (1998) Objects and places: their value in the past, in Bailey, D. W. (ed.) *The archaeology of prestige and wealth*, 106–130. Oxford, BAR International Series 730. Oxford, Archaeopress.

Chapman, J. (2000) *Fragmentation in archaeology: People, places and broken objects in the prehistory of South Eastern Europe*. London, Routledge

Chapman, J. (2003) Domesticating the exotic: the context of

Cucuteni-Tripolye exchange with steppe and forest-steppe communities. In Boyle, K., Renfrew, C. and Levine, M. (eds) *Ancient interactions: east and west in Eurasia*, 75–92. McDonald Institute Monongraphs. Cambridge: McDonald Institute for Archaeological Research.

Chapman, J. (2006) Dark burnished ware as sign: ethnicity, aesthetics and categories in the Later Neolithic of the Central Balkans. In Tasić, N. and Grozdanov, C. (eds) *Homage to Milutin Garašanin*, 295–308. Beograd, Serbian Academy of Siences and Arts and Macedonian Academy of Arts and Science.

Chapman, J. (2007) Engaging with the exotic: the production of early farming communities in South-East and Central Europe. In Spataro, M. and Biagi, P. (eds) *A short walk through the Balkans: the first farmers of the Carpathian Basin and adjacent regions. Quaderno* 12: 207–222 (Trieste).

Chapman, J. (2007a) The elaboration of an aesthetic of brilliance and colour in the Climax Copper Age. In Lang, F., Reinholdt, C. and Weilhartner, J. (eds) *Stephanos Aristeios. Archäologische Forschungen zwischen Nil und Istros*, 65–74. Wien: Phoibos Verlag.

Chapman, J. (2008) Approaches to trade and exchange in earlier prehistory (Late Mesolithic–Early Bronze Age). In Jones, A. (ed.) *Prehistoric Europe. Theory and practice*, 333–355. Oxford, Blackwell.

Chapman, J. and Gaydarska, B. (2006) *Parts and wholes. Fragmentation in prehistoric context*. Oxford, Oxbow Books.

Chapman, J. and Gaydarska, B. (in press) *Spondylus gaederopus / Glycymeris* exchange networks in the European Neolithic and Chalcolithic. (To appear in Hofmann, D., Fowler, C. and Harding, J. (eds) *Handbook of the European Neolithic*. Oxford: Oxford University Press.)

Chapman, J. and Gaydarska, B. (in prep.) The shell ornaments from the Varna Eneolithic Necropolis. (To appear in Slavchev, V. (ed.) *The Varna Eneolithic Cemetery Final Report*).

Chapman, J., Gaydarska, B. and Angelova, I. (2005) On the tell and off the tell: the fired clay figurines from Omurtag. In Spinei, V., Lazarovici, C-M. and Monah, D. (eds) *Scripta praehistorica M. Petrescu-Dîmboviţa Festschrift*, 341–385. Iaşi, Trinitas.

Chapman, J., Gaydarska, B., Angelova, I., Gurova, M. and Yanev, S. (2004) Breaking, making and trading: the Omurtag Eneolithic *Spondylus* hoard. *Archaeologica Bulgarica* 2004/2, 11–34.

Chapman, J., Gaydarska, B. and Hardy, K. (2006) Does enclosure make a difference? A view from the Balkans. Harding, A., Sievers, S. and Venclová, N. (eds) *Enclosing the past: Inside and Outside in Prehistory*, 20–43. Sheffield Archaeological Monographs 15, Equinox.

Chapman, J., Gaydarska, B., Raduntcheva, A. and Petrov, I. (n.d.) *The prehistoric site of Orlovo, South Eastern Bulgaria: from surface finds to past lifeways*. Unpublished report to Durham University Dept. of Archaeology Research Committee, 2007.

Chapman, J., Higham, T., Slavchev, V., Gaydarska, B. and Honch, N. (2006) The social context of the emergence, development and abandonment of the Varna cemetery, Bulgaria. *European Journal of Archaeology* 9/2–3, 159–183.

Chapman, J., Magyari, E. and Gaydarska, B. (2009) Contrasting subsistence strategies in the Early Iron Age? – new results from the Alföld Plain, Hungary, and the Thracian Plain, Bulgaria. *Oxford Journal of Archaeology* 28/2: 155–187.

Chapman, J. and Richter, É., (2010) Geometric order and

scientific principles: a view from the Mesolithic, Neolithic and Chalcolithic of Central and South East Europe. In Bodi, G. (ed.) *In medias res praehistoria. Miscellanea in honorem annos LXV peragentis Professoria Dan Monarch oblata*, 21–58. Iaşi: Institute of Archaeology.

Chapman, J. and Shiel, R. (1991) Settlements, soils and societies in Dalmatia. In Barker, G. and Lloyd, J. *Roman landscapes: archaeological survey in the Mediterranean region.*, 62–75. London, British School at Rome.

Chapman, J. and Shiel R. (1993) 'Social change and land use in prehistoric Dalmatia', *Proceedings of the Prehistoric Society* 59, 61–104.

Chapman, J., Shiel, R. and Batović, Š. (1996) *The changing face of Dalmatia. Archaeological and ecological studies in a Mediterranean landscape*, Society of Antiquaries of London Research Report No. 54, London, Cassell.

Chapman, J., Shiel, R., Passmore, D., Magyari, E. *et al.* (2003) *The Upper Tisza Project: studies in Hungarian landscape archaeology.* E-book 1.(available on: http://ads.ahds.ac.uk/catalogue/projArch/uppertisza_ba_2003/index.cfm)

Chapman, J., Vicze, M., Shiel, R., Cousins, S., Gaydarska, B. and Bond, C. (2010) *Upland Settlement in North East Hungary: excavations at the multi-period site of Regéc-95.* Oxford, Archaeopress.

Charles, J. (1969) Appendix I: A metallurgical examination of South-East European copper axes, 40–42. In Renfrew, C., The autonomy of the South East European Copper Age. *Proceedings of the Prehistoric Society*, 35, 12–47.

Childe, V. G. (1929) *The Danube in prehistory.* Oxford, Clarendon Press.

Childe, V. G. (1935) Changing methods and aims in prehistory. Presidential Address for 1935. *Proceedings of the Prehistoric Society* 1, 1–15.

Childe, V. G. (1957) *The dawn of European civilization.* 6th edition. London, Routledge and Kegan Paul.

Chohadzhiev, S. (2001) *Vaksevo – praistorichecki selishta.* Veliko Turnovo, Faber.

Chohadzhiev, S. (2004) Three-fingered anthropomorphs: origins and territorial distribution. In Nikolov, V., Băčvarov, K. and Kalchev, P. (eds) *Prehistoric Thrace*, 408–420. Sofia, Institute of Archaeology.

Chohadzhiev, S. (2006) *Slatino – praistoricheski selishta.* Veliko Turnovo, Faber.

Choyke, A. (1997) Polgár-Csőszhalom-dűlő lelőhely csont-, agabcs- és agyartárgyainak vizsgálata. In Raczky, P. (ed) *Utak a múltba*, 157–159. Budapest, Magyar Nemzeti Múzeum and ELTE Régészettudományi Intézet.

Choyke, A. (2007) Objects for a lifetime – tools for a season: the bone tools from Ecsegfalva 23. In Whittle, A. (ed.) *The Early Neolithic of the Great Hungarian Plain. Investigations of the Körös culture site of Ecsegfalva 23, County Békés*, 641–666. Varia Archaeologica Hungarica XXI. Budapest, Institute of Archaeology HAS.

Clough, T. H. Mk. (ed.)(1988) *Stone axe studies II. The petrology of prehistoric stone implements from the British Isles.* London, Council for British Archaeology.

Clough, T. H. Mk. and Cummins, W. A. (eds) (1979) *Stone axe studies, archaeological, petrological, experimental and ethnographic.* London, Council for British Archaeology.

Coles, J. (1973) *Archaeology by experiment.* London, Hutchinson.

Comşa, E. (1974) *Istoria comuniţailor culturii Boian.* Bucureşti, Editura Academiei Republicii Socialiste Rômana.

Comşa, E. and Cantacuzino, Gh. (2001) *Necropola neolitică de la Cernica.* Bucureşti, Editura Academei Române.

Comşa, E. and Rauţ, O. (1969) Figurine antropomorfe aparţinînd culturii Vinča descoperite la Zorlenţu Mare. *SCIV* XX/1, 3–15.

Cooney, G. and Mandal, S. 1998. *The Irish Stone Axe Project.* Monograph 1. Bray: Wordwell.

Cotoi, O. (2000) *Uneltele din piatră şlefuită din Eneoliticul subcarpaţilor Moldovei.* Iaşi, Corson.

De Maria, S. (1991) Bologna (*Bononia*) and its suburban territory. In Barker, G. and Lloyd, J. *Roman landscapes: archaeological survey in the Mediterranean region*, 88–95. London, British School at Rome.

Dergachev, V. (1998) *Karbunskij klad.* Chisinau, Institut de Arheologii.

Diáz-Andreu, M. (2001) Marking the landscape. Iberian post-paleolithic art, identities and the sacred. In G.H. Nash and C. Chippindale (eds) *European Landscapes of Rock-art*, 158–175. London, Routledge.

Dimitrov, K. (2002) Die Artefakte aus Felsstein und ihre Nachahmungen. In Todorova, H. (ed.) *Durankulak Band II. Die prähistorischen Gräberfelder*, Teil 1, 207–212. DAI, Berlin – Sofia, Anubis.

Dimitrov, M. (1976) Za haraktera na kultura Karanovo IV, *Izvestia na muzeite v Jugoiztochna Bulgaria* I, 9–16.

Djurova, E. and Aleksiev, B. 1989. Zeolitic rocks in the East Rhodope Paleogene depression. *Geologica Rhodopica, 1*, 240–245.

Dobres, M.-A. (2000) *Technology and social agency.* Oxford, Blackwell.

Dobres, M.-A. and Robb, J. (2000) *Agency in Archaeology.* London/New York, Routledge.

Douglas, M. (1966) *Purity and danger: an analysis of concepts of pollution and taboo.* London, Routledge and Kegan Paul.

Dragomanov, L., Angelov, G., Koyumdjieva, E., Nikolov, I. and Komogorova, I. (1984) Neogenut v Haskovsko. *Palaeontologia, Stratigraphia i Lithologia* 20, 71–75.

Dragomir, I. T. (1983) *Eneoliticul din sud-estul României.* Bucureşti, Academia Română.

Draşovean, F. (1998) Art and black magic in Vinča culture. In Draşovean, F. (ed.) *The Late Neolithic of the Middle Danube region*, 205–212. Timişoara, Eurobit.

Dremsizova-Nelchinova, Ts., Ginev, G., Angelova, I. and Konakliev, A. (1991) *Arheologicheski pametnitsi v Targovishkiya Raion.* Sofia, Natsionalen Institut za Pametnitsite na Kulturata.

Dumitrescu, H. (1958) Deux nouvelles tombes cucuteniennes à rite magique découvertes à Traian. *Dacia* N.S. 2, 407–423.

Dumitrescu, V. (1980) *The Neolithic settlement at Rast.* BAR International Series 72. Oxford, Archaeopress.

Elster, E. (2003) Grindstones, polished edge-tools and other stone artifacts. In Elster, E. and Renfrew, C. (eds) Elster, E. and Renfrew, C. (eds) (2003) *Prehistoric Sitagroi: excavations in Northeast Greece, 1968–1970. Volume 2: the final report*, 178–195. Los Angeles, Cotsen Institute of Archaeology.

Elster, E. and Renfrew, C. (eds) (2003) *Prehistoric Sitagroi: excavations in Northeast Greece, 1968–1970. Volume 2: the final report.* Los Angeles, Cotsen Institute of Archaeology.

Éluère, C. and Raub, C. R. (1991) Investigations on the gold coating technology of the great dish from Varna. In Mohen, J-P. (ed.) *Découverte du métal*, 13–30. Paris, Picard.

Erdogu, B. (2004) *Prehistoric Settlements of Eastern Thrace: A Reconsideration.* BAR International Series 1424. Oxford, Archaeopress.

Evtimova, E., Aladzhov, Zh. and Kamenarov, A. (2006) Sondazhni razkopki m. Keramluka v zemlishteto na s. Krum, Dimitrovgradsko. In Nikolov, V., Nehrisov, G. and Tsvetkova, Yu. (eds) *Spasitelni arheologicheski razkopki po traeto na zhelezoputnata liniya Plovdiv – Svilengrad prez 2004 g*, 267–298. Veliko Trnovo, Arheologicheski Institut BAN.

Filipova-Marinova, M. (2003) Postglacial vegetation dynamics in the coastal part of the Strandza Mountains (Southeastern Bulgaria) In Tonkov, S. (ed.) *Progress in palynology and paleoecology: Festschrift in honor of Prof. E. Bozilova*, 213–231. Sofia, Pencost.

Finlay, N. (2003) Microliths and multiple authorship. In Larsson, L., Kindgren, H., Knutsson, K., Loeffler, D. and Åkerlund, A. (eds) *Mesolithic on the move. Papers presented at the Sixth International Conference on the Mesolithic in Europe, Stockholm 2000*, 169–176. Oxford, Oxbow Books.

Fletcher, R. (1989) Social theory and archaeology: diversity, paradox and potential. *Mankind* 19/1, 65–75.

Fowler, C. (2004) *The archaeology of personhood. An anthropological approach.* London and New York, Routledge.

Gaffney, V. and Tingle, M. (1989) *The Maddle Farm Project: an integrated survey of prehistoric and Roman landscapes on the Berkshire Downs.* BAR British Series B-200. Oxford, Archaeopress.

Galbenu, D. (1963) Neoliticheskaya musterskaya dlya obrabotki ukrashenii v Hîrşove. *Dacia* N.S.7, 501–509.

Gale, N., Stos-Gale, S., Radouncheva, A., Ivanov, I., Lilov, P., Todorov, T. and Panayotov, I. (2000) Early metallurgy in Bulgaria. *Godishnik Nov Bulgarski Universitet*, IV–V, 102–168.

Galović, R. (1959) *Predionica. Neolitsko naselje kod Prištine.* Priština.

Gatsov, I. (1993) *Neolithic chipped stone industries in Western Bulgaria.* Kraków: Jagellonian University Institute of Archaeology.

Gatsov, I. (2000) Chipped stone assemblages from south and south-west Bulgaria and north-west Turkey. In Nikolova, L. (ed.) *Technology, style and society: contyributions to the innovations between the Alps and the Black Sea in prehistory.* BAR International Series 854, 1–28. Oxford, Archaeopress.

Gaydarska, B. (2004) Preliminary research on prehistoric salt exploitation in Bulgaria. In Slavchev, V. (ed.) Todorova Festschrift, *Dobrudzha* 21, 110–122.

Gaydarska, B. (2007) *Landscape, Material Culture and Society in South East Bulgaria.* BAR International Series 1618. Oxford, Archaeopress.

Gaydarska, B., Chapman, J., Angelova, I., Gurova, M. and Yanev, S. (2004) Breaking, making and trading: the Omurtag Eneolithic *Spondylus* hoard. *Archaeologia Bulgarica* 2, 11–34.

Gaydarska, B., Chapman, J., Raduntcheva, A. and Koleva. B. (2007) The *châine opératoire* approach to prehistoric figurines: an example from Dolnoslav, Bulgaria. In Renfrew, C. and Morley, I. (eds) *Image and Imagination*, 171–184. Cambridge, McDonald Institute for Archaeological Research.

Gell, A. (1992) The technology of enchantment and the enchantment of technology. In Goote, J. and Shelton, A. (eds) *Antropology and Aesthetics*, 40–63. Oxford.

Geografiya na Bulgaria. (2002) Sofia, ForCom.

Georgiev, G. I. (1961) Kulturgruppen der Jungstein-und der Kupferzeit in der Ebene von Thrazien (Südbulgarien). In Böhm, J. and de Laet, S. J. (eds) *L'Europe à la fin de l'âge de la pierre*, 45–100. Editions de l'Académie Tchechoslovaque des Sciences, Prague.

Gillings, M. (1998) Embracing uncertainty and challenging dualism in the GIS-based study of a palaeo-flood plain. *European Journal of Archaeology* 1/1, 117–144.

Gimbutas, M. (1974) *The gods and goddesses of Old Europe, 7000–3500 BC.* London, Thames and Hudson.

Gimbutas, M. (1986) Mythical imagery of Sitagroi society. In Renfrew, C., Gimbutas, M. and Elster, E. S. (eds) *Excavations at Sitagroi. A prehistoric village in Northeast Greece. Volume 1*, 225–301. Los Angeles, CA, Institute of Archaeology, UCLA.

Gimbutas, M. (1989) Figurines and cult equipment: their role in the reconstruction of Neolithic religion. In Gimbutas, M., Winn, S. and Shimabuku, D. (eds) *Achilleion. A Neolithic settlement in Thessaly, Greece, 6400–5600 BC.* Monumenta Archaeologica, Vol. 14, 171–227. Institute of Archaeology, University of California, Los Angeles.

Gimbutas, M. (1989a) *The language of the goddess.* London, Thames and Hudson.

Godelier, M. (1999) *The Enigma of the gift.* Cambridge, Polity Press.

Goranov, A. and Atanasov, G. 1989. Lithostratigraphic subdivision of the East Rhodope and Upper Thracian Paleogene. *Geologica Rhodopica, 1*, 14–21.

Grebska-Kulova, M. (2004) Cultural changes in the second half of the 6th mill. BC in Southwestern Bulgaria. In Nikolov, V., Bǎčvarov, K. and Kalchev, P. (eds) *Prehistoric Thrace*, 133–145. Sofia, Institute of Archaeology.

Green, M. (1997) Images in opposition: polarity, ambivalence and liminality in cult representation. *Antiquity* 71, 898–911.

Gurova, M. (2001) Kremuchna kolektsiya ot Vaksevo – tipologichesko opisanie i trasologicheski analiz. In Chohadzhiev, S. (ed.) *Vaksevo – praistorichecki selishta*, 22–27. Veliko Turnovo, Faber.

Gurova, M. (2004) Evolution and retardation: flint assemblages from Tell Karanovo. In Nikolov, V., Bǎčvarov, K. and Kalchev, P. (eds) *Prehistoric Thrace*, 239–253. Sofia, Institute of Archaeology.

Gurova, M. (2007) Review of Manolakakis, L. Les Industries Lithiques Énéolithiques de Bulgarie. Internationale Archäologie, Band 88. Rahden/Westf.: Verlag Marie Leidorf GmbH, 2005, in *Archaeologia Bulgarica* XI/2, 85–87.

Halstead, P. (1999) Neighbours from hell? The household in Neolithic Greece. In Halstead, P. (ed.) *Neolithic society in Greece*, 77–95. Sheffield, Sheffield Academic Press.

Hamilton, N., Marcus, J., Bailey, D., Haaland, G., Haaland, R. and Ucko, P. (1996) Can we interpret figurines? *Cambridge Archaeological Journal* 6/2, 285–291.

Hansen, S. (2007) *Bilder vom Menschen der Steinzeit. Untersuchungen zur anthropomorphen Plastik der Jungsteinzeit und Kupferzeit in Südosteuropa.* Archäologie in Eurasien 20. Mainz, Verlag Philipp von Zabern.

Harbison, P. (1976) *Bracers and V-perforated buttons in the Beaker and Food Vessel cultures of Ireland*. Archaeologia Atlantica Research Report 1. Bad Bremstedt, Moreland Editions.

Haşotti, P. (1985) Noi cercetări arheologice în aşezarea culturii Hamangia de la Medgidia–Cocoaşă. *Pontica* 18: 25–40.

Hawkes, J. G. (1969) The ecological background to plant domestication. In Ucko, P. J. and Dimbleby, G. W. (eds) *The domestication and exploitation of plants and animals*, 17–30. London, Duckworth.

Helms, M. W. (1993) *Crafts and the kingly ideal. Art, trade and power.* Austin, TX, University of Texas Press.

Higgs, E. and Vita-Finzi, C. (1970) Prehistoric economy in the Mount Carmel area of Palestine: site catchment analysis. *Proceedings of the Prehistoric Society* 36, 1–37.

Higham, T., Chapman, J., Slavchev, V., Gaydarska, B., Honch, N., Yordanov, Y. and Dimitrova, B. (2007) New perspectives on the Varna cemetery (Bulgaria) – AMS dates and social implications. *Antiquity* 81, 640–654.

Hillebrand, J. (1929) *Das frühkupferzeitliche Gräberfeld von Pusztaistvánháza*. Archaeologica Hungarica IV. Budapest, Hungarian Academy of Sciences.

Hirth, K. G. (1978) Interregional trade and the formation of prehistoric gateway communities. *American Antiquity* 43/1, 35–45.

Hodder, I. (1990) *The domestication of Europe*. Oxford, Blackwell.

Hodder, I. (1999) *The archaeological process. An introduction.* Oxford: Blackwell.

Hodder, I. (ed.) (2005) *Catalhöyük perspectives: reports from the 1995–1999 seasons: by members of the teams.* London, British Institute at Ankara.

Hodder, I. (2005a) The spatio-temporal organization of the early 'town' at Çatalhöyük. In Bailey, D., Whittle, A. and Cummings, V. (eds) *(un)settling the Neolithic*, 126–139. Oxford, Oxbow Books.

Honch, N., T. Higham, J. Chapman, B. Gaydarska and R. E. M. Hedges (2006) A palaeodietary investigation of carbon (13C/12C) and nitrogen (15N/14N) in human and faunal bones from the Copper Age cemeteries of Varna I and Durankulak, Bulgaria. *Journal of Archaeological Science* 33, 1493–1504.

Iakovidis, S. (1977) On the use of Mycenean 'buttons'. *Annual of the British School in Athens* 72, 113–119.

Ignatov, V., Kuncheva-Ruseva, T., Velkov, K., Popova, Ts., Ribarov, G. and Gospodinov, N. (2006) Arheologicheski razkopki v m. Shihanov bryag do Harmanli. In Nikolov, V., Nehrisov, G. and Tsvetkova, Yu. (eds) *Spasitelni arheologicheski razkopki po traeto na zhelezoputnata liniya Plovdiv – Svilengrad prez 2004 g*, 335–396. Veliko Trnovo, Arheologicheski Institut BAN.

Ingold, T. (2000) The perception of the environment: essays in livelihood, dwelling and skill. London, Routledge.

Ingold, T. (2007) Materials against materiality. *Archaeological Dialogues* 14/1, 1–16.

Ivanov, I. (1991) Der Bestattungsritus in der chalkolitischen Nekropole von Varna (mit einem Katalog des wichstigsten Gräber). In Lichardus, J. (ed.) *Die Kupferzeit als historische Epoche*. Saarbrücker Beiträge zum Altertumskunde 55, 125–150. Saabrücken, Saarland Museum.

Ivanov, I. and Avramova, M. (2000) *Varna necropolis. The dawn of European civilization.* Sofia, Agató.

Ivanov, I. and Bozhilova, E. (1986) Ekologichni usloviya na Varnenskoto ezero prez eneolitnata i bronzovata epoha spored palinologichni, paleobotanichni i arheologichni danni. *Izvestia Naroden Muzej Varna* XXI (XXXVI), 43–48.

Ivanov, S. and Vasilev, V. (1975) Prouchvaniya na zhivotinskiya kosten material ot praistoricheskata selishtna mogila pri Golyamo Delchevo. In Todorova, H., Ivanov, S., Vasilev, V., Hopf, M., Quitta, H. and Kohl, G., Selishtanata mogila pri Goliamo Delchevo. *Razkopki i Prouchvania* V, 245–302. Sofia, Izdatelstvo na BAN.

Jones, A. (2002) *Archaeological theory and scientific practice.* Cambridge, Cambridge University Press.

Jones, A. (2005) Lives in fragments? Personhood and the European Neolithic. *Journal of Social Archaeology* 5/2, 193–224.

Jones, A. and MacGregor, G. (eds) (2002) *Colouring the past. The significance of colour in archaeological research.* Oxford, Berg.

Kalicz, N. (1990) *Frühneolitische Siedlungsfunde aus Südwestungarn.* Inventaria Praehistorica Hungariae IV. Budapest, Nemzeti Múzeum.

Kalchev, P. (1996) Funeral rites of the Early Bronze Age flat necropolis near the Bereket Tell, Stara Zagora. *Reports of Prehistoric Research Projects* (1), Nos. 2–4, 215–225.

Kalchev, P. (2005) *Neolithic dwellings. Stara Zagora Town.* Exposition Catalog. Regional Museum of History – Stara Zagora.

Kamarev, M. (2005) Liavoto i diasnoto v glinenata plastika – idei za niakoi duhovni predstavi ot epohata na kusnia halkolit. In Stoyanov, T., Angelova, S. and Lozanov, I., (eds) *Stephanos Archaeologicos in honorem Professoris Ludmilli Getov*, 371–383. Sofia: Sofia University Press.

Keates, S. (2002) The flashing blade: copper, colour and luminosity in North Italian Copper Age society. In Jones, A. and MacGregor, G. (eds) *Colouring the past. The significance of colour in archaeological research*, 109–126. Oxford, Berg.

Keightley, J. M. (1986) The pottery of Phases I and II. In Renfrew, C., Gimbutas, M. and Elster, E. S. (eds) *Excavations at Sitagroi. A prehistoric village in Northeast Greece. Volume 1*, 345–392. Los Angeles, CA, Institute of Archaeology, UCLA.

Keller, D. R., and Rupp, D. W. (eds)(1983) *Archaeological survey in the Mediterranean area.* BAR International Series I-155. Oxford, Archaeopress.

Kenderova, R. (2006) Geomorfologia i harakteristika na paleosredata. in Nehrisov, G. Yamno svetilishte ot zhelyaznata epoha i selishte ot rannata bronzova epoha pri Svilengrad. In Nikolov, V., Nehrisov, G. and Tsvetkova, Yu. (eds) *Spasitelni arheologicheski razkopki po traeto na zhelezoputnata liniya Plovdiv – Svilengrad prez 2004 g*, 397–398. Veliko Trnovo, Arheologicheski Institut BAN.

Kenderova, R. and Sarafov, A. (2006) Prirodna sreda (morfohidrografska i geolozhka harakteristika) v raiona na mogilen nekropol do s. Vinitsa. In Nikolov, V., Nehrisov, G. and Tsvetkova, Yu. (eds) *Spasitelni arheologicheski razkopki po traeto na zhelezoputnata liniya Plovdiv – Svilengrad prez 2004 g*, 65–67. Veliko Trnovo, Arheologicheski Institut BAN.

Kenoyer, J. M. (1991) Ornament styles of the Indus Valley tradition: evidence from recent excavations at Harappa, Pakistan. *Paléorient* 17/2, 79–98.

King, R. H. (1983) Soils and archaeological surveys: case of the Canadian Palaipaphos Survey Project. In Keller, D. R., and

Rupp, D. W. (eds) *Archaeological survey in the Mediterranean area*, 101–107. BAR International Series 155. Oxford, Archaeopress.

Kokkinidou, D. and Nikolaidou, M. (1996) Body imagery in the Aegean Neolithic: ideological implication of anthropomorphic figurines. In Moore, J. and Scott, E. (eds) *Invisible people and processes: writing woman and children into European archaeology*, 88–112. Leicester, Leicester University Press.

Kopytoff, I. (1986) The cultural biography of things: commoditization as process. In Appadurai, A. (ed.) *The social life of things*, 64–91. Cambridge, Cambridge University Press.

Kopytoff, I. (1987) *The African frontier: the reproduction of traditional African societies*. Bloomington, IN, Indiana University Press.

Korek, J. (1989) *Die Theiß-Kultur in der Mittleren und Nördlichen Theißgegend*. Inventaria Praehistorica Hungariae III. Budapest, Nemzeti Múzeum.

Kostov, R. I. (2006) Pregled na mineralogichnata sistematika na yaspisa i srodnite skali. *Geologiya i Mineralni Resursi, 13*, 9, 8–12.

Kostov, R. I. (2007) *Arheomineralogiya na neolitni i halkolitni artefakti ot Bulgaria i tyahnoto znachenie v gemologyata*. Sofia, Publishing House 'Sv. Ivan Rilski'.

Kostov, R., Chapman, J., Gaydarska, B., Petrov, I. and Raduntcheva, A. (2007) Turquoise – archaeomineralogical evidences from the Orlovo prehistoric site (Haskovo District, Southern Bulgaria). *Geologiya i Mineralni Resursi* 7–8, 17–22.

Kostov, R. Dimov, T. and Pelevina, O. (2004) Gemmological characteristics of carnelian and agate beads from the Chalcolithic necropolis at Durankulak and Varna (in Bulgarian). *Geologiya i Mineralni Resursi* 10, 15–24.

Kostov, R. I. and Machev, Ph. (2008) Mineralogical and petrographic characteristics of nephrite and other stone artifacts from the Neolithic site Kovachevo in Southwest Bulgaria in Bulgarian). In *National Conference "Prehistoric Studies in Bulgaria: New Challenges" (Ed. by M. Gyurova), Peshtera, 26–29 April 2006*, Sofia, 70–78.

Kostov, R. I. and Pelevina, O. (2006) Mineralogical-petrographical structure of the stone artifacts from the Varna Late Chalcolithic necropolis (in Bulgarian with an English summary). *Interdisciplinary Studies, XIX, Archaeological Institute and Museum, BAS*, 25–31.

Kotsakis, K. (1999) What tells can tell: social space and settlement in the Greek Neolithic. In Halstead, P. (ed.) *Neolithic society in Greece*, 66–76. Sheffield, Sheffield Academic Press.

Koukouli-Chryssanthaki, Ch., Todorova, H., Aslanis, I., Vajsov, I. and Valla, M. (2007) Promachon – Topolnica. A greek-bulgarian archaeological project. In Todorova, H., Stefanovich, M. and Ivanov, G. (eds) *The Struma/Strymon valley in prehistory*, 43–78. Sofia: Museum of History Kjustendil.

Kounov, A, Pounev, L., Karadjova, B. (1977) Turquoise, a new mineral for Bulgaria. *Comptes Rendus de l'Academie Bulgare des Sciences, 30*, 8, 1153–1155.

Kovacheva, M. (1995) Bulgarian archaeomagnetic studies. In Bailey, D. and Panayotov, I. (eds) *Prehistoric Bulgaria*, 209–224. Madison, WI: Prehistory Press.

Krauß, R. (2006) *Die prähistorische Besiedlung am Unterlauf der Jantra vor dem Hintergrund der Kulturgeschichte Nordbulgariens (Praistoriiata po dolnoto techenie na r. Iantra na fona na kulturnata istoriia na severna Bulgariia)*. Rahden/Westf, Verlag Marie Leidorf.

Kreutz, A., Marinova, E., Schäfer, E. and Wiethold, J. (2005) A comparison of Early Neolithic crop and weed assemblages from the Linearbandkeramik and the Bulgarian Neolithic cultures: differences and similarities. *Vegetation History and Archaeobotany* 14, 237–258.

Kuhn, T. S. (1962) *The structure of scientific revolutions*. Chicago, University of Chicago Press.

Kunchev, K. (2000) Otnosno prouchvaneto na praistoricheskite kremuchni artefakti v Bulgaria. In Nikolov, V. (ed.) *Trakiya i susednite raioni prez neolita i halkolita*, 133–139. Sofia, Arheologicheski Institut na BAN.

Kunchev, K. and Chohadzhiev, M. (1994) Neolitno selishte v Krumovgrad. In *Maritsa Iztok Arkheologicheski prouchvania*, II. Sofia, 13–38.

Kunchev, M. and Kuncheva, T. (1988) Pozdneneoliticheskoe poselenie "Hlebozavod" u goroda Nova-Zagora. *Studia Praehistorica* 9, 68–83.

Kunchev, M. and Kuncheva, T. (1993) Antropomorphna plastika ot selishtnata mogila do s. Sudievo, Novozagorsko, in Nikolov, V. (ed.) *Praistoricheski nahodki i izsledvania. Sbornik v pamet na professor Georgi Georgiev*, 129–140. BAN, Sofia.

Kutzian, I. (1966) Das Neolithikum in Ungarn. *Archaeologia Austriaca* 40, 249–280.

Lazarovici, Gh. (1973) Tipologia şi cronologia culturii Vinča în Banat. *Banatica* II, 25–55.

Lechevallier, M. and Quivron, G. (1981) The Neolithic in Baluchistan: new evidences from Mehrgarh. In Härtel, H. (ed.) *South Asian Archaeology* 1979, 71–93. Berlin, Dietrich Reimer.

Legge, A. T. and Rowley-Conwy, P. (1988) *Star Carr revisited : a re-analysis of the large mammals*. London, Centre for Extra-Mural Studies, Birkbeck College.

Leroi-Gourhan, A. (1964) *Le geste et la parole. I. Technique et langue*. Paris, Albin Michel.

Leshtakov, K. (2004) Pottery with incised and channelled ornamentation from the Early Neolithic site at Yabulkovo in the Maritsa river valley. In Nikolov, V., Băčvarov, K. and Kalchev, P. (eds) *Prehistoric Thrace*, 80–93. Sofia, Institute of Archaeology.

Leshtakov, K. (2006) Arheologicheski razkopki na praistorichesko selishte do s. Yabulkovo, Dimitrovgradsko. Ranen neolit. In Nikolov, V., Nehrisov, G. and Tsvetkova, Yu. (eds) *Spasitelni arheologicheski razkopki po traeto na zhelezoputnata liniya Plovdiv – Svilengrad prez 2004 g*, 166–204. Veliko Trnovo, Arheologicheski Institut BAN.

Leshtakov, K., Tonkova, M., Mikov, R. and Melamed, K. (2006) Arheologicheski razkopki do s. Yabulkovo, Dimitrovgradsko prez 2000–2003 g. In Nikolov, V., Nehrisov, G. and Tsvetkova, Yu. (eds) *Spasitelni arheologicheski razkopki po traeto na zhelezoputnata liniya Plovdiv – Svilengrad prez 2004 g*, 135–165. Veliko Trnovo, Arheologicheski Institut BAN.

Leshtakov, P. (2004) Graphite deposits and some aspects of graphite use and distribution in the Bulgarian Chalcolithic. In Nikolov, V., Băčvarov, K. and Kalchev, P. (eds) *Prehistoric Thrace*, 485–496. Sofia, Institute of Archaeology.

Leshtakov, P. (2006) The sources and distribution of graphite as a means of decoration in the Bulgarian Chalcolithic. In Dumitroaia, Gh., Chapman, J., Weller, O., Proteasa, C.,

Munteanu, R., Nicola, D. and Monah, D. (eds) *Cucuteni – 120 years of research – time to sum up*, 293–298. Iași, Cucuteni International Research Centre.

Letica, Z. (1998) Anthropomorhpic and zoomorphic figurines from Divostin. In McPherron, A. and Srejović, D. (eds) *Divostin and the Neolithic of Central Serbia*, 173–201. Pittsburgh, University of Pittsburgh, Dept, of Anthropology.

Lubbock, J. (1865) *Pre-historic times, as illustrated by ancient remains, and the manners and customs of modern savages*. 1st. ed. London, Williams and Norgate, London.

Lüning, J. (2005) Eine Weltpremiere: Kleider machen Leute – Kopfputz, Hüte und Schmuck ebenfalls. In Lüning, J. (ed.) *Die Bandkeramiker. Erste Steinzeitbauern in Deutschland. Bilder einer Ausstellung beim Hessentag in Heppenheim/Bergstraße im Juni 2004*, 213–271. Rahden: Marie Leidorf.

Lüning, J. (2006) Haare, Hüte, Hosenanzüge: Trachten der Bandkeramik und ihre Rolle im Ahnenkult. In Keefer, E. (ed.) *Lebendige Vergangenheit: vom archäologischen Experiment zur Zeitreise*, 52–64. Stuttgart, Theiss.

Magyari, E. K., Chapman, J. C., Gaydarska, B., Marinova, E., Deli, T., Huntley, J. P., Allen, J. R. M. and Huntley, B. (2008) The 'oriental' component of the Balkan flora: evidence of expansion into south-east Europe via the Thracian Plain during the last glacial stage. *Journal of Biogeography* 35/5, 865–883.

Makkay, J. (1969) The Late Neolithic Tordos group of signs. *Alba Regia* X, 9–49.

Makkay, J. (1984) *Early stamp seals in South-East Europe*. Budapest, Akadémiai Kiadó.

Makkay, J. (2005) *Supplement to the Early stamp seals in South-East Europe*. Budapest, J. Makkay.

Maneva, B. (1988) Spahievsko rudno pole. In Dimitrov, R. (ed.) *Olovno-zinkovite nahodista v Bulgariya*, 147–160. Sofia, Tehnika.

Manolakakis, L. (2005) *Les industries lithiques énéolithiques de Bulgarie*. Internationale Archäologie, Band 88. Rahden, Marie Leidorf.

Mantu, C-M. and Dumitroaia, Gh. (1997) Catalogue. In Mantu, C.-M., Dumitroaia, Gh. and Tsaravopoulos, A. (eds) *Cucuteni. The last great civilisation of Europe*, 101–239. Thessaloniki, Athena Publishing and Printing House.

Margos, A. (1961) Kum vuprosa za datiraneto na nakolnite selishta vuv Varnenskoto Ezero. *Izvestia na Varnenskoto Arheologichesko Druzhestvo* XII, 1–5.

Marinescu-Bîlcu, S. (2000) Stone tools. In Marinescu-Bîlcu, S. and Bolomey, A. (eds) *Drăgușeni. A Cucutenian community*, 49–57. București, Editura Enciclopedică.

Marinova, E. (2006) *Vergleichende paläoethnobotanische Untersuchung zur Vegetationsgeschichte und zur Entwicklung der prähistorischen Landnutzung in Bulgarien*. Dissertationes Botanicae, Band 401. Gebrüder Borntraeger Verlagsbuchhandlung. Berlin-Stuttgart.

Matasă, C. (1946) *Frumușica, village préhistorique à ceramique peinte dans la Moldavie du Nord*. București.

Mauss, M. (1936) *Les techniques du corps*. Journal de Psychologie 32.

Miličević, M. (1988) A reconstruction of women's dress in the Vučedol culture. In Durman, A. (ed.) *Vučedol – 3000 years b.c.*, 27–29, 54–55. Zagreb, Muzejski-galerijski Centar.

Miller, D. (1987) *Material culture and mass consumption*. Oxford, Blackwell.

Miller, D. (2005) Introduction. In Küchler, S. and Miller, D. (eds) *Clothing as material culture*, 1–20. Oxford, Berg.

Miller, M. (2003) Technical aspects of ornament production at Sitagroi. In Elster, E. and Renfrew, C. (eds) *Prehistoric Sitagroi: excavations in Northeast Greece, 1968–1970. Volume 2: the final report*, 369–382. Los Angeles, Cotsen Institute of Archaeology

Millett, M. J., Carreté, J. M. and Keay, S. J. (1995) *A Roman Provincial Capital and its Hinterland: the survey of the territory of Tarragona, 1985–1990* (Ann Arbor, Michigan: Journal of Roman Archaeology Supplementary Series no. 15).

Mills, N. T. W. (1983) The Ager Lunensis survey. In Keller, D. R., and Rupp, D. W. (eds) *Archaeological survey in the Mediterranean area*, 169–172. BAR International Series I-155. Oxford, Archaeopress.

Milojčić, V. (1949) *Chronologie der jüngeren Steinzeit Mittel und Südosteuropas*. Berlin, Walter.

Milojković, J. (1990) The anthropomorhpic and zoomorphic figurines. In Tringham, R. and D. Krstić (eds) *Selevac. A Neolithic village in Yugoslavia*, 397–436, Monumenta Archaeologica 15, Los Angeles: University of California Press.

Minchev, D., Betsov, M., Grigorov, G., Blank, E., Nedyalkova, L., Vulcheva, S. and Dachev, D. (1964) Vuglenosnost na priabona v chast of Istochnite Rhodopi. *Geofond*, N–IV. 207.

Monah, D. (1997) *Plastică antropomorfă a culturii Cucuteni-Tripolie*. Piatră Neamț, Centrul de Cercetare a culturii Cucutenii.

Mullan, X. and Marvin, X. (1978) *Zoo Culture*. London: Weidenfeld and Nicholson.

Müller, J. (1997) Neolitische und chalkolitische *Spondylus*-Artefakte. Anmerkungen zu Verbreitung, Tauschgebiet und sozialer Funktion. In Becker, C. et alii (eds) *Hronos. Beiträge zur prähistorischen Archäologie zwischen Nord- und Südosteuropa. Festschrift für Bernhard Hänsel*, 91–106. Espelkamp, Marie Leidorf.

Müller, J., Herrera, A. and Knossalla, N. (1996) *Spondylus* und Dechsel – zwei gegensätzliche Hinweise auf Prestige in der mitteleuropäischen Linearbandkeramik? In Müller, J. and Bernbeck, R. (eds) *Prestige – Prestigegüter – Sozialstrukturen. Beispiele aus dem europäischen und vorderasiatischen Neolithikum*, 81–96. Bonn, Holos.

Muraru, A. (2000) A petrographic survey of the Lithic material. In Marinescu-Bîlcu, S. and Bolomey, A. (eds) *Drăgușeni. A Cucutenian community*, 59–62. București, Editura Enciclopedică.

Nandris, J. G. (1970) The development and relationships of the Earlier Greek Neolithic. *Man* N.S. 5/2, 192–213.

Nandris, J. (1972) Relations between the Mesolithic, the First Temperate Neolithic and the Bandkeramik: the nature of the problem. *Alba Regia* VI, 61–70.

Nandris, J. (1972a) *Bos primigenius* and the bone spoon. *Bulletin of Univ. of London Institute of Archaeology* 10, 63–82.

Nanoglou, S. (2008) Building biographies and households. *Journal of Social Archaeology*, 8(1), 139–160.

Nanoglou, S. (2008a) Representation of humans and animals in Greece and the Balkans during the Earlier Neolithic. *Cambridge Archaeological Journal* 18(1), 1–13.

Nehrisov, G. (2003) Spasitelni arheologicheski prouchvania na obekt 'Ada tepe' pri grad Krumovgrad prez 2002 g. *Arheologicheski otkritia i razkopki prez 2002 g.*, 67–68.

Nehrisov, G. (2007) Spasitelni razkopki na zapadnia sklon na 'Ada tepe' prez 2006 g. *Arheologicheski otkritia i razkopki prez 2006 g.*, 173–176.

Neustupný, E. (1998) Otherness in prehistoric times. *KVHAA Konferens*, 40, 65–71.

Newell, R. R., Kielman, D., Constandse-Westermann, T. S., Van Der Sanden, W. A. B. and Van Gijn, A. (1990) *An Inquiry into the ethnic resolution of Mesolithic regional groups: the study of their decorative ornaments in time and space.* Leiden, Brill.

Nikolaidou, M. (2003) Catalog of items of adornment. In Elster, E. and Renfrew, C. (eds) *Prehistoric Sitagroi: excavations in Northeast Greece, 1968–1970. Volume 2: the final report*, 383–401. Los Angeles, Cotsen Institute of Archaeology.

Nikolov, V. (1996) Neolitnata kultura v Bulgarskite zemi v konteksta na Anatoliya i Balkanite. *Godishnik na Department Arheologiya NBU* II–III, 133–144.

Nikolov, V. (1997) Die neolithische Keramik. In Hiller, S. and Nikolov, V. (eds) *Karanovo, Die Ausgrabungen im Südsektor 1984–1992. Band I*, 105–146. Horn/Wien, Verlag Berger and Söhne.

Nikolov, V. (1998) *Prouchvaniya vrhu neolitnata keramika v Trakia. Keramichnite kompleksi Karanovo II–III, III I III–IV v konsteksta na Severozapadna Anatolia i Iugoistochna Evropa.* Sofia, Arheologicheski Institut BAN.

Nikolov, V. (2002) Antropomorfna plastika ot kusnoneolitnoto selishte Ljubimets. *Arheologia* 2, 25–32.

Nikolov, V. (2004) Dynamics of the cultural processes in Neolithic Thrace. In Nikolov, V., Băčvarov, K. and Kalchev, P. (eds) *Prehistoric Thrace*, 13–25. Sofia, Institute of Archaeology.

Nikolov, V. (2005) Prestij i belezi na prestij v neolitnoto obshtestvo. *Arheologia*, XLVI, 1–4, 7–17.

Nikolov, V. (2007) *Neolitni kultovi masichki.* Sofia, Natsionalen Arheologichski Institut BAN.

Nikolov, V. (ed.) (2008) *Praistoricheski solodobiven tsentur Provadia – Solnitsata.* Sofia, NAIM-BAN.

Nikolov, V. and Maslarov, N. (1987) *Drevni selishta krai Eleshnitsa.* Sofia, Sofia Press.

Nikolov, V., Nehrisov, G. and Tsvetkova, Yu. (eds) 2006. *Spasitelni arheologicheski razkopki po traeto na zhelezoputnata liniya Plovdiv – Svilengrad prez 2004 g.* Veliko Trnovo, Arheologicheski Institut BAN.

Nikolov, V. and Petrova, V. (2008) Kusnoneolitno yamno svetilishte Ljubimets-Dana bunar 2. In Vaklinova, M. (ed.) *Po putishtata na vremeto. Katalog kum izlozhba 31 mart-30 april 2008.* Sofia, NAIM-BAN, 6–7.

Nikolov, V, Stefanova, T. and Băčvarov, K. (2001) Spasitelni arheologicheski razkopki na kusnoneolitnoto selishte krai grad Ljubimets, Haskovska oblast. *Arheologicheski otkritia i razkopki prez 1999–2000*, 25–26.

Ninov, L. (1999). Verleichende Untersuchungen zur Jagd und zum Jagdwild während des Neolithikums und Äneolithikums in Bulgarien. In Benecke, N. (ed.) *The Holocene History of the European Vertebrate Fauna*, 323–338. Archäologie in Eurasien, Band 6, Rahden/Westf:Verlag Mari Leidorf GmbH.

Oross, K. and Whittle, A. (2007) Figural representations and other clay objects. In Whittle, A. (ed.) *The Early Neolithic of the Great Hungarian Plain. Investigations of the Körös culture site of Ecsegfalva 23, County Békés*, 621–640. Varia Archaeologica Hungarica XXI. Budapest, Institute of Archaeology HAS.

Ovcharov, N. (2005) *Perperikon. A Civilization of the Rock People.* Sofia, Borina.

Pappa, M. and Besios, M. (1999) The Makriyalos Project: rescue excavations at the Neolithic site of Makriyalos, Pieria, Northern Greece. In Halstead, P. (ed.) *Neolithic society in Greece*, 108–120. Sheffield, Sheffield Academic Press.

Păunescu, Al. (1968) *Evoluţia uneltor şi armelor de piatră cioplită descoperite pe teritoriul Romaniei.* Bucureşti: Academia di Ştiinţe Sociale şi Politice (Institutul de Arheologie).

Peïkov, A. (1972) Sondazhni razkopki na neolitnoto selishte v Kărdzhali prez 1972 g. *Ahrid* I, 7–44.

Pernicka, E., Begemann, F., Schmitt-Strecker, S., Todorova, H. and Kuleff, I. (1997) Prehistoric copper in Bulgaria. *Eurasia Antiqua* 3, 41–180.

Petrusenko, S. I. and Kostov, R. I. (1992) *Skapotsennite i dekorativnite minerali na Bulgariya.* Sofia, BAN.

Popova, Ts. (1995) Plant remains from Bulgarian prehistory (7000–2000 BC). In Bailey, D. and Panayotov, I (eds) *Prehistoric Bulgaria*, 193–208. Madison, WI, Prehistory Press.

Powers, M. J. (2006) *Pattern and person. Ornament, society and self in Classical China.* Cambridge, MA, Harvard University Press.

Prinz, B. (1988) The ground stone industry from Divostin. In McPherron, A. and Srejović, D. (eds) *Divostin and the Neolithic of Central Serbia*, 255–300. Pittsburgh, University of Pittsburgh, Dept, of Anthropology.

Raczky, P., Domborcózki, L. and Hajdú, Zs. (2007) The site of Polgár-Csőszhalom and its cultural and chronological connections with the Lengyel culture. In Kozłowski, J. K. and Raczky, P. (eds) *The Lengyel, Polgár and related cultures in the Middle/Late Neolithic in Central Europe*, 49–70. Kraków, Polish Academy of Arts and Sciences and ELTE, Institute of Archaeological Sciences, Budapest.

Raczky, P., Meier-Arendt, W., Anders, A., Hajdú, Zs., Nagy, E., Kurucz, K., Domboróczki, L., Sebők, K., Sümegi, P., Magyari, E., Szántó, Zs., Gulyás, S., Dobó, K., Bácskay, E., Biró, K. T. and Schwartz, C. (2002) Polgár-Csőszhalom (1989–2000): Summary of the Hungarian-German excavations on a Neolithic settlement in Eastern Hungary. In Aslan, R., Blum, S.W.E., Kastl, G., Schweizer, F. and Thumm, D. (eds) *Mauerschau. Festschrift für Manfred Korfmann.* Band 2, 833–860. Remshalden-Grunbach, Greiner.

Raduntcheva, A. (1986) Obshtestveno-ikonomicheskiat zhivot na Dobrudzha i Zapadnoto Chernomorie prez eneolita. *Vekove* (1986), 15–21.

Raduntcheva, A. (1990) Skalni svetilishta ot kamennomednata epoha v Istochnite Rodopi. *Interdistsiplinarni Izledvaniya* XVII, 141–150.

Raduntcheva, A. (1997) Eneoliten znayatchiisko-proizvodstven tsentur do selo Sedlare, Kurdzhaliisko. *Godishnik na Natsionalniya Arheologicheski Muzei* X, 162–176.

Raduntcheva, A. (1999) Rodopskata i Prirodopskata oblast prez praistoricheskata epoha. *Rhodopica* 1, 5–19.

Raduntcheva, A. (2002). Eneolithic temple complex near the village of Dolnoslav, district of Plovdiv, and the system of rock sanctuaries with prehistoric cultural strata in Rodopi Mountains and outside its territory. *Godishnik na Arheologicheski Muzei Plovdiv* IX/1, 96–119.

Raduntcheva, A. (2003) *Kusnoeneolitnoto obstestvo v bulgarskite zemi*. Razkopki i prouchvania XXXII. Sofia, AIM BAN.

Redfern, D. (2007) *A study of Scythian gold jewellery manufacturing technology and its comparison to Greek techniques from the 7th to 5th centuries BC*. Unpub. PhD thesis, University of Bradford.

Renfrew, C. (1986) The Sitagroi sequence. In Renfrew, C., Gimbutas, M. and Elster, E. S. (eds) *Excavations at Sitagroi. A prehistoric village in Northeast Greece. Volume 1*, 147–174. Los Angeles, CA, Institute of Archaeology, UCLA.

Riggins, S. (1994) Introduction. In Riggins, S. H. (ed.) *The socialness of things. Essays on the socio-semiotics of objects*, 1–10. Berlin, De Gruyter.

Rowland, R. J. and Dyson, S. (1991) Survey archaeology in Sardinia. In Barker, G. and Lloyd, J. *Roman landscapes: archaeological survey in the Mediterranean region*, 54–61. London, British School at Rome.

Sahlins, M. (1974) *Stone Age economics*. Chicago, Aldine.

Sarafov, A. (2000) *Rukovodstvo za prakticheski zaniatia po geografia na pochvite*. Varna

Schléder, Zs., Biró, K. and Szakmány, Gy. (2002) Petrological studies of Neolithic stone tools from Baranya County, South Hungary. In Jerem, E. and Biró, K. (eds) *Archaeometry 98. Proceedings of the 31st Symposium*, 797–804. Budapest, April 26–May 3, 1998. BAR International Series 1043. Oxford, Archaeopress.

Séfériadès, M. L. (2000) *Spondylus gaederopus*: some observations on the earliest European long-distance exchange system. In Hiller, S. and Nikolov, V. (eds) *Karanovo Band III. Beiträge zum Neolithikum in Südosteuropa*, 423–437. Wien, Phoibos Verlag.

Séfériadès, M. L. (2003) Note sur l'origine et la signification des objets en spondyle de Hongrie dans le cadre du Néolithique et de l'Énéolithique européens. In Jerem, E. and Raczky, P. (eds) *Morgenrot der Kulturen. Festschrift für Nándor Kalicz zum 75 Geburtstag*, 353–373. Budapest, Archaeolingua.

Seure, G. et Degrand, A. (1906) Exploration de quelques tells en Thrace. *Bulletin de Correspondance Hellénique XXX*, 358–432.

Shackleton, J. C. and Elderfield, H. (1990) Strontium isotope dating of the source of Neolithic European *Spondylus* shell artefacts. *Antiquity* 64, 312–315.

Shackleton, N. (2003) Preliminary report on the molluscan remains at Sitagroi. In Elster, E. and Renfrew, C. (eds) *Prehistoric Sitagroi: excavations in Northeast Greece, 1968–1970. Volume 2: the final report*, 361–365. Los Angeles, Cotsen Institute of Archaeology

Sheridan, J., Cooney, G. and Grogan, E. 1992. Stone axe studies in Ireland. *Proceedings of the Prehistoric Society* 58, 389–416

Sherratt, A. G. (1972) Socio-economic and demographic models for the Neolithic and Bronze Age of Europe. In Clarke, D. L. (ed.) *Models in archaeology*, 477–542. London, Methuen.

Sherratt, A. (1983) The Eneolithic period in Bulgaria in its European context. In A. Poulter (ed.) *Ancient Bulgaria Volume 1*, 188–198. Nottingham, University of Nottingham Press.

Sirakov, N. (2002) Flint artifacts in prehistoric grave-good assemblages from the Durankulak necropolis. In Todorova, H. (ed.) (2002a) *Durankulak Band II. Die prähistorischen Gräberfelder*, 213–246. DAI, Berlin–Sofia, Anubis.

Sirakov, N. and Tsonev, Ts. (1995) Chipped-stone assemblage of Hotnitsa-Vodopada (Eneolithic/Early Bronze Age transition in Northern Bulgaria) and the problem of the earliest "steppe invasion" in Balkans. *Préhistoire Européenne* 7, 241–264.

Skeates, R. (1995) Animate objects: a biography of prehistoric 'axe-amulets' in the central Mediterranean region. *Proceedings of the Prehistoric Society* 61, 279–301.

Skourtopoulou, K. (2006) Questioning spatial contexts: the contribution of lithic studies as analytical and interpretative bodies of data. In Papaconstantinou, D. (ed.) *Deconstructing Context: A Critical Approach to Archaeological Practice*, 50–78. Oxford, Oxbow.

Skourtopoulou, K. (n.d.) Living Things: investigating technological practices in the Greek Neolithic. Pre-circulated paper presented at Workshop "*Embedded Technologies: reworking technological studies in archaeology*", University of Wales, Lampeter, 24th to 27th September 1999.

Spassov, N. and Iliev, N. (2002) The animal bones from the prehistoric necropolis near Durankulak (NE Bulgaria) and the latest record of Equus hydruntinus Regalia. In Todorova, H. (ed.) (2002a) *Durankulak Band II. Die prähistorischen Gräberfelder*, 313–324. DAI, Berlin – Sofia, Anubis.

Spataro, M. (2007) Everyday ceramics and cult objects: a millennium of cultural transmission. In Spataro, M. and Biagi, P. (eds) *A short walk through the Balkans: the first farmers of the Carpathian Basin and adjacent regions*. Quaderno 12: 149–160 (Trieste).

Srejović, D. (1968) Neolitska plastika centralno-balkanskog područja. In Trifunović, L. (ed.) *Neolit Centralnog Balkana*, 177–240. Beograd, Narodni Muzej.

Stalio, B. (1972) *Gradac – praistorijsko naselje*. Beograd, Narodni Muzej.

Starnini, E., Szakmány, Gy. and Whittle, A. (2007) Polished, ground and other stone artefacts. In Whittle, A. (ed.) *The Early Neolithic of the Great Hungarian Plain. Investigations of the Körös culture site of Ecsegfalva 23, County Békés*, 667–676. Varia Archaeologica Hungarica XXI. Budapest, Institute of Archaeology HAS.

Sterud, E. L. and A-K. 1974. A quantitative analysis of the material remains. In Gimbutas, M. (ed.) Obre I and II. *Wissenschaftliche Mitteilungen des Bosnisch-Herzegowinishen Landesmuseums* Band IV. Heft A (Archäologie): 155–355.

Strathern, M. (1988) *The gender of the gift*. Berkeley. University of California Press.

Szakmány, Gy. and Starnini, E. (2002) Petrographic analysis of polished stone tools from some Neolithic sites of Hungary. In Jerem, E. and Biró, K. (eds) *Archaeometry 98. Proceedings of the 31st Symposium*, 805–810. Budapest, April 26–May 3, 1998. BAR International Series 1043. Oxford, Archaeopress.

Sztáncsuj, S. J. (2005) The Early Copper Age hoard from Ariuşd (Erősd). In Dumitroaia, Gh., Chapman, J., Weller, O., Proteasa, C., Munteanu, R., Nicola, D. and Monah, D. (eds) *Cucuteni – 120 years of research – time to sum up*, 85–106. Iaşi, Cucuteni International Research Centre.

Tasić, N (1973) *Neolitska plastika*. Beograd, Gradski Muzej Beograda.

Tilley, C. (1991) *Material culture and text: the art of ambiguity*. London, Routledge.

Todorova, H. (1975) Arheologichesko prouchvane na selishnata mogila i nekropola pri Goliamo Delchevo, Varnensko. In:

Todorova, H., Ivanov, S., Vasilev, V., Hopf, M., Quitta, H. and Kohl, G. (1975) Selishtanata mogila pri Goliamo Delchevo. *Razkopki i Prouchvania* V, 5–243. Sofia, Izdatelstvo na BAN.

Todorova, H. (1978) *The Eneolithic period in Bulgaria in the Fifth Millennium B.C.* BAR International Series 49. Oxford, Archaeopress.

Todorova, H. (1980) Klassifikatsija chislovoi kod plastiki neolita, eneolita i rannei bronzovoi epohi Bolgarii. *Studia Praehistorica* 3, 38–67.

Todorova, H. (1986) Kamenno-mednata epoha v Bulgaria. Sofia, Nauka i izkustvo.

Todorova, H. (1995) The Neolithic, Eneolithic and Transitional Period in Bulgarian prehistory. In Bailey, D. and Panayotov, I. (eds) *Prehistoric Bulgaria*, 79–98. Madison, WI: Prehistory Press.

Todorova, H. (1995a) Bemerkungen zum frühen Handelsverkehr während des Neolithikums und des Chalkolithikums im westlichen Schwartzmeerraum. In Hänsel, B. (ed.) *Handel, Tausch und Verkehr im bronze- und früheisenzeitlichen Südosteuropas*. Prähistorische Archäologie Südosteuropas Band 11, 53–66. München-Berlin, Südosteuropa Gesellschaft.

Todorova, H. (ed.) (2002) *Durankulak Band II. Die prähistorischen Gräberfelder*. DAI, Berlin–Sofia, Anubis.

Todorova, H. (2002a) Die Sepulkralkeramik aus den Gräbern von Durankulak. In Todorova, H. (ed.) *Durankulak Band II. Die prähistorischen Gräberfelder*, Teil 1, 81–116. DAI, Berlin–Sofia, Anubis.

Todorova, H., Dimov, T., Bojadžiev, J., Vajsov, I., Dimitrov, K. and Avramova, M. (2002) Katalog der prähistorischen Gräber von Durankulak. In Todorova, H. (ed.) *Durankulak Band II. Die prähistorischen Gräberfelder*, Teil 2, 31–162. DAI, Berlin–Sofia, Anubis.

Todorova, H., Ivanov, S., Vasilev, V., Hopf, M., Quitta, H. and Kohl, G. (1975) Selishtanata mogila pri Goliamo Delchevo. *Razkopki i Prouchvania* V. Sofia, Izdatelstvo na BAN.

Todorova, H. and Vajsov, I. (1993) *Novokamennata epoha v Bulgaria*. Sofia, Nauka i izkustvo.

Todorova, H. and Vajsov, I. (2001) *Der kupferzeitliche Schmuck Bulgariens*. PBF XX/6, Stuttgart, F. Steiner Verlag.

Todorova, H., Vasilev, V., Yanushevich, Z., Kovacheva, M. and Valev, P. (1983) Ovcharovo. *Razkopki i Prouchvania* IX. Sofia, Izdatelstvo na BAN.

Tringham, R. (1971) *Hunters, fishers and farmers in Eastern Europe, 6000–3000 BC*. London, Hutchinson.

Tsonev, Ts. (2004) Long blades in the context of East Balkan and Anatolian early complex sedentary societies. In Nikolov, V., Bǎčvarov, K. and Kalchev, P. (eds) *Prehistoric Thrace*, 259–263. Sofia, Institute of Archaeology.

Tsuneki, A. (1989) The manufacture of *Spondylus* shell objects at Neolithic Dimini, Greece. *Orient* XXV, 1–21.

Vajsov, I. (2002) Die Idole aus den Gräberfelder von Durankulak. In Todorova, H. (ed.) *Durankulak Band II. Die prähistorischen Gräberfelder*. DAI, Berlin–Sofia, Anubis, 257–266.

Videiko, M. (2004) Споруди трипільської культури // *Енциклопедія трипільської цивілізації*., 315–341. Київ, Ukrpoligrafmedia.

Vörös, I. (1987) A Tiszalúc-Sarkadi rézkori település állatcsontleletei (Animal bone finds from the Copper Age settlement of Tiszalúc-Sarkadi). *Folia Archaeologica* XXXVIII, 121–126.

Vulpe, R. (1957) *Izvoare. Săpăturile din 1936–1948*. Bucureşti, Romanian Academy of Sciences.

Ward Perkins, J. B. (1962) Etruscan towns, Roman roads and Medieval villages: the historical geography of southern Etruria. *Geographical Journal* 128, 329–405.

Ward Perkins, J. B. (1964) *Landscape and history in Central Italy*. Oxford, J.L. Myres Memorial Lecture.

Ward Perkins, J. B., Kahane, A. and Murray Threapland, L. (1968) The *Ager Veientanus* north and east of Veii. *Papers of the British School at Rome* 36, 1–218.

Weiner, A. (1985) Inalienable wealth. *American Ethnologist* 12, 210–227.

Whittle, A. (1995) Gifts from the earth: symbolic dimensions of the use and production of Neolithic flint and stone axes. *Archaeologia Polona* 33, 247–259.

Whittle, A. (1996) *Europe in the Neolithic. The creation of new worlds*. Cambridge, Cambridge University Press.

Whittle, A. (1998) Beziehungen zwischen Individuum und Gruppe: Fragen zur Identität im Neolithikum der ungarischen Tiefebene. *Ethnographisch-Archäologische Zeitschrift* 39, 465–487.

Whittle, A. (2001) Different kinds of history: on the nature of lives and change in central Europe, c. 6000–the second millennium BC. In Runciman, W. G. (ed.) *The origin of human social institutions*, 39–68. Oxford, Oxford University Press.

Whittle, A. (2003) *The archaeology of people. Dimensions of Neolithic life*. London: Routledge.

Xenophontos, C. (1991) Picrolite, its nature, provenance, and possible distribution patterns in the Chalcolithic Period of Cyprus. *Bulletin of the American Schools of Oriental Research* 282/283, 127–138.

Zidarov, P. (2008) Green bone pin from Pietrele: possible evidence for intentional colouration of bone artefacts during the Copper Age in the Balkans. In Kostov, R., Gaydarska, B. and Giurova, M. (eds) *Geoarchaeology and Archaeomineralogy*. Sofia: ST. Ivan Rilski.

Zlateva-Uzunova, R. (2004) Early Neolithic chipped stone assemblages from the Eastern Rhodope Mountain, South Bulgaria. *Izvestia na Istoricheskia Muzei Haskovo* 2, 19–24.

Plate 1a. The Orlovo site: general view (Photo: John Chapman)

Plate 1b. The Thracian barrow at Orlovo (Photo: John Chapman)

Plate 1c. High terrace of the Harmanlijska reka (Photo: John Chapman)

Plate 1d. Photo of mixed deciduous woodland, near Pchelari, Eastern Rhodopes (Photo: John Chapman)

A

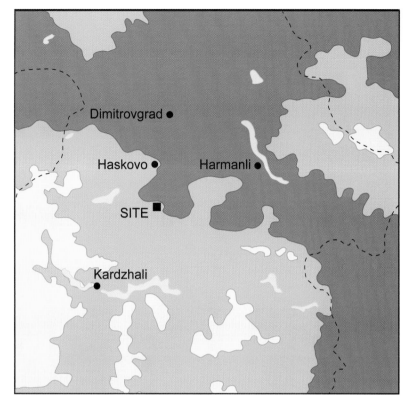

B

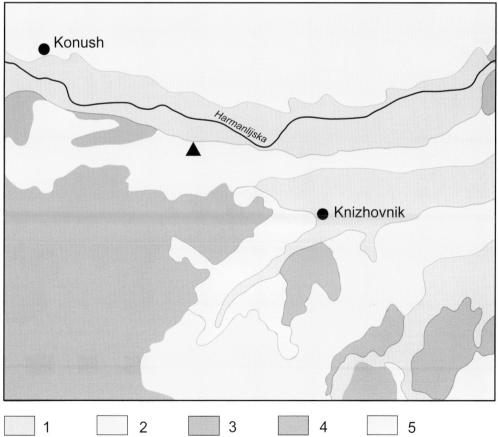

Plate 2. A. Topographic map of the Eastern Rhodopes and Haskovo area. Key: olive green: 100–200m; light green: 200–500m; beige: 500–1000m. B. Geology of the Haskovo area and the Eastern Rhodopes (source: Boyanov et al. 1989; redrawn by Yvonne Beadnell). Key: 1. Quaternary; 2. Neogene (Akhmatovo formation); 3. Palaeogene (coal-bearing and sandy formation); 4. Pre-Cambrian gneiss-granties; 5. Pre-Cambrian metamorphic rocks; ▲ = site of Orlovo

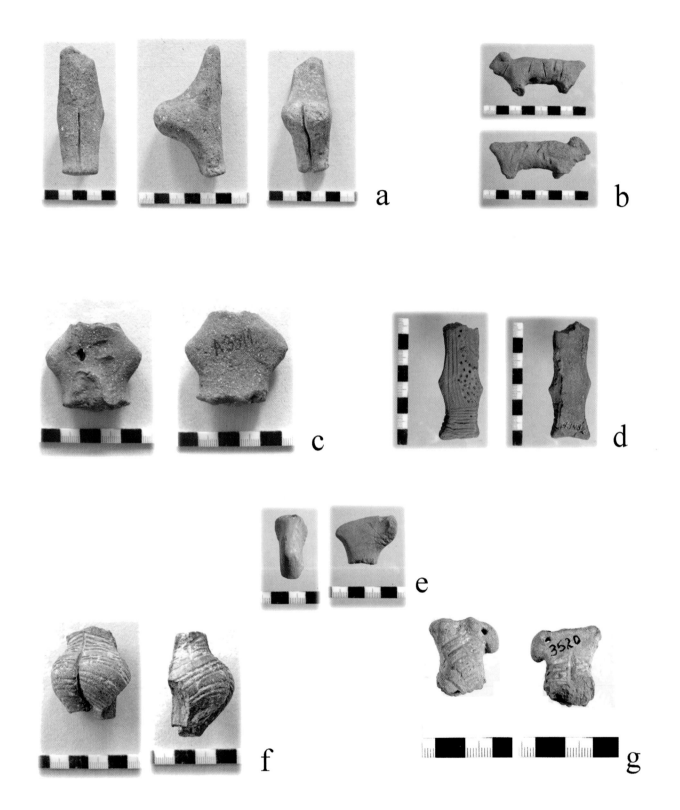

Plate 3. Figurines 1. a. Inv. 3312/1; b. Inv. 3057; c. Inv. 3311/3; d. Inv. 3482/4; e. Inv. 2789/3; f. Inv. 3238/1; g. Inv. 3520/6; (Photos: Irko Petrov)

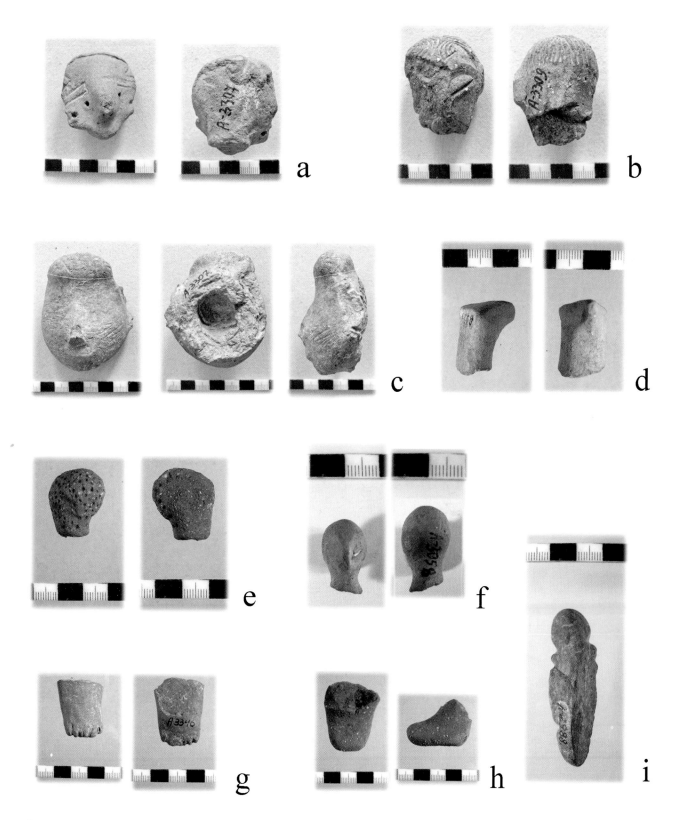

Plate 4. Figurines 2. a. Inv. 3307/2; b. Inv. 3309; c. Inv. 3307/1; d. Inv. 3346/6; e. Inv. 3369/1; f. Inv. 3058/2; g. Inv. 3346/9; h. Inv. 3346/4; i. Inv. 2988; (Photos: Irko Petrov)

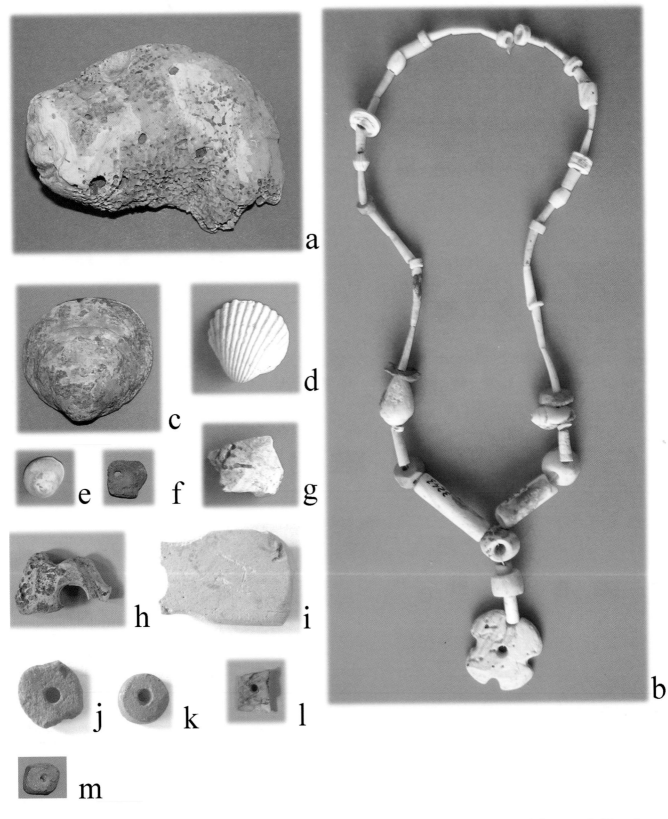

Plate 5. Ornaments 1. Unworked shells: a. unworked Spondylus *shell: Inv. 3224/1; b. reconstructed 'necklace', including unworked* Dentalium *shell: Inv. 3243/51; c. unworked* Glycymeris *shell: Inv. 3243/1; d. unworked* Cardium *shell: Inv. 3350/18; e. unworked* Cyclope *shell: Inv. 3350/68; f. volcanic tuff bead blank: Inv. 3243/22; g. half-finished* Spondylus: *Inv. 3350/3; h.* Spondylus *piece, probably bead or button blank: Inv. 2991/1; i. turquoise sub-rectangular bead blank: Inv. 3316/55; j. turquoise bead blank: Inv. 3316/60; k. turquoise disc bead: Inv. 3316/57; l.* Spondylus *bead blank: Inv. 2781/3; m. volcanic tuff bead blank: Inv. 3243/23 (Photos: Irko Petrov)*

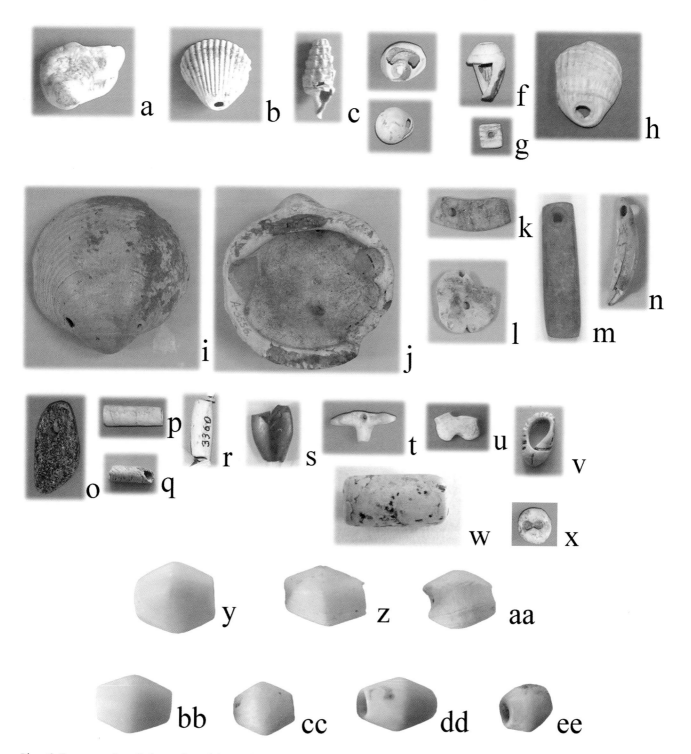

Plate 6. Ornaments 2. a. Débitage, Spondylus umbo: *Inv. 3350/9*; b. perforated Cardium *shell: Inv. 3350/21*; c. perforated Cerithium *shell: Inv. 3350/27*; d. half-finished Cyclope *shell: Inv. 3350/35*; e. perforated Cyclope *shell: Inv. 3224/51*; f. perforated Conus *shell: Inv. 3224/38*; g. Spondylus *pendant: Inv. 3360/35*; h. perforated Ostrea *shell: Inv. 3505/3*; i–j. perforated Glycymeris *shell: Inv. 3556/1*; k. mid-section of Spondylus *pendant: Inv. 3050/11*; l. Spondylus *clover-leaf pendant: Inv. 3050/9*; m. volcanic stone pendant: Inv. 2779; n. boar's incisor pendant: Inv. 3050/23*; o. amphibolite pendant: Inv. 3360/44*; p. cylindrical Spondylus *bead: Inv. 3360/42*; q. Spondylus *cylindrical bead with fine natural lines: Inv. 3316/18*; r. sub-rectangular Spondylus *bead: Inv. 3360/37*; s. fish-shaped bead made of coal: Inv. 2766*; t. marble T-shaped pendant: Inv. 3350/29*; u. fragment of possible Spondylus *clover-leaf pendant: Inv. 3350/15*; v. fragmentary Cerithium *ear-ring: Inv. 3316/52*; w. turquoise cylindrical bead: Inv. 2991/4*; x. marble button (Inv. 3350/37); y. marble polished faceted barrel bead with straight perforation, 8 facets on each half: Inv. No. Private collection No 10; z. Spondylus *polished faceted barrel bead with straight perforation: Inv. No. Private collection No. 7; aa. Spondylus *partly polished faceted barrel bead with straight perforation: Inv. No. Private collection No. 21; bb. marble polished faceted barrel bead with straight perforation: Inv. No. Private collection No 18; cc. marble polished faceted barrel bead with straight perforation: Inv. No. Private collection No 3; dd. Spondylus *polished faceted barrel bead with straight perforation: Inv. No. Private collection No. 20; ee. Spondylus *polished faceted barrel bead with straight perforation: Inv. No. Private collection No. 68 (Photos: Irko Petrov)

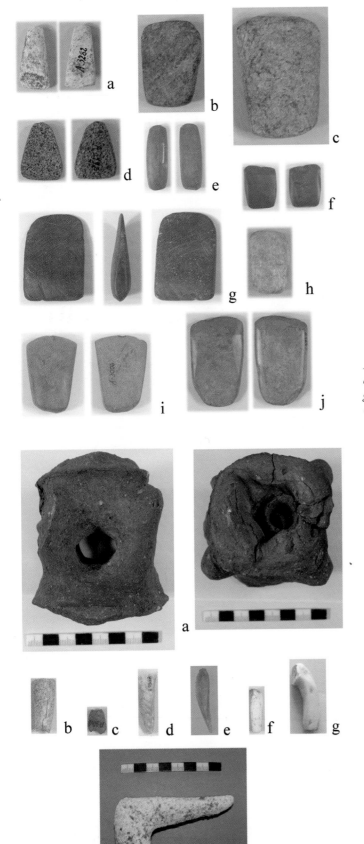

Plate 7. Polished stonework 1. a. Inv. 3282/1; b. Inv. 3193/12;
c. Inv. 2782/5; d. Inv. 3192/5; e. Inv. 2783/1; f. Inv. 3358/1;
g. Inv. 3263; h. Inv. 2755/2; i. Inv. 3006/1; j. Inv. 2755/1;
(Photos: Irko Petrov)

Plate 8. Other objects: a. fired clay 'hora' (Inv. 2778/1); b. horned
stand (Inv. 3067); c. sandstone horned object (Inv. 3068) ; d.
marble horn (Inv. 3368/1); e. flint bladelet (Inv. 3360/46); f.
marble leg (Inv. 3368); g. marble leg (Inv. 3316/62); h. limestone
bird head (Private Collection) (Photos: Irko Petrov)